For Sarah and Anna Claire
and
In memory of my mother,
Clara Bolcskey Gabor

ACKNOWLEDGMENTS

This book would not have been possible without Pam Dorman, my editor at Viking, and Flip Brophy, my agent, who both saw the potential in this book when it was still just a seedling of an idea, and who gave me their backing. The final months of this project, fraught as they were with childbirth and repeated computer failures, were eased by Carolyn Carlson, my "other" editor at Viking, and her insightful editing, warmth, and unflagging support. Arthur Rovine deserves special thanks for convincing me that Sandra Day O'Connor might well agree to be interviewed for this book, as do Beth Brophy and Glen Nager who helped introduce me to the Supreme Court Justice. I am grateful to the many people who granted me interviews, especially Justice O'Connor and Denise Scott Brown, and their families for their time and for their patience. Mary Anne Redding provided valuable help with research in Phoenix. While it isn't possible to mention all of the friends, family members, and associates of the women profiled in this book who lent me their time and help, I would like to acknowledge Scott Alexander, Burton Barr, Jacob Bigeleisen, Gustav Born, Jeanne Bultman, Ted Dragon, Beatrice Challiss Laws, Philip Finkelpearl, B. H. and Abby Friedman, Sanford Friedman, Diana Goldstein, Barry Goldwater, Helen

Harrison, Richard Howard, Steve Izenour, Rena Kanokogi, Peter Mayer, Jason and Diana McCoy, Robin Middleton, Robert Miller, Terrance Netter, Jeffrey Potter, Brian O'Connor, Jay O'Connor, Scott O'Connor, Bryan Robertson, Robert Sachs, Fred Schwartz, Ronnie Stein, Ruth K. Stein, Edward Teller, E.V. Thaw, Jimmie Venturi, Robert Venturi, Helen Wallace, Maria M. Wentzel, Elder Witt.

I also am thankful to the archivists at the American Institute of Physics, the University of California at San Diego, the Archives of American Art/Smithsonian Institution, and Johns Hopkins University who helped me gain access to a rich trove of unpublished material on many of my subjects. Here I must also mention my debt to the countless librarians at the New York City Public Library who were always generous with their help.

Because this book was conceived in the months preceding my first pregnancy, and was completed in the months following the birth of my second child, I owe a special debt to the family members, babysitters, and friends without whom I could never have found the time or concentration to work on this project. Tessie Hogan has been unstinting in her friendship and support even after the ordeal of accompanying me on my first long-distance research trip, during which she helped care for my five-month-old daughter Sarah who was traveling with us. Subsequently, I could always count on my in-laws, Flora and Pepe Fernandez, to help care for my children, whom I now leave at home when I am traveling for work. I also am very grateful to Gladys Mondragon, who has been my right hand for the last two years, helping with the kids and organizing my life. As always, Eva Pomice and Terri Thompson were always there with help, advice, and, when need be, a spare computer. Once again, Hamish Norton helped expand my meager understanding of physics. And, last but not least, my husband Jose deserves a hug for remaining loving and tolerant through the long gestation of another book.

PENGUIN BOOKS

EINSTEIN'S WIFE

Andrea Gabor is a former senior editor for *U.S. News & World Report* and the author of *The Man Who Discovered Quality*, which is available from Penguin. She and her husband have two daughters and live in New York City.

Praise for *Einstein's Wife*

"I read this book with the eagerness I'd bring to a conversation with a friend. I really wanted to hear what Andrea Gabor had to tell about the balancing acts of these extraordinary women, including the architect Denise Scott Brown and Supreme Court Justice Sandra Day O' Connor—and I wasn't disappointed!"
　　　　　—Phyllis Rose, author of *Parallel Lives*

"A fascinating read."
　　　　　—*Newsday*

"The consuming struggle of these women—brilliant, talented, ambitious—to become something more than 'lesser lives' both horrifies and inspires."
　　　　　—Benita Eisler, author of *O'Keeffe and Stieglitz*

"This is a book to gladden every believer in female capability."
　　　　　—*St. Louis Post-Dispatch*

"By setting the experiences of these remarkable women in historical context, *Einstein's Wife* brings a welcome perspective to the sometimes bitter dispute over gender roles. It is a perspective that recognizes the injustices of the past, while pointing toward a more hopeful and equitable future for women and for men."
　　　　　—Diana Chapman Walsh, President, Wellesley College

"[Gabor] brings to life women of whom many may never have heard . . . Gabor's work shows thorough research."
　　　　　—*Houston Chronicle*

ANDREA GABOR

EINSTEIN'S

Wife

Work and Marriage in the Lives of Five Great Twentieth-Century Women

PENGUIN BOOKS

PENGUIN BOOKS
Published by the Penguin Group
Penguin Books USA Inc., 375 Hudson Street, New York, New York 10014, U.S.A.
Penguin Books Ltd, 27 Wrights Lane, London W8 5TZ, England
Penguin Books Australia Ltd, Ringwood, Victoria, Australia
Penguin Books Canada Ltd, 10 Alcorn Avenue, Toronto, Ontario, Canada M4V 3B2
Penguin Books (N.Z.) Ltd, 182–190 Wairau Road, Auckland 10, New Zealand

Penguin Books Ltd, Registered Offices: Harmondsworth, Middlesex, England

First published in the United States of America by Viking Penguin,
a division of Penguin Books USA Inc. 1995
Published in Penguin Books 1996

1   3   5   7   9   10   8   6   4   2

Grateful acknowledgment is made for permission to reprint excerpts
from the following copyrighted works:
Letter from Fritz Bultman to Lee Krasner. By permission of Jeanne Bultman.
Letter from Karl Herzfeld to Joseph Ames, July 13, 1935. By permission of Ferdinand
Hamburger, Jr. Archives of The Johns Hopkins University, Office of the President.
Interviews of and letters by Lee Krasner. By permission of E. V. Thaw & Co., Inc.
Letters from Maria Mayer to Frau Goeppert and letter from Joe Mayer to Frau Goeppert from
Maria Mayer Papers collection, Mandeville Department of Special Collections,
University of California, San Diego. By permission of Maria M. Wentzel.

Photograph credits: Mileva Maric Einstein: Verlag Paul Haupt; Lee Krasner: Sidney Waintrob;
Maria Goeppert Mayer: American Institute of Physics, Niels Bohr Library, Stein Collection;
Denise Scott Brown: © Bachrach; Sandra Day O'Connor: © Zimberoff/Sygma

THE LIBRARY OF CONGRESS HAS CATALOGUED THE HARDCOVER AS FOLLOWS:
Gabor, Andrea.
Einstein's wife: work and marriage in the lives of five great twentieth-century women/Andrea Gabor.
p.   cm.
Includes bibliographical references (p. 319) and index.
ISBN 0-670-84210-9 (hc.)
ISBN 0 14 01.5993 2 (pbk.)
1. Wives—Biography.   2. Spouses—Biography.   3. Celebrities—Biography.   I. Title.
HQ759.G3—dc20
[B]   95–2998

Printed in the United States of America
Set in Weiss
Designed by Francesca Belanger

CONTENTS

There are many dark and thorny crowns which God gives to children in this world, but the most painful that God in his anger has crowned a woman's head with is—genius.

Louise Otto-Peters, in a poem to George Sand

INTRODUCTION

Of Foxes and Hedgehogs

The considerable reputation of Albert Einstein, the father of the relativity theory, whose very name is synonymous with genius, turns out to be, well, relative. Since the 1990 publication of a hidden trove of love letters between Einstein and Mileva Maric, his first wife, the portrait of the great physicist, one of the last Romantic heroes of the twentieth century, has suddenly been revised. Einstein, it seems, was a scoundrel when it came to women and an irresponsible family man. Doubt has even been cast on the exclusivity of his seminal scientific theories; rather than springing fully formed from his great mind, like Athena from the head of Zeus, much of his early work may have grown out of a long and close dialogue with his virtually forgotten wife.

These revelations have sparked a cosmic-sized controversy about Maric, who was herself a promising young physicist, and her role in her husband's life and work. While the scientific community and revisionist historians (many but not all of them feminists) battle over Einstein's legacy, the great man's own letters point to a nurturing and productive relationship with Maric that spanned sexual passion and science. The two young physicists fell in love as fellow students after Einstein had rejected a girlhood sweetheart to whom he used to send his laundry through the mail. Maric and Einstein studied and worked together. And while it is unlikely that anyone will ever know for sure the extent of Mileva Maric's contribution to Einstein's early work, he clearly valued her insight. "I'm so lucky to have found you, a creature who is my equal, and who is as strong and independent as I am! I feel alone with everyone except you," Einstein wrote to her, adding later: "How happy and proud I will be when the two of us together will have brought our work on the relative motion to a victorious conclusion."

Under the pressures of family responsibilities and the all-consuming nature of Einstein's intellectual life, however, the romance soon sputtered. One thing in the entire Einstein-Maric controversy remains clear: Einstein, a man who is revered as both a great scientist and a great humanist, was a terrible husband and an even worse father. "I'm not a family man," Einstein confessed after he had separated from Maric and was about to marry a woman who placed no intellectual demands on him. "I want to know how God created this world. . . . I want to know his thoughts, the rest are details."

Although, as a youth, Einstein craved the companionship of a woman whom he considered his "equal," after the early passionate years of courtship and professional adversity he ceased to accommodate his wife's intellectual yearnings and aspirations. The more successful he became, the more he shut Maric out of his world. Finally, he divorced her and married his cousin Elsa, declaring he was happy she didn't understand science. As for the two sons he had with Maric, Einstein rarely saw them after his divorce and assumed few parental responsibilities. He helped provide a meager living for his family. But Einstein, who moved to Germany in 1914, after eleven years of marriage, made only sporadic visits to Switzerland, where Maric lived with her sons, even though the couple would not divorce until 1919. Nor did he help Maric when his younger child, Eduard, began to show signs of mental instability. Rebuilding her life after her divorce would have been difficult for Maric in any case, but now all was sacrificed to caring for a schizophrenic son. Although Eduard would need to be hospitalized periodically, as long as she was alive his mother refused to institutionalize him and kept him at home with her as much as possible. Not so Einstein. When Maric died, in 1948, Eduard was sent to live permanently at the Sanatorium Burgholzli in Zurich. Einstein, who emigrated to the United States in 1933, never visited his son thereafter. His last letter to Eduard is dated 1944, though Einstein lived for another decade.

If the relationship between Einstein and Maric began as a quintessential modern love affair, Maric's life ended as a paradigmatic feminine tragedy. As students, the two young physicists studied together and supported each other's interests and ambitions; indeed, it was Maric, who had an easier relationship with their professors, who often interceded with them on Einstein's behalf. Later, as a young wife and mother, she would work late in the night reviewing Einstein's papers, and she probably performed the mathematical calculations for some of his theories.

Yet Maric is largely unknown to us because Einstein's executors, and many of his biographers, have tried virtually to expunge her from the record of Einstein's life. For years, the executors of the Einstein estate have sought to suppress details of his personal life, including the love letters exchanged with Maric, that might have cast Einstein in a negative light. Even today prominent members of the scientific establishment, such as Abraham Pais, one of Einstein's most respected biographers, seem eager not only to deny Maric's importance in Einstein's life but to impugn her reputation in the process. Inadvertently invoking Oscar Wilde's ironic play, Pais angrily dismisses Maric as a woman of "utterly no importance." Most of Einstein's biographers similarly dismiss the great man's first wife as a dour and difficult Slav, omitting virtually any reference to her remarkably brave and independent personality, her role as a female pioneer in physics, and her considerable intellectual promise.

Maric's story hit the news during a time when I was becoming fascinated by a well of forgotten potential: the women—most of them wives—whose talent or accomplishments had been virtually obliterated by the work of the more famous men in their lives. I had become aware of Diego Rivera's gifted and long-suffering wife even before the books and exhibitions that would whip up a frenzy of Frida-mania. I discovered Phyllis Rose's insightful book *Parallel Lives*, with its keyhole on the by and large miserable marriages of five brilliant Victorian men, most of whose wives were gifted yet frustrated. And I was captivated by the story of Rosalind Franklin, who made a sizable contribution to the discovery of DNA despite the fact that she was undermined by the three men with whom she worked, who ultimately won the lion's share of the credit for unraveling one of nature's most important biological puzzles.

Newly engaged myself, I was riveted by the metamorphosis of my cousin Magda who, in her mid forties, was getting set to escape a miserable marriage, despite the admonitions of relatives that she would be lonely and destitute without her husband. Defying the doomsayers, Magda won an acting and production role in a major motion picture within a year of her divorce, went on to become one of the most respected foreign diplomats in Budapest, and fell in love. As I prepared for my wedding, I read a spurious but widely published study that seemed to rate a single woman's chances of getting married below the likelihood of her being killed by a terrorist—unless she rushed to the altar at an early age. Soon after my wedding, a controversy erupted over Felice Schwartz's *Harvard Business Review* article advocating that employers acknowledge the special needs of working mothers by establishing in the workplace what has since become known as a "mommy track." At the same time, a media-hyped fertility scare sent many of my thirty-something friends into paroxysms of anxiety and a mad rush to high-priced fertility doctors.

Would professional women never free themselves from the constraints of the biological clock that ticks inside or the professional prejudice that thunders in the world around them?

I felt strongly that I needed to find some role models who could point to an easier route between this Scylla and Charybdis of modern womanhood. While women today have more choices professionally, an easier time getting maternity leave, and more success in finding husbands who will share housework and child care, wives still bear the primary burden of caring for families, especially when these families include children. By examining the marriages of a handful of accomplished women, the obstacles they faced, and whether, and how, they overcame them, I hoped to paint an impressionistic portrait that might lead young men and women to find better ways of handling their own marriages.

My criteria for selecting the women in this book were relatively straightforward: enduring marriages and significant accomplishments that would be remembered after their deaths. (Although Maric and Einstein would eventually divorce, their sixteen-year marriage lasted longer than many today, and their relationship dominated most of Maric's adult life.) Many gifted women marry talented, and often prominent, men. Thus, the test of time is important, because without it, readers might be tempted to credit the accomplishments of these women, no matter how gifted they are in their own right, to the alliances they almost invariably seem to make with powerful men. I wanted to focus on my subjects, not defend the extent of their accomplishments.

It was relatively easy to narrow the field. Even in the twentieth century, some of the greatest female minds chose never to marry, or married only briefly before jettisoning husbands who interfered with their work. Neither Lise Meitner, the cofounder of nuclear fission, nor Rosalind Franklin, an X-ray crystallographer, ever married. Although Margaret Sanger and Margaret Mead both married and had children, they spent their most productive years as divorcées.

I made my final selection with an eye toward portraying the multi-faceted experiences of modern women and indicating the progress they have made over the course of the century. I wanted at least one woman who had several children, and one who had none. I searched for women who worked closely with their husbands, and those who didn't. Some women, like Marie Curie and Frida Kahlo, I eliminated reluctantly because I was afraid their stories were already too well known. I wanted women in a variety of professions. And I wanted at least one happy marriage—and, to my surprise, found two.

As I delved into the lives of the century's most gifted wives, I discovered a number of common challenges and obstacles:

• Marriage is still the primary institution through which even the youngest and most gifted of these women measured their personal success. Partly for this reason, many were attracted to smart and successful men, and I was interested in seeing how this affected both their work and their marriages. So I set out to explore what obstacles the aspirations of men like Robert Venturi—to say nothing of Albert Einstein—posed for their wives.

• From the art world to the bar, it is obvious that most gifted women continue to face formidable on-the-job prejudice. What progress has been made in the professions has largely served to shift the barriers away from the entry-level position to midcareer roadblocks that often stall advancement. And when women marry men in the same profession, as they often do, their presence in the workplace can engender a particularly virulent sort of resentment on the part of male colleagues. Thus, I set out to explore the difficult nexus between marriage and professional partnership.

• Finally, the ancient cultural lure of home and hearth is as strong as ever. I had no intention of taking on the question of whether ambition, nurturance, etc., are in any way gender-linked. Still, it is no accident that the twentieth century has produced a record number of great married women, a list that only begins with names like Marie Curie, Virginia Woolf, and Margaret Sanger, for it is in this century, for the first time, that the combination of birth control and social change has given women a real choice to play a role outside the home. Yet, as I discovered in the course of research, a dirty house, screaming children, and a harried husband can still prompt the most gifted and resilient women to question their commitment to their professions. And so I sought to explore how that potent brew of a traditional upbringing and the birth of children can lead to guilt and crises of confidence, and how these emotions play themselves out in the lives of gifted wives.

This story begins with Mileva Maric because her life is in many respects emblematic of the great promise and potential disappointments of modern marriage. Having come of age at the turn of the century, Maric belonged to the first generation of women who saw the doors to a decidedly masculine profession open a crack, wide enough for her to glimpse a life of both marriage and professional work. Ultimately, she allowed the door to slam shut soon after she had met Einstein and before she had even completed her university studies in Zurich. Her upbringing, the birth of an illegitimate child, her subsequent marriage, and the still formidable gender barriers of her profession all combined to block any real chance she ever had of achieving fulfillment.

Unlike Maric, Lee Krasner had the good fortune to grow up in New York in the 1920s, just when American avant-garde art was being born, in a world that, at least on the surface, offered opportunity to a gifted artist regardless of gender. Although Krasner would face enormous prejudice in an increasingly macho art world, she possessed a penetrating vision and determination that would sustain her commitment to her work. But like Maric, Krasner had had a traditional upbringing. It was her own self-image—a gnawing sense that her life would never be complete without a husband—and her determination to marry not just a good man but a great one, that very nearly cost Krasner her dreams as an artist.

Like Maric and Krasner, Maria Mayer, a Nobel laureate in physics, never questioned her roles as wife and mother. If she had, Mayer might have recognized that motherhood, and perhaps even marriage, were ill suited to her single-minded nature. However, having had the advantage of being born an only child with exceptionally supportive parents, Mayer entered into a marriage of equals, choosing a husband who would provide a vital link to the world of physics. Despite the formidable gender barriers of her profession, this link would prove vital in sparking the work for which she would eventually win a Nobel Prize in the 1960s. Yet while husband and wife treated each other as intellectual partners, Mayer never questioned that she would have to fulfill the traditional role of wife and mother, or fully examined her commitment to those responsibilities. When Mayer found herself sucked into a full-time career, neither she nor her husband ever focused on the special accommodations dual-career couples must make for their children. Thus, the Mayer children soon discovered that science was the first love of both their parents, and suffered as a consequence.

Sandra Day O'Connor and Denise Scott Brown came of age in the years during and immediately following World War II, an era in which the Depression and the war had thrust more women than ever into the workplace. Of the two, Scott Brown was the one who most self-consciously set out to be a pathbreaker. She would anticipate the era of women's liberation, sexual emancipation, and self-awareness that would reach full flower in the 1960s.

Scott Brown strove, with studied deliberateness, to create a family structure that would accommodate her eclectic interests as urban planner and architect, writer and critic, devoted mother and wife. It was in her life that I expected to find the model of a totally liberated wife, to whatever extent such a person exists. In fact, I discovered that Scott Brown was as vulnerable to the traditional marriage myths as any of the women I have studied. But as the only woman in this book who would marry twice, she had the opportunity to question the traditional assumptions that had served as the foundation for her first, short-lived marriage. Scott Brown's struggle to reconcile her commitment to a traditional family life with a determination to reach the top of her profession would represent, I realized, a more realistic model of the challenges that face many ambitious young wives today. What's more, her professional life, as the wife and partner of architect Robert Venturi, would serve as an outsize example of the special prejudice that women can encounter in the workplace when they seek to carve out a claim in what is widely regarded as their husband's territory.

While Scott Brown is a radical who never completely shook herself free of her traditional upbringing, O'Connor's devotion to traditional notions of marriage and motherhood have been a central—if seemingly contradictory—theme of her life. In this respect, the Supreme Court justice and mother of three is an unlikely icon for today's working wives. Yet O'Connor's life proved vitally important in filling out this portrait of marriage, not so much because of her celebrity or because of any desire on my part to endorse her largely conservative views of marriage and motherhood. Rather, she is important because more than any of the other women portrayed in this volume, she possesses the sort of vital self-knowledge that has helped her—and is indeed central—to create a fulfilling life. Like most successful women, O'Connor had, at an early age, developed a belief in her own potential. She also possessed an enduring inner drive to study the law and to engage in civic life. Yet for several years, while her children were small, O'Connor focused on her family. In the end, she succeeded in balancing the two sides of her life because she never lost touch with her priorities, even as they shifted with the changing needs of her three sons. By recognizing the importance of both family and work to her vision of happiness and fulfillment, and finding a way to traverse from one to the other during the course of her career, she was able to pursue her professional interests with a unique clarity of purpose. She wrapped her career around the central ballast of her family, frequently taking detours in her profession but never losing sight of her destination.

Ultimately, each of these five gifted women accepted marriage as the defining aspect of her life—far more so than did most of their husbands. In this respect, the story of these pioneering women serves as testimony to how traditional marital expectations continue to dominate the lives of most twentieth-century women.

At the same time, this chronicle also demonstrates how much more flexible marriage has become since 1903, when Mileva Maric and Albert Einstein said their vows. Unlike Maric, women today need not live in fear of unwanted pregnancies. The Pill, the very real victories of feminism, and the growing tide of women in the workplace have gradually been pushing open the gates of opportunity. For the first time in history, *most* women can envision a life that straddles both the home and a rewarding job; whether they work by necessity or by choice, women can select from myriad vocations, many of which they were barred from only a few generations ago.

Still, the lives of even the most modern wives remain far more bifurcated than their husbands could ever imagine. As recently as May 1993, a *New York Times* front-page article, headlined "Even Women at the Top Still Have Floors to Do," observed that Washington's new crop of female politicians are the principal homemakers in their families. "In a year when more women than ever before took seats in Congress and were appointed to important Government posts, and when the First Lady was given the responsibility for health-care reform, very little has changed at home for women who work, even at the highest levels," stated the *Times*. The news would hardly have come as a surprise to most wives.

As I pondered these familiar problems, I was certain that I had no desire to write yet another chronicle of wifely woes. What I wanted, instead, was to achieve insight into why some women seem to have a far easier time juggling their double lives—an explanation that would go beyond prosaic observations about motivation and organizational abilities. It is a myth that couples marry only for love. But while factors such as timing, the desire for children, financial stability, and religion play a role in many marriages, how many young people probe seriously the professional ambitions and family commitments of their prospective spouse? How many women stop to consider the traditional pressure to marry "successful" men and look at whether the very factors that account for their beloved's success are compatible with their vision of a balanced family life? How many women seriously examine whether—and under what conditions—they should marry at all?

What finally struck me as I examined the lives of these and other gifted twentieth-century wives, and searched, through them, for a new model for a more balanced life, was that I had actually stumbled upon two distinctly different personality types, with radically different approaches to their lives and responsibilities. The first type, regardless of her family obligations, is never as happy as when she is working, and performs her domestic duties distractedly, perfunctorily, a little resentfully. The other type of working wife navigates in and out of her domestic and professional life, craving both, immersing herself in the fine points of, say, the law for half a day and then investing the same attention and dedication to a game of tag or to shopping for dinner, finding satisfaction in both, no matter how pressing the demands on her time.

It was through Isaiah Berlin's *The Hedgehog and the Fox* that the difference between the two personality types I had stumbled across first began to crystallize for me. In his essay, which seeks to unravel the intellectual paradox that defines Leo Tolstoy's life and work, Berlin divides great Western thinkers into two distinct intellectual camps. Drawing on the fragments of a Greek poem, which says, in part, "The fox knows many things, but the hedgehog knows one big thing," Berlin divided the world of great intellectuals into "Hedgehogs" and "Foxes."

Although Berlin conceived his metaphor to describe archetypes of intellectual thought, it seemed a valid and useful way to look at human personality and behavior. Hedgehogs and foxes choose diverging intellectual paths and, thus, radically different personal and professional challenges and dramatically different routes to success. I would echo Berlin's caution that taking the metaphor too far can lead to extremes. But there is a core of compelling logic in his observation.

The Hedgehog's life and work are defined and guided by a single, all-consuming, monistic vision or inspiration. The Hedgehog is priestess to an idea, a lone, Promethean genius. Like Einstein, who was himself a consummate Hedgehog, she is utterly and totally dedicated to the discovery of a unified field theory of her own particular universe.

Applying Berlin's metaphor, I suddenly saw Krasner and Mayer in a new light. The scientist stares endlessly at her shoes, contemplating the structure of the nucleus, impervious to the dustballs that gather around her and the sulking of her children, because she is a thoroughgoing monist. Similarly, the artist marries art—both literally and figuratively—devoting her whole life to the service of her own creativity or that of her husband, the "greatest artist" of her generation; in both endeavors she remains equally dedicated to a specific creative vision.

On the other side of the psychic spectrum scampers the Fox, who glories in a multiplicity of unrelated, often contradictory, interests and perspectives. The Fox craves a vast variety of experiences. As with O'Connor and Scott Brown, her mind moves on many levels. She is a Renaissance woman who is endlessly curious, noticing everything around her and sometimes torn by her varied interests. The architect, for example, brings to her work the sensibilities of an academic, a humanist, and an urbanist, and is, at the same time, a mystery buff, a connoisseur of fine ceramics, a doting wife and passionate mother. The judge, meanwhile, has changed careers three times, distinguishing herself as a lawyer, a politician, and, ultimately, a justice, all the while cultivating a zest for sports and art, a love of cooking, and a passion for her large extended family, as well as for countless lifelong friendships.

For women, Berlin's observation presents a serious conundrum. While, historically, "true genius" has often been associated with the single-minded focus of the Hedgehog, the fact is that for working wives it is extremely difficult to be a Hedgehog. It's not that women are any less likely than men to possess the intensely centripetal vision of the Hedgehog. Indeed, many of the great women of the twentieth century, including Jane Addams, Margaret Sanger, Margaret Mead, and Margaret

Bourke-White, were all Hedgehogs. And not surprisingly, every single one of these women sacrificed marriage, children, or both in pursuit of her vision.

Although Western culture often glorifies the single-focused vision of the Hedgehog as the epitome of "true genius," many Hedgehogs are destined for a lonely life. As Gustave Flaubert, that melancholy exemplar of his breed, once lamented: "I have always lived from day to day . . . pursuing my goal—my only goal—literature—looking to neither the left nor the right! Everything that existed around me has disappeared, and I find myself in a desert." Flaubert, who recognized in himself the ascetic, egoistic "priest," was by his own admission "too decent to inflict himself on another in perpetuity." How much brighter Flaubert's life might have been if he had been able to follow the advice—and example—of his friend George Sand, an exuberant, peripatetic Fox: "I beg you not to be so absorbed in literature and learning. Travel, move about, have mistresses or wives, just as you like; and during such phases, don't work. One shouldn't burn the candle at both ends; the thing is to light each end [and turn it] about."

Indeed, the examples of happily married Hedgehogs are rare. Marie Curie and Robert Venturi are two exceptions. They both found mates who could share—and enrich—the singular passion of their souls. Einstein, by contrast, ultimately opted for a marriage of convenience, taking as a second wife his decidedly unintellectual cousin, Elsa Lowenthal, who was destined to be as unhappy in her role as Mrs. Einstein as was Mileva Maric.

Certainly, a working wife who assumes the burdens of child rearing and homemaking can't afford an exclusive, single-focused intellectual life. Einstein was a disappointing husband and father not because he was a bad person but because he was a Hedgehog. Even if Maric had possessed Einstein's single-minded passion, which she did not, she would not have been able to indulge it; in the absence of a soul mate or a house husband, motherhood would not allow it.

Being a Fox is easier for working wives—yet that too carries a cost. For American culture worships the specialist, the workaholic, the superstar—one might even say the Nietzscheian Superman. Einstein remains the ultimate icon of "intellectual brilliance and creativity" because he was so single-focused.

When one looks through the lens of Berlin's archetypes, it isn't at all surprising that a woman of Maric's eclectic interests failed even to get through university with her ambitions intact. Nor is it surprising that Maria Goeppert Mayer and Lee Krasner, who were both intensely committed to their vocations, led troubled lives. To make it in physics, or in the art world, in the 1930s and 1940s, a woman had to possess steely determination and at least a tendency toward a single-minded dedication to her profession. She might not, at first, recognize that tendency. She might marry and have children and strive to accept her traditional place at the center of her family, but ultimately her heart and mind would be drawn back inexorably to her first and primary love. And unless she had the rare, exceptional marriage of a Marie and Pierre Curie, who shared everything from work to child raising, she would be pulled between the two sides of her life, feeling eternally compromised. She would be torn between her traditional responsibilities as a wife and mother and her intellectual desires, shortchanging one for the other, guilty that she could not take pleasure in what has been viewed for centuries as woman's work.

By the late 1950s and the 1960s, when Denise Scott Brown and Sandra Day O'Connor had come of age and embarked on their professions, the field was a little more open to working wives. Although it was by no means easy, O'Connor could take five years off from her career to throw herself into the lives of her children and into philanthropic work, while still remaining connected to the law. The macho Romantic ideal of the superstar still dominated every sphere from art to science, but complexity and contradiction, diversity and pluralism, flexibility and variety, also had begun to permeate postmodern culture. If you were a Fox and a wife, it had become easier to enjoy a multiplicity of interests, a dual life of work and family.

Studying the lives of the century's most prominent women, I couldn't help but think of the talented, unfamous women of my own acquaintance—not only my cousin Magda, who divorced in order to begin a life of her own choosing, but also Judith Giordan, one of the few women running the research-and-development labs of a major corporation, who married but decided that children were incompatible with her professional ambitions; my friend "Molly," an outstanding lawyer who, at the last minute, was passed over for partnership at one of the country's leading law firms, along with most of her female colleagues; and, of course, my sister, who can't go to a family gathering without hearing the same tiresome question: "So have you met anyone special lately?"

Gifted professional women in the twentieth century have undoubtedly made tremendous progress. Yet that progress has not followed an unimpeded path. The lives of Mileva Maric and the women who tried to improve on the lot of Einstein's wife tell the tale of constructive change. While most of these women achieved some measure of personal happiness and professional success, their lives taken together represent not so much a tale of final accomplishment as an instructive work in progress. My hope is that their stories serve as a blueprint, however impressionistic, for men and women who are themselves struggling to achieve a more creative icon for the union of ambition and love, work and marriage.

Einstein's Wife

Mileva Maric Einstein

What a strange thing must be a girl's soul! Do you really believe that you could find permanent happiness through others, even if this be the one and only beloved man?

Albert Einstein to Marie Winteler, his first love.

The Forgotten Wife

During the fall of 1891, a quiet, dark-haired girl entered the Royal Classical High School in Zagreb. She was painfully shy and not particularly pretty, and she walked with a noticeable limp. But no one who knew her could help but be impressed by sixteen-year-old Mileva Maric. For she possessed an unmistakable spark of genius, a dedication to mathematics and science that was unusual for anyone at that age, and in that time and place, extraordinary for a girl. As a result, she had received a special dispensation to attend the all-boys' school and thus had become one of the first girls in the Austro-Hungarian Empire to sit in a classroom with boys.

Mileva Maric took her place in the Zagreb high school just as Maria Sklodowska (later Marie Curie) was getting her degree in physics from the Sorbonne. Indeed, until she fell in love with Albert Einstein a few years later, the brilliant Serbian student would follow a path remarkably similar to that of her Polish contemporary, leaving behind home and family to become one of the first women ever to study physics at a university.

Mileva Maric was born in a rural Serbian outpost of the Habsburg monarchy, in Vojvodina, a province of what was then Southern Hun-

gary, and an ethnic melting pot of Croats, Slovaks, Hungarians, Roma-
nians, and Gypsies. Mileva's father, Milos Maric, was a successful and
well-to-do civil servant. He and his wife, Marija, would eventually have
three children. Mileva, or "Mitza," as she was affectionately called, was
the oldest. Born in 1875, she was eight years older than her sister,
Zorka, and ten years older than her brother, Milos junior. And she was
said always to have been her father's favorite.

When Mileva was a child, it seemed as though there was nothing
she put her mind to that she couldn't do. She showed an uncanny
knack for mastering everything from mathematics and languages to
handicrafts and painting. By the age of eleven, during her first year at a
secondary school for girls, Mileva had become the top student in her
class.

Before long, the Marics had extracted a long list of special exemp-
tions and dispensations from school authorities and government bureaucrats, which allowed Mileva to break through the rigid gender
barrier in Austro-Hungarian education. First, in 1890, when Mileva
turned fifteen, her parents sent her to a school in the neighboring village of Sabac, across the border in Serbia, where there were no rules
explicitly excluding girls and where the curriculum was probably
stronger in the sciences than it would have been at an all-girls' school.
Mileva, who already had shown herself to be something of a prodigy
when it came to mathematics, also began to show an aptitude for languages and art. She produced sophisticated, highly detailed sketches of
local village scenes. And at the secondary school in Sabac, where typically only one foreign language was taught, she got permission to study
French as well as German, and soon became fluent in both languages.
When she began attending school in Zagreb, where Greek was also a
requirement, she mastered that language too.

It was in Zagreb that Mileva Maric probably first developed a taste
for physics and first demonstrated the grit to pursue an unladylike vocation in the sciences. Mileva began her studies in Zagreb as a "private
student," which probably meant that she received tutoring but did not,
at first, attend classes at the gymnasium, the college-preparatory
school, which was reserved for male students. Her relative isolation
would not have been entirely unwelcome: Since childhood, Mileva had

suffered from a congenital hip deformity that caused her to limp. She had been forced to suffer the taunts of classmates, who ridiculed her as much for her extraordinary intelligence as for her physical handicap. She grew up painfully shy and sensitive, yet also exceptionally determined. At a time when the few women who dared to break through rigid barriers to pursue a higher education were often harassed by male students and faculty, Mileva applied for, and won, permission to attend physics lectures at the gymnasium. Recalling his own days at a Viennese gymnasium in the 1930s, Gerald Holton, an Einstein scholar, said of Maric's feat: "The idea of a girl sitting in on a class [was] so, oh, bizarre . . . the poor girl would have been the subject of attacks in the early years and seduction in the later years." Yet although she was the only woman in her class, Mileva was awarded the highest grades for her work in both math and physics.

If she was to pursue a higher education, a woman of Mileva's generation needed brains, bravery, and an ability to envision a life that ran counter to the norms of her day. However, even for such a woman the chances of succeeding, as Mileva was to discover, were slim indeed.

For it was one of the ironies of nineteenth-century Europe that the very philosophical changes that celebrated individualism and the freedom of human will, that extolled the cult of the hero and established the rights of man, specifically excluded women from the new spirit of liberty. From Rousseau and Hegel to Darwin and Hume, the great thinkers of the eighteenth and nineteenth centuries supported the view of women as inferior beings. Even John Locke, who championed every man's equal right to his "natural freedom, without being subjected to the will or authority of any man," put women in the same category as animals and upheld "the Subjection that is due from a Wife to her Husband."

Such thinking came to be institutionalized in law—and hence, also, in society. When Maric embarked on her career, the increasingly bureaucratized world of the nineteenth century had imposed more, rather than less, explicit restrictions on women. The Code Napoleon, for example, classified married women—along with children and the insane—as legal incompetents; it also vastly expanded a husband's power over his wife, eliminating her right to control her own bank account or even to keep her correspondence private. And universities that had not explicitly barred women from attending in the eighteenth century did so in the nineteenth. Thus, when she set off for Zurich at the turn of the century, Maric did so not only to complete the final step of her education but also to study in one of the only cities in Europe where women were permitted to attend and graduate from the university.

It is against this backdrop that Mileva Maric and Albert Einstein met in Zurich in 1896 and embarked on a bohemian, and decidedly modern, love affair. They were fellow classmates at the prestigious Swiss Federal Polytechnic, which is better known as the ETH, its German acronym. Mileva was the only woman in her class and the fifth woman ever to attend the school. And although she was shy and studious, her first year in Switzerland was academically successful. Though most of what is known about Maric's life during this period comes from recently published correspondence between her and Einstein, it is clear that Maric took to her first year of studies with quiet self-assurance and a belief that a world of opportunity was open to her. What lends exceptional poignancy to the couple's courtship and marriage is that from the beginning, Mileva, who thought at first that she would never marry, seemed to sense the danger to her professional dreams that was posed by her passionate feelings for her brilliant and effusively affectionate "Johnnie." (The nickname Johnnie is a diminutive for Johann and probably a play on the fact that, in German, Johann is a common name for a servant and for everyman.)

Initially, Mileva had not planned to study physics. After completing her secondary education, she entered the University of Zurich, in the summer of 1896, as a medical student—the Zurich university system having become the first in Europe to grant admission to women, in 1867. An interest in medicine ran in the Maric family. Her brother, Milos, would become a well-known expert in histology. And both Mileva and her younger son, Eduard, would develop a keen—though ultimately ill-fated—interest in psychiatry. But for reasons that have never been fully explained, Mileva switched her studies from medicine to math and physics at the ETH, a fact that probably hastened the demise of her career.

It is tempting to surmise that Mileva abandoned her medical studies in response to some trauma she experienced at the hands of hostile classmates or teachers during a time when she was still very much alone in a strange city. Yet she showed few signs of vulnerability during her first years as a university student; on the contrary, Mileva was almost cocky in her zest for independence and learning. Nothing seemed to scare her as she blithely marched from one male-dominated discipline to the next.

What is most notable about Mileva's youth, in fact, is not her dedication to one specific field of study but rather her wide range of interests and her boundless zest for new academic experiences. Long after she had committed herself to studying physics, for instance, Mileva maintained an abiding interest in psychiatry, regaling Einstein with reports of the latest studies in the field, such as the new experiments in hypnotism, just as he showered her with news of the latest discoveries in physics. For if Einstein was consumed by physics, Maric was drawn to math, physics, medicine, music, and, eventually, the raising of both children and exotic cacti.

Legend has it that the couple met when Einstein asked Maric how she had arrived at the solution to a particular problem—probably in mathematics—for which he himself had not found the answer. In the intimacy of a small class of five students, Maric and Einstein, who took several courses together, couldn't help but get to know each other through their shared interest in physics. Einstein, who at seventeen was still virtually a boy, must have been somewhat in awe of his unusual female classmate, who was three and a half years his senior. They discovered a shared love of music and the outdoors. During their first year together, Albert often joined Mileva and her friends for musical evenings. Albert played the violin, while Mileva sang or accompanied him on the piano. Although in later life he developed an aversion to mountains, as a young student in love, he spent some of his happiest weekends hiking with Mileva through the Alps.

Maric told Einstein early in their relationship that she doubted she would ever marry, because although she insisted that "a woman can make a career just like a man," she apparently also believed the two enterprises to be mutually exclusive. What she didn't say, but probably assumed, was that the combination of her physical deformity and what was at the time considered to be her decidedly "unwomanly" intellectual interests made her a less than desirable prospect for marriage. Indeed, one of their classmates once remarked to Einstein that he would "never consider marrying a woman who wasn't completely healthy." (To which Einstein is said to have replied, laconically: "But she has such a sweet voice.")

It is worth noting that from the beginning, Mileva and Albert were drawn together not only by love but also by the disapproval of others. They saw themselves united in adversity, besieged on all sides—by their parents, who opposed their relationship for a long list of reasons headed by their religious differences; by some of their professors, who didn't know what to make of the eccentric young couple; and finally even by some of their friends, who resented the attention the lovers lavished on each other.

Yet even though Maric was very attracted to Einstein and aware that she had few romantic prospects, she wasn't ready to settle down, either to her studies at the ETH or to her relationship with Einstein. By fall of the following year, she had transferred to the University of Heidelberg, one of the oldest and most venerable academic institutions in Europe, where she audited courses for one semester. (Heidelberg was among the many European universities in which women were still not permitted to matriculate, although since 1891 the institution had permitted women to sit in as auditors.) According to Desanka Trbuhovic-Gjuric, a Serbian historian who wrote one of the only accounts of Maric's life, the young woman left Zurich because she feared the consequences of her feelings toward Einstein.

Certainly, the evidence suggests that Maric had good reason to fear her relationship with Einstein. Within a year of her return from her semester in Heidelberg, Mileva would undergo a shocking metamorphosis from a seemingly independent, ambitious, and consummately self-assured young woman to one racked by doubts, disappointment, and resignation.

But at the writing of Maric's first letter to Einstein from Heidelberg, her decision to leave the ETH almost certainly stemmed more from an irrepressible urge for academic adventure than from an instinct for self-preservation. In fact, Mileva was having such a good time that it took her weeks even to get around to writing her boyfriend. And when she did, her correspondence brimmed not only with self-confidence and a hunger for discovery but also with a joie de vivre that was decidedly lacking in her later years: "I don't think the structure of the human skull is to be blamed for man's inability to understand the concept of infinity. He would certainly be able to understand it if, when young, and while developing his sense of perception, he were allowed to venture out into the universe rather than being cooped up on earth or, worse yet, confined within four walls in a provincial backwater. If someone can conceive of infinite happiness, he should be able to comprehend the infinity of space—I should think it much easier. And human beings are so clever and have accomplished so much, as I have observed once again here in the case of the Heidelberg professors."

In that first letter, Mileva also recounted her enthusiasm for a four-hour lecture she had just attended on the kinetic theory of gases, given by Philipp Lenard. The renowned theoretical physicist, who would become an enthusiastic supporter of the Nazis and a nemesis to Einstein, was nevertheless to be an important influence in Einstein's early work. For example, it was Lenard who discovered that a light beam trained on a piece of metal can dislodge electrons from the surface, an insight that paved the way for Einstein's explanation of the "photoelectric effect," an early milestone of quantum theory for which Einstein would win the Nobel Prize. Lenard also would become known for his explanation of Brownian motion, a theory that explained the unceasing and irregular motion of minute bodies suspended in liquid and that in turn would help lay the foundation for Einstein's later work on the electron theory of metals.

Maric's return the following February was due, at least in part, to Einstein's entreaties to his "little runaway." Indeed, there seemed to be no stopping the momentum of their relationship. Although it wasn't until a year later that Mileva began referring to Albert in the familiar *du* form—a usage that connoted far more intimacy at the time than it does today—the couple probably already had become lovers. By September of that year, 1899, when they were both on vacation, Albert wrote to her from Milan, where he stayed with his family, that he wished he could get back sooner to "our place" in Zurich, "the nicest and coziest place I can think of," probably a reference to the Bachtold rooming house where Mileva lived at the time. Upon his return to Zurich, Einstein planned to look for a new room nearby, but to avert "start[ing] any rumors," he would not move into the Bachtold residence itself.

Another profound change was beginning to take place, though, one that would foreshadow the growing difficulties Mileva would have in maintaining an ongoing commitment to her work. That summer, she stayed with her parents in the family home outside Novi Sad, in Vojvodina. It was hot and buggy. And because of an outbreak of scarlet fever and diphtheria, she never ventured into town. Instead, Mileva spent much of her vacation cramming for the first of two major examinations in October, which she would have to pass in order to get her diploma. Partly because of the ETH lectures she had missed during her semester in Heidelberg, she felt insecure about her command of the material in at least two classes. But her letters also hint at a more general sense of foreboding, which seems to go well beyond the natural anxiety of a student who is trying to make up coursework. Toward the end of the summer, she wrote to Einstein: "I'll probably be back in Zurich on the 25th [of September], but rather than looking forward to it, I'm returning with mixed feelings." Her apprehensions seem especially puzzling given the numerous educational hurdles she already had vaulted over.

Einstein, for his part, tried to allay her fears. "I can't think of any other assurances to offer you, other than to say that you shouldn't let this little exam bother you too much," he wrote to her. "That should be easy for you—especially with such harmless competition."

It turned out that, at least for the moment, Mileva's fears were ill founded. Despite missing one semester, she passed her first year's examinations, her highest grade 5.5 out of a possible 6. By contrast, Einstein's final grade in physics was 5.25, and he received his only 6 in electrical engineering.

Yet sometime between that first jaunty letter from Heidelberg and the summer of 1899, something had shaken Mileva's confidence. Had she returned from her leave of absence to a less than friendly reception from her classmates and teachers? Had she compared herself to Einstein's Promethean genius and found herself wanting? Or, having fallen in love with Einstein, and believing in the incompatibility of marriage and a career, had she begun to doubt the strength of her professional convictions?

All three factors probably helped fuel Mileva's growing sense of insecurity. In addition, she was particularly plagued by the thundering disapproval of Einstein's parents. As far as Pauline and Hermann Einstein were concerned, Mileva had no redeeming qualities. They objected to her because she was not Jewish, because she was older than he, and because she was both physically lame and an intellectual. "Like you, she's a book," Pauline Einstein warned her son. "And you should have a wife." While Einstein actually seemed to enjoy goading his parents and flaunting his relationship, the elder Einsteins' disapproval weighed heavily on Maric.

Without ever having met the Einsteins, Mileva surmised Pauline's power. A woman who had held her family together over the years in the face of considerable obstacles, Pauline herself had made a match that was destined to disappoint her. Hermann was easygoing and passive. He had little business sense and was to run numerous commercial ventures into the ground. Pauline, who had come from a wealthy family, found it difficult to tolerate her husband's successive failures; not only did she have to suffer the social stigma of reduced circumstances but both she and members of her family invested, and lost, large sums in several of Hermann's business schemes. After each failure, Hermann uprooted his family; he moved them around Germany, Switzerland, and Italy in search of new opportunities. The relocations were often traumatic. Before the family moved to Italy, for example, in 1894, Albert and his sister, Maya, were forced to watch the contractor who had bought the comfortable villa where they had grown up, in Munich, demolish it, then replace it with an unsightly apartment complex. To make matters worse, Albert, who was only fifteen, was to be left behind to finish his gymnasium education. The plan, which reflected Pauline's driving and unsentimental ambitions for her son, ultimately backfired; for Albert dropped out of school and crossed the Alps to rejoin his family. Where Albert was concerned, Pauline seemed dedicated to nothing so much as ensuring that he would develop the backbone that she felt his father lacked.

Maric lived in fear of Pauline Einstein, whose tirades against her Einstein recounted in almost sadistic detail. On one occasion he described a "scene" in which Pauline "threw herself onto her bed, buried her head in the pillow, and wept like a child." After regaining her composure, Einstein said, his mother asserted: "You are ruining your future. No decent family will have her." Not surprisingly, despite Einstein's assurances that his mother would not confiscate his mail, sometimes Maric wrote to him via registered post to make sure her letters would not be intercepted.

The more insecure Maric became in her relationship with Einstein, the more she came to identify her interests with his, ultimately putting Einstein's welfare ahead of her own. Whether out of love or insight, she had become convinced of Einstein's potential long before his professors recognized it, and served as an indefatigable booster and helpmate to her beloved "Johnnie." Einstein was, in fact, a mediocre student and one of the few ETH graduates who did not receive a position as an assistant upon graduation, which made it difficult for him to get a job. Maric's determination to see Einstein succeed was, at least in part, a result of her own scientific zeal. In championing Einstein's unrecognized genius, Maric also undoubtedly was influenced by the prevailing cultural norms, which put the needs of men ahead of those of women, and perhaps even by a desire to emulate Pauline Einstein's leonine protectiveness.

Since the beginning of their relationship, Maric and Einstein had studied together over vast quantities of freshly brewed coffee. Gradually, and long before they ever married, Maric also came to assume a more traditional, wifely role. Already during the 1899–1900 school year, "Johnnie" would "pound the books as usual while poor Dollie [would] cook." Einstein, who had seemed detached from the world even as a child and, in later years, would become legendary for his rumpled appearance and for eschewing socks and slippers as an unnecessary distraction, craved Maric's maternal attentions. Even at that early stage, he was already so engrossed in his work that he rarely ate unless Mileva fed him, a fact that may have accounted for his chronic stomach problems. Maric saw less of her friends, who came to feel that Einstein was taking advantage of her, so much so that in July of 1900,

Mileva's friend Milana Bota, who had initially liked Einstein, wrote a letter to her own mother complaining that she "rarely sees [Mileva], because of the German [Einstein], whom she [Milana] has come to hate."

Eventually, Maric's protectiveness toward Einstein, who had difficulties with some of his professors, spilled over into their schoolwork and may have damaged her own academic relationships. For example, Einstein eventually developed serious problems with Heinrich Weber, the professor of physics at the ETH; by the time he graduated, there was so much bad blood, in fact, that Einstein was convinced that the reason he had trouble finding a job after graduation was that Weber was sabotaging his efforts. Maric also had her conflicts with Weber, who served as a thesis adviser to both young people. But her relationship with the professor was much better than Einstein's, who had been the only graduate from his class to be turned down for a post as an assistant. By contrast, Maric held a position in Weber's laboratory in 1901 and received an excellent evaluation for her work, according to Desanka Trbuhovic-Gjuric, Maric's biographer. Although the ETH has no record of an official appointment with a salary, it is possible that Maric worked in an unofficial capacity without pay. This scenario would not have been unusual given the fact that most women of her generation worked for little or no pay, if they were allowed into a laboratory at all.

What is clear is that Maric tried several times to intercede with Weber on Einstein's behalf—an effort in which she was unsuccessful and one that may have eroded her relationship with the professor. In the summer of 1901, Mileva wrote to her friend Helene Kaufler Savic: "I've already quarreled with Professor Weber two or three times, but now I am already used to such things. Because of him I have suffered a lot. . . . We still do not know what destiny has determined for us [Albert and Mileva]."

Maric gradually assumed that her destiny was tied to Einstein's. As if in confirmation, Maric suffered her first academic setback in the summer of 1900, when she failed her final exams. Although the final grades for both Maric and Einstein fell below the 5 point average that was necessary to pass, Einstein's 4.9 got rounded up to 5 so that he just barely squeaked by. Maric's 4, on the other hand, meant that she failed outright; once again, she had gotten high marks in physics, but it was a miserable 2.5 average in the Theory of Functions that dragged down her final grade.

When it came to judging her academic performance, probably no one was harder on Maric than she was herself. In the spring of 1901, after Einstein had left Zurich to look for a job in Milan, Maric stayed behind at the ETH, feverishly studying to retake her exams. Just about the only respite she allowed herself was the weekends she spent with Einstein. During one exceptionally romantic trip to Lake Como, where the couple took a boat ride and visited the Villa Carlotta, with its magnificent gardens bursting with azaleas, camellias, and rhododendrons, Maric seemed to almost forget her academic travails. But in May she received another blow, in the form of a letter from home that was probably written by her father. Although the letter itself is lost, Maric's reaction to it suggests that it must have taken her to task both for her recent academic failure and for her relationship with Einstein, which her parents disapproved of almost as much as Einstein's did. It filled her with the sort of despair that would become all too characteristic of her state of mind in the coming years. "I received a letter from home today that has made me lose all desire, not only for having fun, but for life itself," Mileva wrote her beloved Johnnie. "I'm going to lock myself up and work hard, because it seems I can have nothing without being punished."

After years of academic triumph, Maric had lost her momentum. Mysteriously, in the summer of 1901, Maric failed the second round of examinations, and at about the same time, she also gave up the work on her dissertation.

Her friends knew that there was something terribly wrong, but Mileva could not bring herself to confide in anyone. For months, she stopped writing to her friend Helene Savic. "I just wasn't able to bring myself to do it in those awful times," she told Einstein. "I wrote a long letter once and poured my heart out to her, but then I tore it up." Indeed, almost no one but Einstein and the couple's parents knew that sometime in the early summer, just a few weeks before she was to sit for the second round of examinations, Mileva discovered that she was pregnant. The timing of the pregnancy could only underscore her fore-boding that she was destined to be "punished."

If her own growing sense of self-doubt had begun to slow her progress, then surely an unwanted pregnancy must have led her to doubt seriously the feasibility of her professional dreams. Although scientists and historians have pointed to Maric's failing her exams as proof of her intellectual inferiority, this seems hardly fair or logical, especially in light of the fact that Einstein's own performance at the ETH was relatively poor! Certainly, it is hard to imagine that the girl who had repeatedly distinguished herself as a top student in her native Serbia, who had passed the difficult ETH entry examination (which Einstein had failed the first time he took it), as well as the first round of university examinations, and who won at least some kudos from the hard-to-please Weber was simply not gifted enough to pass her final test. Robert Schulmann, an Einstein scholar, suggests that because the finals included an oral component, she might have been subject to the prejudice of her examiners. It is even more likely that Mileva's poor performance was due to anxiety brought on by both the discovery of her pregnancy and the actual physical discomforts of her condition, which in Mileva's case continued well past her first trimester. For Mileva, illness was often accompanied by severe emotional stress, a fact that later in her life would lead to a series of nervous breakdowns that eventually culminated in her death in 1948.

The pregnancy and her failure to complete her diploma ensured that Maric was now more dependent on Einstein than ever. In the intensely conservative world of the Swiss and Austro-Hungarian middle class, which was Maric's world, there could be no greater stigma than being an unwed mother. Even a stronger person—one who was not already overshadowed by the egotistical Einstein—would have had difficulty getting through this problematical period with her ambitions intact. But as things stood, Maric now came to rely on Einstein not only to save her good name by marrying her but also to provide, through his work, the only outlet left to her in science.

For Maric, the first years of the new century couldn't have seemed more bleak, and she clung to Einstein as to life itself. She suffered through the July exams alone while Einstein spent the month on holiday with his mother and sister. Afterward, she was forced to skulk home alone to her parents; for by then Einstein had taken up a temporary, poorly paid job as a substitute teacher in Schaffhausen, twenty miles north of Zurich. Mileva pleaded with him to help cushion her arrival at home: "Write my old man soon, sweetheart, because I'd like to leave on Saturday already, and they should have a letter before I arrive home. . . . Just write a short letter to my Papa. . . . Will you send me the letter so I can see what you've written?"

While she had once frowned upon marriage as unsuitable for a woman of her ambitions, it now remained Mileva's last hope. Yet the prospect of being reunited with Einstein still seemed remote. He had not yet received a position that would allow him to support a wife and child. At the same time, Mileva knew that Pauline Einstein was campaigning against her as hard as ever, an obstacle she tried desperately to overcome. "You should also remember that your parents have a false impression of me and that it's in my power to place myself in a more favorable light," she wrote to Einstein, outlining a strategy. "I think it will take much time and goodwill for reconciliation, but I'm sure it will happen. . . . I've even come up with some techniques to set the thing in motion. For example, if I could ingratiate myself with an acquaintance of theirs whom they look up to a little, then they would already be defeated for the most part (or so I think). I also have a few other ideas on this."

Her best intentions came to nothing, however. Sometime during the fall, when Mileva was in her fifth or sixth month of pregnancy, Pauline Einstein, who would never reconcile herself to the relationship between Mileva and her son, sent a scathing letter to the Maric family, which impugned Mileva's character and heightened her fear that Einstein's family would somehow find a way to stand between them. Maric, whose only contact with Einstein since learning of her pregnancy had been though the mails, now took a train to Switzerland; anxious that his parents not learn of her trip, she booked herself into a small hotel in Stein am Rhein, a few miles outside Schaffhausen.

That November, as she waited for Einstein to visit her in Stein am Rhein, Maric's position must have seemed nothing short of desperate to her. She was by now seven months pregnant, the child visibly rounding out her belly. Yet Einstein left her waiting several days before he scraped together the train fare to come and see her, a fact that should have given her an inkling of his limited capacity for commitment. Although he claimed to be short of money, it is much more likely that he was less than eager to see her, for Einstein's salary, which amounted to 150 francs plus room and board, should have been able to cover transportation.

And so Mileva waited, anxious over Albert's repeated delays, admonishing him to keep her visit a secret even from his sister, Maya— the only member of the Einstein family who supported their relationship—for fear that Albert's parents would learn of it. "I'm afraid that something could happen again, as it always has in the past. . . . Just don't give her my address sweetheart, I'm terribly worried about it. . . . Don't write your parents anything about me. No more fights; I dread the mere thought of it."

Throughout what was becoming known as the "Dollie affair," Maya, who was two years younger than her brother, acted as the family mediator: During Albert and Mileva's courtship, it was Maya who tried—usually unsuccessfully—to ease the tensions between her mother and her brother over the impending marriage. And when Pauline attacked Mileva, Maya was quick to come to her sister-in-law's defense. However, in the end, Einstein's ties to his sister turned out to be far closer than his relationships with either of his wives. By December, the young couple's situation had improved somewhat. Although Maric, who had by then returned home to Serbia, was by this time bedridden with complications of her pregnancy, and Einstein, as usual, had forgotten to remember her birthday, there was good news on the horizon. Einstein had learned that he would get a job in the Swiss Patent Office, a position that would give him a steady income and finally allow him to marry. And sometime at the end of January, following a difficult labor, Mileva gave birth to a baby girl, whom she named Lieserl (Little Lisa). Although Einstein was still in Switzerland, it now seemed to be only a matter of time before the couple could be married. "In two months' time we could find our lives brilliantly changed for the better, and the struggle would be over," wrote Einstein to Maric a month before she was to give birth. "I'm dizzy with joy when I think about it. . . . Together we'd surely be the happiest people on earth."

Yet it took over a year before the promised marriage came off. And when the couple were finally married, on January 6, 1903, the wedding took place under a cloud. In June of 1902, Einstein finally went to work in the Swiss Patent Office. In the fall, Hermann Einstein, who suffered from heart disease, became gravely ill and died, but not before finally granting permission for his son to marry Mileva. In the weeks before the wedding, Einstein busied himself with sorting out the estate of his father, whose business affairs were, as always, in a state of disarray. Now he also had to worry about supporting his mother, who had never made peace with her son's marriage and who had been left with nothing but debts.

In the meantime, one serious "problem" that Einstein couldn't bring himself to focus on was what to do about his daughter. Since the couple was unmarried, and both Pauline Einstein and the Marics continued to oppose their relationship, there had been talk about putting the child up for adoption, a solution that neither Mileva nor Albert seemed to welcome. Yet it is unlikely that he ever even saw his daughter—there is no record of Einstein having visited Serbia in the months after Lieserl's birth or of Maric traveling with her outside of Serbia. And Einstein appears to have left the fate of his daughter up to Maric and her parents. "Ask your Papa," he suggested in a letter written in December of 1901, shortly before Lieserl's birth. "He's an experienced man, and knows the world better than your overworked, impractical Johnnie."

By the time Maric and Einstein were married, shortly after the New Year, the Lieserl problem had still not been resolved. Far from enjoying the anticipation of her long-awaited wedding, Maric seemed to her friends deeply preoccupied in the months before her marriage. If anyone asked her what was wrong, all Mileva would say was that the problem was too "intensely personal." What she didn't need to say, her friends knew, was that Einstein was at the center of whatever it was that bothered her; some even surmised that the romance might be over. Few, if any, of their friends knew the extent of her troubles. Isolated in Serbia, Mileva appears to have kept the birth of her child a secret. Nor would any of her friends have known that the child was stricken by scarlet fever soon after the wedding and might have suffered lasting side effects.

What finally became of Lieserl may never be known. No record of her birth or death survives. Lieserl may have died as a consequence of her illness. But if she was put up for adoption, it was probably due in large part to Einstein's reluctance to compromise his work in the interests of caring for a small and possibly sickly child. Or Einstein may have feared that the stigma of an illegitimate child, especially one born to a Slav, would hurt his career in the decidedly conservative world of the Swiss civil service. In the late summer of 1903, a bittersweet exchange between Mileva and her new husband marks the last known written reference to Lieserl and hints at Mileva's anguish.

Maric was in Budapest, probably at the beginning of her second pregnancy, suffering the first bouts of morning sickness, when she wrote a short, plaintive note to Einstein: "Dear Johnnie . . . It's going quickly, but badly. I'm not feeling well at all. . . . Write me soon, okay? Your poor Dollie." Einstein replied: "I'm not the least bit angry that poor Dollie is hatching a new chick. In fact, I'm happy about it and had already given some thought to whether I shouldn't see to it that you get a new Lieserl. . . . I'm very sorry about what has befallen Lieserl. It's so easy to suffer lasting effects from scarlet fever. If only this will pass. As what is the child registered? We must take precautions that problems don't arise for her later."

To her academic failure, the trials of her courtship with Einstein, and the shame of an illegitimate pregnancy, Maric could now add the loss of her first child. If Maric became "gloomy" and "distrustful," as Einstein's biographers report, who could have blamed her? Yet, at least during the next few years, Maric seems to have handled her grief primarily by pouring all her dreams, love, and ambition into her husband. As long as she could maintain a scientific dialogue with Einstein and feel that she was helping to develop a new understanding of the universe and the scientific interests they had shared since the earliest days of their relationship, then perhaps all her suffering would have been worth it.

Einstein continued to promise Maric a life of shared work. "We'll be students (horrible dictu) as long as we live and won't give a damn about the world. . . . When you're my dear little wife we'll diligently work on science together so we don't become old philistines, right?" he had assured her just a month before Lieserl's birth.

For a time Einstein kept his promise. During the early years of their marriage, which was also the most productive period of Einstein's career, Einstein credited Maric with "solv[ing] all of his mathematical problems," a fact that is confirmed by their son Hans Albert, as well as by at least one student who lived for a time with the Einsteins.

Exactly how much she was to contribute to Einstein's work has become the subject of considerable controversy. Much of the debate revolves around fragmentary evidence suggesting that the original version of Einstein's three most famous articles, on the photoelectric effect, on Brownian motion, and on the theory of relativity, were signed Einstein-Marity, the latter name being a Hungarianized version of Maric. Although the original manuscripts have been lost, Abraham F. Joffe, a member of the Soviet Academy of Sciences, claimed that he saw the original papers when he was an assistant to Wilhelm Röntgen, who belonged to the editorial board of *Annalen der Physik*, which published the articles. (An article in a 1955 Soviet journal of physics quotes Joffe, now deceased, as ascribing the 1905 papers to "Einstein-Marity.")

Although there is no evidence to suggest that Maric came up with any of the original insights for the three most famous papers attributed to Einstein, she probably proofread the articles and performed the mathematical calculations for some of them. Svetozar Varicak, a student who lived with the Einsteins for several months in about 1910, remembered how Maric, after a day of cleaning, cooking, and caring for the children, would then busy herself with Einstein's mathematical calculations, often working late into the night. Varicak said he remembered feeling "so sorry for Mileva" that he sometimes helped her with the housework. At around this time, Maric also joined Einstein and Friedrich Adler for discussions in the quiet attic of the Zurich apartment building where the Einsteins and the Adlers both lived; on those afternoons, Katja Adler, Frederick's wife, watched the children.

During the early years of her marriage, Maric also spoke frequently to her family and friends about collaborating with her husband. She told Milana Bota, for example, about the work she was doing with Einstein. And in 1905, just after the completion of "On the Electrodynamics of Moving Bodies," the initial paper on special relativity, while Einsteins were on vacation in Serbia, Maric boasted to her father and Desana Tapavica Bala, who was married to the mayor of Novi Sad: "Just before we left for Novi Sad, we finished some important work that will make my husband world famous."

To whatever extent Maric managed to pursue science, at least during the early years, she had to all intents and purposes completely subsumed her ambitions and interests to those of her husband. Einstein had begun teaching at the University of Zurich, and she regularly attended his lectures. And even though she would soon be pregnant with her second son, Eduard, and had no household help, Maric took in boarders as a way to supplement the family's income and to free Einstein from financial worries.

Yet her efforts were not to be appreciated. Einstein's reputation had skyrocketed since 1905. And the more successful he became, the more he neglected his marriage. "Albert has devoted himself completely to physics and it seems to me that he has little time if any for the family," Mileva confided to her friend Helene Savic. Einstein spent more and more time away from home, in the company of scientists— gatherings to which Maric was not invited. Always absentminded, Einstein also began to show signs of the callousness and insensitivity that would become much more pronounced as he grew older. In the fall of 1909, Einstein took up a correspondence with Anna Meyer-Schmid, an old girlfriend; Maric was so incensed when she intercepted one of Meyer-Schmid's letters that she wrote a letter to the woman's husband, complaining of the "inappropriate" correspondence.

Relations between husband and wife deteriorated after the family moved to Prague, where Einstein had been offered a position at the university, in about 1911. Neither Maric nor Einstein liked Austria-Hungary's Bohemian capital, a city marked by stark disparities between great wealth and grinding poverty, as well as by growing nationalist hostilities. But the move was hardest on Maric, who was particularly sensitive to the tensions between the Czechs, with whom she identified, and the city's nationalistic German elite. Prague was so polarized, in fact, that there was one university for Germans, where Einstein taught, and one for Czechs (and incidentally, there was anti-Semitism everywhere).

What's more, with the birth of her children, and the burdens of running a household, Maric had become the "philistine" Hausfrau that Einstein had always shunned and that she herself had vowed never to become. She spent most of her time at home with her two small children, especially Eduard, who was an exceptionally sickly infant. Trapped in a city she disliked and a life she scorned, Maric became lonely and depressed.

As for Einstein, he had little sympathy for the difficulties his wife was experiencing. He complained about Maric's moodiness. And he spent more time away from home than ever. While they were living in Prague, Einstein traveled almost constantly. "It must have been very interesting in Karlsruhe," Maric wrote her husband in October. "I would like to have been there and listened a little, and seen all these fine people. . . . It is such an eternity since we saw each other, I wonder if you will recognize me?" Yet, come November, Einstein took off once again, this time to the Solvay Conference in Brussels, a convocation of the world's leading physicists.

The turning point in the Einsteins' marriage came in 1912. At first things seemed to be going better after Einstein accepted a new job at the ETH, which took the family back to Zurich. Day-to-day life in their beloved city, where the Einsteins had many friends, became more pleasant as they resumed their musical evenings with friends like Adolf Hurwitz and their excursions into the Alps.

But the fragile rapprochement would not last long. In the spring of 1912, during a trip to Berlin, Einstein had become reacquainted with his cousin Elsa Lowenthal and declared his love for her—for "I must love somebody," he wrote her in April, in a letter that began a secret correspondence that was to last nearly two years. As if this betrayal were not enough, Einstein maligned his wife in the letters to his lover, calling Maric "the sourest sourpot that there has ever been" and describing his relationship with her as that of a man and his "employee."

Thus, for Maric, it must have been particularly poignant when, in 1913, she met Marie Curie during a trip to Paris, one of the last journeys she would make with her husband. Curie and the Einsteins hit it off so well that they organized a family vacation together (the widowed Curie had two daughters) later that year in the Alps. Unlike Einstein's male colleagues, Marie Curie is likely to have treated Maric with the sort of respect that the young Serbian housewife rarely received anymore. With her two Nobel Prizes, Curie must have been an inspiration but also a painful reminder of Maric's own failed dreams and strained marriage.

Yet Maric wasn't the only woman in her circle whose ambitions had been thwarted by marriage and whose marriage, ultimately, would end in tragedy. In Prague, one of the only people with whom Maric became friendly was a Russian physicist, Tatjana Afansijeva, who collaborated with her husband Paul Ehrenfest for years, until the couple's estrangement eventually led to Ehrenfest's suicide in 1933. Maric would also have felt a kinship for Clara Immerwahr, the first woman to receive a doctorate in chemistry from the University of Breslau, whose research on behalf of her husband, Fritz Haber, an expert on gases, went largely unrewarded. Although no correspondence survives between the two wives, Maric and Immerwahr knew each other well. When the Habers' marriage finally collapsed, it was Immerwahr who committed suicide. Haber, a friend of Einstein's, who, as director of the Kaiser Wilhelm Institute of Physical Chemistry and Electrochemistry, was instrumental in bringing Einstein to Berlin, always blamed himself for his wife's death. Maric also had much in common with Katja Adler, who had given up her studies in physics to marry Friedrich.

Though Maric loved her husband and was not yet prepared to give up on their marriage, she could not live with him on his terms any longer. Just eighteen months after settling back in Zurich, Einstein had accepted a position at the Prussian Academy of Science in Berlin, over Maric's objections. Both of them shared an abiding dislike of Germany, Einstein so much so that he had taken the extraordinary step of renouncing his German citizenship when he was a teenager, an act that left him stateless for several years, until he became a Swiss citizen in 1901. Still, Einstein was drawn to the august Prussian academy, and, initially, Maric agreed to accompany him in April of 1914.

But Maric detested Berlin; she liked neither the city nor its inhabitants, and being there was made all the worse by the fact that Einstein's relatives, including his fearsome mother, lived there. Even at their lowest points, Einstein blamed the bad relationship between his wife and Pauline Einstein on his mother's "perfidious . . . hatred" of Maric. When Maric traveled to Berlin to look for an apartment a few months before they were to move, Einstein suggested that she avoid his family altogether. Instead, Maric stayed with Immerwahr and Haber. By the time Paul Ehrenfest visited the Einsteins in Berlin, a few months later, he found that both Maric and Hans Albert were miserable in their new home. Maric remained as isolated as ever, while her son chafed at the rote learning and discipline he encountered in school. In July, Maric decided to return to Zurich with her sons.

Despite their problems, Maric assumed that the separation was temporary. Bidding farewell to his family at the train station, Einstein had wept bitterly. Maric was convinced that Einstein would eventually leave the hated Berlin and rejoin them. For months, Maric and her sons lived in a rooming house and waited anxiously for his return; it was a period that Hans Albert remembered as "the worst time." When even the outbreak of World War I failed to bring Einstein home, Maric was forced to face the hard truth. "I don't expect to ask you for a divorce," Einstein wrote to his wife in July 1914. "All I ask you is that you send me news of my beloved boys every two weeks." Although Maric sought to foster a long-distance relationship between father and sons, the boys, especially Hans Albert, resented their father's absence. And Einstein soon came to blame Maric for the rift that developed with his sons; he accused her of intercepting his messages and threatened that he would sever all contacts with the family if Maric so much as commented to them on one of his letters.

The break with Einstein represented the end of Maric's hopes and dreams—not because she had chosen to fulfill herself, as have so many bourgeois women over the years, through the career of her husband, but because she had left herself few alternatives. By marrying Einstein, Maric had attached herself not only to one of the greatest and most forceful minds of the twentieth century but also to a potent combination of gender, motherhood, and isolation. While a stronger personality might have overcome even these obstacles, Maric had a pessimistic nature that, ultimately, tipped the balance and ensured her defeat. Her ambition—which once had so resembled Einstein's—could have allowed her to find some satisfaction in his success, if only he had continued to allow her to play even a small, unobtrusive role in it.

As Einstein's own success and intellectual thirst grew, his ability to embrace the needs of even those closest to him virtually evaporated. Einstein himself acknowledged that he had became obsessively absorbed with his ideas, to the exclusion of almost everything else. This man who had no interest in food or clothes, who had to be prodded to brush his unruly shock of hair, who eschewed socks as an unnecessary hindrance, stripped away emotional ties just as ruthlessly. "I'm not a family man," Einstein confessed when he was already in Berlin, separated from his first wife and two sons, and remarried to a woman who placed no intellectual demands on him. "I want to know how God created this world. . . . I want to know his thoughts, the rest are details." Max Born, a friend and rival, both as a physicist and as a humanist, would say of Einstein: "For all his kindness and sociability, and love of humanity, he was nevertheless totally detached from his environment and the human beings included in it."

Unlike Pierre Curie, who amplified his wife's already strong sense of self-confidence and professional drive by ceaselessly reinforcing her ambitions and who saw his own happiness in their shared success, Einstein lacked the generosity of spirit—and the vision—to keep even a small space cleared for Maric on the vast canvas of his scientific universe. The final severing of intellectual ties between husband and wife probably occurred around 1913, when Einstein began collaborating with Marcel Grossman on the general theory of relativity; the collaboration is particularly noteworthy since, according to Einstein's biographer Peter Michelmore, Maric was "as good at mathematics as Marcel [Grossman]."

Although well educated, Maric had few prospects of employment since she had never finished her degree or held a full-time job. Like many single mothers over the ages, she also found herself in deep financial trouble. With the start of World War I and the disruption in the mails, Maric received Einstein's checks only sporadically and often was unable to pay her bills. As the war progressed, the devaluation of the German mark only worsened her situation. Maric began giving music lessons and tutoring in mathematics. And she was often reduced to borrowing money from friends.

The progress of the war brought only more grief. Maric's brother, Milos, was taken prisoner on the Russian front and disappeared in the Soviet Union; although he became a respected professor in Moscow, the family neither saw him again nor, for years, was aware of his fate. In 1915, Maric would have learned that Einstein had rented an apartment around the corner from his cousin Elsa. The arrangement must have been a painful reminder of her own "cozy" living arrangements with "Johnnie" during their student days in Zurich. Worse still, the relationship with Elsa inevitably led Einstein to demand a divorce and to wage an escalating battle for the custody of their children.

It was the fear of losing her children, more than anything else, that probably led Maric to a physical and mental breakdown in the summer of 1916. Although Einstein later acknowledged that he had "the greatest confidence in Mileva's role as a mother" and eventually would thank her for trying to bolster the relationship between father and sons, in the years leading up to their divorce he harassed her relentlessly for turning the boys against him. And although he rarely showed any interest in Eduard, whose emotional fragility he considered a repulsive sign of weakness, Einstein schemed repeatedly to move his older son, Hans Albert, to Berlin. When the pressure finally led to Maric's collapse, Einstein, who happened to be in Zurich at the time, refused to visit his wife, telling his friend Michelangelo Besso that he was convinced she was merely feigning illness as a way to stall their divorce. Einstein finally relented when she was hospitalized.

What exactly was wrong with Maric has never been determined. Some friends assumed she had suffered a series of strokes. Einstein himself believed—or hoped—that she was suffering from tuberculous meningitis, a potentially fatal infection of the brain membranes. Yet over the next several months, Maric gradually got better. She would never fully recover, however, and was to be hospitalized repeatedly during subsequent years.

Einstein enthusiasts might be tempted to attribute the role Einstein played in the dissolution of his first marriage to his "monomaniacal" devotion to his work. But there is considerable evidence that Einstein's growing antipathy for Maric was grounded in malice and misogyny as much as tunnel vision. Certainly, Einstein displayed a particular dislike for intelligent women. In Berlin, he told Esther Salman, a female physics student, that "very few women are creative." Salman objected, noting that Marie Curie was surely an exception. Einstein, who perhaps failed to recognize his own brand of single-focused genius when encountering it in a woman, dismissed the female Nobel laureate as having "the soul of a herring." By the end of his life, his sister, Maya, is said to have been one of the only women Einstein treated with consideration and respect.

Yet it was a tribute to Maric's enduring love and commitment, not only to her sons but also to Einstein, that the couple eventually achieved a reconciliation of sorts. By 1918, a year before their divorce, Einstein would stay with Maric and the children whenever he visited Zurich, even though he was already living with Elsa. And although Einstein's children, particularly Hans Albert, never overcame the resentment they felt for him, it was not for lack of effort on the part of Maric, who always encouraged the boys to be proud of their father.

Most biographers have treated Maric, at best, as a footnote barely worth mentioning in the great man's life or, at worst, as a "gloomy" and "laconic" shadow that clouded his existence. This was due, first, to Einstein's unwillingness to discuss his personal life and, later, to a conscious effort, both by Einstein's executors and by scientists, to protect Einstein's monolithic reputation from even a hint of human frailty, let alone personal scandal. Indeed, in 1958, the executors, Otto Nathan and Helen Dukas, who had been Einstein's secretary, and his stepdaughter Margot blocked the publication of a book by Hans Albert and Frieda Einstein, which was based on Einstein's lifelong correspondence with Maric and his sons; the book, which undoubtedly would have revealed the mortal man behind the great genius, has still not been published. Yet during Maric's lifetime, long after the couple's divorce, Maric continued to command the respect and sympathy of a surprisingly wide array of mutual friends. Scientists like Michelangelo Besso and Fritz Haber, whose sympathies might otherwise have been expected to go to their much-respected colleague Einstein and who

served as go-betweens for the couple during their divorce, often defended Maric's motives, her lifestyle, and her role as a mother. Their
neighbors the Hurwitzs also remained close to Maric until the time of
her death.

Though Maric achieved some stability for herself and her children
after her divorce, she would soon face another domestic tragedy. In
1920, in the dead of winter, Maric was called home to Novi Sad by a
family emergency. Her sister, Zorka, who had stayed with her in
Zurich for a few years during Maric's separation, had begun to go insane. Maric arrived home to find her sister paranoid and hostile; the
only creatures to whom Zorka showed any affection were cats.

Eduard was only ten years old at the time. But within a few years
Maric would come to recognize in him the signs of mental instability
that she had seen in her sister that winter. As a small child, Tete, as he
was called by his parents, had begun to suffer severe earaches that
made his whole head throb. Gradually, the pain took on a more sinister
form, and it seemed as though the sensitive, high-strung Tete was being tormented by ear-splitting noises inside his head. As a teenager, the
thin, handsome boy grew fat and deeply troubled. He suffered mood
swings that swept him from lethargy to nearly suicidal hysteria, as he
ranted and raved in an effort to still the voices in his head. At one time,
Tete, who read voraciously and developed an uncanny ear for music,
was widely believed to have inherited his father's genius; he had even
enrolled at the University of Zurich, intending to study psychiatry. Yet
before long, his intellectual aspirations devolved into a passion for
pornography and the biographies of great men. The youth who had
once adored the great man who was his father and whose visits to
Berlin as a teenager were often followed by desperate, passionate letters
pleading for fatherly love and reassurance, now turned on Einstein, be-
rating him in a deluge of hate mail.

Einstein, for his part, came less and less frequently to Zurich. He
vacillated between feeling guilty for having abandoned his children,
Tete in particular, and blaming Maric and her family's history of mental
illness for his younger son's fate. As a man of old-world upbringing, he
probably couldn't help but see his son's vulnerability as a sign of weakness, an almost inexcusable character flaw. "Who knows if it would not

have been better if he had left the world before he had really known this life," observed Tete's father, even before the appearance of any overt signs of mental illness. When Einstein emigrated to the United States in 1933, fleeing the Nazi tide that swept across Germany, the goodbye he said to Tete and Maric was final; he would never see either of them again.

Separated now by an ocean and, eventually, by another world war, Maric was left to cope with her son's mental collapse. Maric's mother died in 1935, Zorka three years later. Under their divorce settlement, Einstein had given Maric the thirty thousand kronor that he had received for the Nobel Prize. But the costs of Tete's medical care remained an enormous burden to her during these Depression years. His fits of insanity forced her, periodically, to send Tete to the Burgholzli, a mental institution in Zurich. At other times, she took him on trips into the mountains, in the hope of calming his nerves. Eventually, she was forced to sell two of the three real estate properties she had purchased with the proceeds of the Nobel Prize. And in order not to lose the building on Huttenstrasse where she and Tete lived, Maric finally agreed to transfer ownership of the property to Einstein, although she was allowed to keep the rental income from apartments in the building. But in 1947, Einstein sold the house without consulting Maric. Under the terms of the sale, Maric was permitted to remain in her apartment for the rest of her life. Indeed, because she retained Einstein's power of attorney in Switzerland, she was able to keep the proceeds of the sale. But the episode represented a final, devastating act of betrayal by the one man Maric had ever loved, the man to whom she had entrusted, so completely, her life and happiness. To make matters worse, in 1938, Hans Albert, his wife, Frieda, and their son, Klaus, had emigrated to the United States. Shortly after their arrival, Klaus, Maric's first grandchild, who was only about six years old, suddenly became ill and died.

In May of 1948, Tete was home with Maric when, toward nightfall, the demons suddenly returned. As he searched frantically for some imaginary missing object, he began destroying everything within reach. He hurtled books, dishes, mementos, at the walls and finally collapsed on the floor, weeping inconsolably. In the midst of Tete's fit, Maric suffered an emotional breakdown and was rushed to the hospital.

The few friends who came to visit her in the hospital were struck by the severity of Maric's latest breakdown. Utterly confused, she began to complain about Einstein, the hospital, the nurses. She rang her call button so relentlessly, the staff was forced to disconnect it. Over and over she begged to be sent to the Burgholzli, perhaps because she recognized the extent of her mental collapse, perhaps because Tete was there now. Finally on August 4, 1948, Mileva Maric died alone in her hospital room, physically, mentally, and financially broken.

In his later years, Einstein liked to boast that he had survived not only Nazism but also two wives. For in the end, Elsa's lot had not been much happier than Mileva's. Due in large part to Einstein's interest in other women, his second marriage showed signs of strain even before the couple emigrated to the United States, according to Konrad Wachsman, the architect who designed their summer house in Caputh, Germany. "Women were drawn to the world-famous professor like iron filings to a magnet," write Roger Highfield and Paul Carter, two Einstein biographers. According to the accounts of numerous acquaintances, Einstein did not discourage women's advances. He often escorted female companions to the opera and took them on sailing trips near his summer house. These excursions frequently resulted in jealous outbursts from Elsa, who, however, ultimately accepted her husband's marital detours.

Nor was Einstein particularly sensitive to his wife's most basic emotional needs. In 1934, soon after the Einsteins moved to Princeton, Elsa traveled to Paris and found that Ilse, her eldest daughter from a previous marriage, was dying. She returned home with Ilse's ashes and was soon herself bedridden with severe heart and kidney problems. Throughout the long months of Elsa's illness, which culminated in her death in 1936, Einstein stuck "frightfully to his [scientific] problems." In a letter to a friend, Elsa confided: "I have never before seen him so engrossed in his work." After her death, Einstein corresponded with Max Born about his work at Princeton and, with shocking indifference, about the loss of his wife: "I have settled down splendidly here [at Princeton]," Einstein wrote. "I hibernate like a bear in its cave, and really feel more at home than ever before in all my varied existence.

This bearishness has been accentuated further by the death of my mate, who was more attached to human beings than I."

Nor was Einstein moved by the plight of his son Tete, who remained at the Burgholzli for seventeen years after Maric's death. In his lucid moments, Tete spoke of his brother, Hans Albert, who visited Tete occasionally during his trips to Europe after the war, and of his father, who never came to see him and rarely wrote. But after Maric's death, Tete could never bring himself to speak of his mother again.

When Tete died, finally, in October of 1965, his death certificate identified him as the son of the late Albert Einstein, who hadn't seen his son in over three decades. Maric, who lived for years under the shadow of Eduard's insanity and died, as she had lived, struggling to ease his pain, received no mention at all.

The only one whose memory of Mileva Maric remained fresh and loving and lucid was her son Hans Albert. Hans Albert Einstein's own life, in marked contrast to that of his father, was a testimony to his regard for strong and intelligent women. Hans Albert blamed Einstein for his parents' divorce and retained a certain bitterness toward his father throughout his life. The eminent scientist objected when his son became a hydraulic engineer rather than a theoretician. And the tensions between father and son were exacerbated when Einstein opposed his son's marriage. Ironically, Einstein's "explosions" over Frieda, the young woman Hans Albert began to court while he was a student at the ETH, mirrored Pauline Einstein's attacks on Mileva's age and health. In fact, while Frieda was nine years older than Hans Albert, short and plain in appearance, she was also said to be highly intelligent. Soon after Frieda's death, in 1958, Hans Albert married Elizabeth Roboz, a neurochemist who remained active in her profession.

Mileva Maric belonged to the first generation of women who tried to make a place for themselves in the scientific community. Neither society nor the professions made it likely that even the most obsessive female scientist would succeed at her chosen vocation. The combination of Maric's unusual marriage, her peripatetic interests, and her tendency toward defeatism put success even further beyond her reach. It wasn't until the 1970s, when it became more common for women to seek a higher education in the sciences and when nepotism rules began to crumble in the United States under the weight of equal opportunity lawsuits, that women got their first real chance to work in science. It was a world that the young Mileva Maric might have fantasized about during her student days in Serbia and Zurich. It was a dream, however, that all but vanished by the time she reached womanhood in the shadow of Albert Einstein.

Lee Krasner

Of Adam's first wife, Lilith, it is told
(The witch he loved before the gift of Eve,)
That, ere the snake's, her sweet tongue could deceive
And her enchanted hair was the first gold.

And still she sits, young while the earth is old,
And, subtly of herself contemplative,
Draws men to watch the bright net she can weave,
Till heart and body and life are in its hold.

The rose and poppy are her flowers; for where
Is he not found, O Lilith, whom shed scent
And soft-shed kisses and soft sleep shall snare?
Lo! as that youth's eyes burned at thine, so went
Thy spell through him, and left his straight neck bent,
And round his heart one strangling golden hair.

Dante Gabriel Rossetti

Lilith

Although Lee Krasner is regarded as a pioneer of Abstract Expressionism, one of her most telling early works is a very lifelike self-portrait. Krasner was an aspiring art student when she took an easel into the woods behind her parents' retirement home on Long Island, suspended a mirror from a tree, and began to paint her own image. Those who knew Krasner would easily recognize the pose of defiance—one hand clutching brushes and a rag, the other obscured by a corner of the canvas that it is painting. And there was no mistaking the skepticism and intensity that radiated from her blue eyes, or the full, closed lips, high cheekbones, and auburn hair pulled back loosely, almost thoughtlessly, behind her ears. Yet the overall effect was somewhat startling: for Krasner had painted an arresting—one could even say an attractive—face staring quizzically out from the canvas.

It was startling because that was not how Krasner was seen at the time. It says a lot about her generation and the obstacles she faced both as a woman and as an artist that nearly a decade after her death, those who knew her will often dwell on her physical appearance before recalling either her considerable talent as an artist or the formidable power of her personality. Even her friends can't help but marvel at the unmistakable "ugliness" of Krasner's face, a face so striking in its excesses—large, protruding mouth, receding chin, and long nose—that men of her generation recall it with visible revulsion. A neighbor remembers her as "shrewishly unattractive." Her women friends still recoil when they think of the way her lovers, and even her husband, would refer derisively to "that face." And then there are those who would say that she got the face that she deserved.

The self-portrait was no mirage, however, for it portrayed a young and hopeful Lee Krasner, a woman at the beginning of an artistic odyssey that would establish her as both a gifted painter and an almost mythical harridan of American modern art. The portrait was painted in 1929, during the bloom of her artistic passion. She was in love, on the edge of a creative breakthrough, and fulfilling a girlhood dream of becoming an artist. It was a work conceived years before she was to enter into a difficult and painful marriage, before her battles with a fickle and sexist art world would turn her natural combativeness to paranoia, and before the onset of long bouts of artistic alienation that would sometimes make it difficult for her to produce any work at all.

Krasner was not only a gifted and original artist; she was driven to paint. As a young woman, she had possessed a rare combination of talent, intelligence, and passion that would link her with some of the greatest figures of her generation. At a time when Hollywood movies offered the best escape from the Depression and then world war, when most young women dreamed of becoming movie stars or housewives, she had set her heart on a far more quixotic dream. Krasner had joined a small group of pioneering Americans, and just a handful of women, who would venture forth to master the illusive imagery of abstract art and to create the first uniquely American modernist movement.

In the decade following her self-portraiture, Krasner painted and studied and fought for the new artistic idiom, eking out a living as a cocktail waitress in Greenwich Village, with very little hope of ever receiving any reward for her work. She pursued her vision at a time when high culture was largely a European affair; when there was neither money nor prestige in becoming an American artist; indeed, when very few Americans had ever distinguished themselves as painters. New York's Museum of Modern Art had only just opened its doors in 1929, and the works it showed came mostly from the Continent. Even New York's budding avant-garde was dominated by European refugees who carried with them from places like Paris and Berlin the spirit of the modern movement and a familiarity with surrealism and cubism.

Yet even as a young girl, growing up in the aesthetic wasteland of Jerome Avenue in Brooklyn, a community of poor immigrants and drab apartment buildings, Krasner had begun to develop the passion and penetrating eye of an artist. She had managed to gain both physical and emotional distance from her large, devout Jewish family. Having resisted an early marriage, she became the only one of four surviving sisters to pursue an education and a profession. Krasner soon found herself drawn toward the bohemian orbit of émigré artists who were planting the seeds of modernism in New York.

Krasner's talent was first discovered by a mysterious Russian who called himself John Graham. A sometime art dealer and writer who staked a dubious claim to nobility, Graham seemed to reserve his greatest energies for reinventing himself. But he was also a gifted artist, dedicated to exploring the new world of the avant-garde, who saw in Krasner a kindred spirit. Most important, from Krasner's point of view, Graham possessed what one critic called "the visual equivalent of perfect pitch."

Through Graham, who had lived in Paris and now offered his protégés a taste of the international art scene, young American artists were introduced not only to Picasso and the great European masters of modernism, but to African art, mysticism, and the occult. He was an admirer and a companion of Arshile Gorky and Stuart Davis. And significantly, in 1937 Graham had published *Systems and Dialectics*, an opinionated and portentous book in which he referred to several as yet undiscovered artists, including Willem de Kooning, as "young outstanding American painters," some of whom were "just as good as" if not "better than" their counterparts in Europe.

It is hard to say what Graham thought when he first saw Krasner sitting on the stoop of her East Ninth Street apartment building in Manhattan one cold November morning in 1941, her legs spattered with paint, a cigarette undoubtedly dangling from her long, incongruously elegant fingers.

Whatever personal impression she made—Krasner, it was said, was one of the few women whom Graham never tried to seduce—Graham clearly admired what he saw that day in her studio. Soon after his visit, Krasner found a hastily scrawled penny postcard in her mailbox. "Dear Lenore," it began, using the name she had been given by her parents, Russian-Jewish émigrés, a name she would soon abandon. "I am arranging at an uptown gallery a show of French and American paintings with excellent publicity etc. I have Braque, Picasso, Derain. . . . I want to have your last large painting."

For Krasner, Graham's postcard would turn out to be one of those seemingly small but ultimately life-changing events—although not in the way she might have fantasized about when she saw her work exhibited beside that of her artistic idols. To be sure, Graham's exhibition created a minor sensation downtown, in the struggling enclaves of the New York art world. Although McMillan Inc. wasn't really an art gallery at all but a decorators' showroom that occasionally hung modern art as a backdrop for its furnishings, "French and American Painters," which opened on January 20, 1942, turned out to be a landmark exhibition. It was the first time that such unknowns as Jackson Pollock, Willem de Kooning, and Lee Krasner would be hung alongside the works of modern European masters.

With a clarity that would characterize many of his ventures and insights, Graham had located the pulse of a nascent artistic phenomenon. Graham had identified the two men and one woman—Krasner—who would become the center of the first uniquely American movement in modern art, a movement that a decade later would become widely known as Abstract Expressionism. For both Pollock and de Kooning, the show would serve as a foretaste of artistic careers that were both troubled and, ultimately, enormously successful. Initially, both artists battled poverty and an indifferent, if not hostile, public; but their struggles culminated in the sort of international stardom the likes of which few living artists had ever achieved.

Krasner's notoriety would be of a very different kind. Krasner never wavered in her commitment to art. But the path charted by the McMillan exhibition would also lead her to the altar and, ultimately, on a long and painful detour from her artistic ambitions—a life lived, for over a decade, in the service of her husband's talent. As a result, she would become known, first and foremost, as the most powerful wife and widow in the artistic firmament and only secondarily as a gifted pioneer and exponent of Abstract Expressionism.

Torn between her creative and iconoclastic impulse, and the ancient tug of matrimony, she made the decision to throw herself into a marriage that would have tested the forbearance of her strongest ancestors, a decision that became the defining moment of her life. Unlike her sisters, who married as virtual children, Krasner made her choice as a mature woman of thirty-seven, a woman who possessed not only a mission but the promise of achieving it, a woman capable of assessing the risk she was taking with her dream. As the critic Clement Greenberg puts it, albeit unkindly: "she was [still] a Jewish girl who had to snag her genius."

Lee Krasner was born Lena Krassner on October 27, 1908, the epitome of the overlooked middle child. She was the fifth of six children, the fourth of five girls, and the first Krassner born on American soil. (The artist would later drop one s from the family name.) Her father, Joseph Krassner, had left Odessa in 1905, to follow his wife's brother to the United States, where they hoped to escape a life plagued not only by anti-Semitic violence but also by the Russo-Japanese War. In 1908, Krassner sent for his wife, Anna, and their four children. (One daughter, Riva, had died before the family came to the United States.) Lee was born almost exactly nine months after her parents' reunion in New York.

Long after arriving in America, the Krassner clan remained rooted in the patriarchal ways of the shtetl. Although the life of a new immigrant left little time for the synagogue, the Krassners kept a kosher home and spoke Yiddish among themselves. The children attended

Hebrew school. Their lives were imprinted with ancient laws and customs, as indelible as the tightly woven inscriptions of the Hebrew texts that dominated the Sabbath table and that Joseph Krassner gripped in his hands as he davened every day in his prayer shawl and *kipa*. Even Anna Krassner, a hard, practical woman who bore five children before the age of twenty, never shed the mystical beliefs of Yiddish folklore and the cabala on which she had been nurtured in Russia.

In the essentially old-world household, teeming with siblings and relatives, Lee always knew herself to be an outsider. Her father was a remote figure, who had little time for anything but prayer and the fish stall he had opened at the Blake Street Market in Brooklyn. Some of the older children also worked in the market. And although Anna Krassner initially divided her time between the market and her household, she became increasingly involved in the family business, often saddling a horse and buggy at 4:00 A.M. to shop for fish at the docks and spending long hours away from home.

In the orbit of the Krassner family, it was brother Irving who occupied the position of the sun. As she grew older, Anna Krassner increasingly focused her attention on her only boy, relying on him for advice both in making financial investments and, eventually, in raising the younger children. Joseph Krassner gradually abdicated to Irving the role of patriarch, a process that accelerated after Rose, one of Lee's older sisters, died, probably of a ruptured appendix. Rose's death left four daughters—Edith, Esther, Lee, and Ruth. Joseph "fell apart" after Rose's death, says Ruth, the youngest, who, in the pecking order common in large families, had become Lee's responsibility. Soon Irving "took on the role as head of the family." As an only son in a household full of women, Irving also became the primary object of his sisters' attention. Ruth and Lee, especially, would carry on a lifelong contest for Irving's affections.

Just as the Krassner girls learned to treat their only brother as the center of the family solar system, they grew up expecting to transfer those loyalties to their husbands—and at the earliest possible opportunity. Rose and Edith were both betrothed as teenagers. Esther married "late," when she was in her early twenties. When Rose died, leaving behind her husband and two small children, fifteen-year-old Ruth, made restless by the restrictions of her strict family, jumped at the chance to marry her brother-in-law. Only Lee held out until she was in her thirties. Although younger members of the Krassner clan confirm that none of the sisters were happy in their marriages, none resorted to divorce either.

Escaping Jerome Avenue and—at least for a time—marriage, was for Lee an act of ardent individualism. Becoming an artist, a pursuit that challenged her religion—with its ancient taboo against creating graven images—her shopkeeper's upbringing, as well as her gender, was an act of outright rebellion. While her siblings learned to play the piano or the fiddle, Lee refused to take up an instrument. In grade school, at P.S. 72, she wouldn't sing Christmas carols because they professed beliefs she did not hold. And sometime in high school, she rejected Judaism altogether. So when, at the age of fourteen, Lee announced that she would apply to Manhattan's Washington Irving High School, the only school in the city that permitted girls to major in art, her parents apparently did little more than shrug at their daughter's latest sign of willfulness. She made her most decisive break with her Brooklyn upbringing when, after graduating from high school in 1925, she was accepted at the Women's Art School of the Cooper Union for the Advancement of Science and Art, in Greenwich Village, and moved to Manhattan.

Art became a potent outlet for Krasner's exceptionally rebellious soul. Rebellion is, of course, a rite of passage for any artist who seeks to transcend the conservatism of "the academy." As a student, Krasner would have to battle the classical curriculum taught at both Cooper Union and the National Academy of Design, to which she transferred in 1928. From the beginning, many of her teachers, who still taught classical, figurative drawing and painting, saw little potential in Krasner. The sculptor Charles Louis Hinton, who would be one of Krasner's teachers at both Cooper Union and the National Academy, considered her work "messy." She was also widely regarded as "smart-alecky," "impossible," and "too sure of herself." Just four months after she had joined the National Academy, Krasner was put on probation. And a year later she was suspended briefly after she had been caught in the basement, in an area off limits to women, painting a still life that had been set up for another class. However, at least one of her teachers,

Victor Perard, liked her drawings well enough to include them in one of his textbooks.

Rather than bend under the strictures of the academy, Krasner, in her confrontations with authority, eventually came to confirm her sense of vocation as an artist. In 1929, she became determined to advance herself at the National Academy by means of the self-portrait that she painted behind her parents' house on Long Island. Her painting would have to win the approval of a faculty committee. She almost failed because several of her teachers initially dismissed her painting as a fake, refusing to believe that a relatively inexperienced artist could paint a credible plein air self-portrait. But Krasner insisted on its legitimacy. The faculty finally caved in, giving her a promotion under probation, perhaps only because they did not know what else to do with their most truculent student.

Yet early on it became clear that the steely self-confidence Krasner conveyed in her work, and in the pursuit of her career, seemed to crumble when it came to her relations with men. Although, according to one female acquaintance, Krasner exuded "the kind of animal energy and voluptuousness we later came to call sex appeal," she was plagued by the knowledge that many men found her ugly in a prevailing culture of beauty, which placed a woman's physical appearance above all else. "She was not a handsome woman," recalled Axel Horn, who had been a classmate of Jackson Pollock's in Thomas Hart Benton's school. "My impression was that most men, like me, were rather repelled by her." Steven Naifeh and Gregory White Smith, Pollock's biographers, find "the attraction to Lee [hard] to fathom." Naifeh and Smith go so far as to reject categorically the possibility that she possessed any feminine appeal whatsoever, suggesting that the two most important men in her life—Pollock and Igor Pantuhoff—were drawn to her not so much by lust as by their alcoholism, eccentricity, and a latent homosexual's attraction to a maternal figure. Even B. H. Friedman, an art collector who became close to the Pollocks in the 1950s, recalls his puzzlement over the liaison Krasner carried on with a young and handsome British dealer a few years after Pollock's death: "I can't quite imagine—and I hate to be this crude and physical—but Lee really was, by most objective standards, quite homely. I can't imagine his having been attracted to her per se."

To these men, an incisive mind, a sharp wit, luxuriant hair, a stunning figure, and beautiful hands couldn't militate against a face that evoked cubism in the flesh. Worst of all, for Krasner, even the men who grew to love her felt free to disparage her appearance. Her first lover, Igor Pantuhoff, once remarked: "I like being with an ugly woman, because it makes me feel more attractive." In his nastier, drunken moods, Pollock too was known to savage his wife. "Can you imagine being married to that face?" he once exclaimed.

Whatever her attractions, Lee Krasner was rarely without a lover. Pantuhoff, a promising young Russian artist whom Krasner met at the National Academy of Design, was the first of three men who would mark key phases of her life. Although they never married, Igor and Lee lived together for nearly a decade. Igor probably loved Lee more than any other man she would ever know. Lee, for her part, threw herself into her life with Igor with the eager abandon of a woman who not only was raised to cater to men but must have feared that she would never be able to keep one.

When Lee was a twenty-two-year-old art student, she must have felt there couldn't be anyone more perfect than Igor Pantuhoff. Tall, dark, and dashingly handsome, Igor was said to resemble Errol Flynn. While Krasner's roots were in the shtetl, Igor boasted noble blood, a White Russian pedigree, and Parisian upbringing—his parents had fled the Bolsheviks in 1918 for Paris when he was only seven. (As with Graham and many other Russian émigrés, it was hard to verify the authenticity of his lineage.) While Lee's family was stern, dour, and remote, Igor, with his impeccably tailored suits and yellow-and-chrome Lincoln convertible, was ebullient, flamboyant, and eccentric. Yet he was also capable of devotion. Even when he was with other women, long after she had begun living with Jackson Pollock, Lee was virtually all he could talk about. Well into middle age, Igor would send notes of congratulations and encouragement as Lee chalked up her long-awaited successes. And after Pollock's death, on late summer nights in East Hampton, her neighbors would see a much older, inebriated Igor banging on her door, pleading for Lee to let him in. They never resumed their love affair, but "years and years [after Pollock died]) Igor came to see her, and court her," recalls Sanford Friedman, a writer who lived in a small house on Krasner's property during several summers after Pollock's death.

Their affair began through a shared commitment to art. It was important to Lee that Igor was an artist of tremendous promise. Although she would later disavow any great regard for his talent, friends recall her being "wildly impressed" by Igor's work at the time. The year Lee arrived at the National Academy, Igor won four of the school's prizes for artistic excellence and was "unanimously acclaimed the school's most promising student." He also won a traveling scholarship stipend that was considered the equivalent of the Prix de Rome.

He in fact studied in Rome, and soon after he returned, Lee and Igor moved in together, commencing a passionate and sometimes tempestuous life, lived in a series of downtown lofts that they often shared with friends. Igor was a man of extremes: Although he was often broke, he could be boundlessly generous. When he began getting jobs painting society portraits, he would shower Lee with extravagant presents at a time when most artists could barely scrape together enough money for food and art supplies. On one occasion after they had split up, Igor took Lee and another friend for an expensive lunch and presented each woman with a check for one hundred dollars. But Igor had a temper—especially when he was drinking. Friends remember screaming fights that often nearly ended in violence. There was the time, for example, when, at a party, Igor threw Lee into the shower, drenching a dress he had just bought for her.

Yet violent fights never particularly bothered Lee. And despite the differences in their backgrounds, Lee and Igor were tied together by the strongest bonds—their Russianness, a shared youth, and, at least initially, a shared commitment to art. It was a sign of their closeness that Lee's family always treated the couple as though they were married. Ruth remembers Lee and Igor driving out to Brooklyn, and later to Long Island, in Igor's Lincoln convertible. Most curious of all, Lee's flamboyant White Russian lover and dour Jewish father hit it off almost from the start; among the few surviving photographs of the elder

Krassners are the ones that Igor took during his visits with the family. For although the Krassners practiced the Orthodox traditions that they had brought with them from Russia, they were not so devout as to object to Igor solely because he was not Jewish. In fact, in the Krassners' eyes, Igor had a lot going for him. The elder Krassners were, for instance, fervently anti-Communist, and they sympathized with the plight of a White Russian refugee. Igor's elegant clothes, fancy car, and society connections also helped assuage their concern about Lee's living the life of a penniless "meshugena" artist, which later became their chief objection to her living with Pollock. Besides, it was almost impossible for anyone who met Igor not to be charmed by him.

As Igor's girlfriend, Krasner seemed to make the final break with the bleak provincialism of her Brooklyn roots. The couple became fixtures at every museum exhibition and gallery opening in New York. They attended society parties uptown. And between them, they befriended a who's who of New York artists who were beginning to make their names downtown. Lee met Harold Rosenberg, who was to become an eminent art critic, through her work for the Public Works of Art Project in 1934; and for several years Lee and Igor shared an apartment with Rosenberg and his wife, May, on the lower West Side.

The trouble between Lee and Igor probably started when the couple's artistic interests began to diverge. Gradually, Igor had become addicted to the money and glamour of life as a society painter. He spent much of his time painting portraits of the rich and became a regular at their parties. Initially, Lee, who already showed signs of the stubborn, stand-by-your-man loyalty that would later mark her marriage to Pollock, didn't seem to mind. She was always on his arm, wearing outfits that Igor had carefully selected—colored stockings to match a particular dress, extravagant makeup, feathers for her hair.

But Igor began drinking more, and their fights became more frequent and intense. At first, Lee made excuses for his drunken tirades. And when Igor began to cheat on her, boasting to friends that he bedded the society ladies who hired him to paint their pictures, Lee pretended not to know. Inevitably, however, the conflict between Lee's devotion to serious art and Igor's infatuation with high society began to take its toll on their relationship.

Although Krasner finished her formal training in the early 1930s, she had continued to take art courses with a variety of prominent teachers during the decade. After a brief detour, in which she enrolled in a teacher training program at New York's City College, thinking to make a living through teaching, as did many gifted artists, Krasner returned to her artistic studies with a vengeance. In 1933, just a year after moving in with Pantuhoff, Krasner enrolled in a life drawing class given by Job Goodman, who taught a form of realist aesthetics that was reminiscent of his teacher Thomas Hart Benton and whose students would later include Jackson Pollock. It was while working in Goodman's class one day that Krasner signed up for the first of the New Deal public assistance programs.

Not until the late 1930s, when she met Hans Hofmann, a leading émigré painter from Germany, who taught many of the leading Abstract Expressionists, did Krasner encounter her most influential teacher. Indeed, the final break with Igor was probably precipitated by Lee's decision to enroll in the classes Hofmann was giving at his West Ninth Street studio. For in Hofmann, Krasner encountered a celebrated teacher who confirmed her talent, although he never let her forget that she was a woman. Hofmann, it was said, "could teach as much about Matisse's color as Matisse himself." He had known Delaunay, Kandinsky, and Mondrian, as well as Matisse. But he was also a man given to snatching the charcoal from Krasner's hand to redefine the image she was painting and, on at least one occasion, ripping a drawing in two, exclaiming, "Now this is tension!" And in her first year in his studio, Hofmann paid her the sort of dubious compliment that would dog her efforts for the rest of her life: "This is so good you would not know it was done by a woman."

Among her classmates at the Hofmann atelier, Krasner stood out as exceptionally gifted, self-confident, and fervent. One friend vividly recalls the impression Krasner made the first day she "marched into class, wearing black stockings and black elfin boots. She didn't speak to anyone in class. [She was] very intense." Krasner would elbow her way to the front of the studio, where she could see the models better. Once she "had a fit because [a] model cut her hair" between sittings. Although Krasner was already painting abstractions, the model's new hairstyle affronted her because "it changed the volumes of space" with which she was working. Years later, fellow students remembered Krasner "pushing the boundaries of modernism earlier and further than anyone else."

Through Hofmann and the contacts she made at the WPA, Krasner was plunging ever deeper into the world of modernism, while Pantuhoff drifted ever further from it. At the WPA, Krasner won a commission to create an abstract mural for radio station WNYC, which, unlike the more realistic works that were favored by the committee, was canceled before it could be completed. At the WPA, too, she got to know the artists Arshile Gorky, Stuart Davis, Ad Reinhardt, and Willem de Kooning. Through the Rosenbergs, she met Clement Greenberg, and Krasner and May Rosenberg set out to teach the aspiring critic about the new art. And in Hofmann's studio, she studied with Fritz Bultman and Mercedes Carles, the daughter of Arthur B. Carles and the future wife of the photographer Herbert Matter.

It was during this period, in 1939, that Igor took off; only after a week of frantic worry did Lee learn that he had moved down to Florida to stay with his family. It was, very likely, only a dramatic gesture, an unusually extreme conclusion to one of their usual rows. And although Igor would eventually try to patch things up, the love affair was finally over. But Igor continued to carry a flame for Lee. Some three years after his flight to Florida, he took up with Jeanne Lawson, a statuesque young model whom he had hired to pose for him (she would later marry Fritz Bultman). Through the long and tedious modeling sessions, Igor talked endlessly about his artist friends downtown, and especially about Lee. "I was [Igor's] girl then, but all I heard about was Lee," Jeanne Bultman recalls. On one occasion, Igor even took her to visit Lee in the Eighth Street studio she was already sharing with Pollock. "She didn't want to see Igor, and certainly Jackson didn't," Bultman later recalled. "But [it was clear] Igor was still mad about her." Bultman became convinced that Igor's feelings for Lee had remained unchanged.

In the months after splitting up with Pantuhoff, Krasner threw herself into art with angry abandon. She joined the American Abstract Artists, a group of Mondrian followers, many of them fellow students from both the Hofmann school and the National Academy, who rejected any reliance on subject matter in their art. Just a few months before meeting John Graham, Krasner participated in an AAA exhibition—one of three in which she would show her work.

Krasner also became active in left-wing politics. She joined the AAA's protest against the Eurocentrism of the Museum of Modern Art, handing out leaflets emblazoned "Show American Paintings." Although she never became a member of the Communist Party, Krasner was active in left-wing causes; Willie Stein, her sister Ruth's husband, bailed her out of jail at least once following a Party-led protest. And she organized demonstrations for the Artists Union to protest dwindling government subsidies. "New York had no atmosphere then, no ambience," Krasner recalled many years later. "As an artist I felt like I was climbing a mountain made of porcelain. There was little support and few rewards. Paris was the center. . . . One couldn't have imagined in the '30's that the center of the art world would shift to New York."

But with the war, a great tide of talent began moving to the United States. The night of her first AAA exhibition, in 1940, Krasner met her idol, Mondrian, one of a new wave of émigré artists who had fled the war in Europe and moved to New York. For the rest of her life, one of Krasner's most cherished memories was of the anticipation that gripped her as she watched Mondrian work his way around the gallery and waited for him to make his way to her own cubist still life. She would never tire of remembering how he had complimented her on her "very strong inner rhythm" and advised her never to lose it. And she would fondly recount how after the opening, at a party given in Mondrian's honor at Café Society Uptown, Krasner and the Dutch artist, who shared a love of boogie-woogie, had danced together.

In the early 1940s, Krasner found herself riding the crest of an artistic awakening. The public at large knew no more about the abstract artists in Greenwich Village than of the scientists at Los Alamos. But to those in the know, New York had become the center of a promising American artistic movement; it was here that artists were pushing the boundaries of cubism and surrealism, toward complete abstraction. Krasner and her peers, who would come to be known as the Abstract Expressionists, were pioneering a creative idiom grounded in psychological content, the subconscious, and spontaneous gesture.

But the creative Camelot in which Krasner found herself was aggressively masculine. At a time when naive American boys marched overseas to rescue from Fascism what was left of a sophisticated Old World, the New York art scene came to be dominated by hard-drinking, chain-smoking Marlboro men of the avant-garde, men who were drawn together more by opposition than by a set of clearly defined beliefs and whose unwritten motto was: "We agree only to disagree." These were men who lived by Picasso's dictum that women are either "goddesses or doormats," but never painters. Men like Giorgio Cavallon, who dressed up his wife to show off at parties, often in clothes he borrowed from the neighbors. Men like Barnett Newman, who recruited Pollock for an angry protest against the Metropolitan Museum and pointedly excluded Krasner—even though he was still hawking clothes in the garment district long after she was already working as a serious painter.

Few artists, however, seemed to personify the masculine excesses of the era more completely than Jackson Pollock, who came to represent an archetype of unbridled artistic virility. Pollock's exploits were legendary: This was a man who crashed a party given at the apartment of his dealer, Peggy Guggenheim, and pissed in the fireplace; who stood over his paintings ejaculating angry webs of paint onto untethered canvas; who would die in a car wreck beside his lover, hurtling down a dark and narrow road when he was just forty-four years old.

Pollock was, in fact, a complex and deeply troubled man. He could be both brilliant and naive, gentle and aggressive, vulnerable and destructive. Krasner first met Pollock when he was at his macho worst. She was at an Artists Union party, around Christmastime in 1936, long before her final break with Igor, when a balding blond man asked her to dance. He had had too much to drink. And Krasner cut the dance short when he rubbed up against her and remarked in a loud stage whisper: "Do you like to fuck?"

When she first heard the roster of artists that Graham was putting together for his show at the McMillan gallery in 1942, Krasner didn't associate the name Jackson Pollock with the unpleasant drunk she had met five years earlier. Perhaps she just didn't want to remember. Whatever the reasons for her forgetfulness, when Graham gave her a list of the other Americans in the show, she quickly zeroed in on his name as the one artist she didn't know.

Krasner liked to say that when she first learned from a friend that Pollock lived around the corner from her, she wasted no time in going over to meet him. "Something got into me and I just hoofed it over to Pollock's studio and introduced myself," she later liked to reminisce. There, encountering several large canvases, she fell in love with the work and, through it, with its silent, Brandoesque creator from Wyoming. In that moment—according to modern-art history—the thirty-three-year-old Krasner achieved her greatest artistic accomplishment: She became one of the first to recognize, and commit herself to, the man whom critic Clement Greenberg would later name as "the strongest painter of his generation." Long before *Life* magazine ran a story on Pollock, asking mockingly—yet portentously—in its headline: "Is he the greatest living painter in the U.S.?" Krasner had concluded that he was.

Whatever common ground they may have found in art, Krasner couldn't have picked a more unlikely mate. The son of an unsuccessful farmer, Pollock grew up in the arid terrain of rural Wyoming and Arizona. He attended art school in California and, in the 1930s, came under the influence of the social realist Thomas Hart Benton—much more so than Krasner ever had, despite her brief stint in Job Goodman's class. By the time he moved to New York, Pollock was already showing signs of grave mental instability. A serious alcoholic, Pollock had been admitted for several months in 1938 to New York Hospital, in White Plains, both to "dry out" and to undergo psychiatric therapy. While Krasner was known as an outgoing conversationalist, Pollock, when sober, was virtually mute. And while Krasner had demonstrated a steely independence since adolescence, Pollock always depended financially and emotionally on others—on his mother, his brothers, the Bentons, and, finally, Lee.

During Jackson's first years in New York, his older brother Sanford (Sande) had lived with, and cared for, him. Not long after they met, Lee was awakened one morning by Sande, who wanted to know if his brother had spent the night at her place. He hadn't. Sande and Lee later found Jackson at Bellevue Hospital, where he had been taken after passing out on the street following one of his binges. Even though Sande was married and had a daughter, it was not until Jackson met Lee in 1942 that Sande felt he could move his family out of the cramped Eighth Street apartment they had shared with Jackson. Lee moved in almost immediately thereafter.

For all their differences, Krasner probably recognized in Pollock a kindred spirit: a man utterly dedicated to art. She also saw in him a great artist, probably one greater than she, which made it possible for her to muster the sort of respect a wife was said to owe her husband. Although she had made a big show of rejecting marriage—first with Igor and later with Jackson—she may have faced her impending spinsterhood with foreboding. What better way to reconcile marriage and her devotion to art than to give herself to a man whose talent was large enough to contain her dreams and energies, as well as his own?

Jackson had an additional appeal, which was that he needed her— desperately. It was in nurturing him that Lee probably saw the best guarantee for holding on to her man. It also turned out to be a way that Lee Krasner could fulfill both the wifely role for which she had been reared and the artistic destiny to which she had been born.

Although Jackson's reputation would soon begin to eclipse her own, throughout the early 1940s her work continued to catch the attention of a small circle of connoisseurs. In addition to the McMillan show, Krasner's work continued to be displayed in several exhibitions organized by American Abstract Artists during the war years. And in 1944, her work was included in the "Abstract and Surrealist Art in America" exhibition at the Mortimer Brandt Gallery, which had been based on a groundbreaking book of the same name, by the dealers Harriet and Sidney Janis. In the book, another of those seminal works that would help define the burgeoning art movement in New York during the 1930s and 1940s, Krasner's "powerful" work *Composition* occupied a prominent place, toward the beginning of a chapter on "American Abstract Painters" and immediately following a painting by Stuart Davis and one by John Graham.

A year later, in 1945, Krasner came as close as she would ever get during Pollock's lifetime to finding a friend and mentor who was willing to promote her work. A large, blond, effeminate young man, Howard Putzel was a Falstaffian figure, with a florid complexion, owlish glasses, and a tendency to babble incoherently when he was nervous, which was most of the time. He was also epileptic. Yet Putzel possessed a rare knowledge and enthusiasm for art that won him the respect and love of many of the artists and connoisseurs who came into his orbit.

Despite numerous obstacles, Putzel pursued his passion for art with a single-minded determination that would make him one of the earliest and most prescient patrons of the contemporary American scene. Born to an affluent family, Putzel lost his father when he was only fifteen. But the real tragedy of Putzel's life was that his mother refused to support his artistic ventures. As early as the 1930s, he befriended a young artist named Mark Rothko and gave Yves Tanguy his first show in California. But without adequate financial support, he was forced to abandon at least two galleries that he had opened in California, one behind a bookstore in San Francisco and another on Hollywood Boulevard in Los Angeles. At the start of World War II, Putzel packed his bags and moved to Paris, where he became the eyes and nose of Peggy Guggenheim, the American heiress who would soon be credited with discovering many of America's leading abstract artists, including Pollock.

Putzel's influence on Guggenheim, with whom he had corresponded for years while he was still in California, occasionally exchanging artworks for exhibitions, was enormous. Although she was initially taken aback by his somewhat ridiculous appearance, Guggenheim later recalled how "little by little, I realized the great passion for modern art and classical music that lurked behind his incomprehensible conversation and behavior. He immediately took me in hand and escorted me, or rather forced me to accompany him, to all the artists' studios in Paris. He also made me buy innumerable things I didn't want, but he found me many paintings that I did need, and usually ones of the highest quality."

In the early 1940s, Putzel and Guggenheim returned to New York and launched Art of This Century, which became the most important gallery in the making of the Abstract Expressionists. Putzel was involved with every detail of creating the gallery; he even convinced Guggenheim to hire Frederick Kiesler to design the exhibition space. A number of artists and critics, including Greenberg, Rothko, and Krasner herself, contended that Guggenheim would have shown few, if any, of the New York artists if it hadn't been for Putzel. Sometimes he had to go to great lengths to convince Guggenheim to take on a new artist's work. For example, when she repeatedly refused to visit Rothko's studio, Putzel threw a party, hung the painter's work on the walls, and invited Guggenheim. Only then did she see Rothko's artistic merit. Pollock was another artist on whose behalf Putzel lobbied Guggenheim for months.

Krasner was never shown at Art of This Century—but not for lack of interest on Putzel's part. It was a well-known fact that Guggenheim disliked women; by her own admission, she preferred homosexuals. And she probably felt a particular antipathy to Krasner. After Putzel coaxed Guggenheim to visit Pollock's studio, which he already shared with Krasner and where Krasner's works with her signature, "L.K.," were scattered about, Guggenheim sputtered: "L.K., L.K. Who the hell is L.K.? I didn't come to look at L.K.'s paintings." Guggenheim would eventually ask Krasner to exhibit her work in a show of women artists; it probably didn't help their relationship that Krasner, who considered any effort to ghettoize women painters an insult, declined the offer.

What really set the two women at odds was their rivalry over Pollock. Guggenheim was known for falling for her protégés—she had had an affair with Yves Tanguy when he was already married, and she married Max Ernst while he was still in love with Leonora Carrington. Guggenheim, Krasner was convinced, was now trying to get Pollock into bed.

But if Krasner was kept out of Art of This Century, Putzel made sure to include her in his next venture. In 1944, when a backer agreed to bankroll a new gallery, Putzel decided to try once again to make it on his own as a dealer. With financing from Kenneth MacPherson, a handsome man of means, Putzel opened 67 Gallery—named for its street address of 67 West 57th Street—and Lee Krasner was one of the first artists whom he asked to join.

Putzel's gallery was one of a new wave of private galleries that had emerged in Manhattan immediately following the war; in fact, their number would double between 1940 and 1946. From the start, Putzel was prepared to push the boundaries of contemporary art. A few months after opening, in the early summer of 1945, Putzel launched a landmark show called "Problem for the Critics." Convinced that a new artistic movement was being born, Putzel tried to define it with the work of an eclectic array of artists that put Krasner once again in the company of such giants as Arp, Miró, Hofmann, Picasso, and Pollock. Like the McMillan show, "Problem for the Critics" was a historic, defining moment in the evolution of the American avant-garde. Even Clement Greenberg, who disagreed at the time with Putzel's definition of the new movement, later revised his opinion.

Putzel's interest in Krasner's work came not a moment too soon. Ever since she had moved into Pollock's studio, in 1942, his productivity seemed to grow in inverse proportion to her own. In the spring of 1943, he was included for the first time in a show at Art of This Century, one of the few serious venues, at the time, for an avant-garde artist. A few months later, Pollock had secured what was for an American abstract artist an unheard-of $150 monthly stipend from Guggenheim and the promise of a one-man show at the end of the year. Pollock's successive appearances at Art of This Century, as well as a small stream of positive reviews in a number of publications, including *The New Yorker*, identified him as a leading exponent of the new "ism."

If Krasner calculated that she would have to give up some of the dedication to her own talent in order to foster the work of a genius, she could never have anticipated the full cost of becoming midwife to such a legend. The more recognition Jackson got, the more he needed Lee, and the more he needed Lee, the less she was able to focus on her own work. When the nervous anticipation of Guggenheim's first visit to their studio drove Pollock to a binge, it was Lee who had to rush him to the corner coffee shop in a frantic attempt to sober him up before his patron's arrival. In preparation for Pollock's first show at Art of This Century, Guggenheim put Krasner to work addressing and stuffing envelopes. Lacking a telephone at home, Krasner often could be found at a nearby pay phone, scheduling Pollock's visitors and fielding calls about his exhibitions. The woman who had prided herself on not being able to fix a cup of coffee when she first met Pollock also had become an accomplished cook, Pollock's "cordon bleu chef," as Putzel once remarked after a sumptuous meal at their apartment. And when Guggenheim demanded it, she would even whip up a meat-loaf dinner for sixty people—anything to further her lover's career.

While life with Igor had been a whirlwind of socializing, Lee's relationship with Jackson was marked by an intense insularity. At first Lee took Jackson around town to meet her friends. But Jackson wasn't sociable, and as often as not the encounters were marked by long, painful silences. While Igor was a social drinker who sometimes had one too many, Jackson was already a deeply troubled alcoholic.

Working in the same studio with Pollock, struggling to assimilate what she saw in the breakthroughs he was making, Krasner also faced an artistic crisis of daunting proportions. For one thing, their personalities made for a dangerous brew: Krasner's assertiveness and Pollock's volatile swings between sullen sobriety and violent drunken binges often exploded. The day Pantuhoff brought Jeanne Lawson to meet Krasner, for example, they arrived in the lobby of the Eighth Street building to the sounds of a vicious fight emanating from the couple's apartment upstairs. On the occasions when Krasner dared to touch Pollock's work, the incidents would trigger firestorms that lasted for days. And when Pollock faced a particularly difficult deadline, he would go so far as to banish Krasner from the apartment.

Meanwhile, for Krasner, Pollock's presence created an even more daunting obstacle. Like most serious artists, Krasner always painted in cycles, sometimes going through dry spells. But it was during her first three years living with Pollock that Krasner suffered the worst of these "black-out periods," as she called them. Frequently during that period, she later acknowledged, "the pigment would just build up into masses of gray sludge, and nothing happened." Barbara Rose, an art critic and an expert on Krasner's work, believes that the acute artist's block Krasner experienced during her first years with Pollock were due to the difficulties she had reconciling Pollock's breakthroughs in abstract and "automatic" painting, which drew on his subconscious, with her own rigorous training in cubism, which emphasized working both from models and from a grid. For an artist, it was not unlike the experience of an early-twentieth-century physicist suddenly coming upon quantum mechanics and finding that she must reassess her whole view of the universe.

Throughout their stormy relationship, one thing was clear. Krasner was hopelessly and irrevocably drawn to Pollock's talent. Pollock might be sullen and difficult, but he was a genius—and it was this fact that comforted her and that she reiterated over and over again to her friends. She had abandoned religion and family. Like many of her generation, she had given up on socialism when Stalin signed a pact with Hitler. But she believed in the new aesthetic and in a divine, Platonic ideal of the artist that she found embodied by Pollock.

The struggle between her creative vision and the needs and demands of Pollock's career were building to a climax when Joseph Krassner died in November 1944. Although she had not been close to her father for years, it was as though the ancestral spirits had reached out to her once again. The occasion served to remind Lee of just how much of an outsider she was in her own family. Her sister Ruth remembers only vaguely Lee's presence while the family sat shivah. "She was broken up, but I was too involved with my mother and my brother," recalls Ruth.

A few months later, Krasner also lost Putzel. Sometime in early 1945, Kenneth MacPherson, Putzel's friend and backer, began to lose interest in the gallery—or perhaps in Putzel—and withdrew his financing. The gallery was forced to close less than a year after it opened. This time Putzel would not survive the demise of yet another precious venture. In poor health, deeply depressed, Putzel died suddenly in August. Guggenheim called his death a suicide.

To his friends and protégés, Putzel was virtually irreplaceable. He had not been a good businessman and might not have made anyone rich, but he was a beacon of integrity and insight, who "lived for art rather than for what he could sell." As New York's fledgling art establishment was sucked into a centrifuge of money and power after the war, Putzel's brand of integrity could have offered a much-needed antidote to the forces that came to corrupt many influential critics, dealers, and even artists during the go-go sixties.

For Krasner, Putzel's death was a devastating blow. For one thing, with his unerring eye and reputation, he might have done for Krasner what Guggenheim had done for Pollock and his contemporaries. Indeed, even if one accepts that Pollock's talent far outstripped Krasner's by the end of his lifetime, it would have been hard to know that in the early 1940s. In 1944, when Sidney Janis already had decided to include a work by Lenore Krassner in *Abstract and Surrealist Art in America*, he did so before he had even heard of Pollock, whose *She-Wolf* was a last-minute addition and appears toward the end of the book, in a chapter on surrealism. Today William Lieberman, chairman of twentieth-century painting and sculpture at the Metropolitan Museum of Art, notes that Krasner "worked in a mature style considerably before Jackson." But since she lacked the clout and the looks to navigate an increasingly politicized art world on her own behalf, Putzel's death left Krasner without a strong artistic ally.

Blocked, bereaved, and isolated, Krasner gave Pollock an ultimatum. On October 25, 1945, the couple were married at Marble Collegiate Church in Manhattan. (Peggy Guggenheim, who was to serve as a witness, stood them up at the last minute, remarking tartly that Lee was already "married enough.")

The marriage was hardly the culmination of a conventional love affair. Although close friends recall the intense physical attraction Krasner felt for Pollock, she was equally attracted to his genius. As for Pollock, marriage to Krasner had become a matter of survival. Jackson understood that "without Lee, he probably wouldn't have been able to create his work. He would have died falling down drunk in Greenwich Village," says Lee's nephew Ronnie Stein. Notes Jeffrey Potter, a friend and neighbor for many years: "I'm not sure that a person as disintegrated as Pollock was capable" of love. Or that "someone as insecure and ambitious as Lee could really love." It was a compelling need that tied together two people who were "essentially nerve endings."

Yet, consciously or not, Lee Krasner had set herself on the path that gifted wives have chosen for centuries. In her marriage to Jackson Pollock, she succumbed to a potent brew of upbringing, social expectations, and precedent by deliberately choosing to exercise much of her artistic devotion through the work of her husband. In marriage, she had finally given life to a struggle described by Rimbaud, one that she had taken as her mantra years earlier: "To whom shall I hire myself out? What beast must one adore?"

The Invisible Wife

Once married, Krasner set out to create a home where Pollock could work. She was a "city person" and acknowledged that she would never have chosen to leave New York on her own. But to protect Pollock from the temptations of Gotham, she convinced him to move to the country. She later explained her decision this way: It was "a perpetual state of crisis with Pollock. It had been from the day I met him. I wanted to get away."

Krasner took Pollock to a place not unlike the little house in Greenlawn, Long Island, where her parents had lived out the last days of their marriage. Without money or an automobile, the newlyweds moved to a ramshackle farmhouse that had neither heat nor a toilet. Tucked away on the edge of a swamp near the end of Long Island, hours from the galleries and coffeehouses and colleagues that had sustained her for over a decade, Krasner found a creative haven for Pollock and a shallow grave for her own artistic ambitions.

The Pollocks lived on Fireplace Road in Springs, a farming and fishing community nestled in some woods near Accabonac Creek, a short distance from the fashionable society and artist colony of East Hampton. In the wake of the Depression and the gas rationing of the war, the area, which had at one time counted Childe Hassam, Winslow Homer, and Louis Comfort Tiffany among its regular visitors, had fallen on hard times. One longtime resident recalls how the "lawns grew wild, roofs leaked, gravel drives washed out, and bittersweet and bullbriers overran the gardens." So although East Hampton's venerable institutions like the Maidstone Club and Guild Hall had never liked to admit outsiders, they were forced to do so as the old WASP money gradually disappeared during the 1940s. The Pollocks were among the first of a wave of newcomers—new money, Jews, and modern artists—who rediscovered the area after World War II.

While Springs would grow popular and pricey in later years, the village of simple shingle-style farmhouses and cottages was at the time both shabby and inhospitable. The property that the Pollocks bought for five thousand dollars was hot and buggy in the summers, and in the winter, eighty-mile-per-hour winds blew in from the ocean, across unprotected marshes, and through their rafters. The couple, who moved into their new home in November, found the outdoor temperatures so cold that just making it to the outhouse required determination. Indoors, where the only source of heat was the kitchen stove, wasn't much better. The Pollocks were virtually stranded, having as their only means of transportation a bicycle that Jackson bought for two dollars. Nor were their neighbors, the descendants of English sailors who settled there in the seventeenth century and called themselves Bonackers, after the region's Accabonac Indians, particularly welcoming.

Not that there wasn't enough to do around the house. The previous owners had left the place a wreck. There were three different layers of gold wallpaper on the walls, which the Pollocks stripped down and painted white. The house itself was stuffed with old furniture and tools. And the barn across the lawn, which Pollock and, eventually, Krasner would use as a studio, was crammed with rusting farm equipment. To make space for Pollock to work, the couple first cleared out a small upstairs bedroom, barely larger than one of Pollock's five-by-seven-foot canvases.

In the beginning, it seemed as though Krasner had accomplished her goal. With his isolation in their new home that winter, Pollock's drinking binges abated—although they never ceased completely. And he was happier, especially as the woods and meadows came to life in the spring. He enjoyed walking the sandy dunes of Louse Point and the salt marsh around Accabonac Harbor. "He spent hours, sometimes whole days walking around the first spring we were there," Krasner later recalled. "He was like a kid, exploring everything." They planted a large vegetable garden—Pollock hoed and seeded, while Krasner tended the plants and weeded, canning fruits and vegetables at the end of each season. Pollock adopted a pet crow, clipping its wings and naming it Caw-Caw. They acquired a dog named Gyp, and about two years later another, which they called Ahab. Most evenings they spent alone, cooking and listening to records. Weekends often brought visitors and games of penny-ante poker.

By the end of 1946, Pollock had embarked on what would be the two soberest and most productive years of his life. Sometime that summer he began laying huge canvases on the floor of the barn and dripping, rather than painting, images on them. The following January, Pollock's last show at the soon-to-be-closed Art of This Century was a hit. The reviews sang Pollock's praises. And Guggenheim, who was desperate to sell as many Pollocks as she could before relocating to Venice, managed to move several of his new paintings. Later that year, Clement Greenberg, the leading tastemaker of the contemporary art scene, published a sweeping endorsement of Pollock's work, calling him the "most powerful painter in contemporary America and the only one who promises to be a major one." It would be the first of several articles that would help turn Pollock into a popular legend.

While the publicity would eventually help to unhinge Pollock, it also brought new patrons, among them Alfonso Ossorio. Together with his companion Ted Dragon, Ossorio would become not only a patron but also one of the couple's closest and most enduring friends. An eccentric Filipino, Ossorio was the son of a sugar magnate and something of a Renaissance man. They met soon after Pollock's second show at the Betty Parsons Gallery, in January 1949, after Ossorio bought one of his paintings. Later that year, Ossorio and Dragon moved to Paris, where Ossorio was to have an exhibition of his work and where he set about organizing Pollock's first European show, at the Tapie Gallery. While Ossorio was in Paris, the Pollocks stayed in his MacDougal Alley house. And when they learned that The Creeks, a sixty-acre estate on the edge of Georgica Pond in East Hampton, was up for sale, they convinced Ossorio to buy it. In the coming years, both during the more difficult period of her marriage and after Pollock's death, the estate would become a special refuge for Krasner.

Although Krasner continued to paint during the early years of her marriage, her career had gone into self-imposed hibernation. The widely held perception was that she had given up her work. To their friends and colleagues in the art world, Krasner had traded in her palette for a wedding ring. "You didn't ever call on the Pollocks before eleven. So it wasn't until after Jackson's death that I discovered that [the mornings] were Lee's time to work, while Jackson slept," says Josephine Little, a neighbor in East Hampton. In later years, Krasner recalled: "I had three hours to myself. That's what made life possible for me."

Krasner had fallen victim to a kind of invisible-wife syndrome. Although her work usually hung on the walls of their farmhouse alongside Pollock's, few of their friends noticed it. Most remember seeing only Pollock's work on display. "In those days, one related to the man, not the woman," recalls Jeffrey Potter, a little wistfully. By the end of the 1950s, Krasner's transformation from avant-garde pathbreaker to artist's wife was so complete that when B. H. Friedman met the Pollocks about a year before Jackson's death, he recalls, "Lee I met as Pollock's wife. Although I was on the art scene I didn't know Lee's work, and I don't think many people knew Lee's work."

Other than her husband, Krasner remembers only two people who ever took her seriously as an artist after she married. "There were very few painters in that so-called circle who acknowledged I painted at all, except for Bradley Walker Tomlin and Franz Kline, who spoke with me sympathetically of my plight," said Krasner, years later. "But they were the rare exceptions." Tomlin not only admired Krasner's work but may in fact have been one of the few artists, other than Pollock, who was directly influenced by it.

If sexism played a major role in the way her work was perceived by their friends, so did Krasner's decision to cast herself in the traditional role of the self-sacrificing wife. While Krasner orchestrated lavish dinners for dealers and critics who came to look at Pollock's work, she never called attention to her own. Clement Greenberg, who now acknowledges that he underrated the work Krasner was doing when he made his periodic visits to Springs to see Pollock in the 1940s, remembers how easy it had been to overlook Krasner's work. "It was her own doing," insists Greenberg. "In passing I'd see [some of her work, but] she never buttonholed me about her art. I'd go to visit them [in

Springs]—[and] there was Pollock, the main act. It was simply that she was the second one there. That she was No. 2 on the scene."

Nor did it help that Krasner had become mired in a cycle of self-negation and dependency so common to alcoholics and their spouses. "One of the worst things Jackson did to her was to make her a reactor," says Potter. "She lost her essence. There was this constant level of anxiety, sometimes panic, about what he might do. Jackson could go to extremes very fast. First a high, then rage, then depression and despair. She was terrified by his helplessness. And the financial thing was so precarious that if there was an impending sale, she'd be terrified it might fall through."

Carefully gauging his moods, Lee orchestrated the domestic chores, their social life, and even her own behavior, as though she could single-handedly maintain Jackson's fragile equilibrium and forestall another bout of drunkenness. Keep Jackson busy enough around the house, and he might not think of drinking. Surround him with "safe friends," and he might not go on a binge with his drinking buddies. Take him on walks and ply him with good home cooking, and she could avoid the stress that often would lead to the bottle. When visiting friends, she would ask her hosts to hide the liquor. And in the ultimate act of the codependent, Lee bought cases of beer for the house, as though the liquor he drank at home wouldn't be as toxic as what he found in a bar. (Later in their marriage, she even bought whiskey, convincing herself that doing so was safer than letting him drive to a bar.)

As part of her new role, Krasner increasingly accommodated her work schedule to Pollock's needs. Both she and Pollock had been overwhelmed initially with the challenge of making their farmhouse livable. But Pollock, at least, had the relative comfort of the upstairs bedroom in which to work. During that entire first winter and spring, what work Krasner accomplished was done downstairs, in a large room that served as kitchen, dining room, living room, and her studio, where heating was always a problem because the flue in the fireplace never worked properly. It was in this setting, in 1946, that Krasner began working on her Little Image paintings, which would be recognized only decades later, both in their own right and as an influence on Pollock's first all-over paintings.

Although almost no one knew it at the time, the beginning of Pollock's celebrated "drip" paintings coincided with one of the most fruitful periods of Krasner's life with Pollock. Pollock's huge dripped canvases, such as *Alchemy* and *Lucifer*, broke new ground in the field of all-over composition—so called for the way in which they seemed to literally spill off the edge of the canvas in defiance of the picture frame. But at about the same time, Krasner had embarked on her own, far more controlled version of all-over composition. On a much smaller scale than Pollock's, Krasner's paintings typically measured twenty-four by thirty inches. Instead of dripping paint, Krasner began this series by filling her canvases with tightly woven patterns.

On the surface, the Little Image paintings seemed emblematic of the limitations of Krasner's life. Pollock, who had moved out of his small upstairs studio, now spent his afternoons in the spacious barn, hurtling paint onto vast canvases that were laid out on the floor. Meanwhile, back at the house, Krasner had taken over the upstairs studio and was inscribing almost claustrophobic images on her small canvases.

Although even under the best of circumstances the Little Image paintings would have been obscured by Pollock's dripped oeuvre, it was over a decade before they won any recognition at all. The paintings—some with a filigreed, heavily painted design and others with a more ordered "picture writing" that Krasner described as her "hieroglyphs"—resemble Hebrew text and undoubtedly were influenced by her grounding in Judaism. In the tradition of Abstract Expressionism, however, the influence was entirely subconscious. For it was only years after completing them that Krasner realized that she had painted many of the pictures from right to left, the way she had learned to write Hebrew as a young girl.

It is no small irony that the Little Image paintings have come to be considered among her finest work. For although the series established Krasner as an exceptionally gifted and original artist, it was never shown in its entirety during her lifetime. William Lieberman, referring to one of the Little Image paintings in a 1970 letter to Franco Russoli, the director of the Pinacoteca di Brera in Milan, notes: "The painting of 1949 by Lee Krasner . . . is extraordinary in every way and anticipates much that was done by others a dozen years later." Even William Rubin, who insists that Krasner was not a major "breakthrough" painter of her time, concedes: "What she made out of the all-over grid in some ways prophesied what Jasper Johns would do" years later. Bryan Robertson, a British curator who gave Krasner her first retrospective at London's Whitechapel Gallery in the 1960s, believes the Little Image series presaged the work of Robert Motherwell. And Grace Glueck, writing in the *New York Times*, even saw in Krasner's small paintings a precursor to Pollock's most famous and expansive works: "In 1946, [Krasner] began a series of small paintings, such as the lively 'Noon,' in which colors are atomized into a totally abstract field that covers the entire picture surface. . . . Pollock's own explorations with 'all-over' patterning were affected by these works."

The Pollocks established a formal ritual for critiquing each other's work, visiting each other's studios by polite invitation. But while Krasner leaped at the chance to see Pollock's work, she recalled somewhat wryly that she would have to ask two or three times before he would cross the threshold of the upstairs bedroom where she worked. "It would have been very nice if someone had been able to give me the kind of encouragement I gave him," Krasner once conceded. "He did encourage me, but it was not the same kind of encouragement."

Gradually, during their years in Springs, the couple's work developed a kind of complementarity that became key to understanding the work of both artists—Pollock's celebrated dripped oeuvre as well as Krasner's Little Image series. When they first met, husband and wife couldn't have approached their work more differently. As one of the most educated painters of her generation, Krasner was steeped in the images and technique of the great European modernists, so that when she commenced a painting, it was as though the spirits of Matisse and Picasso hovered on the edge of her canvas. Pollock, on the other hand, came into the marriage with very little understanding of—or appreciation for—the Europeans. The difference in their approaches to work was embodied in one encounter between Pollock and Krasner's former teacher Hans Hofmann. Hofmann admonished Pollock to work more from nature, lest he repeat himself, to which Pollock replied: "I am nature." Pollock's artistic spontaneity set an important example for Krasner as she struggled to free herself from the formal constructs of cubism. And Krasner, whose academic training was far superior to Pollock's, probably introduced him to many of the concepts she had learned under Hofmann. When asked whether Pollock had ever been his student, Hofmann would reply: "He was never my student, but the student of my student."

One obvious influence reflected in the work of both husband and wife was an almost pantheistic awe of nature. Lee and Jackson could often be seen sitting silently, for hours, on the back stoop of their farmhouse, staring out at the sky and the marshes. Jackson built a rock garden. And Lee scoured the landscape for natural forms that pleased her, and filled their house with shells, rocks, and plants. It was in large part because of their shared reverence for nature—and the way both artists translated that reverence to their work—that they became each other's most valuable critics.

While some friends and experts detected rivalry between the two artists and charged that Pollock felt threatened by Krasner's work, that was surely an oversimplification. Although, generally, Pollock served more as a hindrance than as a help to Krasner's daily progress, professional jealousy probably had very little to do with it. For one thing, at the time, the efforts of even the most gifted women were so matter-of-factly disregarded, even by discerning critics, that male artists, however insecure, had little to fear. Krasner insisted that she would never have stayed with a man who "didn't respect [her] as a painter." Indeed, when he was sober, Pollock was openly supportive and respectful of his wife's work. In one letter to Ossorio, for example, Pollock wrote proudly: "Lee is doing some of her best painting—it has a freshness and bigness that she didn't achieve before."

Pollock's drinking continued unabated, though, and often undermined the couple's small steps forward. Nothing illustrates this better than the episode of the mosaic tables. Sometime in 1947, Pollock suggested that Krasner use a pair of old wagon wheels that they had found in the barn to make mosaic tables. In addition to helping her get back to work, Krasner saw the project as a way to create some much-needed furniture for their empty house. Pollock helped Krasner haul the wheels, which would be used as armatures for the tables, out of the barn and gave her fragments of tesserae (such as pieces of marble and tile) that he had used for a mosaic project during his WPA days. To Pollock's leftovers Krasner added other fragments—keys, shells, coins, and bits of broken glass. With these materials, Krasner produced two circular tables that measured nearly forty-nine inches in diameter. Working without a preliminary sketch, she created abstract patterns of small circles unevenly spaced on the surface, with other geometric shapes swirling around them. It's interesting to note that some critics suggest that Krasner's work on the mosaic tables influenced Pollock's increasing use of found objects in his paintings.

The next summer, Bertha Schaefer, an interior decorator who also owned a gallery in New York City, came to Springs. Admiring one of Krasner's tables (the other had been given to the Macy family in return for a truckload of furniture that provided the only other furnishings in their home), she asked to include it in an upcoming exhibition, "The Modern House Comes Alive." When the show opened, Krasner's table won rave reviews in a number of papers and magazines, including the *New York Times*, the *Herald Tribune*, and *Architectural Forum*, although the *Times* referred to her as the "wife of the painter J. Pollack [sic]."

As so often happened, even that small hopeful episode ended badly. After the show, Schaefer invited the Pollocks over for dinner to celebrate. Pollock drank too much. And when he insisted on opening a third bottle of wine, he taunted his wife's patron: "What does an old lady like you do for sex?" Pollock then attacked the furniture, smashing several of Schaefer's valuable antiques. The rampage ended only when Pollock finally passed out. Although, at Krasner's insistence, Pollock wrote Schaefer a note of apology, she was not to be placated. Schaefer threatened to have him arrested and sued for damages—although friends of the Pollocks finally talked her out of it. Ultimately, the episode hurt Pollock more than it hurt Krasner, for it cemented his reputation as a drunk who was "more trouble than he was worth" and made it more difficult for him to function in the art world.

The incident was a bellwether of problems to come. Their finances had always been precarious, but with the closing of Art of This Century, in May 1947, the Pollocks lost their only steady source of income, and money problems loomed large once again. All winter and early spring, Peggy Guggenheim, who was preparing to move to Venice, ran up and down Manhattan trying to find a gallery that would be willing to take on Pollock; she was not only interested in unloading a number of the Pollocks that she still owned; she also wanted to find someone willing to pay the $150 monthly stipend that under the terms of her agreement with Pollock she was obliged to pay until the following February. None of the dealers in avant-garde work wanted to take on either Pollock, with his notorious reputation for drunken rampages, or his only slightly less notorious paintings. Finally, just weeks before her departure, Guggenheim persuaded Betty Parsons to sign Pollock on and to give him a show; but under the terms of their agreement, Guggenheim would have to keep paying the stipend until February.

The summer and fall after Guggenheim's departure were unusually calm and upbeat. Riding on a steady stream of good reviews, especially by Clement Greenberg, and months of sobriety, Pollock was diligently at work for his first show at Parsons's gallery. He was so happy, in fact, that Krasner probably didn't mind the constant interruptions to her own work. The house was full of guests all summer. Greenberg was a regular visitor. Pollock's mother, Stella, also came frequently from Green River, Connecticut, where she now lived with Jackson's brother Sande McCoy and his family. (Jackson and Sande's father, LeRoy, had been born a McCoy; but after his mother died, LeRoy was raised by the Pollock family, whose name he ultimately adopted. Soon after Jackson got a WPA job, Sande changed his name to McCoy so that he too could work for the WPA, which wouldn't hire two people who shared both the same last name and the same address.)

The Parsons show turned out to be a disaster, however. The reviews were lukewarm and sales were weak. And under the terms of his old contract with Guggenheim, Pollock, who never made more than eight thousand dollars on a painting during his lifetime, wouldn't see a penny from the few pictures that were sold. Shortly before his last monthly stipend from Guggenheim, Parsons agreed to sign a one-year contract with Pollock. But she would not pay him a regular stipend; Pollock would have to live off a percentage of the paintings he actually sold.

By March of 1948, the Pollocks were destitute. Dan Miller, the one-eyed proprietor of the general store in Springs and by this time a friend, let Pollock pay a fifty-six-dollar grocery bill with a painting. But the Pollocks could no longer afford wood for the kitchen stove, and when the thermometer dipped below freezing, they headed for New York City to stay in Ossorio's MacDougal Alley house. Krasner offered to find a job, but Pollock wouldn't hear of it—even though his own search for employment, first as an art teacher and then at a textile factory in Montauk, didn't pan out.

Finally, it was Krasner's salesmanship that won the couple a reprieve. Ever since moving to Springs, she had worked the phones for hours daily, calling dealers, collectors, artists, and friends. Although they had not had a phone in the Village, they acquired one out in Springs. And when there was business to take care of with Parsons's gallery, Krasner made the calls, not Pollock. Now that they were desperate, Krasner was on the phone constantly, pressuring and cajoling friends to find buyers for Pollock's paintings. In the spring, she persuaded Fritz Bultman, her old classmate from the Hofmann school, to ask his sister to visit the Parsons Gallery. When Bultman's sister, Muriel Francis, finally bought one of Pollock's canvases, Parsons appealed to Guggenheim to forgo the proceeds in exchange for some future work. Parsons gave up her commission and sent the Pollocks a check for several hundred dollars. Then, in June, Pollock learned that he had won a $1,500 stipend from the Demarest Trust, which had been established in 1938 by Pittsburgh heiress Elizabeth B. Demarest to provide a single annual grant to an artist; the award was widely attributed to Krasner's "indefatigable behind-the-scenes" campaigning, according to Pollock's biographers Naifeh and White Smith.

The summer of 1948 was a particularly busy time for Krasner as hausfrau. That season alone, her guest list included close to a dozen visitors, including Betty Parsons, Barnett Newman, and Clement Greenberg—in short, any dealer, critic, or artist who might further Pollock's career. And despite a chronic shortage of funds, Krasner's dinners, which often included roast beef, steak, or leg of lamb, were legendary.

By this time Krasner had also developed a reputation as a particularly fastidious housekeeper. Pollock emptied the garbage, washed dishes, and occasionally baked pies. But it was Krasner who evinced an almost maniacal devotion to her housework, recalling Simone de

Beauvoir's unhappy, sadomasochistic wife who takes "to orderly house-keeping as others take to drink," creating a house "so neat and clean that one hardly dares live in it" and finding, in her frantic Sisyphean endeavor, a chance to "forget her own existence." Every ashtray had its place—one was even nailed to a wall near an armchair she favored, so that no one could move it. She would routinely brush off any offer of help with a curt "I like to do it my way." According to her nephew Ronnie Stein, what Krasner was obsessed with was not neatness per se but the aesthetic placement of every item of furniture, every object, no matter how small or trivial. So much so that in later years, she became notorious for walking into the homes of friends and relatives and literally rearranging the furniture. And near the end of her life, when her arthritis was so advanced that she could barely lift a brush, she wouldn't permit anyone else to load the dishwasher, convinced only she knew how to do it properly.

If Krasner had cast herself in the role of superwife, motherhood wasn't part of the job description. Long before getting involved with Pollock, Krasner had resisted having children; at one time, Pantuhoff had tried to win her over to the idea, but Krasner had refused. "She didn't have a maternal bone in her body," recalled one friend.

But the youngsters who got to know her in the forties and fifties developed a somewhat different view. "I found her interesting and unlike anyone I knew," recalls Jason McCoy, the son of Jackson's brother Sande, who became devoted to his aunt. "She treated me as an adult. There was an assumption of reason. No condescension." Similarly, Ronnie Stein cites the encouragement he got from his aunt Lee as a powerful influence on his decision to become an artist. Of his visits to Springs as a child, he recalls: "Lee always put me to work drawing. She was my alter-mother." In the late 1950s, they even collaborated on a mosaic mural for the Uris Building at 2 Broadway in New York City. And in the early 1960s, she made sure that Frank Lloyd, the Marlborough Gallery's famous dealer, looked at Stein's work.

In all likelihood, Krasner's decision not to have a child was purely pragmatic. Money was one problem, of course. Indeed, many artists in the Pollocks' circle felt that family life was simply incompatible with both the financial uncertainties that plagued most artists and the creative demands of their work. Musa Mayer, the daughter of the artist Philip Guston, a contemporary of the Pollocks', recalled: "what I searched for, incessantly, was evidence of family life among my parents' friends. . . . With few exceptions, artists didn't seem to have children; or if they did, they'd been left behind long before, with their failed marriages."

Some have speculated that Krasner may have feared Pollock's mental instability. It's worth noting that when Pollock lived with Sande and Arloie McCoy, his brother's wife felt so threatened by Jackson's temper that she "vowed never to have children while living under the same roof with him." Krasner certainly understood that even if she were willing to take full responsibility for parenthood, having children with an artist as emotionally unstable as Pollock would be difficult—and doing so as a woman who remained devoted to her own work long after other wives had given it up would have been very nearly impossible.

What's more, despite her legendary strength and willfulness, Krasner was exceptionally vulnerable to Pollock's whims. Like many women of her generation, she had never learned to drive. Until she took driving lessons in the early 1950s, Krasner was completely dependent for transportation on neighbors and on Pollock, who had bought a Model A Ford sometime in 1948.

Life with Pollock also had taken a physical toll on Krasner. She suffered from migraine headaches and developed a debilitating case of ulcerated colitis. By the 1950s, says the writer Patsy Southgate, Krasner "had terrible problems with her intestines—she was a bleeding wreck."

Krasner also was tortured by her oldest self-doubt—her physical appearance—a weakness Pollock didn't hesitate to exploit. Many of the women in their circle, including the painter Mercedes Matter and Southgate, whose liaisons included a love affair with the poet Frank O'Hara, were stunningly beautiful. Rumors were rife during the summer of 1948 that while Krasner visited Elizabeth Hubbard, one of several homeopathic therapists who treated her over the years for both physical and psychic ills, Pollock was running after other women. Pollock stoked the rumors, flirting outrageously with a number of women. He also enjoyed cruelly goading his wife. During a Thanksgiving dinner at the house of their friends John and Josephine Little, Jackson turned to Jeffrey Potter and said, loud enough for Lee to hear: "Jeffrey, you're a lucky man. Look at Penny [Potter's wife]. And look at what I've got." At another party, he turned to his wife and said: "How old are you, Lee?"

Krasner, who was four years older than her husband, never reacted publicly to his taunts. But it is interesting that the one thing this woman known for her uncompromising honesty lied about for years was her age.

By 1950, Pollock had achieved a rare degree of success. The press was already referring to him as the "greatest" living American painter. In June, Pollock would be one of a half dozen artists to be shown at the U.S. Pavilion of the Venice Biennale.

But the genuine joy Krasner felt in his accomplishment must have been tinged with bitterness. For one thing, success failed to temper the demons that haunted him and, hence, continued to make her life a misery. Moreover, Pollock's acclaim inexorably diminished her own efforts in the eyes of the art world. How much so must have become painfully clear in a series of seemingly innocuous events that would, in the eyes of the outside world, both define the "members" of the Abstract Expressionist club and exclude Krasner from it. That spring, Barnett Newman made an urgent call to the house on Fireplace Road. Although Krasner answered the phone, Newman wouldn't tell her what he was calling about, beyond saying that she should get Pollock right away because he had something very important to tell him. Newman had phoned, it turned out, to enlist Pollock to join a group of artists in a protest against the Metropolitan Museum for what they perceived as the museum's bias against abstract art. Eighteen artists, including Clifford Still, Robert Motherwell, and Willem de Kooning, joined the boycott; their protest letter made it onto the front page of the *New York Times*.

In November, Pollock made a trip to Manhattan for another *Life* magazine photo session. Rather than profile Pollock alone, this article would transform an entire group of little-known avant-garde artists into a new creative phenomenon. Fifteen of the original "Irascible Eighteen" would be included in the famous *Life* photo, which had its center in a brooding Pollock and Hedda Sterne, the only woman in the group. Yet Krasner, who was painting and studying under Hofmann long before Barnett Newman had even begun painting, who helped organize some of the earliest demonstrations for avant-garde art, who is at least as important as half the Irascibles, including Theodore Stamos and Hedda Sterne, wasn't even asked to sign the protest letter. Newman, whose own wife, Annalee—a schoolteacher who supported her husband financially as well as emotionally—became a paradigm of the selfless artist's wife, never would have thought to ask Pollock's spouse to join in the group photo. For Krasner, it was a particularly deep and enduring hurt that Pollock didn't think to include her in the group either.

There is a widespread belief that Krasner's exclusion was due to the fact that she had virtually stopped painting at the time the protest was organized. In fact, although few of her contemporaries knew about them, the Little Image paintings were completed in 1950. The real reason for her exclusion was that she was a wife, and Pollock's to boot.

If the episode of the Irascibles marked another public defeat for Krasner, that Thanksgiving ushered in a new domestic crisis. Pollock had been working outdoors that month with the photographer Hans Namuth, who was finishing a film on the artist. Crouched under a sheet of glass that Pollock was using as a canvas, Namuth spent much of Thanksgiving Day shooting a last reel of film that would capture the artist at work, painting directly onto the transparent medium. In the late afternoon, after the sun had set, Pollock and Namuth returned to the house, where Krasner was fixing dinner for several of their friends. Cold and tense after a whole day outdoors and weeks of filming, Pollock headed for the kitchen sink and a bottle of bourbon that he kept in the cabinet underneath. By the time the guests arrived, at eight, Pollock was reeling drunk. When they sat down to dinner, Pollock, at the head of the table, and Namuth, who sat to his right, began arguing. In a scene that would encapsulate Pollock's reputation as a mad genius, the artist suddenly leaped out of his seat. Grabbing the edge of the table, he gave it a ferocious heave. Dishes, cutlery, turkey, and dressing all came crashing down on the floor. For many of their newer friends, including Ted Dragon and Alfonso Ossorio, who had known the Pollocks only since they had moved to Springs, during Pollock's sober period, it was the first time they had seen him in a drunken rage.

Pollock had reached a new low—and one that Krasner couldn't or wouldn't cope with in the way that she had handled previous episodes. It was made all the worse by Pollock's next show, just a few days after Thanksgiving, from which he was able to sell only one large painting—*Lavender Mist*—and that at a deep discount. Worse, Pollock became convinced that he could no longer paint. Frozen in one of the least productive periods of his life, Pollock went on a long bender that stretched from the bars in East Hampton to New York's Cedar Tavern. Over the next few years he was hospitalized several times. Inevitably, his behavior alienated many friends.

At the same time, his growing celebrity, which had been nurtured in part by Lee's unflagging efforts to promote his work with dealers, critics, and patrons, generated hostility among fellow artists, particularly those who admired and befriended Willem de Kooning. De Kooning was the charismatic leader of the diffuse band of artists who were known as Abstract Expressionists. It was said that there was no artist who was "more respected or better liked" by other artists than Bill de Kooning. And while Pollock's reputation had been ignited by the critics, de Kooning's, at least initially, was built on the more comforting and somewhat more reliable foundation of his fellow artists' regard for his work. If you were an artist, "you had to choose between the two camps," observed the dealer and curator John B. Myers, who was a leading connoisseur of the movement. In retrospect, wrote Irving Sandler, "It appears that there was only a de Kooning coterie; those who did not wish to be in it or were not welcome" might gravitate to Pollock. The rivalry was fueled by the critics—Greenberg championing Pollock, Rosenberg backing de Kooning—and by the artists' wives, the beautiful and much "adored" Elaine de Kooning, who was known as the "White Goddess," and the "ugly" and reviled Lee Krasner, who was thought of as the "Black Widow Spider." The artists themselves, who sometimes went drinking together, had relatively little to do with it. Yet the competition, Pollock's increasingly erratic behavior, as well as Krasner's escalating war against de Kooning, whom she accused of sabotaging Pollock's reputation and of plying him with liquor, left Pollock more and more isolated. Mired in depression, alienated from his peers, and often unable to work, Pollock increasingly turned his rage on Krasner.

But it was worse than the old abuse. Starting in the early 1950s, the Pollocks' relationship entered a free fall that wouldn't end until Pollock's death in 1956. What for Pollock had once been mostly unconsummated flirtations turned into real affairs. And neighbors and relatives recall ferocious fights, screaming and yelling that went on at all hours of the day and night. Although Krasner denied that Pollock hit her, artist Harry Jackson, who had married the painter Grace Hartigan at the Pollocks' house on Fireplace Road in 1949, remembered seeing Pollock "[kick] the piss out of her two or three times" during their worst battles in the 1950s. By the summer of 1954, Krasner had stopped giving parties.

Pollock's public flirtations also were becoming more outrageous and indiscreet. At parties he made passes at mutual friends, like their neighbor Patsy Southgate. When Krasner went for a therapy session in New York, he took out Motherwell's first wife, a fiery Mexican actress. On at least one occasion when he and Krasner were staying in Ossorio's MacDougal Alley house, Pollock brought a girl home from a bar; Annalee and Barnett Newman, who had dropped by for a visit, witnessed the humiliating scene. And in February 1955 he took up with Ruth Kligman, the woman who might have ended Pollock's marriage if he hadn't died first.

Pollock's behavior also produced problems with dealers and created another financial crisis for Krasner to solve. A big part of the problem was precipitated by the unraveling of Pollock's relationship with Betty Parsons. While Guggenheim had a reputation for peddling paintings like a Seventh Avenue garmento, Parsons wasn't much of a saleswoman. During her four years representing Pollock, she sold only a few of his paintings. And Pollock wasn't the only artist unhappy with Parsons's salesmanship: During one meeting at her gallery in 1951, seven of the abstract artists whom Parsons represented, including Pollock, Newman, and Rothko, confronted the dealer about the lack of publicity, slipshod recordkeeping, and poor sales at her gallery. They also took Parsons to task for the time and attention she lavished on little-known female painters while their own work went unsold. Yet for all her shortcomings as a businesswoman, Parsons had looked the other way when Pollock made sales directly to patrons such as Ossorio and when he bartered away his paintings. At times, she had even forgone her commission on his sales. Yet when his contract expired, in 1952, Pollock announced that he would leave Parsons and began searching for a new dealer.

But Pollock's reputation preceded him. Sam Kootz turned him down after Pollock created a drunken scene in his gallery. Pierre Matisse wouldn't have him. And when Krasner finally approached Sidney Janis, the dealer was hesitant, put off by Pollock's reputation as a drunk who was "hard to handle." Krasner finally persuaded Janis to take him on, promising that she would help "control" Pollock.

As the 1950s dragged on and Pollock increasingly lost his grip on life, Krasner began to show a new streak of independence. In 1954, she decided to let Patsy Southgate teach her how to drive. "She had no confidence in her driving, or in herself," says Southgate. "I saw my role as [one of] building up her confidence." To bolster Krasner's self-esteem, and to show that she, Patsy, had faith in her friend's abilities, Southgate would pack her two children into the back seat before each driving lesson. At a time when Pollock was drinking more heavily than before and had once again become a regular at the Cedar Tavern, Krasner had finally won a modicum of freedom and mobility.

Alone now for long periods of time, and in both emotional and physical pain from the bouts of colitis that kept tearing at her insides, Krasner was achieving new release in painting. Just as Pollock was finding it almost impossible to work, Krasner entered a new phase of productivity. In a sharp departure from the Little Image series, Krasner began working on a much larger scale. Although she would destroy many of her works during this period, photographs of Krasner at work in 1950 reveal large canvases of "long-necked, long-legged personages."

After a hiatus of several years, Krasner's work began appearing in exhibitions again. Between 1951 and 1956, her work had appeared in at least four shows, two of them solo exhibitions. Despite his differences with Parsons, Pollock convinced his dealer to take a look at Krasner's work. And that spring, less than a year before Pollock was to quit the gallery, Parsons agreed to give Krasner her first solo show in New

York. Emblematic of the turmoil that gripped both her life and her work at the time, the images Krasner embarked on were based heavily on Mondrian's influence. They were not what Betty Parsons had expected, and the show was poorly received; not a single piece sold.

Dissatisfied with her latest effort, Krasner ripped up her own discarded canvases, as well as a few of Pollock's, and began using them in collages. Krasner came to incorporate a wide variety of materials in her collages—a medium she would return to again and again throughout the rest of her life and one that would come to be considered among her most successful efforts. For the first time, Krasner also began signing her full name to the canvases, eschewing the cramped "L.K." The collages increased in scope and size, some of them measuring more than six feet in height.

Even as her marriage disintegrated, the collages seemed to reflect a renewed determination—even confidence—in her work. As though picking up on it, the critics finally took notice. A 1955 show of her collage works at the Stable Gallery attracted a flurry of good reviews. Fairfield Porter noted in *Art News*: "Krasner's art, which seems to be about nature, instead of making the spectator aware of a grand design, makes him aware of a subtle disorder greater than what one otherwise might have thought possible." William Rubin and Clement Greenberg both would come to praise it. And Barbara Rose, a critic whose career was built in part on praising Krasner's work, celebrated *Milkweed*, *Bird*, and *Bald Eagle* as "totally original" and "remarkably advanced works."

By early 1956, Krasner's paintings were erupting in a fresh, agitated spontaneity. There was a new drama in her work of the period, with areas "scratched out vehemently," paint "left to drip in the 'action-painting' mode," and dramatic oppositions of dark and light. In the spring, Krasner set to work on one of her most disturbing works yet—"a hybridized, three-legged standing figure," as Rose described it, that merged male and female anatomical parts. But even as she began to work on that painting, the nightmare of her marriage had become more than she could bear.

That spring, Pollock had taken up with a voluptuous, twenty-five-year-old art groupie named Ruth Kligman, who was, as Jackson liked to boast to his friends "loaded with extras." Kligman, an aspiring artist at the time, had tracked him down at the Cedar Tavern. Initially, it was Kligman who pursued the great artist. But before long Jackson was parading Ruth all over New York and East Hampton, never even trying to conceal his affair from Lee.

Sometime in the early summer of 1956, Lee and Jackson's marriage reached a final crisis. Lee decided to take her first trip to Europe. At first she tried to convince Jackson to join her. When he refused, Lee reluctantly decided to go by herself. A few days before her departure, she discovered that Ruth Kligman had spent the night with Jackson in his studio. White with rage, Lee confronted the lovers, ordering Ruth off the property and threatening to leave Jackson forever. Afterward, she drove to The Creeks. "It's the only time I ever saw her weakened," says Ted Dragon, who remembers her arriving at the house on the verge of tears. "She said she had decided to get a divorce before going to [Europe]." Ossorio and Dragon managed to talk her out of getting a quickie divorce, persuading her that the trip would give her the time she needed to think about the future.

Leaving behind both Jackson and the disturbing painting of her three-legged creature—a work that she would later name "Prophecy" and that Ossorio would eventually buy—Krasner left Pollock for the first time since their marriage and sailed for Europe. Almost fifteen years after the McMillan show had brought her together with Pollock, she was reunited with John Graham in Paris, where the two old friends prowled the galleries on either side of the Seine. On July 21, 1956, she wrote her husband of her impressions of Paris: "It is overwhelming— beyond belief. I miss you and wish you were sharing this with me. . . . The painting there is unbelievably bad. (How are you Jackson?)"

Better she shouldn't ask. Choking on booze and the cloying attentions of his young lover, and cast adrift for the first time by Lee, Jackson was headed for the abyss. July 27 was the birthday of B. H. Friedman, a close friend and patron of Pollock's; the Friedmans decided to celebrate with Pollock and Ruth Kligman. It turned out to be a disastrous evening. Pollock was drinking heavily. He was also driving. When the two couples decided to go to a party together, Pollock stepped on the accelerator and sent his green Oldsmobile convertible careening at breakneck speed down the back roads of the Hamptons.

The ride was so hair-raising that, in a flash of prescient foreboding, Abby Friedman insisted that Pollock stop the car so she and her husband could get out.

Three weeks later, on August 12, Krasner was in Paris, at the home of friends, when the phone rang at 8:00 A.M. Her host, Paul Jenkins, picked up the receiver. It was Clement Greenberg, calling to break the news of Pollock's death. His voice hoarse with exhaustion and grief, Greenberg explained that at about 10:15 P.M., Pollock had killed himself and a young woman named Edith Metzger, a friend of Ruth Kligman's. As Greenberg told Jenkins the news, he recalls, Lee must have "smelled what was coming." Because in the background, Greenberg suddenly heard Lee "break out in hysterical laughter." The laughter turned to screams, as Lee hurtled herself against the wall of Jenkins's apartment, and finally convulsed with uncontrollable weeping.

Over the coming days, Lee would learn the agonizing details of Jackson's death. He had been driving North on Fireplace Road, with Ruth and Edith in the front seat next to him. Edith, who had been sandwiched between the artist and her friend, began to scream as Jackson, drunk and out of control, put his foot hard on the accelerator. The more she screamed, the faster he drove. As the car was going into a curve near his house, Jackson lost control, sending the car skidding off the road and into the trees, just a few hundred yards from his driveway. The car flipped over and the horn blew endlessly, vacantly, into the night. Hours later, the headlights still beamed skyward through the darkness. Of the three people in the car, only Ruth Kligman survived.

The Black Widow Spider

In the hours between Greenberg's call and the landing of Krasner's plane at Idlewild Airport, friends and family rallied to ease the shock for her. Patsy Southgate and other women friends combed through the house on Fireplace Road, ridding it of any sign of Kligman's presence, from bits of pink underwear to dirty sheets and dishes. Ronnie Stein and Ossorio met her at the airport and took charge of the funeral arrangements.

On the surface, Krasner maintained rigid self-control. Although the funeral service at the Springs chapel would become the cultural event of the season, it was fraught with the tensions that had permeated not only the Pollocks' fractured marriage but also their relationship with the art world. While townspeople and art fans crowded the small church, spilling out onto the street, many old friends, still smarting from past conflicts with Lee and Jackson, didn't bother to show up at all. When Krasner asked Greenberg to speak at the funeral, the critic refused, saying that he could not forgive Pollock for getting Edith Metzger killed. In the end, none of Jackson's friends spoke. Kligman, who was still in the hospital, being treated for injuries she had sustained during the car crash, didn't attend the funeral either. And while Ruth and Ronnie, and most of Jackson's relatives, showed up for the funeral, Lee chose to sit alone during the service.

Jackson Pollock would be buried at Green River Cemetery in Springs, a small, scenic graveyard where many of the local celebrities, including Frank O'Hara, would also be laid to rest. Before going to the cemetery, Lee asked her friend Cile Downs to take her to Louse Point, the bay beach not far from Fireplace Road, where she and Jackson used to walk and swim, collecting shells and driftwood on the beach. Afterward, Lee stood alone by Jackson's grave, which would be marked later by a boulder, instead of a conventional headstone, which Lee asked some friends to haul over to the cemetery.

Those closest to her knew Lee was devastated. For months after Pollock's death, Lee was racked by the question: What if she had not gone to Europe? She couldn't sleep, and when exhaustion finally overcame her, the nightmares and demons were so real that she would never again be able to spend a night by herself on Fireplace Road. A string of friends and acquaintances and children of friends and acquaintances became "Lee's sleepers," the night companions without whom she wouldn't remain in the house after dark. If there wasn't anyone to spend the night, she retreated to the Spanish Room at The Creeks, with its comforting rose-colored filigreed curtains and bedcovers and its wrought-iron headboard—the room that Dragon and Ossorio had by now come to think of as hers. It was during this time that she befriended Sanford (Sandy) Friedman, B. H. Friedman's brother, who, together with the poet Richard Howard, rented the house across Fire-place Road and who would write *A Haunted Woman*, a novel based on the trauma of Krasner's early widowhood.

But the problems that most occupied her in the immediate aftermath of Pollock's death had little to do with herself—it was still all about Pollock's work and his reputation. Just days after the funeral, Krasner found among Pollock's papers a note that her friends had failed to intercept during the frantic housecleaning before her arrival from Paris. Addressed to Pollock from B. H. Friedman, it was written shortly after the unsettling "celebration" of Friedman's birthday, and it was the sort of note that could only pick at the scabs of a widow's heart. Sensing the deep turmoil his friend was in at the time, Friedman had written Pollock that he "understood his problem" and that although he had deep affection for Lee, he also understood Jackson's attraction to Ruth Kligman.

Krasner destroyed the note—but not because she viewed it as a sign of betrayal by either Pollock or Friedman. "Lee called me up after she found that note," recalls Friedman. "She knew I had a habit of copying my correspondence, and she said: 'If you have a copy of that letter, I wish you would destroy it.'" Krasner worried that the note, coming from a close friend, would make the relationship with Kligman appear like more than just a passing infatuation. "She saw the historical significance in that note," says Friedman. "That's the kind of calculation she would make." And Friedman, as a favor to Krasner, destroyed his copy of the note.

Krasner was also bombarded with the practical problems of the Pollock estate. For one thing, there was the question of how to value his paintings. If the work was given too high a valuation, Krasner would be faced with enormous estate taxes she could ill afford. If it was priced too low, there would be capital gains taxes to be paid after each sale. Then, too, Pollock's work was insured for "a terrifyingly small sum." To pay higher premiums for his work, she needed money. In the end, Pollock's estate was appraised at about $80,000, with his paintings ranging in value from $2,500 to $20,000; within twenty years, the valuation would soar to $50 million.

Gradually, necessity and grief, guilt and love, as well as the need to justify years of sacrifice to Pollock's career, led Krasner to assume the role of Art Widow. It was a role she took on reluctantly at first, although with time she came to relish her newfound power. In the January 1965 issue of *Esquire*, her old friend Harold Rosenberg declared: "Mrs. Jackson Pollock, besides being a painter in her own right, is often credited with having almost single-handedly forced up prices for contemporary American abstract art after the death of her husband." Krasner was not alone in this regard. After Barnett Newman's death in 1970, his wife would assume the role of Art Widow far more flamboyantly than Lee; Annalee bought Clare Boothe Luce's Manhattan apartment in River House, where she played the "grande dame," establishing a "shrine" to Newman, replete with his work and mementos of his life. Yet it was Krasner, more than anyone else, who was criticized for wielding undue influence.

Racked as she was by grief and the burdens of the Pollock estate, Krasner didn't waste much time returning to her own work. And when she did, she brought a fresh, raw emotional power to her paintings that had rarely been present before. The paintings, she said, were "in homage" to Pollock. For the first time, Pollock's influence on Krasner's work became quite deliberate. One of the stranger episodes of the year immediately following her husband's death involved a work that Krasner insisted she had painted over one of Pollock's discarded canvases. Only recently have tests revealed that it was actually painted over one of her own canvases.

At the same time, after years of serving as Pollock's anchor, years during which she could not afford to give in to her own subconscious impulses, Krasner suddenly found herself emotionally unbound. She began to work in the barn. And during the first eighteen months after Pollock's death, Krasner painted seventeen large pictures that were "of such dazzling color and voluptuous fecundity" that they amounted to "a stunning reaffirmation of life," according to Bryan Robertson. Critic Barbara Rose explained Krasner's newfound creative energy in starker terms: "Krasner was only able to give up control or, to put it more bluntly, to be pushed to lose control, by a real-life accident that shattered her life and left her with nothing but her art to live for."

But the exuberant canvases, with their fuchsias, oranges, and acid greens, that were painted soon after Pollock's death inevitably gave way to a more somber, mournful output. As a wife, Krasner had painted during the morning hours, when her husband slept; as a widow, with her days crowded by phone calls and visitors and the details of the Pollock estate, and her nights racked by insomnia and grief, Krasner, for a time, began painting mostly after dark. Without the benefit of daylight, she banished color from her paintings.

By 1959, it appeared as though she might finally win the acclaim that had long eluded her. That spring, Clement Greenberg had come by one of the many Manhattan apartments that served as temporary residences for Krasner in the years after Pollock's death, to discuss the possibility of putting on a show of her work. Greenberg had recently become an adviser to French & Co., a prestigious Manhattan gallery. A solo exhibition at French would certainly be a coup. But what was even more important was winning the imprimatur of Greenberg, the kingmaker. Krasner knew that his reviews were probably the single most important catalyst that had turned Pollock into a superstar. As Tom Wolfe put it: "Greenberg hadn't created Pollock's reputation, but he was its curator, custodian, brass polisher, and repairman, and he was terrific at it."

But Greenberg's sudden interest would also have brought back haunting memories. For over a decade, coming out to Springs for periodic visits to look at Pollock's latest work, he had never noticed hers. Greenberg also was a drinker; a man who quaffed several shot glasses of liquor per hour, he couldn't have been a good influence on Pollock. This was the same Greenberg whom she had helped introduce to modern art. The same Greenberg who came to pass judgment on Pollock's work and—most galling of all—found his later works wanting. The same Greenberg who rarely came for a visit without bringing with him the young, beautiful, and successful Helen Frankenthaler, whom Krasner hated. The same Greenberg who agreed to give a eulogy at Pollock's funeral, only to change his mind at the last minute.

Greenberg, in fact, represented Krasner's oldest nemesis—sexist Jewish male authority. Like herself, Greenberg was a Brooklyn-born Jew who had sought to put as much distance between himself and his roots as he could. Having established himself as a leading authority on avant-garde art, Greenberg had promoted the boys—Pollock, Still, and Newman (although he later claimed that his support of Still had been greatly exaggerated). Of Krasner, he once said: "Lee should have had more faith in herself and more independence; but then that is the problem of all female artists." Indeed, one of the few female artists to whom Greenberg gave his backing was his lover Helen Frankenthaler.

So it wasn't entirely surprising that Krasner's promised show at French & Co. never came off. That summer, when Greenberg went out to Springs to see her work, he claimed that he didn't like what he saw. "I said that I didn't like the pictures, but that I would tell French to show them anyhow. I would do it for Lee, for an old friend. She said: 'Nothing doing. If you don't like 'em, French isn't going to show 'em.' "

So why did Greenberg offer Lee a show at French's in the first place? "Alas, alas," he sighed. "It was a favor" to a dear old friend.

A much more likely version of the story was recounted in a 1979 issue of *Art World*: Greenberg, "impressed by Krasner's 'Earth Green' phase, proposed she show next at his new emporium, French & Co. When sometime later he stopped by the barn-studio to check on the work in progress, he was confronted instead by an early stage of . . . 'The Gate,' then still impacted with motifs and dark gestures more usually associated with Pollock. . . . He disapproved. His response angered her, the promised show never came off."

Although praised for his insight, Greenberg was a red-pencil critic. He just couldn't resist telling painters how to paint. He criticized Pollock for reintroducing figures in his later paintings. And he would almost certainly have had advice for Lee—just as she almost certainly would have rejected it out of hand. "You weren't going to tell Lee anything," said Greenberg. "When I didn't like her stuff in [1959], she got angry. I know other artists [to] whom [my criticism] would have given pause."

Greenberg remembered how distraught Krasner was the morning after their confrontation. "Her face was swollen and red," like someone who had spent the night crying. Krasner dropped Greenberg off at the train station and wouldn't see him again for several years.

But where did Greenberg ultimately stand in his judgment of Krasner's work? On the one hand, Greenberg conceded: "I discovered that I had been unfair to her [in the late 1940s]. When I saw her things later, I realized the pictures were better than I [had] thought. . . . I got to them by a kind of jump, after Pollock's death, when I saw them again."

On the other hand, he insisted, he hadn't really made a mistake: "Was she as good as Rothko or Newman or Motherwell or Gorky or de Kooning? No she wasn't. Uh, uh. She wasn't in the same league. That's a cruel way of putting it, but that's how I felt."

"She was better than I thought. But not all that good. The retrospective bore me out. [There was] only one picture in the show that I thought was there. This [one picture] hit it."

One picture. Greenberg didn't recall which one. He was not sure whether the retrospective included her Little Image series, which he acknowledged he underrated. (It did.) He didn't remember calling her collage show of 1955 "a major addition to the American art scene of that era," a statement he provided for Bryan Robertson's catalogue for the show at London's Whitechapel Art Gallery. "The fact that I don't remember them is indicative. If I'd liked them that much I would have written about them," he insisted, sitting in his book-laden study, pictures filling up the space between the bookcases and the ceiling.

But then Greenberg was never shy about chopping even the widely acclaimed giants of Abstract Expressionism down to size: "Still wasn't that good—I got misquoted. . . . Bill [de Kooning] lost his stuff after his first show in 1948 or 1949. . . ." As for Pollock, Greenberg wrote off much of his work in the 1950s, saying: "Pollock's first bad show [was] in 1953."

Whatever the final verdict of art history, Krasner's neglect by men of Greenberg's influence was emblematic of the capriciousness that marked the way critical judgments were made in New York's fledgling art establishment. This was, after all, a movement in which theory had arguably become more important than aesthetics, in which a handful of insiders had become virtually the sole arbiters of what was original and praiseworthy. It was a world suddenly infused with so much money, power, and fame that it would lead artists for the first time to hire publicists to promote their work and to create virtual assembly lines to produce it. Ultimately, it would erupt in the sort of all-out scandal that followed Rothko's death and the battle over his estate.

In the early 1970s, Rothko's daughter, Kate, brought suit against the three executors of her father's estate, including the artist Theodore Stamos, and charged them with selling one hundred of her father's paintings to the Marlborough Gallery for far below their market value. She accused them of double-dealing; the motive, she alleged, was that Stamos's work was about to be represented by the gallery, while Bernard Reis, another of the executors, was also a Marlborough officer. The trial put the less than orthodox business practices of Frank Lloyd, the power behind Marlborough, under a microscope and seriously damaged his reputation.

Years earlier, as the widow Pollock, Krasner also became a prime target of art market scoundrels. Sometime in the late 1950s, she was forced to confront the possibility of dirty dealing on the part of Sidney Janis, who was still Pollock's dealer. Krasner became suspicious when she found it difficult to track down a number of Pollock's paintings that she wanted for a traveling exhibition of his work. She kept applying to Janis, who couldn't locate the records for several sales. Krasner assured him that she was interested not in making personal contact with his buyers but in getting hold of the paintings for a show. Janis's vagueness led her to do some detective work. And Krasner discovered that several of the paintings Janis claimed not to know about had been bought by members of the Janis family—and at knockdown prices. "He had told her that they had been bought by struggling young couples who couldn't afford the $30,000 or $20,000 or $10,000," says Bryan Robertson, recalling the story as it was told to him by Krasner. "All the paintings had been marked down. It was a kind of secret cartel at work."

The confrontations with Greenberg and Janis were finally compounded by the death of Anna Krassner in September 1959. Lee had always kept her mother at a distance, resenting perhaps Anna's closeness to her son, Irving, Lee's own status as an overlooked middle child, and her image as the black sheep—the family *kurve* (whore), as her mother had often called her. Although mother and daughter had become increasingly estranged over the years, the death of Anna Krassner must have compounded the sense of alienation and doom that weighed down on Lee after Jackson's death.

The obstacles and indifference she had encountered in the art world had soured her on most of her colleagues, as well as on the New York art establishment, a fact that complicated Krasner's task as she set out to find a new dealer to handle the Pollock estate. The job was made all the more difficult by Krasner's insistence that she wanted a gallery of highest repute. And while several dealers were willing to accept the Pollock paintings on consignment, Krasner also wanted a large up-front payment, possibly to settle the taxes associated with the estate.

These questions weighed heavily on Krasner in 1959 when she returned to Springs for the summer. Thinking, perhaps, of helping her with her problem, Ossorio and Dragon invited Krasner over one Saturday night to meet a young art dealer named David Gibbs. A tall, elegant Englishman, Gibbs, during a visit to New York, had introduced himself to Betty Parsons, who invited him to join her for a weekend at The Creeks. Gibbs remembers sleeping in a room that contained a Dubuffet, a Pollock, and a small painting by Krasner, whose work he didn't know. "I liked [the painting] enormously," says Gibbs, and he told Krasner so the next evening at dinner. He said that he would like very much to see more of her work. The following day, a Sunday, Gibbs came to see Krasner at the barn on Fireplace Road, and he purchased Krasner's *Cool White*. The painting, which now hangs in the National Gallery of Australia, was the first large picture she had ever sold.

Krasner was charmed and flattered by Gibbs's attentions. What ensued was Krasner's last great romance—a relationship that was actually a tangled web of emotions and business motives. Gibbs was, in fact, the first of several Englishmen whose professional advice she trusted, because, as Gibbs puts it: "We were fresh, not tainted by the [New York art] establishment." But while the relationship had its practical uses for both artist and dealer, Gibbs, who was several years Krasner's junior, became the last man she would allow close enough to break her heart.

Soon after meeting Gibbs, Krasner decided to entrust him with the task of finding a dealer for the Pollock estate. Initially, Gibbs had little luck. He recalls "running up and down Manhattan trying to find a dealer." But no one was willing to give Krasner a sizable advance payment for paintings that rarely sold and, when they did sell, fetched only $3,000 or $4,000 apiece. Gibbs finally suggested that Krasner speak to Frank Lloyd, the powerful chief of the Marlborough Gallery in London. Marlborough was one of the world's leading art galleries, and Gibbs knew that its wily Austrian-born owner was about to establish a presence in New York. The Pollock estate could make the perfect vehicle for creating a splash in the New World. Lloyd flew to New York to meet Krasner in April 1961. Wearing the dark sunglasses she often donned to steel herself for a difficult negotiation, Krasner met Lloyd for the first time over lunch at a restaurant near the Santini warehouse on the lower West Side of Manhattan, where Pollock's paintings were stored. Afterward, they pored over Pollock's paintings. Finally, Lloyd agreed to Krasner's terms: Gibbs and Krasner selected a group of paintings and works on paper, from which Lloyd could purchase $60,000 worth of merchandise at wholesale prices. Although Lloyd did not initially have access to the rest of the estate, this purchase, and a later addition of paintings on consignment, provided the nucleus of a one-man European exhibition that started at the Marlborough Gallery in London, as well as of the Marlborough's opening show in New York, in 1964.

Indeed, contrary to the insinuations of her detractors, Krasner was not primarily interested in forcing up the price of Pollock's work just for the sake of cashing in on her inheritance; rather, she was determined to place his paintings with the most discerning collectors and in the best museums. After Pollock's death, "several of us conferred about the disposition of the Pollock estate," wrote B. H. Friedman, who saw in Krasner's stewardship of the estate the same deliberate love for art, and for Jackson, that had always guided her. "We advised Lee to release the paintings in a slow but regular manner, beginning as soon as possible, so that the proceeds could be invested and so she could get back to her own work. She chose to release Pollock's paintings more slowly than we suggested. That decision was uncalculated. It was based upon commitment to the work. It was based upon love, not power politics."

William Rubin remembers Krasner's protectiveness toward Pollock's work and a complicated three-way exchange he tried to negotiate with her and Ben Heller, one of the earliest collectors of Pollock's work, in 1958: Krasner owned *No. 32*, which Rubin wanted. Krasner, however, insisted on selling it to a museum. But Rubin knew that Krasner loved *Blue Poles*, which Heller owned. And Heller was very interested in getting some Rothkos that Rubin owned. So Rubin worked out a deal whereby he would get *Blue Poles* from Heller in exchange for the Rothkos that Heller wanted and some cash, and Krasner would exchange *No. 32* for *Blue Poles*. The deal ultimately collapsed when Heller backed out of the arrangement.

The majority of such negotiations ultimately worked out her way, however. For example, after Pollock's death, Krasner established a new price for *Autumn Rhythm*. Originally, the Metropolitan Museum had considered buying the painting at $10,000 and turned it down. The Met soon caved in, however, agreeing to buy the painting from her for three times that sum. As part of the deal, Krasner agreed to buy back a black-and-white painting from the museum and to credit the Met for $10,000. Nevertheless, the official sale price for the painting was $30,000. Several years later, Sid Janis would buy *One*, the companion painting to *Autumn Rhythm*, for $350,000.

After bringing Lloyd and Krasner together, David Gibbs became a frequent visitor to Springs. Still married to his first wife, Jennifer, he divided his time between London and New York.

For Lee, the dashing Brit, who had served in the Welsh Guards, helped fill a void that had been left by Jackson and provided a welcome relief from the intrigues of the New York art world. His good looks, charm, and foreignness may also have reminded Lee of the old romance with Igor.

It may, ultimately, have been only a "summer" romance, but for at least a few seasons it sizzled. Dragon remembers long summer evenings when David and Lee would spend the night at The Creeks because "they loved it here," and David would mix up huge quantities of Black Velvets in a cut-glass pitcher. Lee was "tipsy all the time." The Friedmans, who remember staying on Fireplace Road on at least one occasion when Gibbs spent the night in Lee's bedroom, remember how uncharacteristically coquettish Lee became around him. In 1961, during one of Lee's trips to London, the Friedmans were taken aback by a phone call from Lee. She was "all giggly," recalls B. H. Friedman. "They were staying at either the Savoy or the Ritz. And David had mixed up all the shoes in the hallway" that other guests had left out to be polished. "I remember us marveling: My God—is this Lee?"

Most of Krasner's friends were concerned about Gibbs's motives. "He was just an opportunist," recalls Dragon. "For a while he did sweep her off her feet. Wined and dined her. He would have married her in a minute, but Lee woke up." Muses Bryan Robertson, whose view of Gibbs was only slightly more charitable: "He wasn't quite a gigolo. A bit of a fancy boy, but not a villain, or cruel. He'd be nice to the woman he was with."

Whatever his initial intentions, Krasner was grateful for the diversion Gibbs offered her. They spent much of the summer of 1962 together in Springs, combing the beach for shells, collecting plants, and gardening. And in July, under Krasner's astute eye and cautious encouragement, Gibbs began to paint. "Your advice, help and encouragement . . . still rings in my ears—'go against the image, not with it—leave it alone, it may look better tomorrow,' " he wrote to her the following spring. "In a few weeks' time I shall have been painting for a year—it all seems so extraordinary. . . ." The letter closes with uncharacteristic passion: "I want to say that I love you very much, think of you constantly, want to see you."

If Gibbs imagined that Krasner would foster his newfound ambition to be a painter, as she had once nurtured Pollock, he was to be disappointed. Krasner, who remained absorbed in her work as she had rarely been during her marriage to Pollock, entered a new creative phase that year. As the darkest period of mourning passed, Krasner reintroduced color into her work, as well as a regenerative imagery that invoked lush, fertile plant life.

Gibbs returned to London and his family when fall began. Gradually, the intimacy that had developed between Gibbs and Krasner during the summer faded. As the holidays approached, David still had not returned. And Lee decided to spend Christmas in Springs with her nephew Ronnie Stein. On Christmas Eve, she joined Ronnie and his wife, Frances, at the home of Jan Church for dinner, even though she had suffered a throbbing migraine headache all day. By the time she got to the Churches', the pain was so severe that Krasner had to excuse herself to lie down. A doctor was called, and Krasner was rushed to Southampton Hospital, where a spinal tap showed blood and indicated a possible brain hemorrhage. Krasner, who had long abhorred traditional medicine and always turned to homeopathic remedies both for her own and for Pollock's ailments, was rushed to St. Luke's Hospital in Manhattan for a battery of painful tests. A few days after New Year's, she underwent surgery for a brain aneurysm.

Confronted for the first time with her own mortality, forced to endure the pain and fear of surgery without Gibbs's comfort, Lee became unusually introspective. At first there was the initial relief at just being alive. Wearing a stocking cap that made her look "a bit like Rumpelstiltskin," she gratefully received a flood of telegrams and flowers, including button roses from David. "Something inside her—her hostility, defensiveness . . . paranoia . . . has relented, relaxed," wrote Sandy Friedman, her closest friend at the time, in a letter to David Gibbs. "She is filled with tolerance, sympathy, even tenderness for her fellow artists and the art world in general. Really David, it is quite a marvelous spectacle."

The feeling wouldn't last long. At the end of January, Krasner checked out of the hospital and into the Adams Hotel. While months earlier she had railed at the intrigue of the art world, now, convalescing in a hotel suite, she seemed lost without it. The tolerance and tenderness that had revealed themselves in the immediate aftermath of her illness were soon replaced by an even deeper bitterness and paranoia, which clung to Krasner like a second skin. It was at about this time that Fritz Bultman quipped to B. H. Friedman that when they removed Krasner's aneurysm, they cut out friendship as well. By her own admission, she exhausted a string of nurses and tested the patience of friends like Sandy Friedman. In February, she wrote David Gibbs: "Once my fury against ART relented it began to waiver [sic] between Elizabeth Hubbard and David Gibbs—though at the moment it seems to favor Elizabeth—no telling how I'll come out with you, David." (In the aftermath of her aneurysm, Krasner lost interest in homeopathy and stopped seeing Hubbard, who had been her doctor for years.)

For Krasner, ardor also was gradually being replaced by disappointment. In the harsh light of a slow convalescence, Gibbs's chivalry may finally have seemed facile and tawdry—and certainly not worth risking her hard-won independence and artistic freedom for. In response to some slides he had sent her to critique, Lee replied, with Sandy's help: "To answer your last question first, Lee feels: Overseas calls at best are inadequate, and as you haven't seen each other for some seven months or so it looms more frustrating than ever. Just what, she wonders, would she say in those two or three minutes? It would all be so artificial and dissatisfying."

For a time, Lee got over her anger. She and David spent time together again that summer. But if she ever harbored any intentions of marrying David, she soon banished them. And few of her acquaintances were surprised when Gibbs, now divorced, finally married Geraldine Stutz, who was for several years the president of Bendel's.

Gibbs wasn't the only friend she would lose. In the years after Pollock's death, Krasner banished legions of her former allies. Patsy Southgate was one of the first to go. Krasner feuded regularly with Ossorio, her friend and Pollock's patron, who, perhaps out of pity or because of turbulence in his relationship with Dragon, had proposed to her after Pollock's death; yet after her surgery they saw each other less and less. She fought constantly with her sister Ruth. In the early 1970s, she broke with B. H. Friedman after he wrote a biography of Pollock, *Jackson Pollock: Energy Made Visible*, a work she alternately encouraged and condemned. And she battled periodically with Fritz Bultman, who after one of their arguments wrote Krasner a letter in which he referred to her "narrow reptilian brain" and concluded: "I want to remove our lives from contact with hateful, cold inhuman types and tell you to take yourself to yourself and never bother us again."

In fact, Krasner had little use for most of her contemporaries. She "never had a kind word to say" about the women, including Helen Frankenthaler, Louise Nevelson, whom she called Luigi, and Elaine de Kooning ("*da* Kooning", she'd say, putting the emphasis on the first syllable). She disliked them, it was said, for their looks, for their connections, and, most of all, for producing what she considered second-rate work and getting away with it.

With Pollock and Gibbs gone, and her health improving, Krasner took a new lease on life, one that came complete with new friends and a new focus on painting. Not even a fall that broke her right arm, while she was recovering from her aneurysm, could keep Krasner from going back to work. With her painting arm incapacitated, she took to squeezing globs of paint directly onto canvas and working them into the surface with her left hand. The results were the dappled all-over patterns of paintings like *August Petals*.

Although the important New York galleries had all but ignored her work for decades, Krasner was about to make her debut in London. After years of enduring the cloying insincerity of curators and gallery owners who had little use for Lee Krasner but salaamed shamelessly before the widow Pollock, she had finally found a connoisseur who truly cared about her work. Bryan Robertson's offer of a retrospective at the prestigious Whitechapel Gallery was particularly meaningful to Krasner because it came *years* after he had asked—and won—her approval to do a catalogue raisonné of Pollock's work.

Indeed, Robertson had discovered Krasner's work quite by accident in 1958. He had come to New York and made an appointment with Pollock's widow to discuss the catalogue raisonné. That evening, at one of her many temporary city residences in the years following her husband's death (this one on East Sixtieth Street), Barnett Newman and Betty Parsons were helping to hang *The Seasons*, an intensely colored canvas that, at seventeen feet in length, was one of Krasner's largest paintings to date. "I was so impressed, I decided then" to give Lee a show, recalls Robertson. However, the young curator must have sensed that Krasner would not trust his interest in her work if he mentioned it *before* he had completed his work on the Pollock book. Thus, Robertson waited two years, until 1960, before even broaching the subject of a Krasner retrospective.

The idea was vintage Robertson, by a man who is known for having discovered and promoted a number of unsung artists, many of them women. For example, he gave Barbara Hepworth her first retrospective in London in 1954. The walls of his modest town house in North London are covered with the work of his favorite artists—the place of honor occupied by Krasner's rose-and-green *Earth Green*.

Not only did Robertson like her work, he had the ability to fill her with girlish enthusiasm. While she chafed under Greenberg's heavy-handed advice, she acquiesced to Robertson's gentle cajoling. In June 1965, shortly before the London show, Robertson concluded a letter to her with the following admonition: *"NEXT, BUT MOST VITAL OF ALL* You must paint a few large and magnificent *new* works for this show or I shall be deeply disappointed. . . . I want 1 superb *very big* long painting for one end wall, at least. The show must end on an upbeat note. . . . Don't stay at the Adams wasting time. Either rent a studio immediately in New York or go out to The Springs immediately and get down to the painting—*NOW."*

And paint she did. That summer she produced at least three large paintings, including *Right Bird Left* and *Combat*.

Now that she was finally getting some attention, Krasner was determined to make the most of her belated debut. As a young woman, Krasner had never had the money for fine clothes. And after Pollock's death, when she could finally afford to indulge herself, her sole sartorial weakness had been for fur.

But several months before the Whitechapel show, Lee began thinking about what she would wear. The Bultmans suggested that she look up Charles James, a couturier for whom Jeanne Bultman had once worked and who had dressed socialites like Diana Vreeland and the Hearsts in the 1940s. James, however, had fallen on hard times; for all his artistry, he had never been able to manage a budget and always lost money on his ventures. He also was known for being chronically behind schedule. On more than one occasion, James had dispatched some unfinished confection in a taxicab, along with an entourage of seamstresses, who continued sewing frantically until the very last minute, when, say, the ocean liner his client was traveling on was ready to set sail.

Despite his reversal of fortune, it soon became clear that James's work habits hadn't changed one iota. Krasner didn't seem to mind, however, and treated James with the respect she would accord any artist *she* deemed great, submitting to numerous fittings, spending thousands of dollars in up-front payments, and enduring several delays. The process dragged on for months. She had wanted the clothes in time to wear for the ocean passage to England. But instead, the outfits had to be sent after her via air freight. When they arrived, it was clear that James had produced the perfect ensembles for Krasner's coming out—a white silk evening gown, a green woolen suit, and a brocade cocktail dress. His clothes celebrated—rather than camouflaged—the random spread of what was by then Krasner's decidedly matronly figure. Rather than hide the artist's broad backside and ample belly, James added a peplum tail and medieval wadding at the waist. "These clothes were a marvel," recalled her friend Richard Howard. "They made Lee look . . . invulnerable, not at all in fashion, but beyond, entirely attractive and secure; and like no one else."

The Whitechapel show, in 1965, was Krasner's long-overdue debut. The retrospective opened to good reviews, and Krasner suddenly became the toast of the town. Kenneth Clark was so taken with the show that he invited her to dinner. She had tea with Bertrand Russell. Henry Moore invited her to visit. She befriended Barbara Hepworth. And, together with Robertson and a young Robert Hughes, she climbed the cliffs of St. Ives in Cornwall to see Virginia Woolf's lighthouse.

The Whitechapel exhibition was to remain a rare moment of unadulterated joy. Nearly twenty years later, she would carp to an interviewer: "Do you realize that to date no goddamned museum in New York City, where I have been born and bred and am part of history—where I fought the battle—no museum has given me a retrospective. When I think of it, I go into a rage."

More and more, as Krasner approached the end of her life, she continued to distance herself from the New York art establishment. Instead, increasingly, she sought solace in her family and in religion—if not in Judaism per se, then in a continuing exploration of spirituality. She was always organizing family dinners that inevitably centered around her brother Irving and that almost as inevitably ended in screaming matches with Ruth. Over the years, Lee and Ruth had maintained the unvanquishable ties of warring siblings—they fought over Irving and Ronnie, both of whom Lee loved, and over their mother and Ruth's husband, William, of whom Lee rarely had anything kind to say. She clung to her nephews Jay and Ronnie. And she sought out her niece Rena (Rusty) Kanokogi, a judo champion who won a long battle with the U.S. Olympic Committee to have women's judo included in the Olympic Games.

Until he died, in about 1980, Lee lavished on Irving the attentions she would previously have invested in her husband or lovers. Irving, whom relatives describe as pathologically cheap (he reused the same tea bag for weeks sometimes and refused to install a telephone so that family members "couldn't call to ask for money"), was said to favor Lee with her hard-driving practicality and success over Ruth, whom he considered too flighty. Although he rarely ventured out of Brooklyn to visit Lee because he didn't like to spend the subway fare, he became obsessed with art; Irving's apartment was stuffed not only with his sister's work but with an eclectic array of sculptures and paintings—the only thing he didn't seem to mind spending money on—by other artists. Krasner, who must have basked in her brother's appreciation of her work, cooked for him and gave him appliances, such as a brand-new television set that he was too cheap to buy for himself. And when she became too ill to venture out of her East Side apartment, she enlisted her niece Rusty to visit Irving and keep him supplied with lox and bagels.

Krasner also became obsessed with "the romance of religion"—that is, any religion but Judaism. Never having been much of a reader, she found it especially difficult after Pollock's death to concentrate on books. But she loved it when friends would read to her during the long nights in Springs. Richard Howard remembers, in particular, her intense interest in Cardinal Newman's *Apologia Pro Vita Sua* and "Lee's absorption, her perfect attention, that power she had of fixing her mind without a moment's wavering upon Newman's vision, upon the argument that 'the human race is implicated in some terrible aboriginal calamity, it is out of joint with the purposes of its Creator.' She made me stop and read again . . . and she knew, she always knew, that what she was hearing could make her *see*. I think she mistrusted words—The Word—but if she did, it was because she knew the consequences of surrendering to their power."

During her last two decades, Krasner cultivated a series of unlikely friendships with Jesuit priests. Krasner's Jesuits helped her gain new insights into her own work and her devotion to Pollock, as well as a better perspective on the order, and disorder, of life. Steeped in Judaism, she enjoyed debating theology with men like Terrance Netter, a Jesuit priest whom she met in the summer of 1964, when Netter was in the midst of his own spiritual crisis, training as an artist and about to leave the priesthood. Frequently that summer, Lee could be seen on Sunday mornings sitting in a pew at St. Filomena's Church in East Hampton, listening to Netter's sermons.

On the tenth anniversary of her husband's death, Krasner asked Netter to participate in a tribute to Pollock that was being held at The Club, a gathering of artists that, ironically, had been organized by the de Kooning coterie in 1949. It had been meeting periodically in Greenwich Village ever since. Sitting on the panel, the only "layman" among the high priests of Abstract Expressionism, which included Ad Reinhardt and Robert Motherwell, Netter began a discourse on the theological implications of action painting, a subject that must have occupied many of his discussions with Krasner. "If the creative act of man is one in which [he] interacts with [the canvas] through dialogue," mused Netter, if, as it were, "God is an action painter, and doesn't control how it will all turn out, then we are really free" to fulfill our own destinies. Netter saw in the act of painting the same dialectic that informed some contemporary interpretations of the Creation: that is, once an artist begins the process of creation, he interacts with the canvas, but he will never fully control it because he cannot know in advance how the work will come out.

Netter, whose presence on the panel had been specifically requested by Krasner, was practically booed offstage. What a "bunch of shit," exclaimed the artists, many of whom believed their own work to be the latest word of God but few of whom would have understood Netter's Hegelian references. (Only recently, Barnett Newman had boasted to Krasner that the Pope himself had congratulated him on his famous work *Stations of the Cross* and for "bringing Christianity into the 20th century.") No sooner had they silenced Netter than an argument erupted among several of the men, who couldn't agree on whether Abstract Expressionism derived from passion or from the intellect. In the ensuing fracas, Pollock was forgotten. Krasner, who long ago had stopped attending meetings of The Club, watched the proceedings in silent, seething disgust. When Netter questioned Krasner afterward about the rude reception his remarks had received, Krasner replied acidly: "You didn't think they actually came here to pay homage to Pollock, did you?"

For Krasner and for Pollock, abstract art had been not an intellectual exercise or some esoteric code of communication, but life itself. And as she neared the end of her own existence, Krasner peeled away everything but art. After the initial months of mourning following her husband's death, she ceased to talk about Pollock, or her marriage, even with close friends—just as she found it difficult to talk about anything as intensely private as her work. Yet not even the growing recognition she received for her paintings could sway her from the obsessions of her past. Just as demons had continued to haunt her nights ever since Pollock's death, by day her ambitions remained, to a large extent, centered on Pollock's legacy—not only because she genuinely believed him to be the greatest artist of his generation, but because she had made his work the raison d'être of her youth. While she continued to paint until the end of her life, Pollock remained a constant presence and preoccupation. It was there in the long, intense negotiations with museums and dealers over Pollock's paintings and in the disposition of her own estate.

Increasingly, Krasner's personal life became as stripped down as a minimalist canvas. She continued to see her nephews and a few friends like Netter and Robertson—men who were as far removed from the New York artistic establishment as she would have liked to be. And she still gave a few dinner parties; but, inevitably, they ended as rancorously as the countless evenings that Pollock had poisoned with his drunken scenes. For Krasner had developed a habit of picking from among her guests one target for attack. Often her victim was Diana, the wife of her beloved nephew Jason, who dissolved into tears on more than one occasion during dinner with his old aunt.

Her experience as a wife in an unhappy marriage and an artist in an unwelcoming profession never inspired in Krasner any sense of allegiance with her natural allies—other women. While she occasionally sought out the company of her niece Rena and at least one young woman artist, Nancy Graves, who also had endured an unhappy marriage, Krasner seemed to bear a special animosity toward women, whom she dismissed en masse as "the skirts." Partly, she had never really overcome the old jealousies over Pollock or the barbs about her own appearance. For Krasner, the shadowy existence of other artists' wives, such as Musa Guston and Annalee Newman, served as an uneasy reminder of a fate that she had only narrowly escaped, and of a husband whom she could never fully possess in life or be rid in of in death. The rivalry with her sister Ruth, which had always revolved in some way around men—either Irving or Pollock—had continued unabated, so much so that after Lee's death, Ruth threatened to disrupt the funeral service by throwing herself onto her sister's grave. Ronnie Stein took the threat so seriously that he forbade his mother to attend the funeral. Thus, Krasner had robbed herself of the one source of support that younger women, in their fight for professional actualization, would seize on—the support of other women.

By the end of her life, Krasner had become an invalid. Unable to leave her apartment without a wheelchair, she continued to paint, working out of a spare bedroom in her apartment on East 79th Street, where she was surrounded by a few beloved objects that she had accumulated carefully over a lifetime—shells and plants, a love seat made of Texas longhorns that she and Ted Dragon had found together in an antique shop, and her paintings. During the last years of her life, the painter had surrounded herself with her own work—dozens of Lee Krasners hung on the walls. But not a single Jackson Pollock.

Yet when Lee Krasner died, she left behind an estate worth about $10 million, which she had earmarked as a final monument to Pollock. Aside from small legacies that she left to a handful of relatives, the bulk of her estate was put into a trust, to be dispensed to struggling artists. Although she had done her share of struggling, there is no doubt that Krasner was thinking of Pollock when she made her bequest. The house in Springs, which remained as spartan as when she and Pollock lived there together in poverty and artistic ferment, was to be preserved as a museum, the Pollock/Krasner House.

Lee Krasner died alone in a hospital room on June 20, 1984; she was seventy-six years old. She had suffered internal bleeding from an attack of diverticulitis. Jason McCoy rushed her to the emergency room of New York Hospital. A few hours later, Diana McCoy and Eugene Thaw, a respected dealer who was to serve as an executor of her will, came by the hospital. None of them guessed that Krasner was in fact dying, and none were with her when death came.

Those who knew her best say Krasner gave up living when she became too sick to paint. Although she did finally have her retrospective at the Museum of Modern Art, it opened in December 1984, six months after her death.

Maria Goeppert
Mayer

"She could succeed even without mathematics."

Anonymous

The Accidental Scientist

It was a balmy spring day in Ann Arbor, Michigan, in 1955, and scientists attending a conference at the university were milling around sharing ideas, debating the latest discoveries, and, of course, being noticed. It was the cocktail hour. A young aspiring physicist spotted an older colleague, whom she admired very much, standing alone on the opposite end of the room. Maria Goeppert Mayer was only forty-nine years old at the time, but she seemed much older. She stood hunched over, absentmindedly sipping a drink. The two women didn't know each other well, but they were often two of the few women at these conferences, so it seemed natural to say hello. "I remember telling her that I had just gotten engaged," recalls Faye Ajzenberg-Selove.

Suddenly, Mayer's gaze moved up from her feet. Maria Mayer took her young colleague up to her room, sat her down, and poured her a large glass of whiskey. Nursing her own drink, Mayer laid out what Faye had to look forward to: how difficult it was to be a woman in science and to be married to a scientist; how hard it would be for Ajzenberg to find a job in the same geographic location as her husband; how her own marriage had given many in academia an excuse not to treat her seriously. It had been twenty-five years since she attended her first physics conference in Ann Arbor, just weeks after getting off the boat from Germany as a new bride. For Maria and Joe Mayer, that first summer in Ann Arbor—meeting fellow scientists like Enrico Fermi, debating quantum mechanics while sprawled out on the campus green, under a hot summer sun—had been like a second honeymoon. And now here she was back in Michigan, at the prime of her career, a front-runner for the Nobel Prize in physics, and still she had not been able to get a full-time salaried position at a university.

Mayer's confession was startling because it was so out of character. She rarely talked about herself. She had long ago given up confiding in women—or in almost anyone else, for that matter. Her colleagues never heard her complain about the discrimination she had been subjected to by the scientific establishment, of the nepotism rules that kept her on the margins of physics for over a quarter of a century, and the frustration and self-doubt she had endured. Nor did she harp on it later, in the public speeches she made after finally winning the Nobel in 1963.

Mayer's confession was particularly poignant because she had always insisted that she could not have done it *without* her husband. "A woman scientist should never marry anyone *but* another scientist," Mayer had always said. For science is collaboration. When all else fails, a scientist should at least be able to collaborate with her husband.

In this regard, Mayer knew that she had been luckier than most women scientists of her generation; luckier, perhaps, than any since Marie Curie. For Mayer's Nobel Prize–winning research on the shell model of the nucleus had followed a lifetime of dialogue with the leading scientists of her generation. She had collaborated with men like the Nobel laureate Max Born, who had been her university mentor; with Enrico Fermi and Edward Teller, two of her oldest friends; with J. Hans D. Jensen, with whom she had both won the Nobel Prize and produced a book on work they had done contemporaneously years before they ever met; and with her husband, Joseph Mayer, a respected chemist, who debated science with her from the moment he came home for cocktails in the evening until they went to bed at night.

Collaboration, she knew, was the great catalyst of science, the yeast of a creative mind. In spite of Western culture's idealization of the lone scientific genius, Mayer was aware that the sort of seminal mind most frequently ascribed to Albert Einstein was the exception—if it really existed at all—rather than the rule. A lifelong denizen of college campuses, from Johns Hopkins to the University of California at San Diego, Mayer understood that Quaker-style meetings and seminars on esoteric subjects ranging from spectroscopy to cosmology were the lifeblood of every physics and chemistry department. She had always looked forward to the social gatherings that inevitably were dominated by shoptalk. And she would have relished participating in the great scientific fraternities of the age, especially Niels Bohr's Institute for Theoretical Physics in Copenhagen, which had attracted the world's most gifted young men between the two great wars, men like Werner Heisenberg, Wolfgang Pauli, and Victor Weisskopf, who had been her teachers and colleagues at the University of Göttingen.

The Copenhagen fraternity may have been off-limits to aspiring women scientists, but in Göttingen young Maria Goeppert had been given a rare welcome into a community of gifted physicists, and it would set the course for her pioneering investigations into the structure of the nucleus. It was as a student in Göttingen, where a disparate group of scientists who shared little more than a determination to unravel the secrets of the smallest units of matter had gathered, that Mayer witnessed the spontaneous combustion that gave rise to the new physics. At a time when gifted women would get into the classroom, only to be given the cold shoulder by male colleagues and teachers, Mayer won full membership in Göttingen's scientific sanctum sanctorum. But marriage and prejudice would keep her on the fringes of the world's greatest academic laboratories for some twenty years. Ultimately, it was her ability to maintain a dialogue with both her husband and a small community of friends whom she had gotten to know at Göttingen that made it possible for her to break the gender barrier in science.

In many ways, of course, Mayer's life followed the pattern that has frustrated the careers of most women scientists. Although she received a progressive education and encouragement from her family, she was raised to believe that her place was always at the side of her husband, as helpmate and friend, but never as rival. At school and at work she was usually the only woman in the lab. And although some of the world's leading scientists would come to respect her as a friend and as a colleague, her academic appointments were so tenuous that she didn't receive a full-time salary until shortly before winning the Nobel Prize. (Indeed, as recently as 1968, women who were completing their graduate studies in science at Yale were still being told: "You are being trained to become research associates and to become the wives of the men you are now going to school with.")

When Mayer embarked on her career, the prejudice against women scientists was so great that, until at least the early 1920s, a woman who chose a life in physics literally had to renounce the possibility of marriage and motherhood. According to extensive studies conducted by Margaret Rossiter at the beginning of the twentieth century, of the twenty-three American women who worked as physicists in 1921, not a single one of them married. "It was generally accepted before 1920 that the pursuit of a scientific career required a single-minded determination, which was incompatible with marriage for a woman," writes Vera Kistiakowski, a professor of physics at MIT. "A wife was expected to be totally dedicated to that role and to subordinate her interests and activities to the aspirations of her husband." In the 1920s, even some women's colleges would not hire married women. Thus, when Mayer completed her Ph.D., in 1929, a month after her marriage, she became one of the first women to attempt balancing family life and physics.

Yet Maria's expectations were quite conventional. She may have thought she could follow the surprisingly unenlightened advice offered by Marie Curie, in the 1920s, to her admirers, whose number must have included the young Maria Goeppert: "It isn't necessary to lead such an anti natural existence as mine. . . . What I want for women and young girls is a simple family life and some work that will interest them." Mayer's success grew almost inadvertently, not out of well-planned ambition or conviction, but out of love for her discipline and the opportunity to practice it as friends, colleagues, and finally World War II repeatedly beckoned her to the laboratory. In fact, in her approach to both marriage and her vocation, Mayer demonstrated the sort of passive fatalism that leads many great women to shrug off their accomplishments as the product of accident rather than as an act of will. As Carolyn Heilbrun noted in *Writing a Woman's Life*: "Well into the twentieth century, it continued to be impossible for women to admit into their autobiographical narratives the claim of achievement, the admission of ambition."

Years after completing her Nobel Prize–winning work, Mayer would hint to a colleague that her marriage to Joe Mayer had been part of a grand plan to keep her connected to the world of science. A Machiavellian strategy, if it were true. But although Mayer felt a strong pull toward science form the day she participated in her first seminar on physics, the truth was that as a twenty-three-year-old bride, she considered dropping the work on her Ph.D. One of the most gifted students at the University of Göttingen, she nevertheless needed the prodding of her American fiancé and a few of her professors to convince her to complete her dissertation.

For Mayer, marriage turned out to be both a huge hindrance and the ultimate asset: It kept her from having an academic career of her own and relegated her to the periphery of academic life, yet it helped to ensure that she always had someone with whom to collaborate. Had she married a man other than Joe Mayer—one less encouraging or one who simply failed to share her enthusiasm for science—she might never have become anything more than a housewife or, at best, a teacher. Still, on the eve of receiving her Nobel honors, sitting in a lounge at the University of Michigan, Maria Mayer warned Faye Ajzenberg to think twice before marrying a colleague.

Maria Goeppert met Joe Mayer, in 1929, at the end of what had been a charmed girlhood—save for occasional bouts of illness. Maria grew up in Göttingen, a picturesque medieval town, embraced by ancient stone walls and forests. She was the only child of Friedrich Goeppert, a respected professor of pediatrics at the university and the sixth-generation academic in his family. Although her mother, Maria Wolff, was a traditional German hausfrau, she too was well educated, having taught French and music before her marriage.

Most important, since he had only one child, Maria's father invested all his hopes and expectations in his daughter. Unlike the fearsome Prussian fathers of lore, Friedrich Goeppert, who ran a children's clinic in Göttingen, was ideally suited to raising a gifted young daughter. Professor Goeppert would have preferred a son, but he solved the problem by treating Maria a little as if she were one. Although she had constant headaches as a young girl, which often kept her home from school, Dr. Goeppert refused to let her become an invalid. Instead, he dreamed up ways to encourage her curiosity and precociousness. When she was seven, he created a special set of glasses through which she could watch a solar eclipse. Father and daughter went on nature walks together, collecting fossils and identifying different trees and shrubs. On one such walk at Eastertime, the child discovered Easter eggs that her father had dropped in the grass and behind some bushes when she wasn't looking. When Maria was a teenager, the two would go off alone on weeklong bike rides into the countryside.

More than anything else, Mayer remembered her father's strange admonition to her: "Don't grow up to be a woman." What she understood by that, Mayer later said, was that he wanted her to develop interests outside of the home and family. She almost certainly didn't take his advice as an invitation to reject traditional womanly virtues. Maria had, after all, also developed a strong bond to her mother, to whom, even as a married woman, she regularly turned for advice on everything from assembling a wardrobe and entertaining to decorating her home and rearing children. Frau Goeppert, Maria knew, could handle almost any domestic problem, for although the Goepperts belonged to Göttingen's elite, Germany's economy following World War I was in such a shambles that starvation was common, and it took considerable ingenuity to keep the family well fed. One year, for example, Frau Goeppert bought three piglets for slaughter—two for patients at the clinic, and one for their home. And she arranged to have her husband's patients make payments in kind for his services; peasants arriving at the clinic knew to bring sausages and poultry, rather than what was then virtually worthless currency.

Maria's upbringing reflected her parents' practical approach to life and their unusual aspirations for their precocious daughter. "It somehow was never discussed, but taken for granted by my parents as well as by me that I would go to the University," Mayer later recalled. "Yet, at the time it was not . . . easy for a woman to do so." After attending public elementary school, Maria was enrolled at the Frauenstudium, a small, elite private school that prepared girls for the university. But Maria wasn't to complete her studies there. Surging inflation would soon decimate the school's finances and force it to close its doors after Maria had completed just two years of what should have been a three-year curriculum. Concerned that Maria wasn't yet prepared to take Germany's daunting *Abitur* for university admission, her teachers suggested that she enroll in a preparatory school for boys to complete her final year. But rather than be the only girl in the class, Maria decided to take her chances with an early *Abitur*.

Maria was one of a handful of girls from her school, plus about thirty boys, who endured the ordeal in Hannover, which consisted of a week of written tests covering history, chemistry, physics, mathematics, French, English, and German, as well as an oral exam. All the boys but one flunked the exam; each of the girls passed. And Maria was the youngest of them.

When Maria entered the University of Göttingen, in 1923, the university was known as the "mathematical center of the world," thanks to the eminent mathematician Felix Klein, who had laid the foundation for Göttingen's math and science faculties. Although Maria planned to get a degree in mathematics, it was not because of any great ambition to emulate "the Great Felix" or, for that matter, any of Göttingen's considerable crop of great mathematicians. Her expectations were probably far more pragmatic; there was a shortage of mathematics teachers in schools for girls, and so for a young woman in Göttingen, in the years before her inevitable marriage, a teaching certificate in mathematics offered the best guarantee for gainful employment during the Depression.

As it happened, it was in the mathematics department that Maria would get to know the university's only female professor. In Emmy Noether, the daughter of the mathematician Max Noether and a noted mathematician herself, Maria would catch an eerie glimpse of the marginal career she would hold for much of her working life. For although Noether worked at Göttingen for decades, she never received a salary.

It was not in mathematics, however, that Maria discovered the first stirrings of ambition. As the daughter of Professor Goeppert, Maria would have become aware that an exciting new academic odyssey was beginning at Göttingen in the 1920s. Just as Klein had made mathematics the fulcrum of Göttingen's intellectual life at the turn of the century, so the arrival of two young scientists, Max Born and James Franck, would make Göttingen the cradle of quantum mechanics.

Before she had even enrolled at the university, Maria Goeppert was already well known to both Born and Franck, two men who would come to have an enormous influence on her career. For it was Maria's reputation as a charming and somewhat ethereal beauty, as well as her family's social connections, that initially won her acceptance in Göttingen's elite circle of scientists. A handful of her male colleagues admitted to being at least a bit in love with "Misi," as she was affectionately known in school. Victor (Viki) Weisskopf, for example, whom she began to date shortly after joining Born's seminar, still holds a grudge against Joe Mayer for snatching her away from him. To Edward Teller, nothing describes Maria Mayer's image in those days better than a caricature drawn of her at Göttingen, and one that she later hung proudly on her office wall in Baltimore, after emigrating to the United States. Beneath a voluptuous likeness of Maria Mayer, wearing a very short skirt, is the inscription: "She could succeed even without mathematics."

After World War I, the roomy Goeppert house was a center of Göttingen's social life. On Sundays, the Goepperts organized teas and dances, to which they invited the town's prominent academics. David Hilbert, a renowned mathematician, who had been Emmy Noether's mentor and who lived next door to the Goepperts, was said to be particularly fond of Maria, who for her own part thought of him as "the King of Göttingen." The Goepperts became friendly with the Francks, whose two daughters went to school with Maria. And the Borns, who lived down the street, also became regular visitors to the Goeppert house. At a time when the gulf between professors and students was so great that it was virtually impossible for a university student to approach her lecturers in person, Maria became known as "the niece of the scientific community."

More than anyone else, it was Max Born who was responsible for introducing Maria to the world of atomic physics. Legend has it that Mayer's career in physics began the day she ran into Max Born as he was hurrying to one of his seminars and he invited her to come along.

Mayer joined him in what was to become an unusual Göttingen ritual. Although Born was shy and reticent, he ran his classes in a manner that was antithetical to the staid, hierarchical formality that characterized traditional German university instruction. Born's seminars were often held in the large study of his home and were frequently followed by bike rides or long walks with his students, which might culminate in a rustic dinner at one of the local inns.

Before long, Maria had abandoned mathematics and was increasingly drawn into the group of scientists who gathered around Born and Franck in a quest to unlock the secrets of the atom. Fortunately for Maria, the students and young professors with whom she studied would come to constitute a who's who of quantum physics. Her fellow students included Robert Oppenheimer, John von Neumann, and Viki Weisskopf, who would become director general of CERN (Conseil Européen pour la Recherche Nucléaire), Europe's largest research center for high-energy physics. Werner Heisenberg, who was in the throes of working out his "uncertainty principle," gave lectures at Göttingen on his insights as the theory gradually unfurled in his head. And it was at Göttingen that Maria was first introduced to Edward Teller, who years later would write her long epistles from Los Alamos, complaining about his colleagues and filling pages with both scientific problems and the poems of Endre Ady, which he translated for her into German from the original Hungarian. Born himself once described Maria's class as "probably the most brilliant gathering of young talent anywhere." In 1926, a science writer named Earle Kennard reported from Göttingen: "Theoretical physics has reached a terrible state. New methods have to be learned almost every day."

More than almost any other institution in the world, Göttingen in the 1920s was charged with a unique scientific spark. Oppenheimer, who initially despaired that he would ever master quantum mechanics, found his much-needed inspiration in Göttingen: "In the sense which had not been true at Cambridge [England] and certainly not at Harvard, I was part of a little community of people who had some common interests and tastes and many common interests in physics," Oppenheimer later wrote of the environment that finally allowed him to complete his Ph.D. at Göttingen between 1926 and 1927.

Like Oppenheimer, Maria found herself irresistibly drawn to the mysterious world of quantum mechanics, which Henri Poincaré, the French physicist, had called "the greatest and most radical revolution in natural philosophy since the time of Newton." The new science would not only unlock the secrets of the most fundamental units of matter; it would also revolutionize technology and lead to both modern electronics—transistors, semiconductors, and computers—and the development of nuclear weapons, an event in which Maria herself would play a role, albeit a reluctant one. "Knowing the circumstances of her life, I was greatly surprised when I learned that Maria was really and sincerely interested in physics," recalled Eugene Wigner, a classmate of hers at Göttingen who later shared the Nobel Prize with her. "When we talked she wanted to talk about physics." Not only did Maria impress her classmates with her dedication to science, but she won their admiration for downplaying her social connections, which, Wigner says, "embarrassed her a little."

Quantum mechanics marked a dramatic departure from classical physics, which assumed that it was possible to calculate precisely both the position and the speed of any particle. The turning point in the new science occurred when Werner Heisenberg postulated, in what is known as the uncertainty principle, that the more accurately one calculates the position of a particle, the less accurately one will be able to estimate its velocity. Explained Born: "The new mechanics makes, in principle, only statements of probability. It does not answer the question, Where is a particle at a given instant? but only the question, What is the probability for a particle being at a given time at a certain place?" Notes the physicist Stephen W. Hawking: "Thus, quantum mechanics does not predict a single definite result for an observation. Instead, it predicts a number of different possible outcomes and tells us how likely each of these are." Despite the important role that the theory of relativity played in formulating quantum mechanics, it is this vision of an apparently random universe that Einstein could never accept and that would lead him to insist: "God does not play dice."

How well Maria was accepted by the boys became clear during an incident involving the brash young Robert Oppenheimer, who had a habit of disrupting Max Born's much-loved seminars on quantum mechanics. The trouble was that Oppenheimer had the very un-German habit of repeatedly interrupting and cross-examining whoever happened to be holding forth—even the beloved and esteemed Herr Professor—snatching the chalk from the speaker's hand with a perfunctory: "This can be done much better in the following manner . . ." and scribbling furiously on the blackboard. The students complained to Born, who, however, was too timid to confront Oppenheimer. Finally, the class decided to compose a written appeal, an idea that Born later attributed to "Misi," and her classmates chose Maria to deliver the entreaty—which they had inscribed, theatrically, on a piece of parchment and rolled up like a scroll—to Born. The next time "Oppie" visited his office, Born left the room on a pretext, leaving the scroll open on his desk for Oppenheimer to read. Upon returning to his office, Born found Oppenheimer "rather pale and not so voluble as usual." Thereafter, the interruptions ceased.

Together with her father and her husband, Max Born turned out to be one of the most important men in Mayer's life. The year Maria switched from mathematics to physics was also the year that her father died of a stroke. Friedrich Goeppert's death was an unexpected blow, and the daughter would almost certainly have found a sympathetic shoulder in the gently compassionate Born. The professor, who was then in his early forties, became literally and figuratively her *Doktorvater*—the term used for a thesis adviser. But the ties reached far deeper than a shared love for physics. Born suffered from a series of debilitating depressions, which were brought on both by a fragile psyche that could not assimilate the chaos of European politics and by a troubled marriage. "Maria was very close to my father," says Born's son, Gustav. "To be tactful, I won't say anything more." Mayer's daughter, Marianne Wentzel, also notes that her mother was "in love with Born"—although she contends that Maria's feelings for her mentor took the form of "hero worship" rather than romantic passion. Certainly, the sight of Mayer and Born setting off on bicycle trips became a common one on campus.

While physical attraction may have played a role in their relationship, Mayer and Born formed a personal and professional bond that lasted a lifetime and was grounded in both deep affection and shared scientific interests. Even after emigrating to the United States, Mayer returned to Göttingen to work with Born during each summer until 1933. That last summer in Göttingen, mentor and protégé published a paper together on the "Dynamic Lattice Theory of Crystals," a much-lauded research project that Mayer and Born must have begun working on when Maria was still Born's student. And although they rarely saw each other after Hitler's rise to power, when Born emigrated to England, they continued both their friendship and a scientific dialogue in letters, regularly reviewing each other's writings through the mails. Long after she had left Germany, the protective wing of her mentor stretched across the Atlantic, offering guidance in her work and introductions to such scientists as Karl Herzfeld, a German émigré who would be Mayer's first employer—and first mentor—in America.

It is noteworthy that it wasn't until Max Born suffered a nervous breakdown that would take him away from Göttingen to a sanatorium on Lake Constance, during the school year of 1928–29, that Maria Goeppert became seriously involved with a man her own age. Maria first met Joe Mayer in January 1929, when he rang the door of the Goepperts' house to see if there were any rooms available for rent. In the years following her father's death, Maria's mother had begun leasing rooms to students as a way to help make ends meet. The Goeppert home had been recommended by an American friend, who told Joe Mayer that it housed "the prettiest girl in Göttingen." The day Joe Mayer dropped by, Frau Goeppert was in bed, ill, and so the maid summoned "a pretty little blond girl," who succeeded immediately in annoying him by "ignoring [Joe's] painfully halting German and talking to [him] with faultless Cambridge English."

Joe Mayer, who had been raised in New York and educated at Berkeley, cut a dashing figure in Göttingen. He was tall and gregarious and—by the German standards of the time—relatively affluent. While the austerity of the 1920s made it difficult for most German students to make ends meet, Joe bought a car as soon as he landed in Göttingen, and he became an enthusiastic participant in the idyll of Göttingen's university life. Both Joe and Maria were athletic, and it was at the municipal swimming pool that Maria was said to have first noticed her new boarder. They played tennis together in the summer, hiked, and went skiing in the fall and winter. Joe also became a regular fixture at local dances, where, on at least one occasion, he got into an argument with Viki Weisskopf over which of the two men would escort Maria home. Mayer, who disliked the fact that Weisskopf always insisted on speaking English in his presence, got the better of his rival when he whipped a coin out of his pocket and said, in rapid-fire English: "All right, let's flip. Heads I win, tails you lose."

In Born's absence, Maria must also have enjoyed Joe's penchant for engaging her in scientific debate. For unlike her more old-fashioned European admirers, like Weisskopf, who never dreamed of discussing physics when they were out on a date with Maria, Joe was attracted as much to her outsize intellect as to her looks. By the end of that summer, Joe's conversation had begun to turn to marriage. And sometime in the fall, Maria accepted his proposal.

For all Maria's physical appeal, Joe knew that he was not getting engaged to a traditional hausfrau. For one thing, although she had been shipped off to her aunt Vera's one summer to learn the domestic arts, Maria didn't know the first thing about keeping house. Years later, her daughter, Marianne, recalled that the Mayers' furniture always gathered dust because the maids soon figured out that Maria, who had a habit of staring at her feet, never noticed the dustballs above eye level. In Göttingen, most of the meals in the Goeppert household were prepared by servants. And when Joe and Maria, shortly before their wedding, decided to throw a dinner party on the day after Christmas—when the servants had the day off—Joe noticed that Maria was completely lost in the kitchen. It was then that Joe struck a bargain with his bride, promising that he would hire a maid to do the housework after their marriage, if she would complete her dissertation.

Indeed, during their engagement, Maria was so swept away by the romance with Joe that she began to neglect her studies. At one point, she even offered to give up working on her Ph.D.—a suggestion Joe immediately rejected. But Maria was distracted enough that those closest to her became concerned that she had lost interest in her academic work. "You'd better get married, or you'll never finish up your degree," Frau Goeppert is said to have chided her daughter. Evidently, her professors were concerned also. One afternoon when Joe and Maria drove over to Leyden to visit Paul Ehrenfest, who was teaching at Göttingen at the time, the professor questioned Maria about the dissertation on which she still had not made much progress. After Maria explained her ideas, Ehrenfest led her to his study, ordered her to commit her thoughts to paper, and closed the door. Three hours later, she emerged with an outline of her dissertation, which examined the probability of an electron, under a given set of conditions, emitting or absorbing two photons simultaneously.

Maria's reticence in completing her thesis is particularly remarkable given her extraordinary talent. Not only would the findings of her dissertation eventually be applied to laser research, but they employed mathematical concepts that were considered advanced for the time— even by Göttingen's high standards. Wigner described Mayer's work on the so-called double-photon effect in atoms as "a masterpiece of clarity and concreteness." Later, she would come to be known by some of her colleagues as "a quantum mechanic" for her mathematical prowess.

Maria also put in a star performance before Göttingen's fearsome thesis committee. One of her oldest friends, Max Delbruck, who would win the Nobel Prize in biology in 1969, had just flunked the examination. What's more, because the German university system eschewed all but a final examination, there was no test run, and Maria had no way of knowing how she would do. She passed without difficulty on her first appearance before her examining committee, which included Born, Franck, and the chemist Adolf Windaus, all three of whom would eventually become Nobelists.

Despite her remarkable academic performance, Maria Mayer had never given a great deal of thought to what, if any, professional path she might pursue. In fact, in those first few weeks of March, following the successful completion of her doctorate, physics was probably the farthest thing from Mayer's mind. Like other women of her generation, she had reconciled herself to following her husband's lead. Joe had been offered a position as associate professor in chemistry at Johns Hopkins University. Maria was about to embark on what was probably the most difficult journey of her life—a voyage to America, and a break with her beloved Göttingen.

The Mayers arrived in Maryland in April 1930. Since they were planning to attend summer school at the University of Michigan, the couple initially stayed at a Baltimore boardinghouse, living out of suit-cases. Ann Arbor's summer symposia on theoretical physics, which had been launched in 1928, attracted the crème de la crème of Europe's sci-entific community. It was there that Maria first met Enrico Fermi, who struck the Mayers as "a very young and pleasant little Italian, with un-ending good humour, and a brilliant and clear method of presenting what he has to present in terrible English." And there, in an atmosphere charged with new ideas and voluble eccentrics, the Mayers were re-united with old friends, like Paul Ehrenfest, who "rule[d] . . . the whole symposium like a somewhat childish Tsar" but who also saw to it that the discussions of quantum mechanics were never reduced to "empty mathematical symbols" or "words pos[ing] as explanations." There, sprawled on a grassy knoll, Maria could regularly be seen with Joe, Ehrenfest, and a handful of brilliant young scientists absorbed in a lively conversation about physics.

It was that summer, too, that Maria set about trying to teach her husband the basics of the Born-Heisenberg system of particle mechan-ics. The Schroedinger system, which Joe had studied in the United States, treats matter as waves, while Born and Heisenberg's system, al-though it is mathematically equivalent to Schroedinger's approach, treats matter as particles. The learning process was punctuated by nu-merous arguments. It is hard to know today if that friction was the in-evitable result of teaching your spouse the scientific equivalent of how to drive, or whether it grew out of the tensions involved in getting ac-climated to each other during the first year of marriage and—for Maria's part—to a new country.

The skirmishes, however, rarely spilled beyond the boundaries of physics. Rather, they helped lay the foundation for a long and fruitful dialogue that would be particularly useful for Maria as she struggled through the long winters of academic isolation that followed her first bright Ann Arbor summer. While Maria had been accepted as one of the boys in Ann Arbor, she remained very much the outsider at Johns Hopkins for a number of years. Although there were no experts in quantum mechanics at the university at the time, no one seized the op-portunity to hire the young physicist from Göttingen. Instead, she was given an office and offered a tenuous position helping a member of the physics department with his German correspondence. The work was unrewarding, but it left her plenty of time to establish a home and to fire off a torrent of letters to her mother.

Mayer was determined, in fact, to make the best of her new life, in part because that was her nature, but partly because she must have felt compelled to justify her decision to leave home, especially to her mother, who missed her daughter and suffered the increasing hardships of life in Weimar Germany. Sitting down to a typewriter in the physics department, Maria wrote to her mother every day or two, painting a domestic portrait of thrifty marital bliss. Her letters are a brave response to her mother's chronicle of woes as a poor economy and political hysteria cast a pall over Göttingen and all of Germany, and a long shadow over Mayer's new life. Hardly a day would go by without Maria thinking of her mother. And every week she would wait anxiously for the arrival of the *Bremen* or the *Europa*, the ocean liners that bore letters from home, as well as comforting packages of sausage and *Quitenbrot*. The young woman who, in Germany, had had virtually no interest in politics would suddenly be riveted by the disturbing news from home. She would scour the papers for news of the latest elections. And finally she would ask her mother to secure a subscription to the *Berliner Illustrierte* and a newspaper from Frankfurt. When the Metropolitan Opera performed *Valkyrie* or *Tannhäuser*, she would sit by the radio, savoring the German lyrics as much as the music. And a German movie, even a bad one, would bring tears to her eyes. "It's really terrible, but the longer one is away from Germany, the more patriotic one becomes," she would write Frau Goeppert, shortly before she applied for American citizenship. Yet even as her homesickness grew, and with it a creeping anxiety over Germany's future, Mayer came to see her very Germanness as a liability. To the Europeans who knew her best, Maria's greatest sacrifice in marrying Joe was not in having to compromise her professional ambitions but in being forced to leave her homeland.

The intensive correspondence, with its carefully numbered installments, and the anticipation each week of the arrival of the mails by sea, also served to anchor Maria in her new life. With relatively little work to do at the university, she set out to document her life with Joe in a house on Cresmont Avenue, not far from the Johns Hopkins campus. No detail was too trivial for Maria, who kept her mother informed of the wallpaper patterns and the color schemes with which she planned to decorate her house. She made note of the purchase of a new set of bookcases, which Maria painted white and black to match their sofa. And she wrote about the lunches that she and Joe shared almost every day. When Joe's mother, Catherine Mayer, came to visit from Manhattan, Maria described the quiet afternoons she spent with her mother-in-law, darning Joe's shirts and Maria's stockings. She recounted the dances she and Joe attended at the university, lamenting the lousy music. And through the mails she celebrated with Frau Goeppert her growing friendship with Kitty Rice, the young wife of Frank Rice, a colleague of Joe's in the chemistry department and one of the few faculty wives who possessed a Ph.D.

Perhaps recalling her mother's resourcefulness during the days of surging inflation, Maria also chronicled the family budget—the $250 from Joe's paycheck, which they spent on household expenses, and the $100 or so in fees from Maria's translations and Joe's scientific articles, which they used to pay off debts. To stretch their dollars, the Mayers would go to the movies a little less frequently. But lest her mother feel sorry for her, Maria reported that, by way of compensation, she and Joe spent more time than ever "making lots of wine and entertaining friends at home." Nor had she sacrificed their once-weekly maid, who came every Wednesday, prepared a roast that the Mayers ate for half the week, and saved Maria the trouble of cooking. "With any luck," she wrote Frau Goeppert in the fall of 1931, "we'll even be able to save a little."

Mayer purged her letters of anything that might sound like bad news. Even so, her correspondence hints at the frustrations of her professional life, as well as the sorrow of being too far from home. "My only concern is that I would very much like to work on a nice article on physics," she wrote her mother in November of 1931. "But I don't have any good ideas. Nor has Herzfeld come up with any ideas for me," she adds, referring to the physicist who would become her principal mentor at Johns Hopkins. Again and again, she concludes her letters on an anxious note: "You are my only other concern. . . . Are you going to concerts at all? Please take care of yourself, and make life a little bit easier for yourself!! This is the greatest favor you could do for me."

For all the girlish mix of earnestness and exuberance in the letters to her mother, Maria Mayer must have seemed the epitome of an elitist bluestocking to her new acquaintances in Baltimore. Trying to fit into her new surroundings, Maria participated in a number of social clubs, especially ones with an international bent, but she never felt wholly comfortable in the Baltimore milieu. Perhaps as a way to establish herself in her new surroundings, in the fall of 1931 she reluctantly agreed to be nominated as president of the Cosmopolitan Club. But this would not prove to be a source of friendships. It was for the wives of her colleagues, many of whom were far less educated than she, that Mayer reserved her greatest disdain. After attending only a few meetings at a local women's club, and finding the company "terribly boring," she renounced her membership. "Kitty Rice and Frau Whyburn are the only two women of my acquaintance here who really work in science," she wrote Frau Goeppert. "And they too find [the club] too dumb. It's full of old ladies and a bunch of silly girls whose only accomplishment is a B.S. degree, which is approximately comparable to our *Abitur*." Again and again, Mayer makes clear that she "could never abide hen parties [*Weibergesellschaften*]."

If Mayer shunned the company of society ladies, she gradually carved out a niche for herself in the mostly masculine intellectual life on campus. Soon after settling down in Baltimore, Mayer met Karl Herzfeld. "Will you look out for her?" Born had written to his old friend. Born couldn't have entrusted his protégé to a gentler soul. Herzfeld, who lived a life of almost monastic asceticism in a dormitory room on campus and was undoubtedly starved for companionship, especially for that of a fellow countryman with whom he could speak German, was more than happy to take Mayer under his wing.

Always, Herzfeld treated Mayer with a combination of fatherly affection and professional respect. On her first day back in the lab after having broken a leg in the winter of 1932, Herzfeld greeted her with roses. Mayer was astonished once again when, upon hearing that she was pregnant, Herzfeld behaved "like a model of consideration" and presented her with a large bouquet of flowers; she had been so afraid of his reaction that she had agonized for weeks before telling him.

Mayer also established a rapport with the chief of the Physical Laboratory, R. W. Wood, an old friend of James Franck. Franck, who moved to Johns Hopkins in 1935, may also have written a letter on behalf of the Mayers. Maria had been given an office next to Wood's, and for a time, she found the eccentric and voluble scientist, whose rail-thin physique reminded her of Mephistopheles, to be "unbelievably kind and civil."

Wood, who never completed his doctorate and was said to be hopeless when it came to mathematics, had a genius for experimentation that he willingly shared with Mayer. "Give Wood a dollar and send him to the five-and-ten store, he comes back with a laboratory," James Franck once said of his friend. Wood taught Mayer how to construct her first spectroscope one day, reaching into his bottomless pockets to extract two old razor blades, a piece of glass or quartz that he used for a lens, and some chewing gum to hold the contraption together; soon afterward, Mayer built a much sturdier machine—one that was still in use at Hopkins some twenty years later.

The old Göttingen connections certainly helped pave the way for Mayer in Johns Hopkins's academic circles. These and Mayer's performance helped secure a place for her at the university at a time when a deepening Depression would, over the course of the decade, throw the scientific community into a "severe crisis" and leave many scientists without jobs. In 1931, her second year in Baltimore, Maria and Joe Mayer began teaching parallel courses in statistical mechanics, a branch of classical mechanics that governs very large assemblies of molecules. The following January, Herzfeld told her that the university was prepared to make her an associate professor, the same position that Joe Mayer held, albeit without a salary.

To many of the students on campus, the Mayers were the epitome of the glamorous modern couple—smart and handsome, and always the life of the party. "They were really jazz age types," recalled Robert Sachs, Maria Mayer's first doctoral student at Johns Hopkins, who took an enormous risk by hitching his star to a professor who, he was warned, would never be able to help him find a job—a major handicap especially during the Depression. In defiance of prohibition, the Mayers drank and smoked heavily—but always with style. While others were content to brew bathtub gin, Joe and Maria figured out a way to crush grapes for wine using an old washing machine. Avid sportsmen still, they frequently joined Sachs on his father's yawl and skied cross-country during the winter, using equipment that Frau Goeppert sent from Germany. They also loved to dance and were often the last to leave a party. The couple's legendary Christmas party—the one holiday feast Maria prepared entirely on her own—was replete with delicacies from Germany, lots of booze, and a large tree festooned with wax candles. The festivities typically would begin on Christmas Eve and often didn't end until the guests finished a huge breakfast of bacon, eggs, and Bloody Marys on Christmas morning.

Day to day, in the sleepy environs of Depression-era Baltimore, it was relatively easy for Maria to juggle her professional, family, and social life. After her daughter, Marianne, was born, in May 1933, the Mayers always employed a full-time housekeeper. (Marianne was christened Maria Ann and later used the name Maria.) Although Maria complained that it was difficult to find a German-speaking maid—a priority since the Mayers wanted their children to grow up bilingual—she always had someone to cook, care for the children, and keep house.

Just as important, Joe seemed pleased to help out around the house. He was an accomplished cook, who probably spent more time in the kitchen than Maria. On one wintry Sunday in November 1931, for example, Joe and Frank Rice banished their wives to the Rice residence and whipped up a gourmet meal in the Mayers' kitchen. Maria and Kitty were told to appear back at Crestmont Avenue, dressed in evening clothes, at 7:00 P.M. There they were greeted with cocktails (despite prohibition) and caviar on toast. The men set the table with candles, roses, and crystal, and served up a four-course meal of chicken bouillon, crown roast, potato croquettes, and peas, followed by an ice cream dessert and liqueurs. "It was all so lovely, and delicious, much better than we had thought it possible," Maria remarked after the meal. She and Kitty racked their brains for days afterward to come up with a comparable feast for Thanksgiving Day.

Joe's help went beyond special occasions. When Maria broke her leg, for several weeks her husband set the table for dinner, carried Maria to her seat, and washed the dishes. Similarly, when the paper-hangers showed up on one of the days when Maria was scheduled to lecture at the university, Joe could be counted on to be there and let them into the house.

In the meantime, their professional collaboration continued. In 1937, about the time Maria found out that she was pregnant with her second child, she and Joe decided to begin work on a book on statistical mechanics, which would encompass much of the material on which they had lectured throughout the 1930s. Husband and wife wrote alternate chapters and then edited each other's work.

For Maria, the project had a less than academic purpose as well. Pregnancy had always made her feel self-conscious. At the time of her first pregnancy, she had confided in her mother: "I'm afraid that rumors would reach my students and that would be very unpleasant." In another letter to her mother, written in November 1932, Maria swore Frau Goeppert to secrecy, saying she wouldn't even tell Joe's mother about her condition because Catherine Mayer couldn't be relied on to keep her mouth shut. Now that she was pregnant again, the book gave Maria a chance to work at home, far from the prying eyes on campus. (The fear of making one's pregnancy public is a recurring theme among women scientists: Some twenty-five years after Maria gave birth to her son, Peter, a gifted woman scientist who had recently graduated first in her class at Cal Tech was so afraid she would lose her job if her male colleagues found out about her condition that she took to wearing extra-large lab coats at work; she kept her secret long after her child was born.)

Whether she was pregnant or not, as Mayer's role in the physics department grew in importance, the university suffered her presence grudgingly. Although she was teaching some of the most formidable scientific courses at Johns Hopkins, Mayer still received no salary. During the course of the 1930s she would teach more than half a dozen courses in the university's physics department, including statistical mechanics, quantum statistics, and classical mechanics. The most she was ever paid was $200 a year, less than one tenth the salary of male professors of similar rank. Yet in 1935, four years into her teaching career at Hopkins, the administration considered eliminating even that token payment.

Indignant, Karl Herzfeld fired off a letter to the university president, Joseph Ames, in defense of Mayer: "Let me take this occasion to state that in my opinion Dr. Goeppert Mayer does at least one third of the work of a full time associate, both as a teacher and in research. She teaches usually two hours for half a year, an advanced course in theoretical physics, and is besides active, on equal footing with Dieke and myself, in two seminaries [sic] throughout the year. In addition, she gives, together with her husband and Dr. Andrews, a two hour seminar in chemistry throughout the year. So far as her research is concerned, she publishes several papers a year, usually in conjunction with Dr. Mayer or myself. . . . In conclusion, I think she is a very valuable member of the department, both as a teacher and as far as the publications emanating from the department go. From the estimate made before ($^1/_3$ time of an associate), the adequate amount of remuneration would be $1,000."

Mayer won a temporary reprieve. She received neither a raise nor a cut in pay. Indeed, she had resigned herself long before to her puny paycheck. Writing to her mother a few years earlier, she had joked: "The university has so little money that I'm always afraid that it will wind up going bankrupt."

By the mid 1930s, Mayer also sensed, for the first time, just how important her work was becoming to her. "I'm beginning to have fun with the lectures," she wrote Frau Goeppert in 1934. "I don't need to prepare as much, and they are much less tiring."

When Mayer arrived at Johns Hopkins, the school was still firmly focused on experimental physics, and she and Herzfeld were the only theoreticians in the physics department. It soon became clear that Hopkins students were in awe of her "high powered" lectures. Attending Mayer's lectures was "like getting in front of a steamroller," recalls Sachs. "She poured it on and the experimental students were hanging by their teeth." By 1935, a degree of competitiveness had crept into Mayer's relationship with Herzfeld, and she was taking obvious pleasure in the fact that some students favored her lectures over his. "It warms my heart whenever students come to me and complain that Herzfeld's quantum mechanics is so lousy!" Perhaps because he was threatened by her popularity among the students, Herzfeld repeatedly refused to allow Mayer to teach a course in quantum mechanics.

Mayer's position, however marginal, was not the only one in danger. The Depression was an inauspicious time for scientific research in general, and at Johns Hopkins, where a fiscal crisis fueled political intrigue, the Mayers would experience a growing sense of unease. The trouble had started in the middle of the nineteenth century, when the school's eponymous founder left much of the university's endowment in the stock of the Baltimore & Ohio Railroad Co. Beginning in the 1880s, the B & O suffered a steady decline; it was finally forced into receivership in 1896, wiping out much of the university's endowment. Although the institution's finances gradually recovered, they were never strong. And at the time of the Great Depression, Johns Hopkins was once again virtually broke.

In fact, research funds at most academic institutions were drying up. In the 1932–33 fiscal year, government funds for scientific research were slashed by 12.5 percent, according to a survey in the congressional appropriations bill published in 1932. Moreover, a Stop Science movement was sweeping the country; the complexity of the scientific developments of the 1920s fueled a public perception that new technology and automation were contributing to joblessness and the growing economic crisis. A backlash against science wasn't the only problem, however. In 1935, a new president, Isaiah Bowman, ushered in a period of xenophobia at the university that would gradually empty it of its greatest thinkers in science and mathematics. Under the guise of austerity, Bowman sought to force out "expensive" senior faculty. In fact, Bowman had come under the influence of Donald Andrews, the chairman of the chemistry department, who had a reputation for being jealous of talented colleagues, and Edward Barry, who served both as dean of arts and sciences and, ultimately, as provost, although he held no degree at all—not even a B.A. What Bowman and his advisers had in common, according to Johns Hopkins officials and Robert Sachs, was a hatred of "foreigners," whom they loosely defined as émigrés, Jews, Catholics, women, and Communists.

One of the first casualties of the new administration was Herzfeld. In the ensuing years, Bowman's administration would force out other "foreigners"—the Mayers; the Rices (who were Catholic); the Irish Francis D. Murnaghan, a world-famous mathematician who had been chairman of the mathematics department for close to three decades; and Maria's old friend James Franck, a Jew who had left Germany in protest over the new racial laws passed in the early 1930s, even though his service in World War I exempted him from them. Although the administration feigned indignation when Franck resigned, Franck told Robert Sachs at the time that Bowman had left him no choice; by first refusing to appoint Franck as chairman of the physics department after Wood's retirement and then withholding research funds that Franck considered essential to his work, Johns Hopkins had effectively forced out one of the most renowned scientists of the age. Ironically, Barry accused Franck of ingratitude toward the institution that had provided him a safe haven from the Nazis. The recriminations echoed the ones that German academics had leveled at Franck when he decided to leave Germany.

The early years of the exodus actually worked to Maria Mayer's advantage. When the administration failed to earmark funds for Herzfeld's successor and found itself, three days before classes were scheduled to begin in the fall, without anyone to teach its major lecture course on classical mechanics, Mayer was asked to give the lectures—without a salary, of course! The move suddenly made her "the most important lecturer in the department." And while Maria was happy for the chance, she was no longer the accommodating Pollyanna.

"Of course, I said yes," she wrote her mother. "Although it's a lot of work, and I'm not at all comfortable with the subject. All of a sudden the roles are reversed, everyone is terribly grateful and ready to grant me any favor I should desire.... The whole Physical Laboratory is swimming in goodwill this semester.... Even Wood came to me and was very friendly and said how happy he was that I would continue lecturing at the university—I, on the other hand, wasn't at all forthcoming. Everything is really very strange."

Mayer's contributions to the physics department were so great that eventually an attempt was made to persuade the Hopkins administration to appoint her to an official, salaried position on the faculty. The proposal seems ultimately to have been rejected at the highest levels of the administration.

The Mayers' Baltimore life was coming to an end anyway. In 1938, shortly before Peter's birth and just as they were completing the manuscript of their book, Joe Mayer was fired. The imminence of war had continued to fuel anti-German sentiments on campus, and Maria was convinced that her German blood was to blame for Joe's dismissal. She may have been at least partly right. Despite the growing xenophobia at Hopkins, the Mayers had never downplayed their German connections: Maria and Herzfeld had acted as secretaries for an organization that helped German refugee scientists during the 1930s. And Joe had joined the Germania Club, to which Herzfeld also belonged.

Although Mayer did finally prevail in her pursuit of science, her willingness to pin the blame for her husband's only professional setback on her own dreams is a measure of the guilt that saddled a woman who attempted to balance her devotion both to her vocation and to her family.

Harold Urey, a Johns Hopkins alumnus from the 1920s, offered Joe a position at Columbia University. But there was no offer for Maria. The prevailing nepotism rules in academia made it virtually impossible for husband and wife to find employment in the same university. Still, with many scientists out of work during the thirties, the Mayers were probably grateful that at least Joe had found work. Maria resigned herself to moving to New York. She packed up her two children and the house on University Parkway, where the family had lived since about 1934, and followed her husband to Manhattan.

A Physicist in the Nursery

In New York, Maria Mayer found herself almost as much of an outsider in her profession as the day she had stepped off the boat in Baltimore a decade earlier. While she had carved out a niche of sorts at Johns Hopkins, at Columbia she was once again persona non grata. George Pegram, the head of Columbia's physics department, didn't want her anywhere near his territory; when someone arranged for her to occupy an empty office in the department, Pegram had her evicted. It was finally Harold Urey who arranged for her to get a toehold in the chemistry department. Urey persuaded the higher-ups to let Maria Mayer give a few lectures, if only because the Mayers' book was about to be published and, for the sake of legitimacy, Urey wanted to see at least "Lecturer in Chemistry" under her name on the title page.

The atmosphere at Columbia with respect to women was best expressed by I. I. Rabi, the distinguished nuclear physicist, who was at the school during the 1930s and who considered women temperamentally unsuited to science. Rabi believed that a woman's nervous system "makes it impossible for [her] to stay with the thing. Women may go into science, and they will do well enough, but they will never do great science."

In most respects, Maria Mayer remained cut off from academia for her first two years in New York. One major reason was that instead of living near campus, the Mayers moved to Leonia, New Jersey, a bedroom community across the Hudson River from Manhattan. Maria threw herself into suburban life, following the examples of Frieda Urey and Laura Fermi, her new neighbors in Leonia, who were both housewives. She became an avid gardener and even struck a bargain with Laura Fermi whereby Mayer would teach her Italian neighbor how to garden if Fermi would do her darning, a task that Mayer detested. Mayer, who had never done much grocery shopping, also took to driving Mrs. Fermi on monthly trips to a large cut-rate supermarket in a neighboring town.

Just as they had once spent long evenings in Baltimore with the Rices, so the Mayers now socialized with the Fermis. In fact, with the start of the war, they clung to one another and envisioned leaving their new country behind. "The Mayers and the Fermis determined to leave the United States together if Nazism should become established in this country," Laura Fermi recalled. "During the many evenings spent with the Mayers between the fall of France and America's entry into the war, we made plans together. Between a philological argument about the origins of some English word and a piece of advice on gardening that the Mayers passed down to the Fermis, we prepared to become modern Robinson

Crusoes in some faraway desert island. . . . Joe Mayer was to be our sea captain. . . . Maria Mayer and Enrico could consult and determine what part of our civilization was worth saving." Ironically, when the Fermis and the Mayers thought of a destination for their getaway, they looked east to the temperate archipelagos between Hawaii and the Philippines. "We could not foresee Pearl Harbor, and we overlooked the Japanese," wrote Laura Fermi.

During the war, Columbia University became one of a handful of command centers from which many of the world's greatest scientists set out to jump-start a revolution in nuclear physics and to build a powerful new bomb. In January 1939, shortly before the Mayers left Baltimore, they attended a conference in Washington, D.C., at which Niels Bohr and Enrico Fermi announced that the first successful experiments in nuclear fission had been conducted in Germany by Otto Hahn and Fritz Strassman. Less than two years later, on the day before Pearl Harbor, the United States committed itself to building a nuclear weapon, a project that would come to ensnare most of the top scientists in the country but that would cause the Mayers special conflicts.

Pearl Harbor marked the end of Maria Mayer's quiet suburban existence. The day after the Japanese launched their attack, Mayer was offered her first bona fide job in the United States—a paid part-time teaching position at Sarah Lawrence College, in Bronxville, New York. Mayer was to teach both mathematics and a unified science course, the latter being taught with a chemistry professor. She was paid about $1,500 a year for a two-day teaching schedule. No sooner had Maria begun teaching in the spring semester than Joe Mayer got a job testing conventional weapons at the Aberdeen Proving Grounds in Maryland, a job that would keep him away from home four to five days a week for several years. (At the time, it would have been unthinkable to turn down a request to do war work, even if it meant leaving behind home and family.) Then, before she had had a chance to adjust to her new job and Joe's imminent departure, Harold Urey offered Maria yet another position. He asked her to join a top-secret research group at Columbia that was engaged in separating the highly fissionable isotope uranium-235 from uranium-238, which was less fissionable and therefore not suitable for a bomb. A year or so later, this secret research group became part of the Substitute Alloy Materials (SAM) project, which was one of the major research sections of the Manhattan Project and was invested with the task of mass-producing uranium for use in atomic weapons.

Mayer could not refuse Urey's offer. During her four years at Columbia, she would work on four separate aspects of uranium research. Aside from a brief period during which she worked on the principal, so-called gaseous diffusion process, Mayer devoted most of her time to investigating alternative technologies. One of these projects—an attempt to extract U-235 via a photochemical reaction—was related to her Ph.D. thesis and was a forerunner of work being done today at Lawrence Livermore Labs, which is believed to hold the key to extracting enriched uranium using far less energy than the still prevalent gaseous diffusion process. By the end of the war, Mayer was taking her orders directly from Edward Teller and heading up the so-called Opacity Project, which involved studying the thermodynamic properties of matter and radiation at extremely high temperatures, as for example during a nuclear explosion.

Once again, Maria Mayer had slipped back into her profession, not as the result of a well-charted game plan but out of her love for her discipline and unexpected opportunities to practice it as friends, colleagues, and finally World War II beckoned her to the laboratory. Almost from the beginning, Mayer's work at Columbia was part time in name only. Except for the few hours that she spent at Sarah Lawrence each week, she was usually at Columbia until after five every night.

As in Baltimore, she developed an intimate relationship with a handful of sympathetic colleagues, who would become particularly important to her as the war progressed. In addition to Fermi, she became close to Teller, who worked at Columbia in 1941 and returned frequently to visit the school after his departure for Los Alamos in 1942, grabbing every chance he could to take Mayer to the Metropolitan Opera. It was during the war that Mayer and Teller established the foundations of a friendship that survived even his testimony against Robert Oppenheimer at the McCarthy hearings and Teller's subsequent ostracism by the rest of the scientific community.

Mayer also became a close companion of Jacob Bigeleisen, a young chemist who had recently received his Ph.D. at Berkeley and who, by his own admission, came to "worship" Mayer both as a woman and as a scientist. "I really liked Maria Mayer. . . . I'll tell you this, if she were younger and not married, I would have tried to marry her," confesses Bigeleisen, who now teaches at the State University of New York at Stony Brook. Some fifty years later, his voice still cracks when he talks about her. "She was a wonderful thing in my life," he recalls. "She was a wonderful person, very smart. She was also beautiful." The relationship between Bigeleisen, a soft-spoken Jew, and Mayer never went beyond friendship, but the two worked together and often ate lunch together. He jumped at her invitations to come out and have dinner at her house in Leonia—evenings that usually included Joe's mother, who frequently visited from Manhattan, and the children's nanny, Miss Forbes, though rarely the children, Marianne and Peter, who were not typically included at dinner when guests were present. Bigeleisen recalls, somewhat wistfully, that the closest he ever got to kissing his colleague was the day he was working on an experiment in the lab that called for a thread of fine fiber, one just about the thickness of Mayer's blond hair. The smitten young scientist leaned over Mayer, who, undoubtedly aware of the temptation that must have seized Bigeleisen at that moment, allowed him to gently pluck a hair from her head.

Maria spent close to four years separated from Joe, save for weekends, and his absence weighed heavily on her. Her unquenchable desire to do research, which began during the war years, grew out of the sense of duty to her new country, and to her increasing loneliness. That loneliness was highlighted by the pain—and the shame—of being a German living in the United States. At home in Leonia, she stopped speaking German with her children. And at Columbia, engaged in work that was leading to the construction of the most powerful bomb ever built by mankind, she could never forget the insanity that had consumed her homeland. Her fears were amplified by the fact that she had virtually no news of family and friends; during the entire war, she received only one letter from Germany, a list of "vital statistics" sent via the Red Cross. "The war was a major burden to her," recalls Bigeleisen. "It was something that occupied her [thoughts] every day. She was concerned that the Germans were going to win the war and destroy

Western civilization. Yet she was also conflicted because she still had relatives and friends in Germany. When I would see her during the day, if there had been bad news with respect to the war, [the subject] would inevitably come up. If things were looking bad with respect to the progress of the SAM project, it would come up. It certainly made her very unhappy."

For all her work on the SAM project, Mayer was still not fully accepted in the academic community. No incident crystallized the point more clearly than the events that led her to stop attending the weekly seminars held by Columbia's chemistry department. Before the war, she and Joe and their friends and colleagues the Kimballs would drive in from Leonia for the early-evening seminars and the dinner that followed. After Joe moved to Aberdeen, Maria and Alice Kimball took to going together, until someone from the chemistry department phoned one day and told Maria that while the two women were welcome at the seminars, their presence at dinner had become—suddenly and inexplicably—awkward. Mayer was so deeply hurt that she never again attended either the dinners or the department seminars.

Nor was Mayer well accepted by Columbia science students, the vast majority of whom were male. Mayer taught a course in physical chemistry at Columbia. Bigeleisen remembers several students complaining about her methods, particularly her rigid grading practices. "She used to give students these problem sets, and if the student didn't report the answer correctly to the proper number of significant figures, it was marked all wrong—no partial credit," recalls Bigeleisen. "She was a tough taskmaster," notes Bigeleisen. "She was a perfectionist."

Though she angered the Columbia students, Mayer was becoming a beloved teacher at Sarah Lawrence. She was even able to recruit one of her more gifted students at the women's college, Susan Herrick Chandler, to come work on the SAM project after her graduation. To teach the Sarah Lawrence students, who had far less exposure to science than the men at Hopkins and Columbia, Mayer practiced her lectures on ten-year-old Marianne: "If I understood nothing, the material was too difficult; but if I understood everything, it was too easy," says Marianne, who retains a fond memory of those practice sessions as one of the rare times during those years that she had her mother's full attention.

Indeed, it was during the early 1940s, between the pressures of her work, her anxieties about the war, and her growing dedication to science, that Mayer began to lose touch with her children. Peter was a sickly child. And although both children disliked their nannies, Mayer left the house each morning for jobs that took her so far away that she could not get home easily in case of an emergency. It isn't surprising that Marianne quickly came to the conclusion that "two scientists in the family are 1.5 too many." Of her mother she recalls: "She was torn. At times she tried very hard to be a mother, but often she wasn't there." Even when Maria was home, Marianne could *feel* her mother's mind wandering elsewhere. And Peter, who was too young to remember the details of the family's years in Leonia, says that he too had a general impression of "being neglected," although, in retrospect, he acknowledges that the war had put a lot of pressure on his mother.

Although Peter had an extraordinary aptitude for science, benign neglect and a misdiagnosed learning disability severely handicapped him in his schooling, causing him to fall behind two years by the time he had reached the fourth grade. Marianne, who at sixty is still a shy, soft-spoken woman, inherited her mother's slight frame, fragile features, and extraordinary intelligence, but decided early on to avoid the path her mother had taken. She studied for a master's degree in German. At twenty-six, she married Donat Wentzel, an astrophysicist, and the son of Gregor Wentzel, the physicist. When the Bigeleisens saw her at Mayer's memorial service, seven years after the Wentzels had adopted their daughter, Tania, and asked her when she planned to return to work, Marianne responded tartly: "I didn't have this child only to leave her the way my mother left me."

Today the issue of whether a mother should work or not still invites polar reactions as extreme as Maria's and Marianne's. We do not know Maria's innermost thoughts on the subject of motherhood, but clearly her initial enthusiasm waned into absentminded care. "It was such an experience to have a child, such a tremendous experience!" Mayer later recalled of Marianne's birth. In her letters to her mother she carefully recorded the antics of her "little creature": the baby's first tooth, her first attempts at crawling, her first words—some spoken in German, others in English.

But soon the novelty wore off. Years later, she confessed her impatience at the occasional interruptions that motherhood inevitably brings with it: "I know if I ever had to stay home because a child was sick, I did it and hated it." And in 1943, Max Born, responding to a letter from Maria, scolded her for writing to him without so much as mentioning either of her children. The letter in question, which Mayer had written on the occasion of Born's sixtieth birthday, described just about every other aspect of their lives, including her teaching post at Sarah Lawrence, Joe's new job in Aberdeen, Maryland, and Maria's concern about the fate of many of the relatives who were caught in Germany during the war. "The only disappointment in your letter is the strange fact that you have not mentioned your children," wrote Born to her a few days later. "As I am a devoted grandpa who likes to here [sic] about his own grand-children, and likes to boast with them, I cannot understand why not at least one page of your letter was occupied by descriptions of Marianne and the little one whose name—shame over me—I cannot remember."

When Mayer visited the home of Lorelei and Willard Libby when their twins were still very small, Joan Dash noted Maria Mayer's reaction: "The men went away, and there she [Mrs. Libby] was. . . . 'How could she stand it?' Edward Teller came by that day and took Maria out for lunch, and she was so relieved to be with him and talking science that she was amazed when he told her at the end of the meal that she had been speaking German all along."

While Frau Goeppert was still alive, Joe and Maria would dispatch Marianne to the care of her grandmother in Göttingen during the summertime, for four to five months at a time—a practice that started when Marianne was just a year old. On one such occasion, when Marianne was just a toddler, the Mayers actually considered permitting their daughter to be sent home on an ocean liner—a five-day voyage—in the care of the ship's nurse, a woman Marianne wouldn't have known. The child was saved from what would undoubtedly have been a traumatic experience by Joe Mayer's mother, who volunteered to go to Europe to bring her granddaughter home. As it was, the summer trips, with their successive separations, first from her parents and then from grandmother Goeppert, were difficult for Marianne. After one such trip, Mayer wrote Frau Goeppert about her daughter's state of mind:

"I'm so glad that the other mother [Catherine Mayer] made the trip with her, after all, because she still doesn't like strangers. On the pier [after the ship's arrival from Germany], she would get terribly upset if Joe's mother left her side even for a moment. And even now she sometimes cries if Joe's mother leaves the room. In general, she loves Joe's mother the best. During the first few days [following her return] she was very quiet, saying nothing at all during the train trip [home]. But now she's chattering like a little bird, and is gradually befriending her parents again."

It wasn't until the early 1940s that her children became conscious of the gulf that was beginning to separate them from their mother. When Mayer returned to work after nearly a two-year hiatus in Leonia, Marianne and Peter were left in the care of hired help. The children's first nanny, a German woman named Frieda, turned out to be physically abusive. When Mayer arrived home early one afternoon, she found Frieda dunking Peter into a scalding-hot bath; the woman was gone by the following morning. But her replacement, Miss Forbes, wasn't much of an improvement, as far as the children were concerned. A taciturn Englishwoman, Miss Forbes scolded the Mayer children constantly. Miss Forbes's child-rearing methods were particularly harmful to Peter, who, showing early signs of a reading disability, was forced to read the same passage over and over again, for hours at a time, until he got it right. Although he was at one point labeled "slow," a test taken when he was in grade school showed him to possess a genius IQ. His learning handicap, it turned out, had been triggered by dyslexia. But in the absence of adequate treatment, and feeling like "the family dummy," Peter developed emotional problems that, in combination with the dyslexia, hampered his ability to learn. Marianne, who was about ten when Miss Forbes joined the Mayer household, says that although she disliked the woman, she never complained to her mother because she was aware that it was difficult to find domestic servants during the war and didn't want to cause any problems for her parents. Mayer never thought Miss Forbes less than an ideal nanny; years later she recommended the woman to Jacob Bigeleisen when he was looking for someone to care for his children.

Indeed, preoccupied with the war and Joe's absence, Maria went through the motions of motherhood but rarely threw herself into the lives of her children. Arriving home at about 6:00 P.M. on weeknights, she would spend a half hour or so busying herself with the final preparations for dinner. If they were not having company, she would eat with Marianne, Peter, and Miss Forbes, whose presence even at dinner—one of the few times Peter and Marianne could have had their mother to themselves—was deeply resented by the children. Maria had stopped speaking German to her children at the start of the war. But perhaps out of homesickness, she tried to reinterest Marianne in the language during the early 1940s. During one six-month period, she took up knitting after dinner as a way to help her stop smoking. And for a short while she had Marianne read German fairy tales to her while she knitted. The fairy tales soon stopped, however, and the smoking resumed. It was usually Marianne who read bedtime stories to Peter. Marianne came to feel that she knew the mothers of some of her friends better than her own mother. In those days, "a lot of things made my mother unhappy," remembers Marianne. "It was very painful for her to have [my father] in Aberdeen. She was listless, not interested in anything. Occasionally she would have a spurt of interest in what the kids were doing, but then it would fade."

Not surprisingly, some of the happiest memories of childhood for both Mayer children were associated with summer vacations. During the war, the Mayers usually escaped to Nantucket for a month of swimming and sailing. In later years, they would drive out West and go camping at a different national park each year. Science talk, Marianne recalls, was kept to a minimum: "It was the only time we had our parents to ourselves." Indeed, sometime shortly after the war, Marianne became so frustrated with the endless discussions about science that, diffident as she was, she screwed up her courage one evening during dinner and demanded that her parents stop the shoptalk at least during the evening meal; thereafter—albeit with occasional lapses—the Mayers did their best to bring their conversations to a level their children could understand.

In February 1945, as the war was winding to a close, Joe Mayer was sent to the Pacific for several months. So on V-E Day, Maria found herself alone in Leonia. Columbia had planned a big victory party, but she couldn't bring herself to go. Though happy peace had finally arrived, she was still sick over the death and suffering of the Germans and couldn't celebrate. She probably did not know it yet, but her family was relatively unscathed. Although several cousins were drafted into the German army, most of the younger generation survived. Older relatives fared much worse; although their deaths couldn't be attributed directly to the fighting, most of Mayer's aunts and uncles died of strokes or heart attacks during the course of the war.

With the end of the war against Germany—with the future of her own relatives no longer hanging in the balance—Mayer's work on the atomic bomb became a little less painful. A few days after the armistice, Mayer answered a summons by Edward Teller and departed for Los Alamos, leaving her children in the care of Miss Forbes. Marianne was twelve, Peter seven. Their mother was away for close to two months, although Marianne says it felt more like six. Joe joined her in Albuquerque, and they returned to New Jersey together in early July. A few days later, Maria ran into Harold Urey at Columbia, who told her that he had been trying all day long, without success, to reach General Leslie Groves in Los Alamos. Of all the people at Columbia, only Urey and Mayer understood the implications; only they knew that the first atomic bomb test had been scheduled for mid-July. A month later, when Joe and Maria were strolling along the beach in Nantucket shortly after the first bomb had been dropped on Hiroshima, Maria was finally able to tell Joe what she had been working on during the entire war.

Although the war was over and the family reunited, Joe and Maria would never recapture the spirit of those early years in Göttingen and Baltimore. Maria had suffered from years of wartime anxiety and from a corrosive blend of mounting ambition and repeated professional disappointments. It was the great misfortune of their marriage that as Maria approached middle age, Joe was incapable of divining—let alone assuaging—the full extent of her rage and sorrow. Bereft of old confidantes, like Frau Goeppert, who had died of a stroke before the war, and Max Born, who was still living in England, and incapable of finding any real release in her children, Maria Mayer increasingly drowned her emotions in work and alcohol.

From the Periphery to the Nucleus

A lot of people began to notice Maria Mayer after Hiroshima. It was only after the war that her abilities first began to be openly acknowledged by a major academic institution that also employed her husband. In 1945, both Mayers were offered faculty positions at the University of Chicago, which had become a fresh magnet for the world's leading scientific minds. Urey, Fermi, Teller, and the Mayers were among a team of gifted biologists, chemists, engineers, and physicists who would come together at the university in the wake of the war. The school wanted to build on the talent that had been assembled by Arthur Compton at its Metallurgical Laboratory during the war, and to create a multidisciplinary group of basic research institutes. Maria and Joe Mayer were both asked to join the newly formed Institute for Nuclear Studies, which is now known as the Fermi Institute. Joe was offered a full professorship, Maria an assistant professorship. But once again, Maria Mayer's position would be "voluntary," due to the university's allegedly inviolable nepotism rules—yet again she had to work without even a nominal salary.

At the time, her status didn't seem to matter so much. Reunited with many of her closest friends and colleagues, in an atmosphere charged with the potential for pursuing new ideas in basic research that had emerged during the course of war work, Mayer took to her research with a fresh élan. While Mayer had usually maintained friendships with one or two women, such as Kitty Rice or Alice Kimball, now, in Chicago, she threw herself into work almost to the exclusion of anything else, virtually cutting herself off from many of her old acquaintances. "Faculty wives like me no longer ha[d] easy access to Maria Mayer, because she was always talking to the men and had a too technical conversation," noted Laura Fermi. Bigeleisen, who followed

Maria to the University of Chicago, also observed that "if there was a social gathering of scientists and their wives, she'd be talking with the men. She wanted to be one of the boys."

The Mayers were together again, but much of their old intimacy was gone. Maria drank heavily and smoked even more. She was no longer the fresh young beauty of Göttingen. The rumor mill around the university campus had it that Joe Mayer had his eye on other women. Jacob Bigeleisen's wife, Grace, recalls the discomfort she felt at the hard-drinking, late-night parties at the Mayers' rambling, fifteen-room mansion in the Hyde Park section of Chicago, where "people had a habit of disappearing in odd couples."

Joe Mayer probably never ceased to care for his wife. But Joe, the only son of an older and somewhat remote Austrian-born engineer, had inherited his father's cool demeanor and was ill equipped to handle the anxiety that had gnawed at his wife ever since the start of the war. Even those who loved and admired him acknowledged that Joe, who was compulsively argumentative and opinionated, found it difficult to be gentle even with those closest to him. To outsiders, he could be a veritable iceberg. Robert Sachs, who worked for Joe in Aberdeen during the war, remembers Maria Mayer's husband as an exceptionally unfeeling person. Those years marked a period of acute personal crisis for Sachs, whose wife had attempted suicide at the start of the war. "I had had to put [my wife] in hospital in New York and was working under tremendous stress," recalls Sachs. "I was working six days a week, and going up [to New York] on the Sunday morning train and then back to Aberdeen the same night. It was very tough. I tried to say something about it to [Joe], thinking that since he and Maria were living in New York he might offer to help, but I got absolutely no response from him, no support at all."

Similarly, Peter Mayer, who idolized his father but grew close to him only during the decade before his death, concedes that Joe Mayer was out of touch with the needs of his family. As a young teenager, still smarting from the burden of repeated academic failures and the fear of disappointing his exceptionally gifted parents, Peter felt that his efforts to win his father's approval often failed.

Hence, Joe's family gradually learned to look elsewhere for emotional support. In 1953, when he was a freshman in high school and his parents were traveling abroad, Peter Mayer went to live with the Libbys for one semester, and developed a close attachment to Willard Libby, a chemistry department colleague of Joe's. Peter credits Libby with giving him the confidence and the impetus to switch from the prestigious University of Chicago Lab School to a public school—where, he says, he realized for the first time that not everyone's parents were Ph.D.'s and where, in a less pressured environment, he was able to improve his academic performance. When his parents returned from the trip, Peter remembers, Joe was very much bothered by his son's attachment to Libby.

Eventually, Maria confided to Peter that she and Joe weren't getting along. By the late 1950s, when Gustav Born, Max Born's son, visited Maria Mayer in Chicago, he barely recognized her: "She was bloated and smoking heavily," he recalls. "I got the impression that she was not happy." Born could not have known that by then the Mayers had begun talking about divorce.

But if the war and four years of separation from Joe had taken a toll on her outlook and on her marriage, at least Maria had her science. She came to Chicago charged with carrying on her work on the Opacity Project. And within a year of arriving in the Windy City, she and Edward Teller began working on a problem relating to the origins of the elements which would lead to her Nobel Prize–winning work on the shell structure of the nucleus. During the 1950s, Teller, Fermi, and Hans Jensen, an eccentric widowed scientist from Heidelberg, with whom she would collaborate on a book about the shell model, would become her closest confidants. Another person who turned up in Chicago at around this time was Robert Sachs, who had been asked to form a theoretical physics division at Argonne National Laboratories and who jumped at the opportunity to give something back to his former teacher. "Maria, wouldn't you like to earn some money?" Sachs asked her one day, and offered her a part-time job at Argonne as a senior theoretical physicist. When Mayer protested that she knew nothing about nuclear physics, Sachs told her, "Maria, you'll learn." He still laughs at the irony of the situation, for nearly twenty years earlier it was Mayer who "not only got me started, but *insisted* that I get started [in nuclear physics]."

For the first time since Göttingen, Mayer found herself in a relatively hospitable environment, excited by new science and new insights. She and Teller dreamed up a seminar on the application of a mathematical concept known as group theory to both chemistry and physics. Group theory, which involves the classification of objects and numbers in groups, already was being used by a small number of scientists to describe the symmetrical properties of atoms and molecules. But the Mayer-Teller seminar—with its scientific orientation—was one of the first of its kind. Mayer was also a regular at weekly seminars held at the Institute for Nuclear Studies, where topics ranged from the nuclear shell structure to carbon dating. And while the faculty club at Johns Hopkins had been off-limits to women, Mayer often attended the luncheons held at Chicago's Quadrangle Club. She also began attending small weekly seminars at Argonne, where she set out to learn nuclear physics, peppering Teller and Fermi with questions about subjects she didn't wholly understand.

Even though Maria Mayer found herself in the most hospitable academic environment she'd come across yet, she still did not seem eager to pursue an independent course of research. Mayer was considered a solid journeyman scientist—smart and competent, but not a pathbreaker. Now in her early forties, an age at which most scientists have either made great reputations or slipped into obscurity, Mayer appeared to be much more of an intellectual follower than a leader. Even though she was treated as a full member of the faculty, participating in teaching, policymaking, and the examination of graduate students, Mayer never complained about the fact that she wasn't paid and worked gratefully on problems tossed out by Teller and Fermi. The judgment Herzfeld had made of his protégé during the 1930s seemed to have proved correct: "Her mind is really brilliant and penetrating, although perhaps not very original." Similarly, Sachs had become convinced that Mayer never developed "a strong driving interest in some particular area where she knew what should be done and needed help from students and others to get it done. What a young physicist has to do is really make his presence known—go to meetings, interact with people and so on. What she did was interact with people who [happened] to come her way. She didn't make a business of making herself known. . . . She didn't have that kind of drive."

Her colleagues could not have known that Mayer had become convinced early in her marriage that to pursue her own ambitions would work to her husband's detriment. For one thing, she had blamed herself for Joe's dismissal from Hopkins, sensing that both her Germanness and her prominence in the physics department irked the university administration. Her son, Peter, recalls that his mother particularly disapproved of at least one woman whom she considered a "pushy" female scientist at the University of Chicago—possibly Franck's second wife, Hertha Sponer. "I was like that once," she told Peter. "But I realized that it was only hurting my husband's career. So I pulled back, and then everything came to me."

Moreover, Mayer's position was so tenuous throughout most of her career that she probably never would have gotten the resources she needed to pursue any long-range scientific inquiry of her own. Often the only course available to her was to collect the crumbs of insight as the men around her sliced off huge chunks of the theoretical pie—a strategy made all the more attractive by the fact that nuclear physics in the forties and fifties was such fertile territory that "you'd go to an institute seminar and the problems just [rained down] on the floor," like manna from heaven.

In fact, although her intensity and single-minded dedication to physics was clearly evident by the time she reached Chicago, Maria Mayer didn't begin to realize her full scientific potential until relatively late in her career. It was only when she conceived the shell model of the nucleus that her colleagues finally perceived Maria as coming out from under Joe's shadow. Edward Teller had gotten Mayer thinking about the origin of the elements soon after she came to the University of Chicago. But Teller, as always, was working on a number of projects at the same time. One day while he was out of town, Mayer gathered the information about the elements and nuclei that they had been studying and systematically inspected the data she had gathered. Suddenly, she discovered that "in all these nuclei either the number of protons or the number of neutrons were very special." Eventually, Mayer discovered a host of "special" numbers in the nuclei of elements, which she came to refer to as "magic numbers." What Mayer had discovered was that the most stable nuclei have any one of about half a dozen magic numbers—that is, they have either 2, 8, 20, 28, 50, 82, or 126 neutrons or protons. Although some of the magic numbers had been discovered earlier by other physicists, their existence wasn't considered important to nuclear structure. And Mayer, who initially didn't know about the discovery of some of the early magic numbers, would add new ones to the known list.

When Teller returned from his trip, Mayer tried to interest him in her discovery. But he had by now become fixated on the development of nuclear weapons and wasn't interested in the magic numbers. So Mayer took to collecting more data on nuclei from nuclear experimentalists at the University of Chicago, who were observing nuclei that had been bombarded in a cyclotron, and to dropping in on Fermi, the only physicist in Chicago who seemed interested in her work.

Over and over in her research the magic numbers kept popping up, pointing to a nuclear symmetry similar to that of an atom wherein electrons orbit the nucleus. The magic numbers indicated the potential for great stability *within* the nucleus—much like the structure of certain atoms that contain nuclei with such tightly bound electrons that they do not combine easily with other chemical compounds by losing or gaining an electron. Thus, the existence of nuclei with tightly bound "shells" of neutrons and protons that prevent them from breaking down into other elements could help explain why some elements are much more abundant in nature than others.

The structure that was beginning to reveal itself in Mayer's research would help explain the central conundrum that other hypotheses about the structure of the nucleus had left unsolved. For while some alternative models treated the nucleus as though it functioned much like the atom itself, with a central force that held each nucleon in its unique orbit and each orbit together within the nucleus, none of these models could accurately predict why certain nuclei had magic numbers and others didn't. One problem was that, unlike the atom, the nucleus has no central force holding together its galaxy of nucleons, and the earlier models of the nucleus were unable to account for the absence of a central force in a way that also would account for the magic numbers.

Initially, Mayer's investigation would lead her against the tide of conventional wisdom. For example, Edward Teller concedes that at least initially he was "completely opposed to the magic numbers. I disagreed with her conclusions." When they met in Stockholm, in 1963, to receive the Nobel Prize, Eugene Wigner also confessed to Mayer and Jensen that he had long considered the magic numbers "mere charming nonsense." (Wigner won the prize for the body of his work in physics.)

But Fermi believed in her results. And it was while speaking with him one afternoon that Mayer hit upon the final piece of the puzzle. "Fermi and Maria were talking in her office when Enrico was called out of the office to answer the telephone on a long-distance call," Joe Mayer later recalled. "At the door he turned and asked a question about [so-called] spin-orbit coupling." In a sudden flash of insight, Mayer was able to explain why certain magic numbers fit inside certain nuclei. Fermi "returned less than ten minutes later and Maria started to 'snow' him with a detailed explanation. . . . Maria, when excited, had a rapid-fire oral delivery, whereas Enrico always wanted a slow detailed and methodical explanation. Enrico smiled and left: 'Tomorrow, when you are less excited, you can explain it to me.' "

What Mayer had figured out was that the value of the magic numbers inside each stable nucleus was a function of two interrelated quantities—the so-called spin and orbital angular momentum of each particle: Each nucleon spins around its own axis. At the same time, it has a momentum within an orbit. Scientists knew that nucleons had both spin and orbital angular momentum. It was Mayer who figured out that the relationship between the two had a significant effect on the energy level of each nucleon and hence determined whether or not it contained magic numbers, and the value of those magic numbers. The reason no one had thought to connect the two forces was that in the atomic model, the spin of an electron has very little interaction with its orbital angular momentum.

Although she had written important papers before, this was perhaps the first time that Mayer experienced the physical and emotional exhilaration that accompanies a profound leap of creative insight. Forgetting the promise she had made to her daughter to suspend scientific talk during cocktails and dinner, she ran home every night bursting with ideas and problems. One night, Maria rushed home and, as usual, began spilling out for Joe the latest results of her work. Joe, however, wouldn't let her finish. "I want you to go upstairs right now and write it down," he demanded.

For if her relationship with Joe had grown to be emotionally frustrating for Maria, her husband remained an important scientific ally. For one thing, although he was always careful to remove himself from faculty meetings at which her status was being discussed, he privately always encouraged Maria in her work. Moreover, he helped infuse her thinking with a chemist's sensitivity to natural patterns and systems; and it was that willingness to study the patterns that emerged from nuclei, even in the absence of an applicable theory, that would lead Maria to the magic numbers.

Joe also was careful not to intrude on her territory. Notes the writer Joan Dash: "There were times, Joe recalled, when he had felt himself drawn into the work, ready to succumb to his interest in it and become a partner. Yet he felt unmistakably that Maria was letting him know: Hands off, this is mine. He kept to his original role, therefore, finding satisfaction in the thought that no one would be able to imagine now that Maria was riding on his coattails."

Joe would, however, have to give Maria one more push to get her to stake a claim to her discovery. Maria Mayer knew she had something important. In April 1948, she wrote up some of her preliminary findings. But she was reluctant to present a detailed account of her ideas to the scientific community at large, fearing that the ideas were not as original as she thought they were. It is a fact that few great creative insights are ever wholly original—rather, there is a certain zeitgeist that can lead both artists and scientists in remarkably similar directions. Thus, a few artists in California and at least one in England began painting in an abstract expressionist style at precisely the moment when the movement was said to have been born in New York. Similarly, several scientists, in addition to Darwin, had been working on a theory of evolution in the mid-nineteenth century; indeed, although Darwin has become known as the father of evolutionary theory, much of his work draws heavily on a paper written by a colleague, Alfred Russel Wallace.

Mayer was concerned that the work of two scientists, Lothar Nordheim and Eugene Feenberg, two veteran physicists who also had tried to account for the magic numbers and whose papers she had read before publication, may have influenced her—even though their conclusions were very different from her own. So instead of writing up a detailed explanation of her theory, she composed a brief letter that was published together with short statements by Nordheim and Feenberg for the *Physical Review* in June 1949. It was only after extensive prodding by Joe Mayer that Maria subsequently published two lengthy papers in the *Physical Review*. What's more, Mayer had to be talked out of publishing her work under both her name and Fermi's, which she wanted to do as a way to recognize the inspiration their conversations had given her; Fermi had to persuade her that not only had the theory been her own but putting the name of a famous scientist on her paper would forever obscure her own contribution.

As it was, in the potently competitive world of physics, Mayer very nearly ceded her victory to yet another rival. After publishing her brief explanatory letter in 1949, and as she was agonizing about publishing her theories in full, Hans Jensen, a respected physicist at the University of Heidelberg, rushed into print with his own version of the shell model—one that was identical to Mayer's. As it turned out, Jensen's research would spark a close friendship between the two scientists and lead to the last major collaboration of Mayer's career.

The coincidence of two physicists making discoveries across the Atlantic at the same time caught the imagination of the scientific community. Before long, the Mayer-Jensen model had won over such eminences as Bohr and Heisenberg.

When Mayer and Jensen met for the first time, during the summer of 1950, the two scientists apparently hit it off immediately. That summer, Joe and Maria had traveled to Germany as State Department consultants charged with renewing contacts with German physicists and chemists. In Heidelberg, Jensen received his rival graciously and imme-diately arranged for Maria Mayer to receive an invitation to the Uni-versity of Heidelberg for the following summer. The invitation was quickly reciprocated by the Mayers; in the fall of 1951, Jensen set sail for the United States, where he traveled around the country as a guest lecturer for several months, always returning to stay for several days with the Mayers in Chicago. All in all, by February 1952, Jensen had spent a total of close to two months in the Mayers' house.

In Jensen, Maria encountered not just a collaborator but something of a soul mate. Jensen, who had been widowed for several years, was a playful, procrastinating eccentric. An avid gardener, he lived alone in a small apartment-cum-office, overflowing with books and plants, on the Heidelberg campus. Perhaps in response to the rumors that swirled around campus about Joe Mayer's infidelities, and to the unusual cir-cumstances of a lone woman working closely among men, some col-leagues speculated that Maria Mayer and Jensen were having an affair.

To be sure, Jensen's playfulness often turned to flirtation. In one letter to Maria, just before he wangled an invitation to the Mayers' for Thanksgiving, he enclosed a dialogue between Casanova and Giuliana, which read in part:

" 'You love me Giacomo,' " said she: " 'What you call love is proba-bly desire, which in your opinion is a commendable impulse in accord with the will of nature. For my part, I love you, and what I call love in this instance is probably desire. . . . In my opinion, as in yours, to sat-isfy this desire would be to chime with nature's plans, but I have not the slightest intention of doing so. . . . I love you, but you are a scamp, a spoiled boy, a conceited male. Of course, I'll be sorry I said no, but I'd also be sorry if I said yes. In either case my breast will ache, but I'll get over it quicker if you don't have your way.' "

The thank-you note he mailed immediately following Thanksgiv-ing is signed: "yours sincerely, the scamp, the spoiled boy . . ."

Rather than a lover, it is much more likely that in Hans, Maria dis-covered the sibling she never had. Where Joe was often gruff, obtuse, and arrogant, Hans was gentle, mischievous, and self-effacing. Hans and Maria also shared a love of music. (Joe was tone-deaf.) And they found special meaning in the fact that they shared the same birthday and the same eyeglass prescription. The two friends sometimes joked that they were twins who had been separated at birth. Jensen even took to signing his letters to Maria, "with love, your twin brother."

But in this brother-sister act, Maria emerged as the dominant player. Sometime early in their acquaintance, Mayer and Jensen decided to collaborate on their book *Elementary Theory of Nuclear Shell Structure*, which was published in 1955. But in the face of Jensen's constant procrastinations, Mayer spent much of the early 1950s coaxing, cajoling, and fuming over Jensen's slow progress. When the book was completed, most colleagues assumed that Mayer had done the bulk of the work; in this case, they were probably right. Years earlier, most of the scientists who knew about Joe and Maria's collaboration on *Statistical Mechanics* were happy to assume that Joe had done most of the work, especially because statistical mechanics—the application of statistics to the study of large molecules—was the field to which Joe dedicated most of his career. There was, however, one notable exception to this view: Ed Teller had always thought much more highly of Maria's intellectual abilities than of Joe's. "Compared to Maria, Joe Mayer was a zero," says the outspoken physicist.

Nor was it just in her relationship with Jensen that Mayer started to take charge. At Argonne, Mayer began to assume a clear "leadership role," recalls Sachs. A small coterie of graduate students became the focal point of a shell-model theory group at Argonne that gathered around Maria until she left the University of Chicago in 1959. "Members of the group became known in their own right as experts on theoretical problems of nuclear structure," notes Sachs. At the same time, Mayer's own "style changed from the eclectic style reflecting broad interest in many kinds of physics to a single minded concern with the consequences of the shell model."

Yet even as her work was opening new horizons for Mayer, life in Chicago was beginning to lose some of its appeal. Fermi died in 1954. Franck suffered a series of heart attacks and would die in 1964. In the aftermath of Ed Teller's testimony against Oppenheimer in the McCarthy hearings, Teller, who was by now living in California, virtually dropped out of sight. He was so deeply shaken by the outcry against him that he lost touch with even those few old friends who were willing to overlook his politics.

So in 1959, when both Joe and Maria Mayer received job offers from the University of California at San Diego, they were ready to move on. The Ureys already lived in La Jolla. And best of all, Maria was finally offered a professorship in physics, with a full salary. Not even a last-minute about-face by the University of Chicago, which suddenly forgot its nepotism rules and offered Maria a salary as an incentive to keep the Mayers from leaving, would change their minds.

Ironically, Maria's departure from Chicago for her first fully paid academic post also marked the end of her most productive years as a physicist. Shortly after arriving in La Jolla, Maria Mayer became ill; although the doctors never determined whether her malady was due to an infection of the nervous system or to a stroke, she lost the feeling in her left arm and found it difficult to speak. Thus, the news that she had won the Nobel Prize became particularly important in keeping Mayer connected to the scientific community—without it, notes Teller, with a bitterness that no doubt reflects his own exile from the scientific community, "she would have been completely isolated."

On November 5, 1963, Joe and Maria were awakened at about 2:00 A.M. by a call from Stockholm. "But I don't know anyone in Stockholm," said Maria as she reached for the receiver; meanwhile, Joe, who had answered the telephone, ran to the kitchen to chill a bottle of champagne. By the time they got around to calling Marianne, two hours later, to tell her that Maria had become the second woman ever to win the Nobel Prize in physics, husband and wife were already a little drunk. "I got this call in the middle of the night, and I was sure my mother was tipsy," recalls Marianne. "In the morning I called them back because I was sure I had dreamt the whole thing."

Even after the news had sunk in, Maria remained strangely subdued. To the Mayers' closest friends, it seemed that Joe was far more excited than she. Initially, Maria was overwhelmed by the flurry of congratulatory phone calls to the house—many of them from people, like Laura Fermi, with whom she had virtually dropped out of touch.

When the big day came, Maria worried about how she would make it up to the podium without tripping over her floor-length green brocade evening gown, and how she would manage to give the king her right hand while holding the gold medal and elegant leather-bound diploma with her virtually paralyzed left hand (as it turned out, an attendant discreetly stepped up to assist her). She also wondered whether she could make it through the ceremony without a cigarette. With the television cameras and blazing lights of the auditorium shining down on her, she could not see that, sitting in the audience, Joe had burst into tears.

For Maria, the prize didn't represent the unalloyed triumph that it might have been for a younger, healthier scientist. With both her speech and her movement impaired by her illness, Mayer was unable to take full advantage of either the celebrity or the professional opportunities available to a Nobel laureate. Nor could the prize begin to fill the void of illness, age, and estrangement from her family that had come to mark her life, or to compensate for the opportunities she had missed when she was younger and had all her faculties. Mayer would say of the experience: "To my surprise, winning the prize wasn't half as exciting as doing the work itself . . . *that* was the fun—seeing it work out!"

Yet there were moments during the weeks leading up to the Nobel ceremony that Mayer cherished. In particular, Born, who then was living in retirement in Edinburgh, was bursting with pride over his protégé's accomplishments; he sent Mayer an enormous bouquet of flowers and released an account of her life to the newspapers. Mayer couldn't help but bask in the glow of Born's obvious affection and approval.

The trip to Scandinavia was also one long celebration. Joe and Maria stopped in Denmark for a brief holiday before the ceremony. They then joined Jensen in Stockholm, where the Mayers found to their amusement that the normally disheveled professor from Heidelberg had ordered a whole new wardrobe for the week of celebrations and was strutting around Stockholm like a dandy. Maria's relationship with Joe had been on the mend ever since they moved to La Jolla. Peter remembers his father rallying to Maria's side after her illness. Maria hated the fact that Joe was now saddled with an "invalid" wife; yet more than ever, Maria depended on her husband for both mundane household chores and companionship. The problems of work were compounded by the frustrations of getting dressed and doing household chores with a crippled arm. Now that the children were grown, the Mayers spent more time alone together than they had in years—even on holidays, like Thanksgiving and Christmas, which they frequently shared with Peggy Griffin, Joe Mayer's pretty and vivacious secretary, and her husband. Never particularly sensitive to the emotional currents that coursed through her family, Maria Mayer was probably too preoccupied to notice the bonds that began to develop between her husband and his secretary, whom Joe would marry within six months of his wife's death.

The chasm between Maria Mayer and her children had widened. Marianne was living in Michigan with her husband and rarely visited. Peter, who received a B.S. in physics from Cal Tech, had decided, to Maria's dismay, to abandon science in favor of a master's degree in economics. So eager was he to emerge from the shadow of his parents that even though they pleaded with him to go to Stockholm for the Nobel ceremony, Peter refused. (Peter would go on to become an itinerant academic, moving from job to job around Asia.) Marianne, who says she would have been delighted to go to Stockholm, was never invited; Maria's daughter insists that her parents' reasons for not inviting her weren't so much a question of favoritism as the fact that she was married and had family responsibilities.

When Maria Mayer died, in February 1972, eulogies and editorials celebrated her as one of the century's most important physicists. A few months later, at a symposium of the American Physical Society in New York, several scientists who had known Mayer, including Eugene Wigner, reminisced fondly about their soft-spoken and unflaggingly pleasant colleague. The memories they cherished were of an agreeable, noncompetitive woman who had never allowed her frustrations to end in bitterness, who had never been anything but a lady.

To the female physicists gathered at the symposium, these colleagues' perception of her as a pleasant woman was precisely the problem: They did not see her—and never really had—as a top physicist. "Obviously, they weren't listening," says Fay Ajzenberg-Selove, who attended the APS symposium in the midst of her own struggle for tenure at the University of Pennsylvania. Maria Mayer "was extremely angry about the fact that she had not had a full professorship until shortly before winning the Nobel Prize."

Ajzenberg-Selove belonged to a younger generation that was not about to let the male establishment dictate her professional future. Having held a tenured position at Haverford College in Pennsylvania for several years, Ajzenberg-Selove switched jobs to the more prestigious University of Pennsylvania in 1969. But at Penn, where her husband, Wally Selove, had been a professor in the physics department for many years, she was turned down for tenure. Ironically, Ajzenberg-Selove's tenure application was rejected at the very moment when she had been nominated as vice chairman of the Nuclear Physics division of the American Physical Society—a highly prestigious post and one that made her the first woman ever to serve as an officer of the hallowed scientific association. Convinced that prejudice and her status as Wally's wife were the principal reasons for her denial, Ajzenberg-Selove filed a formal complaint against the university with the Equal Employment Opportunity Commission of the federal government and the Human Relations Commission of the Commonwealth of Pennsylvania. A year later, concluding that Ajzenberg-Selove had demonstrated a prima facie case of gender discrimination, the HRC ordered the university to grant her tenure.

Thus, Ajzenberg-Selove became one of a small army of women on campuses across America who, during the 1970s, helped overturn the nepotism rules that had kept Maria Mayer on the periphery of science and academia for most of her career. It was a strategy to which Maria Mayer could never have resorted—in part because the EEOC had only been founded in 1965, but also because she would never have wanted to saddle Joe with the embarrassment of having an outspoken, strident wife.

Maria Mayer was lucky in being able to navigate a circuitous route to Stockholm. She had been fortunate in her upbringing. She may have been smarter than Mileva Maric, but Maria also had the good fortune to be considered both beautiful and charming. She was born with better connections than Lee Krasner and, thus, received an early introduction—and a much warmer welcome—in her chosen profession. Although at one time she would have been ready to give herself over to a traditional role as wife and mother, Mayer had had the foresight to marry a man who refused to let her squander her professional training and who was happy to see her succeed. While she was a Hedgehog at heart, Maria Mayer's ambitions often had to be rescued from her own impulses to lead a conventional feminine existence.

By contrast, Maria's daughter, Maria M. Wentzel, decided consciously, and somewhat defiantly, to devote her life to her husband and child. Her choice was a common one at the time; for as Ajzenberg-Selove's experience had proved, it was still enormously difficult for a woman to succeed at both a profession and family life. Maria M. Wentzel and Fay Ajzenberg-Selove, two women of about the same age, chose radically different paths. But it was the women of their generation and educational level—women with one or more degrees who came of age after World War II—who began to inform their choices with a deliberateness and self-consciousness hitherto unimaginable to their female forebears.

Denise Scott Brown

Denise is a true intellect who structures the world around ideas. Bob is a great hand and eye to which is harnessed a pretty good brain.

Steve Izenour

The Masterful Planner

The eccentric art nouveau mansion in the Mount Airy district of Philadelphia was dark and quiet when a colleague dropped Denise Scott Brown off at home one spring night in 1991 after a long day at the office. In recent years, Denise and her husband, Robert Venturi, had grown used to spending more time apart than they would have liked. A few choice commissions to design museums had made them famous, but not rich. As their lives had come to be filled not only with travel—as much in pursuit of new architectural commissions as to fulfill ones they already had won—but also with countless speeches and public appearances, they found themselves robbed of the two things they valued most: time together and time to work. But as Denise opened the leaded-glass entryway of her house and stepped into the foyer, with its soaring ceilings, riotous stenciled decorations, and sweeping mahogany staircase, she felt strangely relieved to be spending that night alone.

As on most nights, Denise headed straight for the kitchen, bypassing the generously proportioned—and little used—living room and parlor. Moving noiselessly across the grayish-brown linoleum floor, she prepared a plate of vegetarian pasta on an old gas range; Nancy, the

157

airedale, padded softly around behind her. As was their custom—hers and Bob's—Denise ate her dinner in the laundry room, a spartan, apple-green chamber just off the kitchen. She sat in one of the floral deck chairs across from the washer, dryer, and ironing board. The laundry room, which also houses the family television set and Nancy's blanket, is their refuge from the passion and pressure of work. It is a little unseemly, she knows, for the first couple of American architecture to relax in the glow of an overhead fluorescent light or to put their feet up in a space as "ordinary" as a laundry room—but then that is partly why they find the place so comforting.

Normally, Denise would have taken advantage of Bob's absence to retrieve, from the foyer, the drab, utilitarian Sportsac bag that she keeps stuffed with papers and to finish some work. Usually, this means editing an article, one of hers or one of Bob's. But she found it hard to concentrate. She thought about watching the news, or perhaps a mystery—Denise always enjoyed a Miss Marple episode—if one was airing. In the end, she settled for the cryptogram puzzle, which she thinks of as a final treat before going to bed—like the morsel of chocolate left on a crisply starched pillowcase at a fine hotel.

But that night the puzzles did not offer much satisfaction. For once again Denise found herself torn between her love for Bob and her rage at the architectural establishment. Tonight Bob was in Mexico City, receiving the coveted Pritzker Prize. Tonight marked his public coronation, the ultimate feather in his cap, and yet another snub of her work.

Denise didn't for a minute begrudge Bob his reward; it had come late enough, she knew. Only after honoring virtually every other great American architect of his generation, and even a few obscure foreign ones, had the Pritzker Prize committee finally seen fit to honor Bob. After all, how many times could the committee overlook the acknowledged father of postmodernism before casting doubt on the integrity of the prize itself?

Besides, Bob and Denise *needed* the Pritzker Prize. With all that publicity, perhaps the financial worries of the firm, Venturi Scott Brown & Associates, which Bob established in 1960 and Denise joined formally seven years later, would finally be over. For twenty-five years, they had lived a hand-to-mouth existence, flourishing on the crumbs of architectural patronage—a retirement home here and a firehouse there—even as other architects made off with commissions for the modern-day cathedrals of office buildings and airport terminals. Corporate clients had never felt comfortable with the offbeat look of the firm's buildings—too gaudy when modernism was the fashion, not decorative enough when postmodernism became mainstream. Some famous architects, especially Philip Johnson, who influenced many lucrative architectural commissions and controlled the Pritzker committee, had never really liked Bob or Denise. Bob, with his quiet, tweedy intellectuality, and Denise, with her wire-rim glasses and "schoolmarmish" feminism, were often the butt of jokes in the high-design architectural fraternity. More and more, as the firm began to win prestigious—if often financially draining—public and civic commissions, the couple also became the subject of a quiet, venomous envy. So Bob and Denise kept to themselves, in Philadelphia, far from the architectural epicenter of New York.

After he had been notified about the prize, Bob, for the first time in their marriage, publicly decried the treatment of his wife, saying that her exclusion from the prize was unfair. Coming as it did just as she turned sixty, the snub hurt even more than she expected, and Denise could not bring herself to go to Mexico. Instead, she finished her pasta in the laundry room, mounted the mahogany staircase to her bedroom, and went to bed alone.

Denise Scott Brown has been at odds with the architectural establishment almost since the beginning of her career, in the 1960s. She came of age in an era when women were beginning to grapple not only with the force of their own emerging ambitions but also with a growing awareness of the obstacles—both professional and personal—that they would have to overcome to achieve their dreams. Like Bob, Denise had built her career on criticizing the prevailing orthodoxies of modernist architecture. But while Bob won the sometimes grudging respect of his peers, Denise has been ridiculed and reviled by many leading architects—though not by the clients and students who know her work well. Part of the problem lies in the fact that, by her own choosing, Denise initially focused her efforts on urban design and planning, disciplines that, at most firms, have always taken a back seat to building design. The problem has been compounded by her insistence on working with Bob rather than setting up a business of her own. But equally important, it is informed by what Martin Filler and Rosemarie Haag Bletter, a husband-wife team in architectural criticism, describe as a "deeply misogynist streak" that pervades the "realm of high-art architecture" at its most illustrious and influential level.

The decision to award the Pritzker Prize, the most prestigious honor in architecture, to Bob but not to her was Denise's most painful clash yet with her most powerful peers. It came after decades of struggle to establish both their firm and her place within it. It came after years of collaboration in which she and Bob had helped frame the critical debates of their profession. It came at the end of the 1980s, when she finally had amassed a cadre of prestigious clients and projects of her own, for which she had beaten out some of the biggest names in architecture and urban planning. Now, in denying her claim to the prize, the architectural establishment had officially declared its unwillingness to recognize the intimate, collaborative partnership that had shaped the iconoclastic aesthetics of the firm.

Still, most architects can be excused if they fail to understand Scott Brown's work and marriage, both of which defy easy categorization. For one thing, her role in the firm as Venturi's in-house critic, fellow theorist, and architectural collaborator is both misunderstood and resented by other architects. Yet Denise has insisted on standing by her man, not only because of decades of fruitful collaboration but, quite simply, because she loves him, enjoys working with him, and relishes the atmosphere of a family business.

Indeed, on the surface Denise has constructed a personal and professional life every bit as ambiguous as the lives of other gifted wives who, no matter what their promise, put their husbands' needs before their own careers. Instead of forging a career of her own, as a talented young architect and urban planner she allied herself with a brilliant husband who seemed destined to overshadow her. And overshadow her he has. For one thing, her particular talents as a planner and architectural theoretician are much less easily understood than Venturi's seminal work as a designer and an architectural draftsman known for his "golden hand." Moreover, as a gifted teacher who is regarded by colleagues and former students as an educational pathbreaker, Denise nevertheless abandoned a tenured teaching post at UCLA, where she had helped found the School of Architecture and Urban Planning in the mid 1960s. She did so to join her new husband's firm in Philadelphia, to which she committed herself as surely as she had to her marriage, even though she acknowledged: "I could [have] improve[d] my chances for recognition as an individual if I had returned to teaching or if I had abandoned my collaboration with my husband."

While Scott Brown's choices often were informed by the same values—gleaned both from her family and from the prevailing cultural norms—that have detoured the careers of other gifted women, they also illustrate just how complex and ambiguous decisions relating to family and professional life have become. In defining her work and marriage, Scott Brown was driven not only by genuine love and traditional expectations but also by the strong sense of intellectual and artistic kinship she shares with her husband. The marriage has flourished on the apparent paradox of near-obsessive work and close-knit intimacy, an unlikely combination that has nurtured their relationship with each other and also with their son, Jimmie. Although Bob has an intellectual appreciation for complexity and contradiction, it has been Denise who has embraced the messy ambiguities and conflicts that both infuse a working wife's life and define the whole environment of American life, as she sees it. So although Denise's relationship with Bob has been fraught, at times, with difficult compromises and conflicts—although she occasionally succumbs to the professional disappointments and rivalries that have gnawed at her over the years—it is a way of life she would knowingly and willingly choose all over again.

Scott Brown's life has been a portrait in complexity and contradiction. Vaguely Victorian and academic, Denise has the look of a Vermeer portrait and the elocution of a nineteenth-century diarist. Yet she fell in love in Las Vegas—both with Bob and with a vision of American urbanism that seeks to learn from the "ugly" and ordinary every bit as much as from classical beauty and romanticism. Condemned by many of her colleagues as a strident and noisy feminist, she won legitimacy in her husband's firm by working long hours and by helping to keep the firm afloat during tough times with her planning projects. And although she has been vocal in her demand that the architectural establishment give her equal credit for the firm's creations, she has been steadfastly reluctant to pick up a pencil and draw.

Denise's taste for ambiguity was cultivated at an early age, during a girlhood spent in Africa. Denise Lakofski was born in rural Rhodesia and raised in a prosperous Johannesburg suburb, and her world embraced, precariously, the mystique of the African veld and the bourgeois values of a well-to-do Jewish household. While, on the surface, life in the Lakofski family was dominated by the traditional values of Denise's father, Shim, it was heavily influenced by the artistic and intellictual sensibilities of her mother, Phyllis, who insisted that her husband build a thoroughly modernist structure in which to raise her family. Of Phyllis and Shim's four children, it was Denise who came closest to absorbing—and achieving some harmony between—Shim's old-world practicality and Phyllis's metaphysical impulses.

Denise's father, the descendant of Lithuanian Jews, was a self-made man who had begun his career roaming the bush country of Rhodesia, working in the general stores that serviced remote mining communities around the country. It was at one of these outposts, in southern Rhodesia, that he met Denise's mother. A precocious free spirit, Phyllis had always chafed against the standards of her own mother, a Latvian girl who, despite her frontier spirit, had never shaken the bourgeois values of her own upbringing. Instead, Phyllis's mother was married off to Willie Hepker, a handsome and quixotic dreamer whom she met for the first time the day she stepped off the boat in Cape Town, as a mailorder bride. Although Phyllis was taught to play the piano and to pour tea in the afternoons from a silver tea service, which had been hauled to the remote farm by oxen, she preferred to be outdoors. She wore khakis instead of dresses, was more familiar with guns than with dolls, and roamed the family farm with her brothers. In an effort to tame her, her parents eventually sent her to a convent school in Natal. The nuns, however, were so taken by the exceptionally agile mind of their young Jewish charge that they overlooked Phyllis's exploits, such as her penchant for doing homework while crouched high up in the branches of an avacado tree. When she graduated, at fifteen, Phyllis set her heart on what was then the almost exclusively male domain of architecture. She spent five years in the bush, working in gold mines before an uncle agreed to finance her studies.

Her career plans ended early, however. Phyllis was forced to return home after just two years to help run a small hotel, which was her father's latest scheme for eking out a living. It was there, in 1930, that she met Shim Lakofski, whom she married just a few months later and whom she followed to South Africa after the birth of their daughter Denise on October 3, 1931.

Within the constraints of her traditional Jewish marriage, Phyllis sought to create a life as richly patterned as that of her Rhodesian girlhood. She taught her children how to identify rocks and different grasses. To summon her brood she would let out the ear-splitting whistle of African cowherders. She chafed at the social restrictions of the provincial, racially stratified world of Johannesburg, where ethnic groups tended to cluster together. The British country clubs, top preparatory schools for boys, and business organizations were off-limits to Jews. Although the Lakofskis were an established, affluent Jewish family, Phyllis and Shim shunned the insularity and showiness of the well-to-do Jewish community, from which her husband hailed, and preferred instead a more eclectic social circle. Thus, the Lakofskis socialized with a mix of European refugees from World War II, Americans, and even Chinese, who, in the byzantine hierarchy of South Africa's racial laws, were—unlike the Japanese—considered second-class nonwhites.

Yet for all her enlightened views, within the glass-and-concrete frame of the International-style house that Phyllis had commissioned hummed the soul of a decidedly traditional family. The house often sheltered several generations. When Denise was just four years old, her beloved grandmother Rose, Shim's mother, died in the bedroom next to hers. Soon afterward, her maternal grandmother moved in. It was to Granny Rebecca's room that Denise and her siblings escaped for afternoons of milk and cookies. There they would listen to Granny's stories of Czar Nicholas and to Hitler's speeches crackling over the shortwave radio as Granny railed back at the disembodied voice of the dictator. An assortment of aunts, uncles, and cousins passed through the house during Denise's childhood. Denise's paternal grandfather and her cousins also lived nearby.

Day-to-day life in the household was dominated by Shim Lakofski, who had built a series of successful businesses, including a real estate development company, after his return to South Africa. In his personal life he was sometimes stern and remote, and given to depressions and black moods that could last for months. In the mid 1930s, four-year-old Denise saw a black cloud descend on the family—one that in retrospect, she realizes, coincided with the death of Granny Rose, the Great Depression, and the rise of Nazism. Granny Rebecca agonized over the fate of her relatives in Latvia; in 1944, she learned that all but one had been killed. And there was always Denise's own childhood fear that the Germans would bomb Johannesburg.

As the war ended and the clouds lifted, Denise found herself in a hopeless struggle for her father's attention. Years later, Denise says, she realized how much he loved her. But as an old-fashioned patriarch, Shim Lakofski found it difficult to show affection to all but the youngest of his brood, while at the same time he expected Denise—as the oldest—to look after her siblings. "Her father must have been hell to grow up with," says Robin Middleton, a friend from South Africa and an architectural historian at Columbia University. "No one could talk when he came home tired. No one could make a noise. Everything was subordinated to his moods."

Of all his children, it was Denise who resembled Lakofski most—in her character, if not her appearance—and who was most influenced by him. Just as her early relationships with men were informed by her girlish efforts at pleasing her father (though she was too proud to admit it)—and by an acute sensitivity to her father's moodiness, which eventually took a heavy toll on her parents' marriage—so she also inherited his strength and integrity, as well as a special mix of idealism and practicality. For Lakofski was known for building good, orderly, well-serviced buildings. He cared enormously about what these buildings looked like, not only choosing the building materials but even going so far as to tear down structures that were not built to his precise specifications. He was determined to build buildings of good value and would rail at the "WASP" architects who designed five-foot-wide corridors (because architects' fees were based in part on a percentage of the construction costs) when a width of three feet would do just as well.

Denise was always earnest and hardworking, but she also had a streak of stubbornness and defiance. As one of the few Jewish girls at the exclusive—though racially progressive—Kingsmead school for girls, she wasn't accepted by her wealthy Protestant classmates, nor did she quite fit in with the school's small clique of Jewish girls. Possessing a keen and precocious intelligence, Denise was—just as her mother had been—always a year or two younger than her classmates. So when the other girls donned stockings and lipstick and took to going to the movies on their own, Phyllis kept Denise at home, well scrubbed and in socks, for fear that her daughter would become "too blasé" if she grew up too fast. ("Can you imagine me ever being blasé?" Denise now says, laughing.) At first Denise longed to emulate the older girls in her class. But by the time she turned thirteen, she had begun to relish her status as an outsider. In a photograph of her bas mitzvah class, Denise stands defiantly, her head turned away from the camera, wearing the only pair of socks amid a sea of stockinged legs. "You can tell from the picture that that girl is going to go far," she quips—far, that is, from the world of Johannesburg's bourgeoisie.

By the time Denise enrolled at the University of Witwatersrand, she already stood out as something of an iconoclast. Diana Goldstein, a university classmate who went on to practice architecture in San Francisco, noticed immediately "a kind of intensity and passion and ambition and moral fiber" about her. Like her mother, Denise had blossomed into a young woman of delicate Pre-Raphaelite beauty, thin and pale, with a mane of wavy copper-colored hair. But she resisted pressure from her peers—and even, ironically, from her parents—to wear makeup or to "do something" with her unruly hair. Rather than buy fashionable clothes, she often bought boys clothes—simple cotton camp shirts and trench coats that couln't be found in the women's department. And on weekends, while her classmates went to parties and movies, Denise was just as likely to embark on a camping expedition with a club of amateur archeologists, in search of stone-age implements in the hills around Johannesburg.

In those days, South Africa was a cultural backwater. Denise allied herself early on with an intellectual group of "horribly precocious pip-squeaks" who looked at paintings, read Camus and F. Scott Fitzgerald, and spent long hours lying in the grass debating the future of cities. Her intimates would come to include Diana Goldstein, Robert Scott Brown, whom she would later marry, her sister, Ruth, and Robin Middleton, who would become an eminent architectural historian and a close companion of Ruth's. "We thought of ourselves as pioneers in modern architecture," recalls Goldstein, whom Denise initially shunned for being loud, "vampy," and boy-crazy but who won a prize as the most gifted woman student at the university. Gradually, Denise and Diana became fast friends, their lives shadowing each other through their marriages and across continents, until both became architects in the United States. In a pattern that would repeat itself over and over in her most important relationships, the soft-spoken redhead found a soul mate in one who was—at least on the surface—her absolute opposite.

Yet it was Denise's relationships with Robert Scott Brown and with her sister Ruth that would prefigure most tellingly Denise's marriage to Robert Venturi. Her relationship with Ruth highlights both her competition with and her attraction to an iconoclastic creative spirit. As the two oldest children—Ruth is two years younger than Denise—the Lakofski girls grew up as strong, if often reluctant, allies. "She and Ruth are totally unalike," notes Robin Middleton. "Denise [is] rational, Ruth intuitive. Denise [is] prosaic, Ruth poetic." In high school, Denise was the good girl, Ruth the rebel. This was precisely the image Denise always fought against. Yet, the two girls shared a kinship that belied their apparent differences. During the Depression, and during the bleakest moments in the Lakofski house, Ruth clung to Denise. The younger sister followed the older one's lead both intellectually and socially. Both girls were drawn to the arts—architecture in particular. Soon after Denise went abroad to finish her studies at London's Architectural Association, Ruth followed her there.

When it came to men, Denise found herself drawn to Robert Scott Brown even though his credentials didn't quite fit those she expected of a prospective mate. Raised in the 1950s, with old-world European Jewish values, she had never questioned that she would marry young and marry a Jew. Yet she was tired of Jewish men who dated her as an attractive prospect, as Lakofski's daughter. Worse, from Denise's perspective, few of the Jewish men she met came even close to being her intellectual equal. She rebuffed one such suitor by telling him that she would only marry an architect. She had kept her distance from Scott Brown initially because she knew his father to be a "WASP," a "club man," and an anti-Semite.

But Denise also was drawn to him, particularly to the combination of "intelligence" and "idealism" that she sensed in him. Robert Scott Brown was tall and muscular, but he spoke with a slight lisp. It was Diana Goldstein who had first pointed him out to Denise, insisting that he was not his father's son, that while the senior Scott Brown was Presbyterian and reactionary, his son took after the iconoclastic liberalism of his half-Jewish mother.

During her third year at the university, Denise and a clique of architecture students set out to organize an exhibition entitled "Man-made Johannesburg," which was to be modeled after a similar show that had been mounted in the United States. Denise was put in charge of the project. She appointed Robin Middleton and Robert Scott Brown—the two men whom she found most attractive—to committees on the project. Robin was to be the exhibition's designer. So Robert and Denise took off in search of the city's best buildings on Robert's motorcycle, Denise in her "snazzy" black corduroy pants suit. Soon the two were inseparable, racing around Johannesburg for weeks on end on the bike, looking at buildings, visiting architects' offices, and collecting photographs and drawings. "It was a fantastic education, learning about the 1910s, 20s, 30s, and 40s," recalls Denise. "Looking at hundreds of buildings. Figuring out which were good and which weren't. Doing school work in the evenings and on vacations."

One afternoon, it began to rain. Robert and Denise pulled over to a shelter on the side of the road to protect the photographs that Denise had been balancing on her lap. They spent more than an hour there, waiting for the rain to stop. "Robert started talking about the 'dear' cows his mother raised on her farm in Natal," Denise recalls. It continued to rain. As Robert kept talking about the farm and the "dear" cows, Denise remembers wondering, "Is that all the conversation he's got?"

But there was something alluring to Denise about this man who was so drawn to the city and yet so rooted in the land his mother farmed. A few weeks after the rainstorm, during another run for photographs, Robert suggested going to see a film. They picked up a package of photographs, went to the movies, and then returned to the university to continue working on the exhibition. A few weeks before the opening of their exhibition, Robert asked her out on a proper date—to a Gilbert and Sullivan operetta. The performance wasn't scheduled until after their final exams, though, filling Denise with anticipation as they made the final preparations for "Manmade Johannesburg."

The exhibition opened in the spring of 1951 and was widely praised by the faculty. Denise and Robert couldn't savor the triumph, though, because exams were upon them and they were thoroughly unprepared. The two architecture students had done little of their schoolwork. "There was nothing left for us to do but to go straight on working together to learn for the exams," recalls Denise. "So we went to my house and swotted together, as we called it," for over a week.

It was after one of these study sessions, just as Robert was preparing to leave her house, that he blithely remarked to Denise, "One day I'll tell you what I think of you."

"Well, what do you think of me?" she demanded to know then and there.

"Stop being so serious," he said, and leaned over and kissed her.

"And I just kissed him right back," says Denise, as though she is still quite proud of her daring.

By the time of their date for the Gilbert and Sullivan operetta, Denise and Robert were in love. Robert invited Denise to his mother's farm, where she and her second husband practiced organic farming and herded cattle on a 120-acre triangle of land that abutted a canyon known as Oribi Gorge. Denise learned that Robert was, indeed, partly Jewish. In Robert's mother's house, she discovered a world much like the one her mother had described of her own girlhood. She learned that Robert clashed with his own father much as Denise feared Shim Lakofski and, in response to his father's reactionary conservatism, had cultivated a fervent idealism about architecture and South Africa that mirrored her own. It was a magical summer, spent hiking through the gorge, helping one of the family servants build a house, and mostly just talking—about architecture, about South Africa, and about sex. "We talked a whole lot about sex." Denise chuckles. "We weren't doing it, of course—we were very proper and felt we were too young. But we talked about it," endlessly.

Their talks—and in many respects the initial magic that comes with first love—ended with the summer. During the fourth of their five-year architecture program, students were encouraged to take an apprenticeship in an architect's office. Denise had made plans to try to find work in London. Although she was very much in love, she set off for Europe in March 1952. After a few months in England she even took a European tour, stopping in Germany along the way for a look at the vanquished Reich. Robert remained behind, living on his mother's farm and apprenticing in an architect's office in Natal.

Swept up in the excitement of postwar London, Denise found a job in an architect's office almost immediately and enrolled at the Architectural Association School of Architecture, one of the leading outposts of Modernist architecture. Her arrival in England in the early 1950s coincided with a period of utopian excitement in architecture that melded Modernist aesthetics with a socialist sensibility and the need to rebuild after the war. At the AA, she came under the influence of men like Arthur Korn, a German refugee who had helped design the MARS plan for postwar London—a visionary blueprint that called for linear bands of buildings that would run perpendicular to large roadways with parks in between. (Like many such architectural thought pieces, the MARS plan was influential in design circles but never implemented as such.) Korn's "communist rhetoric . . . Utopianism . . . social view of architecture . . . and great-hearted pedagogic style imbued us with a mission," Denise later recalled. "We were to be commandos for social change and regeneration through architecture." In those heady days after World War II, young architects saw themselves not as lone master builders or superstars but as soldiers in a great municipal crusade to rebuild shattered cities, and Denise was eager to become part of the campaign.

She was further buoyed by the letters from home. Robert wrote frequently and passionately. Although he remained in Natal, he lived away from the farm and shared with Denise such exploits as his unsuccessful attempts to cross the color barrier by befriending a young Indian whose father owned the local general store where Robert and Denise had often stopped to admire exotic fabrics. He proudly wrote to her of running across some young women whom he and Denise had met during a visit to Natal, and his decision *not* to look them up again; Denise interpreted the reference as Robert had meant her to: as a declaration of love and loyalty.

But time and distance would eventually take their toll. When Denise returned home for a visit in about July 1953, more than a year after leaving Johannesburg, she sensed that Robert's ardor had cooled. At first he seemed happy enough to see her. But there was the gnawing issue of commitment. Left behind, Robert seemed to resent Denise's greater independence. Eventually, he had even begun to see other women. What was most disturbing, however, was the fact that Robert seemed sometimes not to be there at all. "I'd be talking to him," recalls Denise, "and he'd suddenly switch off. At those times I called him Brick Wall Brown."

It took years for Denise to figure out that however much fickleness might have contributed to his mood, Robert probably also suffered from depression—periods of lethargy and uncommunicativeness. Having lived for years with her father's dark clouds, she found Robert's bouts of coldness particularly frustrating. As she prepared to return to England, though, Denise was plagued by the knowledge that Robert had invited another woman to the architects' ball, which was to take place shortly after her scheduled return to England. If only Denise would remain in Johannesburg, Robert insisted, he would of course be taking her.

If she thought about putting off her return to England, she overcame the impulse and was back in London in time for the next term. But Denise was devastated. For the first time in her life, she felt as though she was "going to pieces." She was overwhelmed by a terrifying "crisis of meaninglessness," a feeling that would return two or three times during her relationship with Robert.

Her reaction to the crisis with Robert couldn't have seemed more out of character. Denise was, after all, a young woman of boundless inner strength and courage. She had been a bulwark for her family, a leader at school, an adventurer who had gone halfway around the world to work and study in a strange city, and a fearless traveler who, during her trip through Germany, had associated with former members of the Hitler Youth just "to figure out how their minds work[ed]." Yet somehow Denise had fallen into a miasma of lovesick despair.

There was, indeed, more to her pain than the fear of personal loss. For all her commitment to learning and to architecture, she also had developed a particularly "feminine dependence" on Robert. Denise had been reared, after all, to marry. And although she scorned the girls at university who were there only for their Mrs. degrees, she too had measured every man she dated as a potential husband. Was he Jewish? Was he an architect? After Robert kissed her for the first time, she had admitted as much to him. "Well, of course I'd never marry you because you're not Jewish," she exclaimed the very next day.

"I didn't ask you," he replied, an answer that, she acknowledges, "scared" and embarrassed her.

Yet for now, anyway, her adventurous side had won out. She took leave of Robert and returned to the AA. In Johannesburg, she had discovered how dependent she could become on a man. Back in London, she learned an even more valuable lesson: If she could throw herself into her work, into the study of buildings and neighborhoods, and surround herself with like-minded, sympathetic colleagues and teachers, she could find her bearings again.

It was at about this time that Denise discovered so-called Brutalism, an architectural movement that captured her imagination for several reasons. For one thing, the movement's principal proponents were the Smithsons, a husband-wife team who were as well known for their critique of architecture, which "opened [our] eyes to machines, folk architecture, even popular architecture and advertising," as for their buildings. Although Peter and Allison Smithson were not yet teaching at the AA, they were being sought out by a small group of maverick students—among them Denise—who were drawn to the way the couple seemed to flout "the canons of architectural taste," especially the sterile, monolithic sameness that constituted much of orthodox Modernism in the 1950s. It was through the Smithsons that Denise would first come to view urbanism as the study of "communities of varying degrees of complexity," in which "complexity" was to serve as the guiding principle for design and planning.

But Robert was never far from her thoughts. Stubborn and determined, Denise had probably already decided that she would marry him—although Robert was still a long way from asking her. Despite their difficulties, he had spoken of coming to England, but there was a major obstacle: Robert had no money and refused to ask his father, who always had seemed determined no to "spoil him," for any. Finally, Lakofski, who perhaps feared that a woman of Denise's temperament—a "handful," as she must have been thought of in those days—might have difficulty finding a husband, hired Robert to investigate new construction techniques in Germany. The job would pay Robert's way to Europe, although he would have to win a scholarship to pay his expenses at the AA.

On his way to Germany in the spring of 1954, Robert suggested that Denise meet him in Israel. She got to Tel Aviv before he did and was filled with anticipation as she waited for him at the airport. They set off through the Promised Land on a journey that promised to be a magical reunion, but the experience was too much for Robert. Embarking, with Lakofski's backing, on a trip to the new Jewish State, where an expectant and determined lover awaited, Robert once again became "Brick Wall Brown." Soon he wouldn't even hold Denise's hand. When she prodded him to learn what the matter was, Robert would only say that he just needed a little time. For Denise, meanwhile, the trip turned into a nightmare. They hitchhiked around the country, most nights staying in kibbutzim, where, in keeping with the liberal mores of the communal culture, Denise and Robert were always put in the same room. Here she was, still a virgin, longing for the man she loved, forced to share a room with him. Although Denise wasn't yet ready to sleep with Robert, she wasn't prepared for the fact that he wouldn't even touch her!

After Israel, Robert went on to Germany to complete his assignment for Lakofski, while Denise returned alone to London, in a worse tailspin than before. She was utterly depressed, incapable of concentrating on her schoolwork. She had planned to complete her architect's certificate in less than one year, and she hadn't even chosen a thesis topic. "I simply didn't care whether I finished on time," she recalls.

Yet not once did she ask herself why she was willing to put up with Robert's insecurity and uncommunicativeness. Not once did she question the wisdom of her commitment. She was, after all, nearly twenty-three. It was time to get married. And Robert, she had decided, was the man for her.

Whatever she thought of herself during her worst moments, it was Denise's good fortune that her teachers and classmates saw her as something of a gifted pioneer, not as a lovesick bluestocking on the verge of spinsterhood. Although women were a rarity at the AA, Denise was accepted as one of the boys—as much as any woman was in those days. "I was the subject of considerable interest at the school," recalls Denise. "I was South African, and a girl, and pretty." It probably helped that she had a reputation for being exceptionally bright. Her design projects, which included a circular auction hall, were widely praised, and she was in line for an honors diploma. Just as she was once again ready to wallow in lovelorn self-doubt, she got a call from a classmate, asking whether she would like to collaborate on a thesis project.

The prospect of a real project once again shook her out of her lethargy. Brian Smith, Denise's collaborator, had chosen a hilly site in a Welsh mining village on which to design workers' housing. From the beginning, Denise and Brian agreed to eschew the sort of massive housing complex à la Le Corbusier that was then in vogue among the Modernist architects. Instead, they planned a pueblo-like honeycomb of two-story buildings, each of which would accommodate six to eight families grouped around a landscaped courtyard. Because the site was hilly, the duo positioned the buildings so that each apartment would open onto terra firma—either the courtyard within or the street behind the buildings. "We were trying hard not to do Ville Radieuse," says Denise, referring to the Corbusian ideal of high-rises surrounded by parks and roadways. She already had come under the influence of the

Brutalists and was looking to design something on a more human scale. Subtlety, however, wasn't high on the academic agenda. "At the AA if we were given a building to design between two others on a London street, most students would change the brief and replan the whole block," she recalled. "Those who stuck to the requirements and produced a town building were often called dentists, cavity fillers, by the faculty."

While the rest of the class had spent months putting together their projects, Denise and Brian completed theirs in just six weeks. If their teachers frowned on the speed with which the two knocked off their thesis, they were aghast at the results. For although a "community-oriented" approach might sound sensible and attractive today, in that era of avowed utopian Modernism it was heresy. The faculty couldn't fault their methods or the feasibility of the final design, which was neatly detailed and bound in a book, but, notes Denise, "they wouldn't praise it" either. They especially objected to the uniformity of the units, even though she and Smith pointed out that because the development was designed to be built into a hill—as in San Francisco—each unit would be uniquely positioned and hence have a unique feel. The faculty, which in the past had frequently praised Denise's work for its "sensitivity," deemed the housing project "insensitive"—a particularly egregious breach for a woman—and withheld the honors from her diploma.

Denise couldn't have cared less. By this time, Robert had arrived from his assignment in Germany. He was broke and surly, uneasy about being so far from home and insecure about his abilities as an architect. With determination, Denise set about the delicate task of boosting his confidence and of introducing him to her London life. She invited Arthur Korn to tea, counting on her teacher's passion for architecture and Modernism to fire Robert's imagination. She introduced him to Brian Smith and to her other friends at the AA—where he did win a scholarship. Conscious of the fact that their relationship had been born in the excitement and shared work of the "Manmade Johannesburg" exhibition, Denise decided to enroll, together with Robert, for a one-year course that focused on planning and building problems in tropical countries. Although she had already completed her architect's certificate, she justified the decision by telling herself: "We're Africans; it would be good to have this. And to do some studying with Robert."

With a new city to explore, and a community of common friends and interests, Robert and Denise grew close once again. They visited the Smithsons, roamed through London looking at buildings and taking photographs, and worked together on school projects.

They also began sleeping together. After years of talking about sex and reading every book they could find on the subject, including the books of Eustace Chesser, a British expert on birth-control, Denise decided it was time to consummate the relationship. Like most young women of her generation, she had never been to a gynecologist and had been taught nothing about contraception. Her mother had talked with her about sex years before, but these were childhood discussions about "the greatest mystery on earth," and not at all informative for a young woman. To find out what she needed to know, Denise turned once again to self-help books and even phoned Chesser, who referred her to a gynecologist. The doctor examined Denise and fitted her with a diaphragm. During her next visit, Denise "horrified" the doctor by bringing Robert with her and showing him a diagram that illustrated how the diaphragm fits over the cervix. "The doctor took me aside and said, 'This is something you do by yourself and don't tell your husband about.' But Robert was a farm child—and I knew he'd be interested."

Of course, Denise and Robert weren't actually married yet. And soon their conversations about London and about architecture shifted, once again, to the old arguments about commitment. Denise wanted to get married. Robert worried that he was too young, that he wasn't ready. Eventually, his resistance eroded. By the time Denise was ready to visit her family again, Robert told her that she might as well ask her parents for permission to marry—although he also told her that he still thought he was too young.

While Denise was certain that she "belonged with Robert," her friends weren't so sure. Elizabeth MacCrone, her closest friend from Kingsmead, asked her: "Will he be enough for you? Will he be intelligent enough for you?" Several acquaintances commented on Denise's extraordinary force of character and wondered aloud if, during the course of a lifetime together, Robert would be able to keep up with her.

Ironically, it was Robert's father who tipped the balance. After Denise paid him a visit to tell him of their plans, James Scott Brown fired off a letter to his son, telling Robert he was making a grave mistake—that their religious differences were insurmountable. That was all Robert needed to firm up his resolve.

Denise returned to London to prepare the wedding. Like everything else she put her mind to, the ceremony, rooted in architecture, was executed with exacting detail. To avoid a religious confrontation, Denise and Robert agreed to be married in a registry office. So Denise searched out a registry office in Kensington that was intimate enough for the occasion. There was just one problem. By law, couples were assigned to registry offices based on their residence, and neither Robert nor Denise lived in Kensington. To establish the required residency, Denise moved in with Ruth, who *did* live in Kensington, for several weeks. After the ceremony, the newlyweds and guests were to gather at a reception in the Gorham, a small old hotel that she and Robert had picked because, although a little frayed at the edges, it was pretty and intimate as well.

If traditional architecture served as the venue for their wedding, then modernism was the leitmotif. Denise designed a rectangular, Brutalist wedding cake and roamed the London bakeries until she found the baker to Fortnum and Mason's, who agreed to help modify Denise's original design so that it could be built out of eggs and butter. Instead of rectangles, which couldn't sustain the weight of the structure, the baker created two double-decker oval shapes. In the Brutalist tradition, the edges of the cake were left hard-edged, bare of icing. Refusing the usual flourishes of colored flowers and doodads, Denise asked the baker to decorate the cake in soft leaves and petals, made of the same white icing that covered the horizontal surface of the cake.

Her dress was just as painstakingly planned, researched, and executed. Denise had set her heart on a simple, modernist wedding suit that was to be a straight-edged Brutalist structure, devoid of curves or decoration. She roamed the London boutiques and pored through magazines until she found the right dressmaker to produce it for her. Discovering that her chosen designer was located on the Isle of Wight, she made the daylong journey there by train, boat, and bus. Again negotiations ensued. The designer insisted that Denise's angular design wasn't suited for her curvaceous figure. Agreeing that function must sometimes follow form, Denise gave in to a more curvy, baroque confection.

Finally, Denise and Robert were married at the Kensington registry office on July 21, 1955. Denise's parents hadn't planned to attend the wedding but flew to London at the last minute. Although James Scott Brown had softened in his opposition, neither of Robert's parents made it to the wedding, though one of his favorite cousins, Melo MacRobert, showed up, also at the last minute, and performed a Zulu war dance.

From a room at the Savoy Hotel, where she spent the last few days before the wedding, Denise orchestrated the flurry of final preparations, confident and ecstatic. For even as her long-awaited marriage to Robert approached, Denise was already busy planning a new adventure for their first years together as husband and wife.

While Robert had frequently been plagued by doubts about his relationship with Denise and his abilities as an architect, the one thing he was certain of was his commitment to Africa. Although Denise loved England and had often thought she would like to stay there, she never questioned that the broad direction of her life would be shaped by Robert's ambitions, particularly his determination to return to Africa, the continent of his birth, and "give something back." While she agreed to follow him home eventually, Denise convinced Robert that their architectural education was still not complete. Through the Smithsons, Denise had discovered the American architect Louis Kahn, who was, according to Peter Smithson, the only American architect with whom it was worth studying. So the Scott Browns made plans to enroll in the University of Pennsylvania, where Kahn was teaching at the time. Philadelphia was put off for more than two years, though, until Robert turned twenty-six, in 1957, when he would no longer be subject to being drafted into the U.S. Army. In the meantime, the couple set off for Europe, including Rome, where they had gotten jobs in an architect's office for six weeks.

During their Roman hiatus, Denise's doubts about the orthodoxies of modernism grew. Denise and Robert roamed the streets and squares of the city, photographing signs and storefronts and street life amid an eclectic array of Baroque and Romanesque architecture. They discovered a humanized monumentality and the special intimacy of the piazzas.

Nine months later, they returned to Johannesburg, where they discovered a low-income housing boom that Denise found both "horrifying" and intriguing. The plan called for "endless regimented rows" of single-family houses in the black townships around Johannesburg, including parts of Soweto. When Denise wondered why the architects hadn't designed the sort of utopian, Le Corbuisier–inspired high-rise apartment complexes that were the modernist ideal, one of the planners gave her an answer she would never forget: "The South African way of life is to have your own little house with a piece of ground around it. Why would we want it for ourselves and not also give it to Africans?" Although she chafed against the inherent paternalism of the planner's message, architecturally it made a great deal of sense.

What Denise had discovered was a massive poor man's Levittown that would be, in many respects, far more successful than the drab high-rise housing projects—many of which became urban tenements—that were built in the United States at about the same time. The plan called for the South African government, together with the Anglo American Corporation, a gold- and diamond-mining concern, to build about 300,000 units of housing over three years. What's more, the black bricklayers who worked on the project were each given two different colors of brick, which they laid in a variety of patterns, lending each tiny structure a unique character. Each house also was allotted two fruit trees, providing shade and breaking up the monotony of look-alike houses.

By the time the Scott Browns reached Philadelphia, in 1958, Denise was ready to develop her own critique of modernism. For one thing, the social tensions that would rock America during the sixties were already being keenly felt at Penn. In fact, Denise found the environment there so intellectually stimulating that she wondered how she had made it through life, thus far, without it.

Although the Scott Browns had initially moved to the University of Pennsylvania to study under Louis Kahn, it was only after their arrival that they learned that Kahn did not teach at the planning school. So initially, Denise and Robert immersed themselves in social planning and urbanism. With their studies financed through grants and funds supplied by their parents, the couple planned to complete their master's degrees in city planning during the next two years and to have a baby. (Denise would go on to get a master's degree in architecture from Penn in 1965.) The 1950s were a time in which social planning would come to alter the practice of city planning and the urban landscape for several decades. Penn was one of the first places where social scientists were challenging the competence of architects to deal with urban blight. The social planners saw that the problems and solutions to urban decay were often rooted more in poverty and party politics than in the way buildings and streets were designed. Architects were perceived as elitist, utopian do-gooders who did more harm than good, especially for the urban poor. Denise recognized that the critique was often incorrect—eliminating architects would hardly solve the ills of urban America—but for the pair of idealists out of Africa and indoctrinated in the modernist dogma of the AA, the debate at Penn related to the ideas they had first learned about in South Africa and expanded with the Smithsons, and opened a whole new way of looking at urban problems. Among the professors who would have a marked influence on Denise was Herb Gans, who had just moved to Levittown as a participant-observer of the new community. It wasn't until 1960 that Denise—though not Robert—finally took a design class with the famous Lou Kahn.

The Scott Browns—stunningly attractive, intense, and a little mysterious—found themselves in an intellectual environment tailor-made for Denise's temperament, much more so than for Robert's. Since their days of cramming together in Johannesburg, Robert had always gotten slightly higher grades than Denise, but at Penn the scales tipped in the other direction. At first most of their teachers gave husband and wife the same marks. But by their second semester, Denise had clearly emerged as a star. "I once saw them presenting a project to a jury," recalls Bob Venturi, who wouldn't meet Denise formally for another two years. "She was [clearly] a leader, and she had a certain presence and grace." Chester Rapkin, now professor emeritus at Princeton, calls Denise one of the "star students" of his career. "She was confident, subtle, and forceful at the same time. Very soon, she captivated the whole school." Robin Middleton contends that had Denise and her first husband remained together, eventually "she might have had to leave Robert. He might have been so driven into the background that there may have been no place for him to exist."

Indeed, by their second semester at Penn there already were growing signs of competition—and tension—between husband and wife. "Robert was somewhat depressed," recalls Denise. He was perturbed that she was doing better academically. As always, Denise was determined to defuse the tension between them. By her own admission, she had not yet developed a sense of feminist defiance and accepted, almost without thinking, the role of wife as a somewhat secondary one. She agreed with David Crane, her student adviser at the time, when he told her that although she might do better than Robert at school, in life her "place would be behind her husband."

By the time their exams were over in the spring of 1958, both Denise and Robert needed a vacation. They decided on a short visit to New Hope, Pennsylvania, and set off in a Hudson Rambler that Robert had purchased soon after they arrived in the States. But Denise could feel the brick wall descending between them. Robert lit his pipe, even though he knew that his smoking irritated her, and then announced that a spark had burned a hole in his polyester trousers. "I'll murder you," she muttered in reflexive exasperation. No sooner had the words left her lips than she regretted them. A "great feeling of remorse" swept over her, and she took his free hand—the one that wasn't holding the wheel. They sat quietly, hand in hand, as though to apologize to each other. Suddenly, as they were crossing an intersection near Doylestown, an elderly man in a large old Chevrolet ran a stop sign and swerved into the lane of oncoming traffic. The hulking car crashed into the tiny Rambler, which flipped over, throwing Denise free. Robert remained trapped inside. Several minutes later—what at the time seemed like hours—Robert was loaded into an ambulance. He died on the way to the hospital.

There was probably nothing Robert could have done to avoid the accident. He had turned the wheel in an unsuccessful attempt to avoid the oncoming car. But Denise, who had driven thousands of miles with Robert, was convinced that his reaction time had been slow. Robert had been disappointed with his performance at school—especially when he compared it with Denise's. He had wanted to be an architect and suddenly didn't know what he was doing in Penn's planning school. He didn't want to be in America or England. He wanted to be back in Africa. No matter how many times Denise replayed the picture of Robert turning that wheel, it was as though she could see the old depression and lethargy sweep over him, filling him again with a "sense of hopelessness," slowing his reflexes.

For months, she hovered between depression and fear over Robert's death. Bereft and stranded half a world away from home and family, Denise was taken to the home of a cousin on Long Island. There she would pace the lawn of the suburban house, heavily sedated, Robert's watch strapped to her wrist, saying over and over again: "It's a game; he'll come back," not fully believing or accepting his death. She couldn't shake the thought that only a few inches had separated the two of them at the instant of the crash—inches that had meant the difference between her life and his death. Although she fought to maintain control, Denise was haunted by the fact that she had chosen their route, carefully mapping out a way to circumvent the weekend traffic. And then there was the knowledge that Robert had died depressed, and the fear that her accomplishments might have somehow soured the last few weeks of his life—indeed, that they might have contributed in some small, but perhaps final, way to his demise.

With time, Denise would overcome her grief, but as with every other important experience of her life, Denise integrated her memories of Robert Scott Brown into the fabric of her ongoing life. Long after his death, she kept in touch with his parents—even the fearsome James Scott Brown. Because Robert had been an only son, and because she had published under his name, she kept Scott Brown even after her marriage to Robert Venturi. Scott Brown's watch remains strapped to her wrist. And while she learned to drive when she was just eighteen— one of the few women of her generation to do so—since his death she has never been able to bring herself to sit behind a wheel.

The autumn following Robert's death, Denise returned to Penn to complete her degree. Together, she and Robert had been the most romantic couple on campus; after Robert's death, her mystique as the "tragic" widow took on almost mythic proportions. Before long, her fellow students, most of whom were men, discovered that she ate breakfast every morning at seven-thirty in the law school dining hall, and some of them could be counted on to turn up at her table. "Half of the architects were in love with her," recalls Steven Izenour, who was a student of Bob Venturi's at Penn and has worked at the firm almost since its inception. Her teachers too were "so horrified" at what had happened that they were ready to do anything for her.

Like Lee Krasner, Denise Scott Brown had been suddenly, violently—albeit unwillingly—liberated from her marriage. And as with Krasner, that liberation allowed her to accomplish a body of work that she may well never have mastered at the side of a husband whose needs often came close to overwhelming her own. Robert's death initiated a period of mourning and a five-year bout of intense work and study in which grief clarified Denise's intellectual interests and helped lay a foundation for her career as an architect and urban planner.

Denise remained deeply shaken during her final year at the university—so much so that when it came time to graduate, she still wasn't "emotionally ready to leave Penn." She had served, informally, as a teaching assistant during her final year, and so when she searched for something to do after graduation, she looked for a job that would allow her to maintain her ties to the school. In the end, Denise proposed offering a studio course that would serve as an introduction to urban design for city planners—a request the faculty was more than happy to grant.

Her decision to become a full-time academic was driven in large part by the fact that it was still difficult for a woman to get a job at a leading architectural firm. At the same time, it soon became obvious that, in teaching, Denise had found her vocation. "If I had any pangs or stage fright, they didn't last more than twenty minutes," she recalls. "I realized that I was born to do this." Her course for urban planners was a model-building approach to architecture and urban planning that came to be a Scott Brown trademark. "She was a brilliant designer," notes G. Holmes Perkins, who was dean of Penn's architecture school during the 1950s and 1960s, and who recalls how Denise distinguished herself from the very outset. "She developed an entirely original program for teaching studio to beginning city planners."

Indeed, Denise's studios were a pedagogical tour de force, a multidisciplinary exercise in planning and in cultivating the imaginations of her students. Denise's studios were designed to dissect a wide range of planning challenges, whether developing a deserted island or redesigning a commercial strip in Houston. Over the years, these courses became a sort of laboratory where she would develop her ideas about urbanism. The studios "involved a process of learning—reading, researching, immersing yourself" in a community or a building form, recalls Fred Schwartz, who taught a studio with her at Harvard during the late 1980s. "It involved far more preparation on the part of the professor," he adds, recalling how he and Denise spent an entire summer putting together a fifty-page syllabus that was meant to serve, among other things, as a total immersion in the sociological, economic, and urban fabric of their subject.

Unlike traditional studios, which centered on real cities that could be visited and analyzed, Denise's first design course, "The Shipwrecked Planner," was built around an entirely imaginary world and was aimed at teaching students in the planning achool about architecture and urban design. Her students were expected to invent an island, complete with topography and climatic conditions, and then work out an architectural and urban plan based upon their own assumptions and needs.

Later on, she devised studios around real—but entirely unorthodox—planning problems. In a studio entitled "The Architecture of Well-Being," which she taught at Harvard, her students were expected to look at the whole subject of personal health and hygiene. They were to design something "small and personal," a space, such as a sauna, that was to be an ideal place for rejuvenation. In the process, the students were expected to look at the subject in its historical context, from Roman baths to the nineteenth-century spas of Europe, and they were to look at the institutional aspects of the problem, including hospices and communal showers for the homeless.

Similarly, through a studio on Las Vegas, which would evolve into the controversial book *Learning from Las Vegas*, her students discovered that urban space does not need to be defined, as it has been historically, by bricks and mortar, but that signs can serve the same purpose. The Las Vegas studio also served as a vehicle for helping students to recapture an appreciation for variety, which, Denise argued, had been jettisoned by the Modernists along with vulgarity.

Most important, perhaps, Denise's studios set out to drive home how dangerous it is for planners to impose rigid guidelines on a community. Urban design is, after all, a little like building a skyscraper in an earthquake zone; you never know when a tremor will hit, and when it does, the fissures could erupt anywhere, with untold consequences. Thus, the best defense is to build in maximum flexibility. To substantiate the point during a studio at Rice University that focused on a vast commercial strip in Houston, Denise asked half the class to come up with the strictest—and thus, by conventional standards, the best—design guidelines and zoning codes they could imagine; the other half of the class was told to design buildings that, while sticking to the letter of the guidelines, would seek to subvert them as much as possible. So when the "planners" asked for "Spanish-style" architecture but failed to specify "Spanish colonial," the architects came up with bizarre Gaudíesque edifices with towers and turrets—buildings that turned out to be "quite wonderful," according to Denise.

Just as the era of urban renewal was picking up steam, Scott Brown embraced what was then a relatively visionary message, put forward primarily by urban theorists at Penn and Berkeley and later by Jane Jacobs: To build effective buildings, architects and planners must understand the sociology and economics of a neighborhood. But at this time many ignored these factors—with dire consequences. The 1960s marked the apogee of a misguided effort on the part of urban planners to reduce the squalor of the inner cities. In places like Buffalo and New Haven, vast swaths of tenements and storefronts were razed. Destroyed in the process was the cultural and sociological fabric of the cities themselves, creating stretches of desolate wastelands of what would more accurately be described as "urban removal." In some urban areas, the demolished neighborhoods were replaced by highways that only served further to empty the city by giving middle- and upper-income residents easy access to the suburbs. Denise Scott Brown realized that even the "ugly" and "outdated" had its uses, that preservation was almost always better than demolition. She embraced the mantra of Paul Kriesis, a Greek planner whom she had met in London in the 1950s, who said: "I'll be happy if I can say I have saved one street."

Kriesis's motto is key to understanding the complex ledger of Denise Scott Brown's accomplishments. While she would become known for some of her planning projects, specifically the design guidelines for Main Street in Miami Beach's Deco District and has always worked on the firm's architectural projects, some of her most important contributions are theoretical. These include her writings, particularly *Learning from Las Vegas*. They also include her efforts to protect some communities from the wrecking ball, from overzealous planners, and, on more than one occasion, from transportation authorities whose plans for new highways cut through poor inner-city communities.

In fact, Denise and Bob Venturi met over just such a "transparent" problem. During her first semester as a junior faculty member, Denise took part in a Penn faculty meeting at which her colleagues discussed plans to tear down a library that had been built on campus by Frank Furness. The year was 1960, and Furness's heavy Victorian edifice, with its short, squat columns and forbidding red brick facade, was considered, according to Perkins, to be "the second-ugliest building" in Philadelphia. (Some believed the ugliest building to be City Hall.) Modernism was in, Victorian architecture was definitely out. Yet Denise loved Furness's quirky edifice, which Lewis Mumford had described as "bold, unabashed, ugly, and yet somehow healthily pregnant." Knowing that her colleagues were likely to vote for the building's demise, she stood up and delivered an impassioned plea to save the structure.

When the meeting was over, she was approached by a quiet young instructor whom she had seen before but to whom she had never been formally introduced. "You know," he said, "I agreed with every word you said."

"Well, then, why didn't you speak up?" she demanded.

The young architect was Robert Venturi, and that initial encounter would speak volumes about the relationship as it was to evolve over the next several years. Ironically, some twenty-five years later, Venturi Scott Brown & Associates was chosen to renovate the building. Now architects and Philadelphians have rediscovered Furness, and the university treats the once-maligned edifice as its crown jewel.

Marrying a Genius

By the time Denise met Bob, she was no longer a coed hellbent on marriage. She had left her home and family, buried a husband, and come up against a well of sadness in herself. If work had been a refuge during the troughs of her courtship with Robert, it was her salvation after his death. During those years, Denise threw herself into work and wasn't thinking about a serious relationship. It was a good thing too, because the old Denise would probably never have had the patience to wait out a glacial courtship with Bob Venturi. It's not that Bob was antisocial or reclusive; it's just that as far back as anyone could remember, he lived for architecture.

Bob Venturi insists that the story his friends like to tell about how he was introduced to great art when he was still in the cradle is entirely apocryphal. But it says a lot about both Venturi and his upbringing that his aesthetic education was said to have started immediately after birth, the day his mother brought him home from the hospital and put him in a cradle above which she had hung a copy of one of Michelangelo's paintings. As an only child born into a strong, close-knit, and somewhat eccentric Italian-American family, Bob Venturi was almost certainly destined to distinguish himself in some way.

Bob's father, Robert senior, was an Italian fruit and vegetable merchant who came to Philadelphia at the age of nine from a small town in the Abruzzi. Although Robert had dreams of going to college, he dropped out of high school at sixteen, when his father died suddenly and he was obliged to take over the family store. Family lore has it that Robert senior had dreamed of becoming an architect. He certainly developed both intellectual and aesthetic aspirations: In 1922, he commissioned Edmund Brumbaugh, a well-known local architect, to design a new store on South Street in Philadelphia. Two years later, he married a fiercely independent and eccentrically intellectual young woman named Vanna Luisi.

It was Vanna Venturi who became the most seminal influence in the life of her only son. Although Vanna had been born to an Italian immigrant family and, like her husband, had been forced to drop out of high school, she educated herself, filled her house with books, and developed a particular interest in George Bernard Shaw, whom she frequently quoted. Possessing a particular passion for vintage costumes and interior design, she amassed a collection of antique furnishings. Emulating a much respected teacher who had been a mentor to her as a young girl, Vanna Venturi wore tailored Chanel-style suits, midcalf in length—no matter what the fashion—and crisp white blouses, a style she adhered to for the rest of her life. Years later, Bob Venturi, who lived with his mother off and on until his marriage, at the age of forty-two, was said to possess an encyclopedic knowledge of furniture and could date any dress since the eighteenth century to within a few years of its manufacture—information no doubt picked up from his mother.

An active pacifist and socialist who voted for Norman Thomas each of the four times he ran against Franklin D. Roosevelt, Vanna cultivated in her son a taste for subversive ideas. She also nurtured in him an abiding love and respect for strong women, which would be reflected not only in his marriage to Denise but, according to one leading critic, also in his work. Vincent Scully, the eminent Yale art historian, notes, in an essay on Venturi's seminal first house (appropriately, the one he built for his mother), the way Venturi's vision seems to be reacting against the traditional heroic male image of "an athletic, aggressive being who fits into but basically dominates the essential shapes of the world." Of the most well-known photograph of the Vanna Venturi House, a direct frontal shot in which an elderly Vanna sits demurely, cross-legged on a kitchen chair, with a pot of geraniums beside her, framed by the doorway of her new home, Scully notes: "Contrasted with the traditional male figure, Vanna Venturi is at once anti-heroic and feminist in meaning. She is stronger than he."

Despite the considerable influence of his family, Bob Venturi's affinity for architecture seemed inborn as much as bred. As a mere toddler, family and friends remember, his near obsession with building blocks and his ability to construct imaginative structures amazed the adults around him. At the beach during summertimes, he spent hours molding sand castles. One night at a dinner party at the Venturis', Phineas Paiste, a well-known Philadelphia architect, got down on his hands and knees and built an imposing structure of blocks for the child. Bob, who was only five years old, is said to have swept the construction away with his hand and announced: "Now I'll show you how to do it."

By the time he got to college, Bob Venturi had developed a serious love affair with architecture. "There was a caringness, not just an undergraduate crush," recalls Philip Finkelpearl, a noted Shakespearean and Jacobean scholar, who was Bob's roommate at Princeton. "You had a sense that in his head he [had stored] all the great buildings that were ever built. . . . And on a Saturday afternoon when there was nothing else to do, he would dream over his architecture books," turning their pages and imagining he was walking through the Baths of Caracalla or Palladio's Villa Rotondo.

Most impressive of all was his uncanny ability to draw. "He had this fantastic drawing ability that we all could respond to," recalls Finkelpearl. Adds Steve Izenour: "Bob Venturi has got the greatest instinctive hand I've ever seen. I've never seen anyone as good as him at putting the right line" in the right place. During his student days at Princeton, a story circulated that Bob could spend all day "deciding on, and drafting, one line." To this day, Venturi doodles endlessly on the backs of envelopes, when he is at the office, or on napkins, if he is at a restaurant, just as in childhood he used to fill up the margins of his schoolbooks.

Bob and Denise were formally introduced sometime after the Furness library debate, at a dinner party given at the home of Denise's mentor David Crane—the same professor who had once told her that as Robert Scott Brown's wife she was destined to take a back seat to her husband. Crane, who apparently still didn't think Denise's life could be complete without a spouse, told her that he thought she and Bob would eventually marry.

Not long after their dinner at the Cranes', Bob asked Denise to accompany him to a football game at Princeton. They got to Bob's eating club in time for the pregame lunch, but to Denise's surprise, when everyone else set off for the football field, Bob steered her to the Princeton architecture library instead. They spent the afternoon roaming through the stacks, poring over architecture books and talking about the things that interested them—Modernism, and the new rage of pop art, and the history of mannerism. That was the afternoon when Denise suggested to Bob that he look once again at the work of Sir Edwin Lutyens, not just as a designer of buildings but as a mannerist architect who distorted the rules of strict classicism, especially in his commercial buildings, with which Venturi wasn't familiar. (Years later, Venturi would be credited with rediscovering Lutyens.) When Bob and Denise returned to his eating club for the postgame party, Denise found that she and Bob were in for some ribbing; since they hadn't bothered to show up at the game, Bob's friends weren't going to tell them the score.

Bob's approach to women was almost as cerebral as his interest in football. Before marrying Denise, he had seriously considered marriage only once before, to his teenage sweetheart, Joanne Mott. After Mott turned him down, probably recognizing their relationship to be one of deep friendship rather than true love, Bob fell occasionally into romantic crushes, but always with intellectual women. After his first tentative proposal to Joanne Mott, however, it would be twenty years before he ever considered marriage again.

Although it would take them years to marry, there was a certain inevitability to Venturi's relationship with Scott Brown. "We were comrades in adversity," Bob said, years after they first met. "Neither of us had been to Harvard. Intellectually, we were the black sheep" at Penn. Friends remember them as two bookworms whose attempts at being "hipsters were always amusing." They liked "mod" talk, but words like "cool" and "groovy" just didn't fall trippingly off their tongues. And while Bob and Denise occasionally bumped into each other at trendy

Philadelphia restaurants while out on a date with someone else, their evenings together invariably were spent at the Quaker Lady, an old-fashioned tearoom that served up "tipsy parson pudding" but no liquor and where Bob also frequently took his mother. In 1961, Denise took on the tutorials for Venturi's course, which covered material that would lay much of the foundation for his seminal book, *Complexity and Contradiction in Architecture*, his opening volley against the orthodoxies of Modernism. Denise's involvement with the course deepened the dialogue between the two architects, which continued to grow in intensity over time. Often in the coming years, Denise and Bob would have dinner early and then return to one of Denise's studio classes on urban design, where Bob would critique her students' work. Or they would go to Bob's office at Penn, where Denise would pore over drafts of *Complexity and Contradiction in Architecture*, or the latest drawings for his mother's house.

Their early courtship provided interludes in what was, for both of them, an intensive career-building odyssey. For Denise, the early 1960s was a time when she immersed herself in work, teaching herself "almost everything she needed to know about her field." For Bob, the same period was devoted to years of such monastic productivity that it became the subject of a running joke among his students: "What does Venturi do all the time? He designs his mother's house." That was almost literally true. For it was during the five or so years leading up to 1965 that Venturi completed both *Complexity and Contradiction in Architecture* and the Vanna Venturi House.

These two projects would establish Venturi's reputation as a leading force in contemporary architecture. The house, with its flat, pale-green facade, incorporated the traditional: a gabled roof; the modern: an airy "Corbusian" interior—that is, an open plan, but with some columns that fall within the room rather than inside the walls; and the mannerist and symbolic: an arched molding over the entryway that looked sketched on, like a sign, the antithesis of a functional support. Vanna's house was hailed as the first "Postmodern" house and the "most important building of the late twentieth century."

Meanwhile, *Complexity and Contradiction in Architecture*, which was published in 1966, was praised by Vincent Scully as "the most important writing on the making of architecture since Le Corbusier's *Vers une Architecture*, of 1923." Drawing on a vast reservoir of historical references, from the Roman Pantheon to the giants of Modernism, Venturi assailed the glass-and-concrete blueprint of the Modern movement as "bland" and "boring." Instead, he praised an architectural aesthetic that is "hybrid rather than 'pure,' compromising rather than 'clean,' distorted rather than 'straightforward,' ambiguous rather than 'articulated.' " In his book, Venturi traced the roots of complexity and contradiction throughout architectural history, including those of such key Modernists as Le Corbusier, who, Venturi points out, often disregarded his own polemical writings, to the benefit of his buildings. Even as Venturi was enduring the creative "agonies" of designing Vanna's house, in his book he pleaded for an aesthetic that would accommodate diversity and sophistication, ambiguity and distortion.

Despite Bob and Denise's shared intellectual interests, the course they taught together, and the beginnings of a collaborative professional relationship, work was so central to their lives that for years they remained little more than casual friends. "We weren't too close," says Bob. "I was too focused on getting to shore. We grew together [only] after she left" Penn.

Sometime in 1965, Denise realized that her interest in Bob Venturi was more than just academic. Bob had invited her to watch the annual Mummers Parade from a house on Broad Street that belonged to friends, which he had just finished renovating. That day, Bob also invited another guest to watch the parade, a two-year-old girl named Helen, who lived in the same building in which Bob shared an apartment with his mother. "I watched Bob with [Helen, and, seeing] him handle this little girl, fell in love," recalled Scott Brown years later. Denise realized that there was something about the image of Bob and Helen that hit a nerve: "It was something to do with what I wanted from my father that he was giving to this little girl."

A few weeks later, while she was preparing to leave for California, to take a job at the University of California at Berkeley, it occurred to Denise that Bob Venturi was the person with whom she wanted to spend her last evening in Philadelphia. "I thought that I would be quite sad the night before I left. So when Bob said 'Let's have dinner together a final time,' I arranged for it to be the night just before I left. I felt I needed a good friend to help me through, and he was a very simpatico person."

Bob was clearly reluctant to see her go. They talked about California, and Bob insisted that she keep in touch and look up some friends of his in Los Angeles.

It was sometime during their dinner and the drinks they had afterward, at the Frank Sinatra Bar, that Denise told him he was wasting his affections on Helen, a little girl who wasn't his. Although Denise had not seen Bob and Helen together since the Mummers Parade, Bob spoke of her often. In response to her comment, Bob didn't say a word.

Eventually, Bob escorted Denise back to her apartment building— as always, to the front door, never beyond. And as the evening drew inexorably to a close, he remarked, as he had often done before: "There's something else I wanted to say, but I can't remember what it is."

"What he was wanting to say was all the things he couldn't say," says Denise, with a knowing chuckle. "That night a funny look crossed his face, and he kissed me, which he didn't normally do." It was, in fact, the first time Bob had tried to kiss her. And he was so nervous that, aiming for her cheek, his kiss landed, instead, on her ear.

Friends speculate that Denise moved to California as the only way to get Bob away from his mother. Although Denise concedes that leaving Philadelphia might have helped their courtship in the long run, at the time of her departure she still had "no intention of marrying Bob."

After a semester at Berkeley, Denise moved to Los Angeles to help start a new school of architecture and urban planning at UCLA. The head of the urban planning department at Berkeley, William Wheaton, one of Denise's mentors, had recommended her for the position. George Dudley, a city planner who was to head the UCLA school and who had gotten to know Denise when they both worked on an ambitious planning project for New York State that had been commissioned by Governor Nelson Rockefeller, was happy to hire her. In her new position, Denise had virtually no full-time faculty, but she did have a budget for visiting professors. One of the first of these she invited was Bob. The plan was for Bob to lecture for four days. The students were then given four days to work alone on their projects, which Bob would critique before returning to Philadelphia. It was during that four-day hiatus that Denise took Bob to Las Vegas for the first time.

For Denise and Bob, Las Vegas delivered a powerful message: It is the people and the atmosphere, every bit as much as the architecture, that give the place definition. Denise was fascinated by the juxtaposition of signs, the "low reader" placards—as they are called by outdoor-sign manufacturers—which mark the entryways to hotels or gas stations, and the "high readers" which tower above the buildings and highways, coaxing drivers to take the next exit ramp to El Morocco or the Stardust. Years later Las Vegas would remind Denise that at the AA in London, she had been taught to view London's Trafalgar Square, with its vast dimensions, low buildings, and ill-defined perimeter, as a failure of urban planning. For all Las Vegas's "vulgarity," wasn't it all a little like Lord Nelson looming above Trafalgar Square, visible from the Strand and beckoning passersby to the fountain and the National Gallery?

"We had a marvelous time, and we began to fall in love," recalls Denise. "And at the end, when we came back to L.A., the last day or two [of Bob's visit] it became a real relationship."

Las Vegas was also important to the relationship, and to Denise in particular, because it served as an inspiration for one of the couple's most important and controversial projects, the "Learning from Las Vegas" studio, which later became the infamous book by the same name. Unlike *Complexity and Contradiction in Architecture*, which had aimed to be a "gentle Manifesto," *Learning from Las Vegas* distilled some of Venturi and Scott Brown's most provocative ideas, including the importance of symbolism in architecture and even the value of things ugly and ordinary. Both books marked an open rebellion against the "less is more," stripped-down aesthetic of Modern architecture—a rebellion that marked Venturi and Scott Brown as outsiders within their profession and locked them out of many major, mainstream commissions.

Learning from Las Vegas, published in 1972, urged architects to become more sensitive to the tastes and needs of "common" people. Scott Brown and her collaborators on the Las Vegas studio, Venturi and Izenour (who was the third author of the book), condemned Modernist architects for failing to understand the symbolic content of classical forms, such as the Baroque duomo, which is far bigger outside than inside in order to create an impressive presence in the city. They saw Las Vegas's Strip, with its bold and gaudy signs, its casinos and neon-covered wedding chapels, not only as a symbol of American vernacular taste but as a valid architectural form. In all its huge, exaggerated form, the Strip illustrated the logic of signs in a country of vast spaces and in a fast-moving, car-driven culture; the billboards and signs of Las Vegas, they argued, beckoned drivers much the way duomos and piazzas attracted pedestrians in Florence.

To make their point, the authors went out of their way to be provocative. They underscored the importance of variety and symbolism in architecture by legitimizing two building forms, which Denise dubbed the Duck and Bob the Decorated Shed. The former was named after a duck-shaped drive-in on Long Island, and refers to a building that is "submerged and distorted by an overall symbolic form"; the latter refers to a functional structure to which the "ornament is applied independently."

By urging architects to embrace a historic eclecticism that could accommodate the "pluralist, mobile, pop, mass culture" of America, the couple redefined the architectural zeitgeist of the 1970s and 1980s. Suddenly, "less [was] a bore," decoration was in again; the car culture was something to be worked with rather than merely despised. After more than a decade of building steel-and-glass boxes surrounded by barren plazas, architects everywhere began rediscovering columns and archways, Queen Anne and Chippendale. Together, the two books succeeded in "chang[ing] a whole generation, enabling architects to move [away] from the very reductive aesthetic of late Modernism," notes Robert A. M. Stern, a prominent New York architect.

But something peculiar happened on the way to the drive-in: *Complexity and Contradiction* was finally embraced by an elite cadre of critics and academics. *Learning from Las Vegas* was something else altogether. A few brave souls praised it as "perversely brilliant," "a book to be disagreed with, challenged and read." While the book was intended to serve as a defense of variety, which the Modernists had discarded along with vulgarity, most critics interpreted it literally, as a celebration of the "worst" of the American landscape, including freeways, neon, billboards, and kitsch in general. *Learning from Las Vegas* was vilified by most architects. Little by little, Venturi came to be credited with inventing postmodernism, the source of all the good that emanated from the firm, while Denise, who was considered the principal instigator behind the Las Vegas book, was viewed as a corrupting influence, a grasping interloper, who was responsible for the firm's "excesses."

Whatever architects may have thought of it, the Las Vegas study was very much Denise's inspiration. "The Las Vegas [project] was totally dependent on Denise for the intellectual rigor of it," says coauthor Steve Izenour. As such, it represents one of the clearest keyholes through which to see Denise's intellectual influence on her husband and on the firm. Venturi concedes that as an outsider, as a South African, Denise helped him "resee" the American landscape. Notes Aldo Rossi, the great Italian architect: "The authors discovered part of the American city, something that we all seemed to know but that is now clearer." It was Venturi who asked, in *Complexity and Contradiction*: "Is not Main Street almost all right? Indeed, is not the commercial strip of Route 66 almost all right?" But "the actual application of such ideas to the larger urban setting increased dramatically after Denise Scott Brown joined the firm in 1967," observed the critic Rosemarie Haag Bletter, referring to the Las Vegas study.

Thus, when the manuscript was finally completed, it was suggested that, in all fairness, Denise's name should go first on the title page. Nothing doing. Both Denise and Bob backed off when the publisher, MIT Press, insisted on leading with the better-known name of Venturi.

In the year or so following their first Las Vegas trip together, Bob and Denise shuttled frequently across the country between UCLA and Yale, where he was then teaching. (Venturi still maintained his base in Philadelphia, where, together with a new partner, John Rauch, he also struggled to establish his fledgling firm.) But it was a cautious courtship. Although Denise had been promised tenure when she moved from Berkeley to UCLA, the faculty had reneged, passing her over before she even began teaching. Her boss, George Dudley, backed her application, but the university's tenure committee turned it down, charging that she had not published enough. In retaliation, during the first preparatory year of the program, before classes had commenced, Denise stayed at home for almost a year to work on a book; she also refused to accept her salary, which had been pegged at the level of an assistant professor, until the department raised her pay to that of an acting associate professor. While some members of the administration perceived her as troublesome, her mentor Dudley continued to give her his backing.

Though assured that she would get her promotion the following year, 1967, Denise was determined to keep her relationship with Bob a secret, for fear that news of the romance—and a potential marriage— might derail her chances. They spent romantic weekends together in places like Palm Desert, or "hiding out" in Santa Monica. And when they once almost ran into a UCLA colleague on the Santa Monica boardwalk, the couple ducked around a corner. "I wasn't about to let anything affect my tenure," says Denise, who notes that even a hint of marriage could stall a woman's career in those days. For one thing, it was assumed that married women would leave to have children. The bias against wives was also fueled by the nepotism rules that had stymied Maria Mayer's career and that still prevented women at many universities from working in the same institutions as their husbands.

Still, Bob and Denise kept up a long-distance romance for close to a year, during which they saw each other no more than three or four times, for periods of only a week or two. Denise was drawn to Bob in large part because of his dedication to architecture and to an architectural vision that, to an uncanny extent, they shared. But Bob's single-minded devotion to architecture also reminded her of Le Corbusier, who had refused to have children because he was afraid they would squelch his creativity. Bob, however, insisted that her concern was unfounded. Although he couldn't quite bring himself to propose, he insisted that he had overcome his reticence, that he was ready for marriage, that he wanted children. So when Shim Lakofski came to New York for a visit, occasioning another trip East for Denise, she invited Bob to join her there. It was sometime during that weekend, holding hands in a New York taxi, that Denise finally popped the question that had been on both their minds for quite some time. "Will you marry me?" she blurted out as the cab careened down the potholed pavement of a wide Manhattan avenue.

"Yes, yes, and yes," replied the perennial bachelor.

Indeed, in Bob, Denise had found both a soul mate and a man who would become an exceptionally affectionate husband. The physical intimacy that developed between Bob and Denise during their courtship is still palpable today. Whether they are standing on an auditorium platform or discussing a design problem at the office, Bob's fingers inevitably find their way to the small of Denise's back or gently grasp her hand. He never fails to notice what she is wearing, and it is not beneath him to accompany her on a shopping expedition to purchase an evening jacket for one of the many formal functions they must attend.

Soon after their secret engagement, the UCLA faculty finally announced that Denise would receive tenure. And not a moment too soon. Denise's students were beginning to suspect something. She and Bob had been spotted at Yale during one of her visits back East. They pressed her to reveal her plans for the following year. "When I got tenure I announced my engagement," says Denise. She pauses a moment, knowing exactly how that sounds. "That's exactly what they say women do, isn't it? But they deserved it," she says, a little defensively, recalling the battle she had had to fight to win tenure.

The Venturis were married in 1967, on the veranda of Denise's bungalow in Santa Monica. Initially, Bob had been aghast at the prospect of so public a ceremony. But Denise had pointed out that their guests could not all fit into the tiny house. By incorporating the street and having their guests stand on the sidewalk, while Bob and Denise said their vows on the veranda, they could accommodate everyone.

Once again, Denise designed a wedding tailored to her own ideals and those of her future husband. The wedding party did indeed spill out onto the street, which had been decorated with pink, yellow, and white paper streamers that spanned the street, suspended from an old-fashioned streetlight and from a large banner that blew in the breeze. An old Chevy painted with daisies and Pollock-like drips, and emblazoned with "God Is Love" on the front grille, was parked in front of the house. The lovemobile belonged to Bill Dubay, a former Catholic priest, who performed a civil marriage ceremony.

Eclecticism was to be the theme of the day. After the ceremony, the guests gathered on the back patio for cocktails and canapés, which were served on napkins embossed "Marriage is almost all right," a pun on Venturi's famous motto, "Main Street is almost all right." Meanwhile, children scampered around the patio, eating ice cream. To feed her adult guests, Denise had hired the best caterer from Beverly Hills, while her wedding cake was produced by a kosher baker in Santa Monica. Just as her first wedding cake had been born of the Brutalist ideals that she and Robert Scott Brown embraced in the 1950s, the dessert for her second wedding was a florid confection, brimming with baroque decorations befitting the "Age of Las Vegas." For the occasion, Denise wore a minidress with a swirling black-and-white art nouveau pattern, while Bob sported a jacket with wide lapels and a wide zooty tie.

What's in a Name?

After their marriage, the newlyweds returned to Philadelphia. Initially, they maintained the fiction that Denise's return was just temporary. She had secured a one-year leave of absence from UCLA. Both she and Bob had loved Los Angeles, and UCLA was more than happy to give Bob a position on the faculty. But uprooting Bob from Philadelphia never seemed very likely. The city had been his home for more than forty years. He had gone to school there. His mother still lived there. He had fought to establish his firm there. The costs of moving to California, especially for his partner, John Rauch, who had five children, were just too steep, Bob argued. What's more, for Bob there was nothing more important than the firm.

The first months of marriage were filled with smaller disappointments as well. A romantic weekend in the country that Denise had planned during the winter after her wedding backfired when Bob, who went along only grudgingly, because he didn't want to be away from the office, insisted on staying in their hotel room and brooding about work. Then too, the newlyweds lived with Bob's mother for the first few months after moving to Philadelphia, so that Denise found herself having to adjust to two strong personalities instead of one.

Yet Denise made no bones about the fact that now Bob and her marriage came first. In the delicate calculus of even a thoroughly modern marriage, she was ready to assume the principal responsibility of establishing a family, even if it meant staying in Philadelphia and giving up her prized position at UCLA. She was thirty-six years old, she "had proven [herself] in a man's world," and she "was going to have a baby." Thus, she came to Philadelphia accepting an open-ended arrangement in which she had no official position in Venturi's tiny firm, even though, as a tenured UCLA professor, she might have expected one. Denise claims that the situation suited her perfectly at first. Her plans, however, went a little awry. After suffering a series of miscarriages, she found herself gravitating more and more toward the office, where she worked on a series of projects, initially without pay.

One thing Denise was sure she was not prepared to do, at first, was work for Bob's firm. "I did worry that Bob's strength would create a crisis of confidence for me," Denise recalls. So she went to the office to work on some articles, and helped manage the fruit and vegetable business that Bob had inherited from his father, who died in 1959. Occasionally, crises would crop up with Bob's clients, and, being there, she would help solve them. John Rauch, who joined Bob in his practice in the early 1960s and served essentially as the firm's business manager until he left in the mid 1980s, began asking for Denise's help in writing the firm's proposals for new work. And she started to help Bob plan and teach his studios at Yale—including the "Learning from Las Vegas" studio. Then she began getting planning projects of her own, and what better place to work than Bob's office? Before long Denise was ensconced full time at the firm.

Yet Denise was leery of invading Bob's turf. Although she had earned a master's in architecture in 1965, Denise never applied for an architect's license. She rarely drew. "Bob is a better designer than I am," she freely concedes. But during her early years at the firm, it was clear that "no one wanted me to draw. Bob has been happy to have me for my complementary skills. I'm not sure he would be so happy if I had

had the same skills." While she always had relished the joys of collaboration, no one needed to tell Denise about the damage professional competition could do to a marriage.

Over the years, the offices the firm bought in Manayunk, an erstwhile warehouse district in Philadelphia that has gradually been infiltrated by trendy restaurants and antique shops, became their home away from home. At all hours of the day and night, including weekends, the spartan renovated warehouse buzzed with activity. Even after their son, Jimmie, arrived, he could frequently be found playing amid the drafting tables and model buildings of the office, in the "spaces between adults," as his mother would say.

In the early 1970s, Bob and Denise bought their house in West Mount Airy, a neighborhood nestled between upper-crust Chestnut Hill and working-class Germantown. The setting was, in its unique eccentricity, vintage Venturi Scott Brown. Denise and Bob had bought the ramshackle mansion knowing that the land around the long private driveway that led from Wissahickon Avenue to their new home had been subdivided and sold by the previous owners. In the first years of their residence, the Venturis had hoped to design their neighbors' homes; instead they were forced to watch as split-level ranch houses sprouted along their narrow drive, creating a touch of Levittown on the doorstep of the elegant stone mansion.

The house, with its fourteen rooms, was perfect for a family. But in the hands of Bob and Denise, it became a design laboratory and perpetual work in progress. Here Bob could experiment with his hand-stenciled wall decorations, many of which are a play on American arts-and-crafts designs. And Denise would pick wallpaper patterns for the bedrooms that would later be invoked in some of the firm's signature buildings and furnishings. As befits the champions of vernacular taste, the generously proportioned living room and parlor are a clutter of mismatched objects, with every horizontal surface crowded with the mementos of their life and travels—a giant pencil, a model of the Desert Inn in Las Vegas, a giant ketchup bottle and ice cream cone. Amid the pop art are fine ceramics and porcelain—the product of Denise's intrepid scavenging through junk and antique shops—and stacks of exquisite architecture books. Rows of chairs, some antique, some new, some merely old, others designed by Bob, snake from room to room. In the parlor, beneath a firmament of exuberant stencils—an explosion of geometric and organic shapes—lies a beautiful antique Oriental rug. But the living room, next door, is lined in industrial carpeting and encircled by institutional steel bookcases.

The dining room is far less cluttered but no less eclectic. The frieze is festooned with one of Bob's art nouveau decorations and the names of his idols—among them, Loos, Le Corbusier, and Toscanini. At its center stand a large wooden library table and chairs, which the couple purchased in the bankruptcy sale of an old Philadelphia hotel. Like the parlor, the living room, and the garden—so beautiful and spacious and located as it is at the edge of deteriorating Germantown that friends have dubbed it the Garden of the Finzi Venturi—the dining room is almost never used. Since Jimmie has grown, just about the only time it is set for a meal, with china featuring a riotous Venturi-designed pattern of the wall stencils in the entryway, is when Bob and Denise ask their housekeeper, Molly, to roast a chicken—a rare departure from the couple's vegetarian diet—for an important client.

Denise had been back in Philadelphia less than a year when she got her first commission. She was asked to join a crusade led by a group of community organizers who were intent on saving South Street, a dying commercial street in center-city Philadelphia. While it had once been a popular thoroughfare of shops, restaurants, and jazz clubs, South Street had fallen on hard times. It suffered from the twin scourges of modern cities—the exodus of wealthier residents to the suburbs and the city's stated intention of cutting a highway through the neighborhood. Having lost both its carriage trade and any incentive to reinvest in the community, South Street underwent a precipitous decline in the 1960s. Denise was chosen for the project because, as one social planner told her, "If you can like Las Vegas, we trust you not to neaten up South Street at the expense of its people." It may have helped that the family's fruit and vegetable business was still located on South Street.

South Street was Denise's first "Main Street" project, and would pave the way for her particular brand of urban and advocacy planning. Denise recommended a number of incremental changes—finding new uses for many of South Street's dilapidated buildings as a way to attract people to the area without displacing the local residents, many of whom are black or ethnic. She also encouraged the community to renovate a few buildings to show that people in the community "cared." But, most importantly, she challenged the transportation department to replace the planned expressway with a network of one-way streets, just as it would be likely to do in a more affluent community. Coupled with the work of neighborhood advocacy groups, Denise's alternative proposal beat out the new highway plan. Over the years parts of South Street have been revitalized. Although some blocks are still poor and rundown the eastern end has been taken over by galleries, restaurants, and craft stores. Further west a new hospital has breathed life into another stretch of South Street. As Denise likes to point out, the tax revenues that would have been lost if the highway had been built instead increased sharply as property values have begun to recover along the street.

It was toward the beginning of the South Street project, in 1968, that Denise was given an official position by Yale, and a salary, for the work she was doing with Bob in the Architecture School. When asked to draw up a contract for herself, she pegged her salary at $8,000, exactly $1,000 less than what Bob was getting. Enmeshed in Bob's work, and trying to have a baby, Denise (and Bob) turned down several offers to teach at Penn, although she did periodically offer studio courses there. At about this time Denise also asked Bob and John for both a partnership in the firm and a salary.

She was given both. But John Rauch drew the line at putting her name on the shingle. He insisted that since the firm had recently had a name change—the firm became Venturi and Rauch after Rauch replaced Venturi's previous partner, William Short—it was too soon for another one. Bob, meanwhile, was afraid to rock the boat, angering John, whose skills as an administrator he valued. "We need John," Bob would say. "He's got five kids; don't push him." Over the years, there never seemed to be a good time to change the firm's name, a detail that would aggravate the perception of Denise as "the boss's wife" and haunt her efforts to gain recognition for her contributions to the firm. Although she sporadically pressed her cause, Denise ultimately left the decision on changing the name of the firm to Bob. "The issue of feminism, woman's role, was something that I debated with those two over many years," says Denise, who notes that she and John Rauch developed an amicable working relationship over time. "John's view was: 'I don't understand what this is all about.' Bob's view was: 'Denise, we've got so many problems, why must you bring up trivia?' "

It wasn't that Bob lacked sufficient regard for Denise's talents. In fact, he had married her in large part because she was a soul mate in adversity. Today it seems unthinkable, even to Bob, that so much time elapsed before Denise's name joined his and Rauch's on the firm shingle. "I think of it as having been in the mid 1970s," says Venturi. When someone points out to him that it actually took more than a decade, until 1980, for the firm to become known as Venturi Rauch and Scott Brown, he protests and says that it wasn't nearly that long.

But of course, it was. Although Bob was to redeem himself in the end, the issue lodged itself inside Denise like a grain of sand within an oyster. Outwardly, she showed few signs of the irritant. She turned her attention, instead, to the problems facing the firm, which, in its early years, suffered the usual growing pains of a fledgling architectural office, and then some. Most corporate clients were scared off by Bob and Denise's antimodernist philosophy, as well as by the somewhat unconventional design of some of their early buildings, such as the Philadelphia retirement home known as Guild House. Although the simple brick structure is quite sedate by today's standards, critics at the time attacked some of the building's more daring features, such as the symbolic oversized TV antenna on top. The problems were compounded in the mid 1970s by a recession, which hit the real estate business particularly hard. Business got so bad that although in good times the firm had employed as many as twenty people—a figure that would rise to a hundred during peak periods in the 1980s—the head count fell to just ten. At one point, almost all the architects in the office were on unemployment, drifting in because they had nowhere else to go and because work, even without pay, was better than doing nothing at all. While the Venturi grocery business helped subsidize the firm in its early days, during this period Denise invested some of her family's money into keeping the office afloat, an investment, according to one longtime associate, that alone should have won her name a place on the letterhead.

Even as the firm lurched from crisis to crisis through the 1970s, a precarious balance emerged not only in its finances but also in Denise's working relationship within it. South Street brought new planning projects. In 1977, Denise was asked to restore the historic district of Jim Thorpe, Pennsylvania, a once-wealthy coal-mining town with a Main Street that was still lined with formerly sumptuous Victorian mansions. In the late 1970s, Denise took on planning projects for both Miami Beach and the town of Princeton; although only the former was implemented, as part of the historic renovation of South Beach in Miami, the firm won prestigious awards for both designs.

Denise also began collaborating with Bob on some of his buildings. In 1972, the office was commissioned to build Philadelphia's Benjamin Franklin Memorial. Because the site was relatively small, Denise came up with the idea of locating the memorial itself underground, so as to retain the ground level for a pedestrian plaza.

Then, in 1979, the firm built the BEST Products Catalogue and Showroom. One of its most striking features, the riotous patterning on the outside wall that was to become a Venturi signature, was sparked by Denise. Shortly before the BEST job, Denise had taken one of her frequent trips to New York to search for wallpaper for the upstairs bedroom of their Mount Airy house. Looking for something domestic, but large enough to match the scale of the house, she had brought back a few sample swatches of paper. From these, she and Bob selected a lively 1950s-style pattern of stylized buttercups, colorful buds on pale-blue and pale-green backgrounds. When the BEST project came along, they decided to blow up for the showroom the floral pattern that still graces their bedroom and guest room, working together on the size and spacing of the giant Warhol-style appliqués, which invoke a Las Vegas–style symbolism. "It is a fairly large, boxy building, a simple container without much spatial or conventional architectonic definition," wrote Rosemarie Haag Bletter of the BEST building. "The totally two-dimensional flowers provide the only detail and make for a tension-provoking confrontation between man-made technology and man-made nature."

Over the years, Denise would come to leave her mark on a number of other "Venturi" designs. She suggested placing a sculpture depicting a stylized tiger cub outside Princeton's Gordon Wu Hall, which Bob designed (a tiger because it was Princeton's mascot, a cub because she wanted to achieve "irony not savagery"). The sculpture has become as much of a landmark at Princeton as the lions outside Chicago's Art Institute. She conceived the idea of positioning a new student union at the University of Delaware so that the principal campus thoroughfare would cut through the building, rather than around it. And recognizing that the site sits opposite several academic buildings, she ensured that the design of the student union would leave enough space for the construction of additional classrooms, should expansion become necessary. Denise would influence countless other "details," including the layout and configuration of the capitol building of the Haute Garonne district in Toulouse, France.

During the 1970s, Denise was preoccupied with the thorny question of juggling her growing workload and motherhood. After several miscarriages, she had finally despaired of ever carrying a child to full term. In May 1971, the Venturis adopted six-day-old Jimmie, who would soon become a "pert, tart" little child with unruly blond hair, and who filled her with love and the special anxiety of a first-time mother. During the first two months of his life, Denise spent most of her time at home, getting to know her infant son. Then in August, she and Bob took off with Jimmie for what has since become a twice-yearly trip to visit Phyllis Lakofski in Switzerland, where she now lived; Denise's parents finally gave in to the tensions that had long marred their marriage by getting separated—they were in their eighties at the time. When the Venturis returned to Philadelphia, Denise resumed work, at first for only a few days a week, and finally full time. They hired a housekeeper named Molly, a mature Trinidadian woman with grown children of her own. Although Denise was confident of Molly's care and love for Jimmie, she was plagued by the fear that this little creature who had miraculously appeared in her life after years of childlessness would somehow not recognize her as his mother.

Even without the complicating practical and emotional issues of adoption, Denise had few role models to look to when attempting to balance a vocation and motherhood. Indeed, the opprobrium of society at large toward the working mother was echoed by her own family. One summer, during a visit to London to see her sister and Robin Middleton, who now lived together, childless themselves, Denise was accused by Ruth of neglecting her responsibilities as a mother by continuing to work while Jimmie was still a small boy. The attack was so vehement and hit so close to the core of Denise's greatest vulnerability that it precipitated a break between the sisters that lasted for years.

In fact, Denise approached motherhood with all the creativity and studied resourcefulness that she unleashed on a planning project or a studio. In the beginning, she felt as torn between her commitment to Jimmie and to her work—which quickly escalated to a forty-to-fifty-hour workweek—as any professional parent. Returning home from a six-day trip with Bob, during which she had left six-month-old Jimmie in Molly's care, Denise was devastated to find Jimmie clinging to Molly and having, apparently, no memory of his mother. She was racked by guilt, once again, while attending a two-week architecture conference in Iran during Jimmie's first week in kindergarten.

Although she knew it was irrational, often she couldn't help but feel in competition with Molly. "I had no idea how riven I would feel about Molly becoming very important in Jimmie's life," says Denise, acknowledging that over the years it proved to be "a very big problem" for her. She resented it if she found herself making lunch while Molly looked after the baby. If Jimmie was ill, she couldn't help but feel jealous when Molly comforted him. And yet she understood that without Molly, a life of work and family would have been virtually impossible.

At the same time, through Jimmie, the teacher in Denise bloomed again. To help him learn how to chart graphs, she dreamed up a scheme for having him time the passage of insects across the ground with a stopwatch and keeping a record of the creatures' progress. Although Denise belonged to a synagogue, Jimmie didn't like to go. So Denise sought out the Jewish Children's Folkshul in Philadelphia, an institution that focused on the culture of Judaism, in the hope of giving him a grounding in Jewish history and Judeo-Christian ethics, without the religious dogma. She even served on the curriculum committee of the Folkshul's board. And years later, Jimmie would affectionately recall the patience with which she sat with him in the early evenings over his schoolwork. "I would ask her for help because she was good at it. She's better, more patient" than Bob, recalls Jimmie. But "she could drive me crazy because she was such a perfectionist. We'd fight about it" all the time, he says, quipping: "We finally stopped fighting when I dropped out of school."

Although both Bob and Denise worked long hours at the office, it was Denise who took on the role of caregiver, making arrangements for after-school and summer activities, researching schools, and—most important—gauging the delicate seismograph of adolescent development. Jimmie's relationship with his father blossomed more slowly. Since neither father nor son is particularly athletic, they never shared an interest in sports. And when Bob tried to kindle in his adolescent son some of his own passion for architecture, pointing, for example, to a castle flashing by the Bavarian landscape during a train trip in Germany, the best Jimmie could muster was a sarcastic "Oh . . . wow." Jimmie's reaction was in sharp contrast to the awe Bob had experienced when his father first took him to see the original Penn Station in New York.

It was also Denise who established the tone of deliberate calmness in the face of Jimmie's adolescent exploits. Although he was unquestionably bright, Jimmie as a teenager showed signs that he had imbibed his parents' zest for rule breaking all too well. He challenged his teachers, cut class, and failed courses such as music appreciation. In response, Denise patiently searched for new schools and new ways to stimulate his development. To shake him out of his academic ennui, she also planned extracurricular activities that she hoped would be both educational and inspiring. While working on a planning project for the city of Memphis, for example, she took thirteen-year-old Jimmie out of school for four days so that he could sit in on town meetings, catch a glimpse of the jazz clubs on Beale Street where Elvis had learned about music, and, of course, visit Graceland. When he developed an interest in computers, she encouraged him to visit fellow hackers as far away as Ann Arbor, Michigan.

Most of all, she found creative solutions to the unique demands of their work-consumed family life. Although both she and Bob worked all week and often on weekends, they made a point of getting home in time for dinner with Jimmie. At least at the dinner table, shoptalk was suspended, and the conversation focused on subjects like politics, which interested Jimmie more. Sometimes, though, Bob and Denise were so tired at the end of the day that the family would retreat to Bob and Denise's bedroom. There, Jimmie would set up his train set amid the books, files, and old magazines in a space that looks more like the war zone of perennial students than the habitat one might expect of two of America's premier designers. Bob and Denise, meanwhile, would collapse, exhausted, on their queen-sized bed, Jimmie's locomotives whirring around their heads.

Conscious of the difficulty of being an only child, especially with ambitious parents, and remembering the comfort of a house filled with relatives, Denise also developed a scheme for infusing Jimmie's life with surrogate siblings. Soon after Jimmie's arrival, Denise hired the first of her Harvard Handymen, so named because many of these family helpers came from Harvard's architecture school. The students would live with the Venturis during the summers, do repair work on the house, tend the garden, and play with Jimmie. The scheme worked so well that Jimmie remained close to several of the Handymen (and women). Indeed, one of them, Fred Schwartz, a gifted architect with a slight frame and a rumpled, phlegmatic air, who began spending summers with the Venturis in 1975, became virtually part of the family. Years later, Schwartz, who established his own firm in New York, would frequently work with the Venturis. He also helped Jimmie get started in a computer consulting business for architects and provided the youngest Venturi with a home away from home during visits to New York. The two remain close friends.

Even when it came to revealing the details of Jimmie's adoption, Denise came up with insightful solutions. While he was still a baby, she read and consulted with doctors and debated with Bob about how and when to broach the subject with their son, finally concluding that they would tell him early, so that there would never be a time when he didn't know. More surprisingly, she decided not to wait for Jimmie to probe her with questions about his parentage, choosing instead to tell him the facts of his conception when he was twelve and, when he was sixteen, encouraging him to look up his biological mother, with whom Denise had maintained contact. Jimmie was initially shocked by the suggestion, but he eventually mustered the confidence and equilibrium to develop a relationship with the woman who had conceived him, as well as with the children to whom she had given birth later in life, without his ever questioning that Denise was his real mother.

Denise was ultimately vindicated in her decision to balance professional life and motherhood. A handsome, slouchy youth, with a quick mind and a wry sense of humor, Jimmie has taken on his parents' values without falling victim to their celebrity. The antithesis of the organization man, he dropped out of high school in the tenth grade but passed a high school equivalency exam at his parents' urging. Sensing well the burden he would bear if he tried to pursue architecture as a career, Jimmie assiduously avoided his parents' vocation. "I have an interest in architecture. If my parents weren't who they are . . . ," he muses, recalling how much he enjoyed computer drafting during the six months he worked for the Italian architect Aldo Rossi, soon after dropping out of college. But "I'd always be Venturi's kid and Scott Brown's kid." So instead, in his computing business, he built on his knowledge of architecture and a love of electronics.

Now in his early twenties, Jimmie has none of the postadolescent's love-hate ambivalence toward his parents, whom he refers to affectionately as Bob and Denise, as though they were his closest friends. Jimmie lives in New York now, and if Denise is lecturing anywhere in the New York area, he invariably shows up, frequently with a girlfriend or Fred Schwartz. He adores his father and accompanied Bob when he was on his first major building commission in Japan. There Jimmie scoured the showrooms of Sony and Panasonic for the large video monitors that Bob plans to use in two of the firm's projects, and, in the process, picked up valuable contacts for his own fledgling business. He also traveled to Mexico City when Bob won the Pritzker Prize, yet understood and empathized with his mother's decision to remain at home. "The Pritzker Prize hurt her very much," explains Jimmie. "It has to do with her turning sixty this year. It meant she would not get the same recognition as Bob, at least not while she is living."

Jimmie is, in fact, every inch his mother's son, with his shoulder-length blond hair cut bluntly—and deliberately—like Denise's, and the tweedy sports coats he buys at thrift shops, and his air of gentle, sardonic wisdom. Ultimately, says Jimmie, it's what "Denise does in urban planning—dealing with people—that meshes most with what I'm interested in."

Of Stars and Satellites

In 1980, just as the firm was expanding into its Manayunk offices, Bob finally decided to put Denise's name on the firm. They were spending a weekend in Massachusetts with Bob's Princeton roommate Philip Finkelpearl and his wife, Kitty, when, over breakfast, Bob explained that with all the problems they had faced, the time had never seemed right to worry about a name change. "Well, when will the time ever seem right?" inquired Finkelpearl, who had spent his career teaching at women's colleges, most recently at Wellesley, and had grown sensitive to the plight of many of his graduates. Thus, prodded by his old school friend, Bob finally accepted the need for a change.

The rechristening came none too soon. After nearly twenty years of partnership, the relationship with John Rauch was coming to a bitter end. By most accounts, Rauch, who had just divorced his wife and whose kids were, for the most part, grown, was increasingly losing interest in the firm. Although he had worked amicably with Denise for several years, her growing reputation and assertiveness also had begun to rankle. Finally, in the mid 1980s, Rauch withdrew from the partnership. With his departure, Denise was forced to take on many of the administrative duties that Rauch had shouldered—and that Bob detests—as well as continuing her planning projects and her role as Bob's collaborator and principal critic.

Meanwhile, her own projects continued to flourish. Her most memorable undertaking, in the late 1970s, was a revitalization plan for the commercial district of Miami Beach. It had been a decade earlier, during a cross-country trip from California a year before her marriage, that Denise first discovered Miami Beach. Although a single individual can rarely take credit for revitalizing an entire neighborhood, Denise was probably the first person to call attention to the area as an architectural treasure worth saving. She coined the moniker "Deco District" and later developed a planning proposal for Washington Avenue, its principal commercial thoroughfare.

From the beginning, Denise was charmed not only by the neighborhood's pastel-colored, cubist-shaped buildings and its tropical, pink-flamingo mystique but also by its unique atmosphere, which Denise thought of as both "tawdry and vital," young and old, East European and Latin. Miami Beach was an enclave of elderly Jews, many of them from New York's garment workers' union, and young Cuban arrivistes. It was a place of "Blood Pressure: $1" signs, where one group of retirees presented Denise with her very own copy of *Sex and the Senior Citizen*. Here delis vied with bodegas for clientele. At the large discount stores, you could see a Venezuelan tourist buy forty thousand dollars' worth of appliances, peeling bills off a money roll to pay for them.

During her first visit to Miami, in 1966, Denise spent two days at the grand Fontainebleau Hotel, discovering, and photographing, some of the smaller, less prepossessing stucco structures in the surrounding neighborhood. A few years later, she returned with Bob. They roamed the South Beach section beyond the Fontainebleau and took more photographs. Upon returning to Philadelphia, Denise penned a letter to the Miami chapter of the American Institute of Architects, praising the South Beach neighborhood as "a priceless heritage of the early 1930's, the more valuable because [the buildings] occur together in a precinct, which makes them extremely rare in world architecture."

Although she received no response to the letter, Denise followed up with a succession of missives, phone calls, and planning proposals. When, in 1975, she heard that Miami was proposing to replan the southern tip of the beach, she submitted a formal proposal. "The art deco structures could form a 'Deco District' for Miami Beach in much the same way that the 'Vieux Carré' enhances New Orleans and brings tourists to its other, new facilities," she wrote. What's more, she pressed for slow, evolutionary change, which would take a gradual approach to introducing new tourist attractions to the area, thereby hoping to preserve the human character of the neighborhood and to "avoid excessive and unpopular relocation of elderly and poor residents."

Again no response.

Back in Philadelphia, Denise discovered a one-paragraph item in

Preservation News about a citizens' group that had taken up the cause and that was being led by a Miami matron named Barbara Capitman. Denise decided to give Capitman a call. During their first long phone conversation, Denise discovered that she had an ally. When plans were hatched to bulldoze the southern tip of Miami Beach to create a Floridian Venice, replete with canals and moorings, Capitman led a local battle to stop the effort. Then, when planning designs were requested for Washington Avenue, Capitman lobbied behind the scenes for Denise's proposal, which finally won the competition.

Of course, when it comes to urban planning, it is hard ever to really win. Denise complains that her guidelines were mostly honored in the breach. She had suggested planting palm trees and flowers in a median strip, for example, and warned against planting flowers along the sidewalk. The municipal authorities ignored her advice. Flower beds were located beside the pavement, and as Denise predicted, they were soon overrun by pedestrians and dust. Then there was little money left for planting a median strip.

Yet her commercial guidelines were remarkably successful. One of the greatest triumphs of the plan, notes Fred Schwartz, who worked with her on it, was that it "took into account the reality of economics. It was designed to be affordable to Cuban and old Jewish immigrant" shopkeepers. Indeed, several merchants followed her suggestions for replacing worn-out awnings with broad-striped canvas ones. She also established a palette of colors for repairing the masonry and trim of storefronts on the street. On a visit to Miami a few years after the project was complete, Denise discovered that a local designer who had been hired for several renovations on the street had taken up the idea of a unified color scheme, albeit with a slightly modified palette, and it was catching on throughout the neighborhood. Notes Denise: "His interpretations of our design guidelines resulted in color combinations that were less deco, sweeter and more abundant than those we would have selected; but they were suitable, and from his efforts a new image and continuity were emerging, not only on Washington Avenue, but elsewhere in the Deco District."

Her plan won the prestigious *Progressive Architecture* award for urban design. Years later, she and Bob, eating their late dinners in the laundry room, would often tune in to *Miami Vice*, turn down the volume, and feast their eyes on the "pale pastel violence and swirling movement" that danced across the rich art deco panorama that has become synonymous with Miami.

"And yet . . . and yet," laments Denise. "The proportion of elderly in the Deco District has dropped from 90 percent to 30 percent. Social services are reduced; cultural and social development has not kept pace with commercial." The social planner in her looks back with nostalgia to a high point of "real" preservation in 1983, when preservation meant just that for both the community and the buildings in which they lived and shopped.

Denise emerged from the Miami Beach project at the start of the Reagan era, when municipal planning budgets were being eviscerated. Yet even during that period of austerity she won a number of municipal planning projects. For example, in the early 1980s, the firm was hired to chart a center-city redevelopment plan for Memphis, which had spawned Elvis and rock and roll but had fallen into a state of suspended animation ever since Martin Luther King was assassinated at the Lorraine Motel. Recession and political turmoil were to foil some of the major portions of her revitalization plans for downtown, which called for creating a small residential community on a narrow sliver of land that juts into the Wolf River, facing the commercial district. But some of her more "conceptual" suggestions succeeded. For example, Denise exposed a transportation department plan for building a highway that would cut downtown off from the Mississippi. By mapping all the existing expressways, as well as those that had received funding but hadn't yet been built, Denise was able to show that only one small segment was missing from a loop that would isolate the city by running straight down the banks of the Mississippi. Knowing that there's nothing like a highway to kill the heart of a city, Denise showed up with her maps at citizens committee meetings—to the fury of the transportation commissioner—which promptly put an end to the highway construction plans.

Denise didn't have much time to brood over the fate of Memphis. In the late 1980s, she found herself besieged by work. In 1991, she was hired by the town of Denver to create the development plan for a civic center that would draw together three of the town's leading cultural institutions. The same year, her team was chosen to do what is known as the programming for the Smithsonian's Museum of the American Indian, which will occupy the last major site on Washington's Mall. (While planning generally refers to the orienting of several buildings, open spaces, and transportation systems within a wide geographic area, programming lays out the spatial and functional requirements of a specific building or group of structures.)

Meanwhile, Bob Venturi suddenly found himself catapulted out of his role as an architect's architect and into full-blown stardom as he won a series of prestigious museum commissions. In 1984, Venturi Rauch and Scott Brown, as it was still known, began work on the Seattle Art Museum. Soon thereafter, in a contest that pitted the world's leading architects against Britain's Prince Charles, the firm emerged as the unlikely winner of one of the most coveted architectural commissions of the era.

It is in the saga of the Sainsbury Wing of the National Gallery in London that Denise's role in the firm, and the difficulties she had in winning recognition from the architectural establishment, were placed in sharp relief. The Sainsbury Wing was a truly monumental project, with larger-than-life protagonists and an outsize battle over structure and form that has rocked the National Gallery since its inception in the 1830s. Denise was not the principal architect on the addition, nor was she even listed as the project manager, but as Venturi's wife and partner, she played a role far greater than either the critics or most of those closest to the enterprise were willing to recognize. On a precarious project that already had been derailed once—plans drawn up by Ahrends Burton and Koralek, a British firm, were ditched after Prince Charles dismissed the proposal as a "monstrous carbuncle on the face of an old and beloved friend"—and that was riddled with byzantine politics, Denise became Bob's principal troubleshooter, a vital though thankless role, for which she would be vilified rather than praised.

Sometime in the early 1980s, Bob and Denise were returning to Philadelphia from Switzerland, when they decided that Denise should make a detour to London to learn more about the Sainsbury commission. In London, she met with Michael Levey and Michael Wilson, the museum's director and assistant keeper, respectively, and over tea described the sort of building the firm was likely to propose for the site. She described a vision for the museum that would "maintain the cornice heights" of the old museum, incorporate its pilasters, and use the same sort of Portland stone. She described a building that "would extend classicism to give it modern form." After decades of developing a common approach to architecture and urbanism—and without discussing with Bob the specifics of what she would say at the meeting— Denise anticipated the materials, the scale, even the controversial pilaster to the left of the building long before Bob was to draw a single line.

By deciding to go after the Sainsbury Wing commission, Bob and Denise were throwing themselves into a fight for one of the most prestigious, and contentious, monuments in recent architectural history. By most accounts, Denise's trip set in motion a series of events that eventually would result in the firm's selection for a project named after the British supermarket moguls who agreed to finance the building after the Ahrends Burton and Koralek scheme failed. Venturi's whimsical facade, with its irregularly spaced pilasters, closely packed at the end adjacent to the old museum, as if they were a folding screen, was meant to invoke the lines of the original building in a jazzier, syncopated rhythm. In fact, Venturi's mannerist design became almost as controversial as the fact that an American architect—the offspring of a grocer, no less—had been chosen to design the last available spot on one of London's great squares.

What few Britons realized was that in selecting such a controversial husband-wife team from the "colonies," the museum was following a tradition of alien infiltration that had begun with the inception of the National Gallery itself in the early nineteenth century. From the outset, Britain's first national museum was the product of an encroaching middle class. Long after the French government had established the Louvre as a museum, London's elite kept "high culture" as the sole province of the aristocracy, housing artistic treasures in so-called public galleries that were, however, no more "public" than a British public school.

The calls for a national museum had been, in fact, part of an intense class struggle in the early part of the nineteenth century. Most significantly, the cornerstone of the National Gallery, without which it would never have been built, was a vast collection of art that had been amassed by a financier, John Julius Angerstein, and sold to Parliament for £68,000. Angerstein was a Russian Jew, illegitimate, a man who was always described in the press as "vulgar," a man who belonged to the powerful emerging merchant class.

So in a very real sense, both the Venturis and the museum, in devising an addition to the National Gallery, labored under the burden of 150 years of controversy, which had acquired a particularly sharp edge since Prince Charles helped torpedo the Ahrends Burton and Koralek plan. From the beginning, the Venturis felt captive to a large and nervous client committee, which included not only the museum trustees and staff but the three Sainsbury brothers who were financing the project, a group of architectural advisers, local town planners, and the ubiquitous prince. Here Bob had finally gotten a commission worthy of his artistic talents, yet more than ever he felt like a lone Christian in an arena filled with gladiators. Every line, window, and paint color was subject to minute hair-splitting scrutiny by an army of overseers, many of whom felt that, given the project's contentious history, the odds were against the wing's ever being built.

Bob needed Denise more than ever. "From the first meeting, she was a vital part [of the process], the support she was giving was palpable," recalls Simon Sainsbury. When the clients balked at their low entryway, with its thick columns that recall the exaggerated proportions of the Furness library, Denise composed for the client committee a presentation designed to show the historic precedents for their design, including the crypts often found beneath cathedrals and old Italian houses, in which a low stone entryway leads to the *piano nobile* on the second floor. Even as the delicate official meetings between the architects and the town planners of the City of Westminster were under way to ensure approval for this final addition to London's historic Trafalgar Square, Denise met privately with one of Westminster's top planners. Unbeknownst even to the Sainsburys, she let the planning representative know that if they compromised the design too much, the firm might be forced to resign. "Her negotiations with Westminster were one of the most fruitful products" of her involvement with the project, says Colin Amery, who became an architectural adviser to the project.

Early on, however, there were tensions between Bob and some members of the client committee—whom he accused of meddlesome micromanagement—tensions he often left to Denise to resolve. "During our first row with Venturi, I was shocked that he'd sit in the room and sulk," recalls Amery. "We were made to feel contemptible." When Bob finally threatened to resign over one of several disputes about the design, it was Denise who, by all accounts, saved the day. One of the biggest disagreements centered around a half column that Venturi had proposed, initially, as a freestanding entity to the left of the entryway. Learning from Las Vegas, it mirrored the Corinthian columns of the main museum and alluded to the "column base" of Lord Nelson. However clever the historic symbolism, the client hated the idea.

"After a bit Bob felt he couldn't take the strain," recalls Sainsbury. "Then Denise held it together. There's no question. She presented the designs, and defended them more strongly than [Bob] would have. If she hadn't been there, [the project] wouldn't have happened. I had great admiration for her." Adds Amery: "It was she who helped him back on the rails, who kept the dialogue going. He might have resigned" if it hadn't been for Denise.

Years later, Venturi described the process as a "Kafkaesque" ordeal. If so, the role of "K" was played by Denise. For more than a year, Venturi snubbed the client, staying away from meetings. It was assumed by some members of the client committee that although Bob wouldn't attend meetings, he was actually holed up in a hotel in London, giving Denise instructions by phone and in the evening. In fact, Bob remained behind in Philadelphia. Denise, together with the project manager, David Vaughan, returned alone to London to make presentations, fight for the design, and negotiate modifications. Thus, slowly, painstakingly, the Sainsbury Wing emerged, along with a curved, fluted pilaster.

When the wing opened in 1991, it was alternately hailed and vilified by a welter of critics who had gorged themselves on the most delicious controversy in recent architectural history. But when the dust settled and the headlines were forgotten, what remained was a whimsical, mannerist structure, a part modernist, part classical, thoroughly American confection in the midst of Trafalgar Square, facing Lord Nelson and rubbing shoulders with the National Gallery itself. The building is unmistakably a product of Venturi Scott Brown—not so much because of its lines, but because of its historical whimsy and the way it relates to the square. From the front, it maintains a faux classical facade, with the folding-screen effect of irregularly spaced pilasters. The entryway is decidedly modern—large rectangular glass sections cut out of the stone facade and big enough to drive a truck through. The side of the building that faces the original structure, across a narrow alleyway, is sheer glass; it has the effect of an optical illusion, a transparent curtain dividing the main museum on one side from Venturi's sweeping stone staircase, which leads to the main gallery space at the top of the Sainsbury Wing and the entryway to the main museum.

In assuming the role of mediator on so contentious a project, Denise could hardly expect praise, let alone credit. What's more, with an undertaking of its size and complexity, notes Steven Izenour, who is otherwise extremely sympathetic to his boss's plight, "there were ten people who made as many key decisions as she did." In all, twenty-seven architects worked on the plan. The star system may not be fair, but when it comes to losing credit for a project like the Sainsbury Wing, Denise had plenty of company.

Yet not even her role as Venturi's troubleshooter quite accounts for the viciousness of some the criticism leveled against her. For while Bob was viewed as a prima donna, and the two together as "a pair of spoiled children," it was Denise who attracted a special, particularly personal sort of animosity from some of the Brits. "She was pretty fierce, with her angular hair and glasses," recalls Colin Amery, who prides himself on being one of a small coterie of architectural tastemakers who have the ear of Prince Charles. "I remember the first time we went out to their house. It was me, Simon [Sainsbury], and [Jacob] Rothschild. And she lectured us on high-rises and public housing. It didn't go down very well."

Of course, since it was *after* the clients' first trip to Philadelphia that the firm won the commission, the visit couldn't have gone that badly. Still, the critic muses, momentarily forgetting Denise's more useful moments on the project: "She lacks the charm and wit that are necessary at that sort of occasion. I always felt like she was something out of an Edward Albee play. I suppose she's never been domesticated."

In elite architectural circles, dumping on Denise has become something of a sport. She is widely perceived as an interloper, "an irritating wasp flying around the buildings" of her gifted husband. The woman whom clients and colleagues have come to respect as an intelligent and thoughtful professional is often derided by her peers as a "strident," "finger-wagging," "teacherly" crusader. When her ideas aren't being openly ridiculed, they are either pointedly ignored or attributed to Venturi. Even the speaking engagements and panel discussions to which she is invited never seem to pass by without some famous male architect sniggering: "Why doesn't Bob come out and play with the big boys? Why does he send this surrogate?"

This is emblematic of Scott Brown's position vis-à-vis the most powerful kingmaker of the architectural establishment, Philip Johnson. Critics Filler and Haag Bletter, for example, attribute the "misogynist streak" in architecture directly to Johnson's circle. "And Johnson," as one prominent architect points out, "has a tremendous effect on people's practices. More than I would care to know."

Certainly, Johnson and Venturi Scott Brown represented opposing aesthetic factions in the 1960s—at the time, Johnson was a leading exponent of the "whites," who represented the purity of Modernist architecture, while Venturi led the "grays," who rebelled against it. It is telling that *Complexity and Contradiction in Architecture* opens with a scathing indictment of Johnson's work. Referring to two houses designed by Johnson, Venturi wrote: "Where simplicity cannot work, simpleness results. Blatant simplification means bland architecture. Less is a bore."

Whatever anger Johnson may have felt over this postmodernist critique was taken out on Scott Brown rather than Venturi. Sometime in the late 1970s, Johnson invited Bob Venturi to join his Penguin Club, so named for the tuxedos worn by its members, prestigious architects who gather monthly at Manhattan's tony Century Club; Denise was pointedly not invited. Indeed, the Penguin Club, which by dint of Johnson's enormous connections and reputation has become a valuable network for finding and winning new work, never has admitted women to its inner circle. Thus, it serves as a formidable professional barrier to women architects. In the end, partly in deference to his wife, partly because he preferred to stay at home and work rather than become part of the "New York scene," Venturi declined to join the group.

At about the same time, Fred Schwartz, the couple's protégé and former Harvard Handyman, vividly recalls, there was a symposium at the New York Architectural League on the award-winning plans for restoring the art deco district in Miami Beach. Following a presentation on the design, an "eminent New York architect," in the course of making some comments on the presentation, referred repeatedly to "Bob Venturi's plan for Miami Beach." Schwartz, who was new to the profession but who had worked on the project with Scott Brown, finally screwed up his courage and corrected the eminent architect, explaining that the plan was actually Denise's. "But [the architect] just kept on referring to it as Bob's plan," he recalls. "This guy just refused to acknowledge that it was Denise's work."

Clients of Her Own

Denise often rails against a star system that has cast her own career as a satellite to her husband's—yet time and again she succumbs to its standards. Like a straight-A student with Coke-bottle glasses who is despised by her classmates for her brains and her unmodish appearance, Denise strives for the approval of her peers. And of course, she is mocked even more for striving, for being so unseemly, so uncool as to care.

Still, at a time when few women ever get major commissions, Scott Brown's work and marriage have served as valuable examples for younger women architects, many of whom continue to marry their colleagues despite the professional risks inherent in doing so. "She was really a groundbreaker," notes Elizabeth Plater-Zyberk, who worked for a short time in the Philadelphia firm and now practices in Miami with her husband, Andres Duany. Indeed, Plater-Zyberk is one of many women architects who, having begun their careers working with Scott Brown, grew to like and admire her and benefited from her mentoring. Although Duany and Plater-Zyberk consider the Venturis to be their "heroes" and are themselves regarded as one of the most gifted couples of their generation working in architecture and urban planning, Plater-Zyberk has made an assiduous effort to learn from Scott Brown's experience. She has "consciously" fought to maintain a "competitive posture" and to be perceived as an equal partner to her husband. Although some leading architects imagine Duany to be "the designer"—a false impression—the pair are perceived as a much more equal partnership than their Philadelphia counterparts. Vincent Scully, for example, not only knows precisely what Plater-Zyberk's role is in the firm but praises her work.

What is most striking about Scott Brown's work, especially as she has taken on larger and larger projects of ever-increasing complexity and prestige, is that her modus operandi marks a jubilant rejection of traditional notions of heroic artistry. If compromise and accommodation form the leitmotif of a feminine existence, then Scott Brown's mission has been to infuse architecture and urban planning with just such a feminine sensibility. While fellow architects and planners arrive at competitions with pretty drawings and blueprints with which to put their stamp on a project, Scott Brown frequently walks away with a commission precisely because she refuses to commit herself to a solution until she has studied all the ramifications. Scott Brown's plans aren't about building new buildings or imposing a specific style. Rather, they are about analyzing the maps of the existing neighborhood or city, listening to the multiple voices of a community, and trying to coax from them a vision that will suit its needs and last the test of time. "I often talk about the macho as opposed to the feminist approach to transportation systems," she explains. "The macho plan would be to run an expressway straight through the city, ignoring existing communities and the like; the feminist plan would do a little widening [of the street] here, a little narrowing there, changing in the traffic pattern rather than the street plan. I prefer darning and mending."

Scott Brown's approach has won her recognition by a growing

cadre of clients. For example, she was hired to help create a plan for bringing together three disparate Denver cultural institutions, which among them house one of the greatest collections of Western American art, artifacts, and archival material in the United States. In keeping with the all-American penchant for "healthy competition," the three institutions were always administered independently and had a rich history of rivalry and, in some cases, outright hostility. Thus, the collection was never shown in a unified exhibition.

It was her reputation as a thoughtful, and receptive, problem solver that led the three institutions to select her team over those of several major architectural firms, including Skidmore, Owings & Merrill and Frank Gehry, to help plan a new civic center. Her ability to hammer out a planning blueprint that takes into account the needs of all three institutions—the Colorado Historical Society, the Denver Public Library, and the Denver Art Museum—won rave reviews from each of her clients. "The brilliant thing Denise has done for this process is to bring institutions and the community together in a desire to collaborate," noted Lewis Sharp, director of the Denver Art Museum, toward the end of the planning process.

The rivalry that had once represented merely a loss to the public, suddenly, in an era of funding shortages and belt tightening, came to threaten the institutions themselves. At some point during the Reagan era, it became clear that the three cultural entities were increasingly in danger of cannibalizing each other's sources of funding and wasting valuable resources in duplicated efforts and facilities.

Denise's challenge was to build a vision of what collaboration would mean for the three erstwhile rivals. She also had to create a blueprint for physically drawing together the three institutions, which border a wasteland of parking lots and abandoned buildings. And she had to do so knowing that it might be years before funding became available for a single new building! Within less than a year, Denise had developed a plan that drew unqualified rave reviews from her three clients. Although she sketched out ideas for the center's physical look, landscaping, and long-term new construction, the most important feature of the blueprint was that it created a framework for sharing resources and know-how. If the historical society needed new exhibition space, couldn't it share expenses by building a facility that also could be used by the museum? Couldn't the library, with its vast collection of archival material and information, defray the costs of computerization by sharing the databases with its neighboring institutions?

Like a professor who teaches her students to find their own answers, Denise created a structure within which her clients could develop a vision for their complex. Over a period of months, she held dozens of meetings with the directors and employees of the three institutions, as well as representatives of city government and community groups.

Denise's meetings were part academic seminar, part quality-management circle. Her style never failed to inspire confidence in her clients. She had a way of strolling into a conference room quietly and confidently, toting her bedraggled beige nylon Sportsac stuffed with books and papers. She would sit down at the head of a long conference table, slowly scan the room, and remove seven or eight freshly sharpened No. 2 pencils from her bag, laying them in front of her. Then Denise would open the meeting by recapping the previous sessions' proceedings, often punctuating her talks with slides and maps, "fearlessly laying out her ideas. If they're wrong, fine," says Jim Hartmann, director of the historical society. Denise, her clients know, can handle criticism. She would then sit quietly again, listening to a debate unfold, her hands alternately taking notes and lying neatly folded on a long yellow legal pad. "She was conducting a seminar," recalls Hartmann. "It was tremendously participative. She never got frustrated. And she seemed to know whose judgment to trust. She didn't kill ideas, she encouraged them."

The first major design challenge involved rescuing the historical society, which is set apart from the other two institutions by a busy commercial street teeming with traffic, from the margin of the civic center. To solve this problem, Denise suggested creating an arc of landscaping that would embrace all the buildings on the north side of Thirteenth Street, including the historical society, and spill over onto the south side of the street. At its center, the arc would cross Thirteenth Street and overflow into the parking lots that face the civic center to the south. To sharpen the separatation between the parking lots and the civic center, Denise envisioned framing the arc with a series of tall, pylonlike structures, indented about a third of the way up, to symbolize human scale, and topped off with flags or lights. These structures would create a "high reader" for drawing visitors to the civic center, while at the same time serving as dividers for fairs and markets that could be planned as an additional amenity for Denverites.

Long-term, the city and the civic center could expand southward, filling up some of the parking lots with new structures that could house additional galleries, auditoriums, storage space, production shops, and even government buildings—most of which would be shared by the three institutions. In the gradual conversion of the empty lots between Eleventh and Twelfth Streets to civic uses, Denise envisioned the possibility of creating housing on the southern edge of what would soon be a vibrant area of civic and cultural life, drawing middle-class and affluent residents closer to downtown.

By 1993, Denise's preliminary plans for the civic center were unanimously approved. But even as she began gearing up for the next phase of development, Denise was girding herself for a far more difficult battle—the programming for the American Indian Museum in Washington, which is likely to be one of the most important, and most problematic, projects of her career.

Denise had come to the elegant Victorian Pension Building in Washington, D.C., on a chilly February morning in 1992, to introduce before the Commission of Fine Arts one of the most important assignments of her career. As she waited, Denise witnessed the commission's review of the latest designs for another project, the Franklin Delano Roosevelt Memorial. Her heart went out to the artists who had spent years struggling to win the approval of the capital's culture constabulary for a project that already had languished for over two decades.

For over two hours, five commissioners, headed by J. Carter Brown, the former director of Washington's National Gallery, scrutinized the dozen or so artworks assembled before them. A sculpture of Eleanor Roosevelt by Niel Estern, for example, posed a political problem for the commissioners. The figure itself was fine, but that fox-fur boa!

Surely it would would bring down the wrath of the animal rights move-ment, argued Brown. The coordinating architect fought valiantly for Mrs. Roosevelt's signature fur piece. But in the end, it was clear the boa had to go.

Nor did the commissioners like the shallow relief of FDR's head by Leonard Baskin, who was too ill to attend the hearing and defend his work. "This ovoid shape [of FDR's mouth] looks as if he is sort of screaming—[like] somebody, you know, stepped on his toe or some-thing," exclaimed another commissioner.

As the critique finally drew to a close, Denise leaned over to the sculptor George Segal, whose own work made it through the proceed-ings relatively unscathed, and asked why none of the artists had come to Baskin's defense. Segal, who sat a few seats away from Scott Brown, shrugged his shoulders. Recalling the way the commission had torpe-doed one of the Venturi firm's own designs for Washington nearly twenty-five years earlier, Denise said sadly: "This is why I hate the Fine Arts Commission—they want to design sculptures and buildings." They had all the power, yet they lacked the vision to see the drama in Baskin's sculpture of FDR: "the power of the face . . . the shallow relief, and the power and fear of [its] expression contrasted with the inscrip-tion above it: 'We have nothing to fear but fear itself.' "

Denise had returned to this star chamber of the arts, where a stroke of the pen could eviscerate a design or keep projects languishing for decades without the requisite approvals, precisely because she under-stood its power. In hopes of averting a culture war, she had persuaded her client, the National Museum of the American Indian, to launch a preemptive strike by appearing before the commission at an early stage, before a single line had been drawn. By working with the com-mission and anticipating its objections, Denise and W. Richard West, Jr., the NMAI's first director, were trying to protect what promises to be one of the most important projects in recent Washington history: the programming and construction of a vast institution that eventually will house the largest collection of Native American art in the country and will occupy a number of buildings, including the last available site on the Washington Mall.

Some architects were nonplussed when Venture Scott Brown took on a programming project that automatically disqualified them for any role in the more prestigious business of designing the museum itself. Yet in many respects the firm was a natural choice for a project as delicate in its early planning phases, and as inherently controversial, as the American Indian Museum. In selecting Denise's team, the museum gets the backing of a firm that is well enough respected to make it a match for even the most hidebound of Washington's culture czars. At the same time, because Denise has been both a victim of discrimination and a lightning rod of criticism for her unorthodox views, she is a natural ally for her Native American clients. As the doyenne of complexity and contradiction, she also can be counted on to help devise a program that will seek to reconcile the conflicting requirements of ultra-establishment Washington and the ancient spiritual culture of Native Americans.

What's more, in laying the conceptual foundation for a brand-new museum that is grappling not only with the design of its first building but also with its very definition as an institution, the programmers would have a particularly broad role. Denise's team would, for example, help the client plan the size and spaces of both the Mall facility and a separate building in Suitland, Maryland, that will house many of the institution's artifacts and ceremonial materials. The firm conducted a transportation survey for both buildings that helped plan everything from loading facilities to nearby bus stops and subway stations. While many of the Smithsonian's museums keep their archives in Suitland, the NMAI structure there was to be significantly different. Denise's team helped articulate the wishes of her Native American clients who envisioned a gathering place that would safeguard valuable artifacts, as well as offer ceremonial spaces for Native American visitors and computer databases and videotapes for constituents who couldn't travel to the center.

Denise's initial strategy for the NMAI bears her imprint of gentle intervention. To start with, Denise and her project manager, Ann Trowbridge, were asked to organize a series of meetings with Native American tribes, from Washington to Alaska, from which the firm culled dozens of suggestions and impressions that it is using to inform the planning process. To accommodate the social and ceremonial needs of Native Americans, Denise sought to accommodate her clients' vision of a museum that will open into "a large gathering space, probably round, where performances and social events can occur. It might be the place where gifts of building materials from each tribe are incorporated or where the names of Native nations, extant and extinct, might be recorded upon the walls." She also sought to incorporate private ceremonial spaces that will "have access to the sky and the outdoors and will permit the safe use of fire and smoke."

All the while, she sought to embrace all the ideas of her clients, which are as complex and contradictory as the traditions of the hundreds of tribes that are to be represented by the museum. From the beginning, planner and client agreed on one requirement above all else: to make the project inclusive, rather than exclusive, collaborative whenever possible, rather than confrontational. "In this get-acquainted meeting, we don't have any design . . . to show you," Denise told the fine arts commissioners. "We think this is the time to begin to try to get a little bit of input from the Fine Arts Commission, on what [you] feel in particular [about] the Mall site so that we can put this, too, into our set of directives to the design architects."

The meeting was amicable enough. However, culling through a long list of quotations made by Native Americans and collected by the firm at the planning conferences, Carter Brown warned Scott Brown not to indulge in any Las Vegas–style symbolism. "I would agree with the phrase 'I've never seen a tepee out of other materials look good,' and I am glad to hear Scott Brown say the same. . . . At the same time there are quotes in here that would give one pause, like 'I see a sign, not a building—a building that says something—a billboard,' " said Carter Brown, quoting the survey of Native Americans, not the planners. "I think that very neatly summarizes exactly what this Commission would be dead against."

Then, departing from his notes, as though remembering some old grievance, Carter Brown continued: "We are trying to reduce billboards in our City, and we have very tough standards about signs and for a whole building to be, in a famous architect's phrase, 'less of a decorated shed and more of a duck' I think would be too bad."

It has been nearly a quarter of a century since Denise and Bob together first coined those two phrases, yet the architectural establishment still can't forget those offensive references, although they never get the attribution right.

The sun has almost set on a wintry Sunday in Philadelphia, and Bob and Denise are still at the office. They stand side by side in the reception area, so close they are almost touching, going over their schedule for the following week. Absentmindedly, Bob fingers a few painted beads hanging from Denise's throat on a narrow strand of silk. "That's very pretty," he says.

"Thank you. I strung it together this morning," says Denise, who still occasionally finds time to browse through junk stores and flea markets for fabrics and vintage clothing and decorative objects. She blushes girlishly at Bob's compliment.

Denise prepares to retreat back into the conference room with a visitor, while Bob returns to his office. "Can I get you something to eat? You must be hungry," says Bob, noticing the time. "There are some sandwiches left over from yesterday"—a reference to a meeting with some prospective clients who came from Korea to meet with the architects.

"That would be lovely," says his wife.

A few minutes later, Bob reappears with sandwiches, napkins, and sodas. He sets two places at the conference table, which is piled high with books on Korean culture, art, and history, volumes of planning documents that Denise fingers with loving care, and, at the far end, an enormous blowup of an aerial photograph of Denver, which is marked in bright reds and greens and yellows to highlight public, residential, and commercial districts. Bob leaves Denise and her guest and returns to his office.

It is around this conference table that Bob and Denise do their "crits," debate designs, and confer with clients. In just a few months' time, Denise will win a second contract in Denver, for the realization of the civic center arc that she designed in 1992. Bob, of course, will do the drawings. They will spend days in the conference room, debating how the structures that define the arc should look: Bob initially will favor concrete pylons, and Denise will reject the ideas as too "heavy" and too expensive; Denise will counter with a proposal for a more minimalist, filigreed, flagpole-like solution, but Bob will reject it as not strong enough; finally, Bob will suggest three narrow poles and Steve Izenour, a colleague since he graduated from Penn in the 1960s, will suggest connecting them with a tracery of horizontal and diagonal lines. It is this last concept that the firm will finally adopt and modify. To make the structures visible at night, Denise will suggest adding lights at the top; a high reader, to be sure, but the lights will be "small and civic," not too bright, "not Las Vegas" at all. Behind these poles, Denise envisions a series of concrete wall panels to obscure the parking lots to the south, but spaced so that pedestrians can have easy access to their cars. The poles themselves will have seating areas around them; grass and crab-apple trees and park benches will create a civic space between the poles and the wall, which will carry signs and notices for upcoming events at the civic center.

The phone rings, and Bob pokes his head in through the door. "It's Jimmie," says Bob. "He wants to talk to you." Jimmie has called to get some advice for a marketing brochure he is putting together for his computer firm. Bob sits down to chat with his wife's visitor, while Denise spends half an hour advising her son. She returns to the conference room, and they wind up the evening at 7:30 P.M.

Since the Sainsbury Wing was completed, work has flowed in to the firm much more steadily. More and more of their work is overseas, in both Asia and Europe. The combination of work, travel, and the absence of a full-time administrator has meant that Bob and Denise now routinely work seven days a week.

They are no longer as controversial as they once were. Modernism was followed by postmodernism, which is now rivaled by deconstructivism. For the client with just a little chutzpah, Venturi Scott Brown is increasingly becoming the first choice. During slow periods in the late 1980s as much as half the firm's revenues came from Denise's plans and programs, projects like the NMAI and the Denver Civic Center.

Denise's influence also is beginning to be felt outside the firm. The new plan for New York's Times Square, which seeks to preserve the billboards and neon signs that give Broadway its character, owes much to the Las Vegas study of a quarter century ago. Some of the country's most gifted young architects and designers credit Scott Brown as an important influence on their work and development—and not just women like Miami-based Plater-Zyberk. Another architectural couple, Bill Morrish and Catherine Brown, who were recently hailed by the *New York Times* as "the most valuable thinkers in urbanism today," were inspired early on by both Scott Brown and Venturi. Says Morrish, who grew up in California and attended some of Scott Brown's studios: "*Learning from Las Vegas* was one of the first books by a major architect and theoretician on anything in the West. Their work began to address where I was coming from, the street vs. just buildings . . . also the vernacular landscape—the signs, casinos, the parking lots. Both of them looked at ordinary landscape as a resource to make grand." Like their role models, Morrish and Brown have rooted their partnership in a years-long dialogue as designers who work in different but related disciplines—he in architecture, she in landscape design. Their work at the Design Center for American Urban Landscape, a think tank within the University of Minnesota's College of Architecture and Landscape Architecture, in Minneapolis, is based on an appreciation for different disciplines and the "connective tissue"—highways, buildings, and the natural environment—that defines urban relationships.

Over the years, some of Denise Scott Brown's most important work in architecture and urban design has been like the thin steel supporting rods that run through a cement structure—often invisible, but vital nonetheless. It is not surprising that many of the symbols of architectural recognition, like the Pritzker Prize, have eluded her. Denise and Bob's roles are complementary but fundamentally different. Years ago, Denise removed herself from the mainstream of architecture—the conceptualizing and drafting of building designs. She did so because of the real barriers of her profession, because she loves and excels at theory and planning, and in order not to jeopardize her marriage to Bob. She is unlikely to get full credit for the complex ledger of her contributions until decades from now, when the work of the firm—her own and Bob's and what they have done together—is reassessed with the perspective of time.

Denise's path was partly self-chosen and partly thrust upon her. But she has emerged with a rich body of work that few of her contemporaries can match. It is now clear that she helped redefine the architectural zeitgeist of the late twentieth century—a fact that most members of the architectural establishment have to admit—however grudgingly. It may not at first seem obvious, but anyone strolling through a handful of neighborhoods, in places like Miami, Philadelphia, and Memphis, will experience regenerative changes in the urban fabric that draw directly from Scott Brown's vision for preserving the eclectic vitality of America's cities. And she has helped legitimize a collaborative, contextual approach to both family life and urbanism that serves as an inspiration for younger generations—of both architects and married couples.

Sandra Day
O'Connor

You can't be shining lights at the bar because you are too kind. You can never be corporation lawyers because you are not cold-blooded. You have not a high grade of intellect. I doubt you can ever make a living.

Clarence Darrow

The dilemma is this: If society does not recognize the fact that only woman can bear children, then "equal treatment" ends up being unequal. On the other hand, if society recognizes pregnancy as requiring special solicitude, it is a slippery slope back to the "protectionist" legislation that barred women from the workplace. . . . I would hope that [the next] generation of attorneys will find new ways to balance family and professional responsibilities between men and women . . . in a way that . . . frees both women and men from traditional role limitations.

Justice Sandra Day O'Connor

Desert Flower

There are few places farther from nowhere than the Lazy B Ranch. From Phoenix or Tucson it's several hours' drive. The well-paved single-lane highway leads through Arizona's San Carlos Indian reservation, between the majestic Gila Mountains, covered in scrub and sagebrush, past a few giant saguaros that stand like sentinels in the sun-baked earth. The nearest grocery store is in Safford, one and a half hours from the ranch—two days if you were to make the trip by horseback, the way the ranchers once did. There used to be a 7-Eleven in Duncan, which is just eighteen miles from the Lazy B, but that burned down several years ago.

Duncan is itself little more than a ghost town. No trains have stopped at the depot since long before the 7-Eleven fire. And as you leave town, the road flattens out, barren and still—the only visible movement the air itself, wavy from the heat rising up from the desert. Not far outside Duncan, a sign marks the invisible border between Arizona and New Mexico, where the ranch is situated, straddling both states.

The Lazy B headquarters lies hidden off the highway, eight miles farther down a winding dirt road. With its small adobe houses, barn, windmills, trailers, and reservoir tanks, the headquarters is a crowded oasis in a vast stretch of desert. At its center, a small, precious grass lawn leads to a modest adobe house that has been home to the Days for over fifty years. Mulberry and fruit trees provide a few patches of shade. But the best view is out back, from the shaded veranda, where the Lazy B stretches farther than the eye can see, a primeval, undulating expanse of creosote, mesquite, and sun-burned grass. There isn't a cow in sight, even though the ranch boasts two thousand head of Barzona cattle, specially bred for the desert. On most days they fan out across the 200,000-acre property in search of scarce water and grass.

But this seemingly boundless demesne isn't quite what it seems. No more than seventy percent of the land has ever belonged to the Days. The rest is federal land, under perpetual lease from the government—which lends the entire enterprise an air of perpetual uncertainty. One reason the Days never owned more was that, by law, 640 acres was the most anyone was permitted to homestead at the turn of the century. What additional acreage the family acquired was painstakingly pieced together in a series of purchases from other homesteaders and Indians.

That ratio of homestead to government property became a defining issue in the life of the Days. For the Homesteading Act's 640-acre limit was based on the optimal acreage needed to farm the fecund lands of the Midwest. Harry Day, whose father founded the Lazy B, used to rail against the Homesteading Act as a prime example of what happens when the federal government sticks its nose into matters it doesn't understand. For in the Arizona desert, 640 acres would barely sustain ten head of cattle and their calves, let alone a flock of hundreds, which is what it takes to support a family of ranchers. Consequently, the Days' livelihood would depend on the whims of distant bureaucrats in Washington. Like a tornado cloud hovering perpetually on the horizon, even a seemingly modest rise in leasing fees could put an end to their precious—and precarious—existence. So the family, which learned to survive droughts and flash floods and vermin, came to fear nothing more than the federal government.

Even without the threat of remote bureaucrats, life on the Lazy B can be rough on humans and cattle alike. Early on, the house was just four small rooms with a screened-in porch. There was no electricity or running water. The nearest neighbor was twelve miles away, and there was no telephone. It wasn't until after the Depression that the Days acquired a butane refrigerator; until then someone made weekly trips to town to buy a block of ice. To catch whatever breeze might cut the hot summer nights, the family slept out on the covered veranda, together with the ranch hands. Only a wire-mesh screen offered protection from the rattlesnakes, black widow spiders, and scorpions that rise up out of a desert night like mist from the sea. Every once in a while, a ragtag band of stragglers would appear on the horizon, wending their way through the mesquite and creosote, barefoot, half-starved, and dying from thirst; they would collapse near the house, saying their prayers, grateful for the sign of life, for whatever food and water the Days could spare, and mostly for having survived the ninety-mile trek from the Mexican border.

The ranch is lucky to get nine inches of rainfall each year. But some years there is no rain. If a drought comes, the cattle waste away to skin and bones, until they topple over onto the seared earth. A man who grew up on the ranch remembers that as a small boy during one of the droughts, he pushed at a mature cow that had grown weak from lack of sustenance, and watched it collapse, almost in slow motion.

But then, some years, a torrent of rain descends from the heavens so fast it washes away the soil without penetrating it at all, depriving the earth of much-needed nourishment. Once, a flood even swept away a small boy, the child of a Lazy B neighbor.

To survive, it wasn't enough just to be resourceful. People had to rely on one another. If you were one of the cowboys—someone, say, like Rafael Estrada, who ran away to the Lazy B when he was seven and died there, unmarried and childless, when he was in his seventies—the ranch was the only home you ever knew. And if you were one of the Days, well, the family was your support and salvation. The only thing that you could count on from the outside world—from the land, from partners, or from the government—was trouble.

Long before she would ever have given it any thought, a devotion to
and a respect for family penetrated Sandra Day's being like particles of
fine Southwestern dust. It emanated first from Harry and Ada Mae Day,
who loved each other the way only two people who find themselves
isolated in a remote and inhospitable world can do—if they don't wind
up hating each other instead. It penetrated Sandra's persona, as their
firstborn, as a child adored, by Harry especially, as though she were
some spectacular desert flower coaxed out of the dry and inhospitable
earth. And it was fueled throughout a childhood of long periods spent
away from the ranch, wrenching absences that she accepted stoically
because her parents wished her to have opportunities that the Lazy B
could never offer, but that only sharpened her yearning for home.

To hear her brother tell it, Sandra never did have much of a childhood. She was barely five years old when her parents first drove her to
El Paso to stay with her Grandma Wilkey so that she could attend the
exclusive Radford School for Girls. Years later, her brother, Alan, and
sister, Ann, would make the same journey, but neither would last more
than a few semesters in Texas before begging to return home to the
ranch. Only Sandra had both the personal resilience and the deep, un-
questioning faith in her parents' wisdom to stay in El Paso throughout
most of her schooling.

While she lived the school year in Texas and adored her grandmother, an eccentric, energetic, and fiercely independent woman, Sandra's heart remained on the Lazy B. Had she been forced to stay at the
ranch year round, she might have been lonely without children her
own age to play with, she might have found the local schools in Duncan, Arizona, and Lordsburg, New Mexico, unchallenging and dull,
and she might have found the unrelenting heat and dust and the arid
terrain oppressive. But from the distance of city life, the Lazy B seemed
like a dream. Sandra would count the days until the end of school,
when she could return to the ranch, often with her cousin Flournoy,
who also lived at Grandma Wilkey's for a time. She yearned to go riding with the cowboys, or to walk along the banks of the Gila River and
roam the hills and caves of the ranch with her mother, searching for ar-

rowheads and pictographs. And she looked forward to the spring and autumn roundups, when she would rise with Harry Day and the cowboys at 3:00 A.M., saddle up her horse, and gallop to the remote corners of the ranch to corral the herd, so the calves could be branded and the steers readied for market. After a day of riding or mending fences, no lake could ever have felt as cool and welcoming as the water reservoirs, the tall vertical tanks that offered the only respite from the dry desert temperatures.

If the ethos of the Day family was to be her touchstone for life, then, in the impressionable mind of a young child, her long stays in El Paso had two crucial consequences: They prepared her for a world far beyond the Lazy B, reinforcing her instinct for self-reliance and independence, and they also transformed the world of the Lazy B, her image of her parents, and through them the institutions of marriage and family, into an almost fictional paradise. Long before she would ever meet John O'Connor or discover her love for the law, Sandra Day recognized the core commitment that would define virtually every decision of her life: an almost mystical devotion to family.

In her thoughts of home, Harry and Ada Mae must have seemed like the greatest miracle of all. More so than the dreams she and her husband shared after their marriage, it was the ideal of her parents' marriage, and of their lives as individuals, that guided the key decisions of Sandra's life. While many young adults wrestle for years to form an identity, Sandra had known since childhood who she was and what was important to her. It was this clarity of vision that would later make her a pioneer not only in the judiciary but also in navigating the uncertain ground between her profession and motherhood.

As marriages go, Harry and Ada Mae's was an unusually harmonious one. The two were inseparable. Their children remember Ada Mae often sitting in her husband's lap in the evenings; they cannot recall them ever fighting. In fact, the children came to suspect that the real reason they were sent away to school was that Harry Day didn't want Ada Mae away from the ranch; for taking the children to school in Lordsburg, as she would have to do when Alan and Ann refused to stay in El Paso, meant that Ada Mae had to drive them to town and stay until school let out, fixing them lunch in a rented apartment, because the two-hour round trip journey was simply too arduous to make twice a day.

To Harry Day, the family and the Lazy B meant everything. Among the eclectic group of adults who anchored Sandra's life, including her parents, ranch hands, and Grandma Wilkey, it was Harry Day who was the most powerful influence. From him she inherited a deep curiosity and a thirst for learning, which in Sandra's case also translated into an irrepressible sense of adventure.

Harry was a gentle rancher, who rarely carried a gun. The years had long passed since Geronimo and his Chiricahua Apaches raided the territory that was settled by Harry's father, Henry Clay Day. But Harry Day would have preferred books to guns anyway. He gave up his dreams of an education at Stanford University after his father died unexpectedly, forcing the eighteen-year-old student to return to the Lazy B.

Neither Harry nor his father had ever planned to become a rancher. Henry Clay Day had made a fortune in the lumber business in Wichita, Kansas, when, in 1880, he agreed to put up fifty thousand dollars to purchase five thousand head of cattle for what was to become the Lazy B Ranch. Henry Clay had no intention of moving to Arizona, and planned, instead, to let his nephew, Lane Fisher, run the ranch. But when a letter arrived one day from an acquaintance, warning Henry Clay that his investment was in jeopardy, he packed his bags and took the first train out of Wichita. On the ranch, Henry Clay discovered that Fisher had been stealing half of his calves. Henry Clay chased his nephew off the ranch, promising that if Fisher left with nothing but the shirt on his back, he wouldn't have him sent to jail.

No one ever heard of Lane Fisher again, but apparently Henry Clay Day hadn't learned his lesson. To make sure that Harry and his four siblings got a decent education, Henry Clay moved the family to Pasadena in about 1912 and took on another business associate, who would get a partial interest in the ranch in exchange for managing it. After his father's sudden death, Harry discovered that, once again, the ranch had been so mismanaged that its equity had dwindled to almost nothing. He abandoned his educational plans, returned to the ranch, and kicked his father's partner off the property. With just three hundred dollars he had brought from California, Harry set about rebuilding the enterprise. But the failed partnership left Harry with a long legal battle to regain full control of the ranch.

Maybe it was the legal wrangling or just the hair-raising process of trying to rebuild the ranch and keep it going during the Depression, but Harry Day became an intensely conservative man. He ran the entire enterprise on just five hundred dollars per month, squeaking by when, like the plagues of Egypt, the Lazy B was buffeted not only by the lawsuit and the Depression but also by a long drought in the early 1930s. Shortly before his marriage, a drought had led Harry on a year-long cattle drive through Mexico—Sandra still proudly refers to it as a "real *Lonesome Dove* experience"—to save his livestock. But during the Depression there was no money for a cattle drive, and even if there had been, the price of livestock wouldn't even cover the cost of their freight. In the end, the cattle got thin and sick, and Harry had to shoot many of them. "The conditions were awful," recalls Sandra Day O'Connor, almost shuddering at the vividness of those memories. "I don't know how they survived that period."

Although his hardships in running the ranch would have a profound impact on his political outlook—one that he passed on to his daughter—Harry never seemed to resent his sacrifice. He became something of an autodidact, reading books and magazines on everything from engineering to politics. When he married, he picked a college-educated bride who also had a voracious appetite for reading and who would subscribe to everything from *Vogue* and *National Geographic* to the *Los Angeles Times* and the *Saturday Evening Post*.

Although it was Harry Day who became the lodestar of Sandra's life, much of her feminine self-assurance—and her no-nonsense intelligence—came from her mother's side of the family. Ada Mae herself was said to be a consummate lady: She wore dresses and stockings on the ranch, even in the hottest weather. The women of Lordsburg, New Mexico, about thirty-five miles down the road, would gather outside the post office every Wednesday, the day Ada Mae came to town to fetch the mail, to see what she was wearing. And dinners at the Lazy B were always served on fine bone china, at a table set with candles and silver cutlery. Harry would sit at the head of the well-laid table and hold forth, while Ada Mae sat to his right, nodding encouragingly as he spoke and remarking every so often in her soft voice, barely more than a whisper: "Why, yes, Harry, that's just the way it was."

But Ada Mae also had a nose for business. She played the stock market, for example, quietly, as she did almost everything else, but successfully. She invested the wages of the Lazy B's ranch hands, building nest eggs for men like Rafael Estrada, who didn't know how to read or write or drive. Every year or two, Ada Mae would say: "Rastis, how much money do you have?"

"Well, Ada Mae, how much do you need?" he'd reply. Estrada, who never spent his wages, was said to walk around sometimes with three or four thousand dollars in his pockets.

"Just count it out and give it to me," Ada Mae would say. The cash would be invested. And pretty soon the cowboys were taking in more money from the dividends on their stocks than from what they earned on the ranch. By the time Estrada died, he was worth over $100,000, even though he had never made more than $150 a month in his life. Alan Day, for one, was convinced that "the cowboys would never have given that money to my dad."

Ada Mae inherited her business sense from her mother. It was in Grandma Wilkey's house that Sandra encountered a female mind as sharp as her mother's, but far more stubborn. Mamie Scott Wilkey was the first woman to work outside the home in Sandra's family. Like many working women, Grandma Wilkey got her experience in a business started by her husband, W. W. Wilkey, who made and lost several fortunes over the course of their marriage, in everything from cattle trading to merchandising. When Ada Mae first met Harry Day as a young girl, the Wilkeys were living in Duncan, where they owned a general store that was mostly run by Mamie Wilkey. (Ada Mae would wait several years to marry Harry, until she had graduated from the University of Arizona.) W.W. was a sort of hail-fellow-well-met, who brought in much of the business, accepted hay or grain or cattle in lieu of payment, and could never turn down a request for credit. Mamie, on the other hand, minded the store, kept the books, and harassed late payers.

The Wilkeys made a small fortune in Duncan and eventually returned to El Paso, and to W.W.'s cattle business. But for all Mamie Wilkey's vigilance, her husband's lackadaisical nature eventually cost them their small fortune and hardened Mamie Wilkey's already stiff back into steely resolve. One afternoon, after making a large sale, he brought $100,000 to his local bank. Finding the doors closed, W.W. went around to the back, where he met some bank officials whom he knew well. They told him the bank was closed for inventory, and W.W. left his money with the bankers. It was the late 1920s, a time when a series of small-bank failures would lead to the big crash of 1929. Wilkey never saw a penny of that deposit again.

W.W. continued trading cattle, a business that Sandra Day O'Connor describes as "a little like going to Las Vegas and playing craps for a living." It was shortly after Sandra first came to live with the Wilkeys in El Paso that W.W. died suddenly, during a business trough. "I hadn't been there more than two or three years, when he had a heart attack and died in the bed next to my grandmother," recalls Justice O'Connor, the memory of that morning still fresh in her mind. "She woke up and he was gone." Mamie Scott Wilkey, who cared enormously about financial security and living comfortably, would never forgive her husband for dying at the moment when he had just lost "a bundle of money," leaving her without any assets.

For Sandra, just seven years old at the time, life with Mamie Wilkey after her grandfather's death turned out to be a far more unorthodox and unsettled existence than her parents had planned. After W.W. died, Harry Day bought his mother-in-law a house in a quiet neighborhood near Sandra's school. But Grandma Wilkey had other ideas. She sold the new house to buy one that was much larger on a busier street in a less affluent neighborhood near the railroad station. Soon Mamie was taking in boarders, renting rooms for the night to engineers and brakemen who passed through El Paso on the railroad, an arrangement of which the Days heartily disapproved. Sandra grew up amid a steady stream of strangers. Even when business was relatively slow, it was never quiet in Grandma's house. Mamie Wilkey was a "nonstop talker," and Sandra would do her homework with the steady hum of Grandma's chatter in the background. "I always said that the reason I became a judge was that I learned as a child how to just listen and still get my work done," O'Connor would say years later.

During those early years in El Paso, it was her cousin Flournoy Manzo, more than her eccentric grandmother, who served as the anchor in Sandra's life. Flournoy came to live in El Paso after her own father's sudden death, which had forced her mother to take a job and leave her daughter in the care of Grandma Wilkey.

Flournoy was a year older than Sandra, and for five years the two girls were inseparable. When Flournoy's mother remarried and took her daughter back to live with her, the cousins saw each other only on summer vacations at the ranch, a fact that would make Sandra's memories of home rosier still. She began to yearn for the Lazy B with growing intensity. Eventually, she persuaded her parents to let her attend the eighth grade in Lordsburg. But she found the commute long and the classes unchallenging, and finally she agreed to return to El Paso.

The sudden deaths in the family—which left women in economic trouble—coupled with the hardships of the Depression, left a lasting impression on Sandra. Years later, she would talk her husband out of building a tennis court behind their house, because it would involve going into debt. In the state legislature, she became known as a fiscal conservative. Indeed, the knowledge that a wife could not always depend on her husband for financial support undoubtedly underscored her determination to develop her own career.

Sandra had always been mature for her age. Now, as she was about to enter high school, she was also intellectually precocious, curious and restless. Perhaps it was a zest for new adventure or just a growing interest in boys, in the coeducational Lordsburg school, but Sandra decided to switch to a public school instead of returning to Radford. She breezed through her high school in just two years and graduated at the age of sixteen.

No one who knew her well was surprised when Harry Day's oldest daughter decided to enroll at Stanford University. "At a relatively early stage, she had her sights set on Stanford," says Alan Day, who remembers his father reminiscing about how he had missed his chance to attend the school. Alan had the feeling that Sandra was going to "make up for what [Dad] couldn't do. They'd talk about world events, and the people who make world events happen, and that so-and-so had been a Stanford graduate. I remember more than one conversation about getting preparation for life, and [Dad saying that] Stanford's the place to go for a blue-ribbon preparation."

Sandra majored in economics as an undergraduate and, initially, had no clear plans to attend law school. But more than one would have thought possible on a remote ranch in Arizona, questions of law and public policy had loomed large in the lives of the Days and in Sandra's own consciousness. When Sandra was a teenager, one family vacation consisted of a car trip that took the family to every state capital west of the Mississippi. It became an important bit of family lore that the day Sandra was born in El Paso, Harry Day was sitting in a courtroom in Tucson, trying to extricate himself, finally, from his father's last, ill-fated business partnership—the one that had brought Harry Day back to the Lazy B immediately after Henry Clay's death.

Although he was often the first to try innovative technology for the ranch, such as the solar-powered water heaters he installed in the 1930s and the windmills that still draw water from the wells, when it came to money and politics, Harry was utterly reactionary. No matter how attractive a business venture looked, Harry Day would forgo it rather than have to take out a loan. He got New Mexico license plates for his car because they were cheaper than plates from Arizona. During the Depression, he worried endlessly about Roosevelt's "giveaway programs," that the nation would "spend itself into poverty." He railed against the New Deal, even though the Civilian Conservation Corps had set up camp right on the Lazy B and built erosion control projects, some of which function to this day, as well as most of the fences that still mark the outer boundary of the property. Years later, he would call Harry Truman a "pinko, Communist, no account." While Arizona became a bastion of the Democratic party, Harry Day became one of a handful of prominent Republicans in the state.

Harry Day had his opinions, for sure, and out on his remote ranch, who better to discuss them with than his sharp-witted elder daughter, Sandra? "She and Dad would have heated debates," recalls Alan Day. "Usually they would argue about who was more conservative on various points." Although Day admits that his dad was "right of Genghis

Khan," he remembers that the one subject "they agreed on is that they both hated Earl Warren and his impact on the court and the nation."

Yet as much as she adored her father and was influenced by him, Sandra showed her intellectual independence long before she became involved in politics. Already as an undergraduate student, she developed a special interest in—and sensitivity to—social issues that Harry Day would have considered anathema. "I can recall her defending desegregation and the early stirrings of race equality," says Alan Day, "[while] dad would say that's just not the way of the world."

Not surprisingly, when Sandra was finishing college, it was an inspirational, larger-than-life Stanford professor who persuaded her to go to law school. Sandra met Harry J. Rathbun when she enrolled in a business law course he taught to undergraduates. And it was Rathbun's seminars, which may have reminded her of the spirited debates with her father, that helped solidify Sandra's commitment to a life devoted to both family and community service.

What captured Sandra's imagination had nothing to do with the nuances of contracts or torts, however. Rathbun, with his white beard and spectacles, was more of a preacher, a latter-day Martin Luther, than a teacher. A founder of such philosophical movements as Creative Initiative and Beyond War, Rathbun taught his students that every human being has a destiny and that personal fulfillment can come only from discovering one's true potential and by contributing to the greater good of one's community. "The future of every one of us and of our earth rests on the attitude and actions of a creative minority of people who are living the universal religious life of spirit and truth," wrote Rathbun in his manifesto, *Creative Initiative*. Rathbun's philosophy was rooted in the Judeo-Christian ethic of love, forgiveness, and charity. In an era of mass destruction, he saw the mobilization of large numbers of "fulfilled individuals," working in a "collective cooperative" for the good of the community and against war, as a key to the survival of mankind.

For Sandra Day, who had grown up in a place where "the forces [of life] were largely uncontrollable," where survival depended on the weather, the market price of cattle, the presence—or lack—of a cattle buyer, Rathbun's outlook was a revelation. On the ranch, Sandra had come to believe that while an individual could try to make the most of her fate by adopting high standards and by striving to be well read, a kind employer, and a good parent, ultimately she must "accept the hand that's dealt." It was in Rathbun's seminars, for the first time, that she learned to consider the possibility that "history turns on the actions of individuals," that a person's destiny is largely determined by her own choices. To Sandra, Rathbun's insistence that each "individual could make a difference," that by doing something "meaningful" every person has the opportunity to "leave the world a better place," was a "fabulous" insight.

Significantly, Rathbun endorsed monogamous marriage, rather than the alternative lifestyles that would soon become commonplace, as the most important civilizing influence on mankind. He perceived a direct link between the notion of "brotherhood," which he saw as "the highest common *commitment* . . . to 'do the will of God,'" and the commitment men and women make when they marry. If couples really believed, and acted on, the vows they made to each other at the time of marriage, Rathbun argued, what better vehicle could there be for transforming society? "The breakdown of marriage and family relationships [is] one of the root causes of our world crisis," wrote Rathbun. "The primary family is the most basic educational agency developing fundamental understanding of the true and enduring values upon which meaningful survival depends."

If Rathbun saw the family as the primary unit of civilization, then he saw the marginalization of women as its greatest waste. Although Rathbun recognized crucial differences between the "feminine" and "masculine" of the species, he saw women and men as equal partners in the creation of "truly human beings." "Egocentric male dominance has brought our world to the brink of disaster," Rathbun would say, albeit recognizing some female complicity in the world's sorry state of affairs. But, he argued, "If the world's crisis is to be met successfully, the need is that woman shall be given, and shall take, her proper place. That place male domination has heretofore denied her. It is one of complete equality with the male of the species. . . . In achieving this equality, not only must woman claim her place, but the male must make sure that it is accorded her. Together, they can make a new world."

Although Sandra had no clear goals when she enrolled at Stanford

Law School, Rathbun's teachings would take on a rich resonance in her life. "I didn't know where [law school] might lead, if anywhere," recalls Justice O'Connor, with her penchant for understatement. "I just thought I would like to try." O'Connor was never driven by a fanatical devotion to the law. But it was at law school that she first became aware of her intellectual and civic potential. Under Rathbun's tutelage, she would come to approach her education with a quiet determination to make something of her talent, to give something back to society, and to live life to its fullest.

Sandra would have been well aware that acceptance in law school, for a young woman of her generation, offered a historic opportunity. And it was one she didn't take lightly. In the years following World War II, the nation's law schools were flooded with applications from veterans. At the time, many prominent law schools, including Harvard, didn't accept female students at all. Her Stanford law school class of about one hundred fifty students graduated only five women. And many among the law school faculty felt that even those five places, a record number at the time, were too many to squander on students who, it was assumed, would marry anyway and never put their law degrees to use.

Friends who knew Sandra in law school always marveled at how "tremendously well prepared" she was. Sandra lived in Cubberly House, which was, at the time, one of the only residences for women law students anywhere in the country. Fellow Cubberly House resident Beatrice Challiss Laws, who became a lifelong friend, is still impressed by the way "Sandra use[d] time better than anyone else I know. She [had] remarkable powers of concentration, a remarkable talent to just stop, focus on just one thing. [In law school] she would be reading through her torts notes, and if a letter arrived from her mother, she would stop to read the letter, immediately write out a response, and return to her homework without skipping a beat."

Already in law school, Sandra displayed the work habits that would later help her in successfully juggling a number of responsibilities—as a wife and mother, and as lawyer, politician, judge, and, finally, justice. Although O'Connor was brutally disciplined about getting her work done, her classmates also remember her for never passing up a chance to have a good time. Sociable and athletic, Sandra was always up for a tennis game, an afternoon swim, or beer and potato chips at Rosatti's beer garden, a university hangout. And after a long evening of partying, it wasn't unusual for Sandra to get up before the crack of dawn to study. "I'm darned if I know when the homework got done—but it got done," she liked to say. Sometimes she didn't sleep. "I can remember getting up to study at 3 A.M.," says O'Connor. "But that's not unusual for a cowgirl."

Although it is often said that Sandra ranked third in her class, Stanford didn't publish a class ranking. Sandra did, however, outperform most of her classmates. She was chosen for *Law Review* in her second year. She took first prize in a moot-court competition. And upon graduation, O'Connor was elected to the Order of the Coif, an honorary legal society reserved for the highest ten percent of the each class. It was William Rehnquist who stood out as the star legal mind in the class, but professors remembered Sandra as a bright and "very popular" student, who was "easy to get to know."

Although the brainy women in her law school class were not always in great demand socially among their male classmates, Sandra never had trouble getting dates. For a time, Sandra and Rehnquist dated regularly. The relationship became serious enough that she invited him to the Lazy B to meet her family during one Easter break. According to a close family friend, Harry and Ada Mae told her to get rid of him; "they didn't like his table manners." Manners might not have been a determining factor, but soon after the trip, the two future justices stopped dating, although they, with their spouses, would become fast friends again in Phoenix, years after they had graduated and had become part of Arizona's up-and-coming Republican elite.

When it came to social graces, John O'Connor, another law school classmate, whom she began dating sometime after her trip home with Rehnquist, would have been eminently acceptable to the Days. Sandra Day met John O'Connor one night on the *Law Review*, when they were assigned an article to cite-check and proofread. After laboring in the library for several hours, John suggested that they finish their work over a beer at Dinah's Shack, a bar down the road. That evening led to a marathon series of dates—forty nights straight without a break. Finally, the couple decided to take some time off from each other, because although Sandra always showed up in class after their evenings out, John couldn't always make it, and his schoolwork was beginning to suffer.

Although John O'Connor was unquestionably intelligent and well spoken, it wasn't his brain that first attracted Sandra. A tall young man, with a wiry, Fred Astaire physique, John was the son of a well-to-do physician whose family had emigrated to San Francisco from Ireland. Those who know him say John inherited his forebears' gift of blarney. Although he is not universally loved, everyone agrees that there are few men funnier than John O'Connor. As for Sandra, she loved the fact that "he made me laugh. It kind of bubbles out of him at any time of the day or night, he just always comes up with funny things."

The relationship with John was serious, and the couple soon began talking about marriage. But Sandra did not want to marry while she was in law school. What's more, as she approached graduation, Sandra knew she wanted to get a job in a law firm. She was committed enough to her goal to apply for positions in southern California, even though John still had another year at Stanford law school.

Sandra did not have a realistic picture of the job market, though. One summer during law school, she had worked as a clerk in a law office in Lordsburg. But high-powered summer jobs and recruiting were unheard-of in those days. So when, shortly before graduation, she applied for positions in several of the California law firms that had posted notices at Stanford, she was "startled" to learn that "none of them were interested in hiring a woman."

"I don't think I had realized that that would be the case," says Justice O'Connor. Her only offer in the private sector came from Gibson Dunn and Crutcher, a white-shoe law firm in Los Angeles that was looking for a legal secretary. "To receive as my only offer [a job] as a secretary was quite shocking. That made me pause," she says, adding with characteristic pragmatism: "It also made me get busy looking elsewhere."

At last Sandra got a job as a deputy county attorney for San Mateo County. By that time, she was busy planning a wedding. Her female classmates also would marry, and all but one would defy their more skeptical professors by continuing to work full time, with just brief interruptions for childbearing.

For Sandra, the whirlwind courtship with John seemed destined to lead to the altar. Not only was he adoring and attentive, but they shared many of the same interests. Both of them loved to ski and play tennis, they were both interested in politics, and they talked about one day traveling the world together.

Moreover, John O'Connor was, for his day, unusually tolerant of his wife's ambitions—embryonic though they were in many respects. "He knew I wanted to work," says the justice. "That was understood. I don't know why, really, because [none of the women] in his family had worked. I don't think he had any experience at all that would lead him to understand what it would involve being married to a working wife. But he accepted that."

The O'Connors were married on December 20, 1952, at the Lazy B. The ceremony took place in the Days' tiny parlor, and the reception was held in a new barn that Harry had just constructed. Pine and juniper boughs decked the rafters. A hundred guests, including Edward Mecham, the governor of New Mexico, feasted on Lazy B beef barbecued in a covered pit in the old cowboy style, and danced to the strains of a country and western band.

Forty years later, the O'Connors would still be dancing. And Sandra would "still [be] laughing." In hindsight, she insists, it helped that bride and groom were young when they married. "We were only twenty-two, and that was probably a good thing," says Justice O'Connor. "We were so young, we grew up in the process of adjusting to each other and to each other's respective careers and needs. I think marrying late can present more problems than marrying young. Once you're set in your ways it's much harder to adjust. We weren't set in anything; we just worked it all out."

For all their youth and willingness to make accommodations, Sandra wasn't about to redefine the institution of marriage. Years after her marriage and her appointment to a seat on the Supreme Court, when one of her young protégés told her he couldn't leave Washington because his wife didn't want to move, Justice O'Connor quipped: "John never made any sacrifices for my career until this appointment." But if that was true, it was in large part because she didn't expect it of him. Even when she was being beckoned to run for the U.S. Senate or for governor of Arizona, Sandra's decisions weren't so much influenced by John as by her own vision of the ideal family.

Just as Ada Mae had moved from El Paso to the Lazy B, Sandra embraced a traditional pattern of married life, always deferring to John's choice of where to work and live. After John graduated, he was drafted and sent to Germany; Sandra left her job in the San Mateo Attorney's office and accompanied him to Frankfurt, where she got a job as a civilian attorney in the Army Quartermaster Corps. The O'Connors lived in Germany for three years. When they returned, Sandra would have liked to return to the Bay area, where she had put down roots and made several friends. But John was eager to move someplace else, and Sandra acquiesced when he suggested that they settle in Phoenix, where he had been offered a job with an eminent firm. Sandra, however, had no ties to her state capital, a boom town of new businesses and state politics that was physically and culturally far removed from the New Mexico border and the Lazy B.

John's reasons for moving to Phoenix explain a lot about the man and why he turned out to be a surprisingly good choice for Sandra. John had come from a family of physicians. His grandfather, the first John Jay O'Connor, was one of the founders of St. Francis Hospital in San Francisco, where John's father, John Jay II, and two uncles also worked as doctors. John's father had few interests outside of medicine and, not surprisingly, hoped that his only son would follow in his footsteps. The son did, in fact, go to college expecting to become a medical student, but he soon changed his mind, deciding to become a lawyer instead.

Perhaps his decision to reject medicine put some distance between John and his family. Perhaps he simply wanted a change. Whatever the reason, when he married Sandra Day, John insisted on leaving California. Following their stint in Frankfurt, the O'Connors considered staying in Germany, until they realized that most of the American couples they knew there "were never really part of the German community, and at the same time had lost their links with the U.S."

"We recognized that what we wanted was a life where we had a deep involvement with our community," says Justice O'Connor. The move to a small, growing community out West, where newcomers were easily absorbed and a little initiative could take a person—even a woman—far in civic life, would prove to be a fortuitous training ground for national office.

To John, Phoenix seemed ideal. It was a prosperous state capital, yet it wasn't too big. And he had been offered a job by Fennemore, Craig, von Ammon and Udall, a fine old law firm that "wasn't too big" either.

"It's a small town and I can make a name for myself," he told Beatrice Laws, the couple's old law school friend, at the time. "In San Francisco, he would have been swallowed up," says Laws.

That wasn't, of course, entirely true. With his family and school ties, John O'Connor would probably have done well in San Francisco. John always had a knack for making the right connections. At St. Ignatius, the prestigious Jesuit academy he had attended, two of his closest friends were Peter Armstrong, who became a monsignor in the Catholic Church, and George Mosconi, who became the mayor of San Francisco.

Whatever his reasons for deciding to leave the Bay area, John O'Connor seemed content to become a big fish in a small pond. The O'Connors would move to an exclusive Phoenix neighborhood, fittingly known as Paradise Valley. They bought a cabin in Iron Springs, a retreat in the mountains above Tucson, where, in the days before air-conditioning, "all the top families" went for the summer. With a brilliant and beautiful wife at his side, John befriended a crowd of young Phoenix Republicans and became involved in Richard Nixon's 1960 election campaign. If Sandra's ambitions were inspired by Rathbun's vision of creative, cooperative citizenship, John was moved more by his desire to be a pillar of Phoenix society. He became prominent in the Phoenix Rotary Club and was president of the United Way and of the Maricopa County Young Republicans Club. And in the mid 1970s he won admission to California's exclusive, all-male Bohemian Grove club, which by most accounts became one of the "most important things in his life."

John was building an "inventory" of connections that would make him the leading rainmaker at his firm and would also turn out to be a huge asset for his wife. When Henry Kissinger visited Phoenix in the early 1970s, Sandra was chosen to accompany Mrs. Kissinger for the day. At the Paradise Valley country club, Sandra showed up on the tennis court one afternoon with Kit Bond's wife, the first lady of Kentucky. Nor was there doubt in anyone's mind that it was "John O'Connor [who] worked many of those connections. [For John] it was a 'Who do you know?' type of game," says Scott Alexander, a former colleague of Sandra O'Connor's in the Arizona State Senate and her sister Ann's ex-husband.

John was smart, funny, the perfect master of ceremonies, and, there was no getting around it, an elitist—some even said a snob. "The difference between Sandra and John is that Sandra has a unique ability to penetrate, and he has a unique ability never to ask what's doing with you," says Jerome H. Lewkowitz, a Phoenix attorney who used to work with Sandra Day O'Connor in the Arizona Attorney General's office in the early 1960s. "It's always Sandra and I did this, or I did that. He's just self-satisfied."

"John's John," says Alan Day. "If John were talking to me and someone more important walked by, he'd stop in midsentence and walk the other way."

Yet like almost everyone who knows them well, Day is quick to point out that Sandra O'Connor has no greater fan than John O'Connor: "He's very, very supportive," says Day, pausing for emphasis. "I've never heard him be negative about her goals."

Since their days as students together, John understood and accepted that Sandra was an exceptional woman, one who, for all her commitment to family, was driven by a sense of destiny, albeit one that would take years to unfold fully. Early on, he must have recognized that his wife's growing interest in politics and in community affairs—to say nothing of her brains and poise—served as a perfect complement to his ambitions. Even as she set up a small legal practice, Sandra became involved with a number of charities and community organizations, including the Junior League, the Salvation Army, and the Heard Museum. "John loves to be social, to be around people," says Alan Day, who notes that through Sandra Day's life as a public figure, John had the opportunity to meet a lot of "movers and doers around the world," which is what John thrives on.

Indeed, in some ways, Sandra Day O'Connor's ascent in public life represents an inverted tale of frustrated ambitions, the flip side of the mythic 1950s ideal of marriage between an accomplished breadwinner and a dependent homemaker. For in the beginning, it was John O'Connor who was most interested in getting involved in politics. As a high school student in San Francisco, John had dreamed of one day running for public office. After the couple moved to Phoenix, it was John who first decided to join the Arizona Young Republicans. Years later, when his wife was already in the state senate, John continued subscribing to obscure political newsletters that kept him informed of every proposed statute and bill that was wending its way through the legislature.

But the need to provide for a growing family put public office beyond John O'Connor's reach. In the 1960s, the salary of an Arizona state legislator was only about six thousand dollars. And the job of a legislator was too demanding to be compatible with a full-time position in a law firm. John O'Connor had no problem earning a good living in his law practice. It would have been virtually impossible for husband and wife to reverse roles, however, even if they had wanted to—the jobs simply weren't there for women.

Thus, for a man of his generation and his interests, genuine love and a strong ego were important factors in the pleasure John O'Connor was able to take in his wife's accomplishments. So although he rarely volunteered to do any domestic chores, and the O'Connors' family life was, on the surface, quite traditional—with Sandra doing everything from getting dinner on the table to planning after-school activities for the kids—John did more than just stand out of her way. It was clear to the kids how "impressed" Dad was with Mom's abilities. They could see competition between other couples, but that was "never an issue" for John, who liked to boast that he had made "the best marriage decision in the country." To the couple's friends, it was obvious that a "sense of partnership" pervaded their relationship. To anyone who knew them well, there was never any doubt that "John [was] the raison d'être for Sandra—her primary support system, her primary promoter." If you asked John, "How's the family?" he was apt to sing Sandra's praises.

But Sandra O'Connor also knew how to return the compliment. Alan Day notes that when called upon, his sister Sandra "will sit quietly, and encourage [John] to tell jokes; the family joke is that Sandra promises to laugh, if John will take out the garbage." Even her colleagues noticed her knack for playing the role of (doting) wife. "It was always John this or John that—she's always building him up," recalls Jerome Lewkowitz.

It also helped that Sandra O'Connor was the sort of person who could make running both a five-person household and the state senate seem effortless. Because it was so unusual at the time, "John's support of [his wife's career] was in some sense a sacrifice," says Ruth McGregor, a judge in the Arizona Court of Appeals, who served as Justice O'Connor's clerk during her first term on the Supreme Court. "But her ability to organize and be efficient decreased the impact of her career on their marriage."

"This is not meant as a criticism of my dad," says Jay, the couple's youngest son, but "Mom did it all. Even the day-to-day financial stuff. Dad did overall finances, investment decisions. And he had certain household responsibilities, like taking out the trash and cleaning the pool. He's incredibly fun, and good at organizing trips. But Dad is a disaster in the kitchen. He's not Mr. Mechanic. He would have starved to death if left to his own devices."

When the O'Connors returned to Phoenix from Frankfurt, Sandra was pregnant. She was still unable to get a job in the private sector, but while taking her Arizona bar exam, she met another young attorney, Tom Tobin, who was looking for a partner to start a storefront legal office—a "dirty shirts" operation—in a run-down section of Phoenix known as Maryvale. Sandra found a baby-sitter and began working "pretty much full time" within a month or two of Scott's birth. In 1960, a second son, Brian, was born, and again she returned to the office after just a few weeks.

But within months of Brian's birth the O'Connors' baby-sitter suddenly quit. "When the baby-sitter left, I had two children—small," recalls Justice O'Connor. "It certainly wasn't possible for me to continue working without the kind of baby-sitter whom I wanted to leave my children with day in and day out. [It would have to be] somebody really lovely. My sitter had been a woman named Cora Shell. She was arthritic and a little handicapped, but she was the dearest person. She was loving and warm and darling with the children."

Although there were plenty of migrant workers in Arizona, Sandra decided she didn't want to leave her children with someone who wasn't English-speaking. Try as she might, she was unable to find a replacement for Cora. "Without someone like that, I felt I had to stay home and take care of things. John was plugging away, and we were able to live on what he made. It was not an economic necessity [for me to work]. It would have been nice. But I had that special freedom. Many women don't have that choice, because they have to make ends meet. So I decided that I would just have to stay at home for a while. I settled into the life of a suburban housewife."

Sandra O'Connor would take a five-year hiatus from her life as a full-time professional. But even as a self-proclaimed housewife, O'Connor took pains to make sure she didn't drop the threads of her profession. "I was very concerned that I not totally lose touch with the law while I was out of the paid-employment sector," says Justice O'Connor. "I wanted to be able to go back to work as a lawyer. [But] I hadn't had enough experience to feel that my future was assured as a lawyer. I was concerned that if I didn't keep my hand in some way, doing lawyerly things . . . And of course it still wasn't easy for women to be hired in law firms."

So O'Connor picked up odd jobs wherever she could. She started out writing bar-review exam questions and grading the answers; the pay, as for much of what she did during this period, was minimal, but it allowed her to "continue focusing on certain areas and to read up [on the law] and stay in touch." She also agreed to sit as a voluntary referee in juvenile court, passing judgment on the less egregious cases.

Gradually, over the course of five years, O'Connor took on a number of both legal and philanthropic responsibilities. On behalf of the Maricopa County bar association, she set up an office for a lawyer referral system for the poor and hired a director. She did legal work for the Salvation Army. She also took on bankruptcy trustee work, marshaling the assets of the estates entrusted to her, filing court documents, and handling disputes among creditors. Knowing little about bankruptcy law when she got started, O'Connor had to read up on the subject, which made the projects all the more "fascinating to do."

By this time, spurred on by John's interest in politics and in Arizona's fledgling Republican party, Sandra also had become involved with local politics and community affairs. She started out as a precinct committeeman, working her way up to the chairmanship of her legislative district, a job in which she spent hours helping to register voters and serving as a conduit between her community and its legislators. Today C-SPAN and electronic media have made the job largely obsolete, but in O'Connor's day the precinct committeemen served as a crucial information pipeline for constituents. The job also turned out to be the perfect political apprenticeship. "In the process, I got to know a number of Republican officeholders," says Justice O'Connor, who befriended Barry Goldwater, the man who would come to be one of her most important political mentors, during this period.

O'Connor's responsibilities kept mounting. Soon she found herself sitting on the county planning and zoning commission. She did work for the local YMCA. And in 1962, she gave birth to her third child, Jay. At about the same time, she also became an active member of the Junior League. "After five years of scrambling, I decided it would make more sense to unload all this voluntary activity and to get a paid job to have a little peace and quiet in my life," says O'Connor, only partly in jest. "It just got *very* busy. I had to get baby-sitters constantly."

Going back to work wouldn't be easy, however. "I was afraid I wouldn't get a job," says the Supreme Court Justice. "I didn't, of course, get one in a law firm. I didn't press it. What I did think I could do is work in the attorney general's office." When O'Connor first began pursuing the idea, the attorney general was a Democrat, and she didn't stand a chance. When elections brought a Republican to office, O'Connor tried once more. Although the new attorney general wasn't much more enthusiastic than his predecessor had been, he finally agreed to give O'Connor a job. At first, O'Connor says, she got "the least desirable position" in the office, which involved straightening out the legal morass at the Arizona state hospital for the mentally ill.

O'Connor would distinguish herself in her new job and her first project. At the time, Arizona was going through a difficult transition from institutional to community-based care, when inmates were being released from years of confinement in ever greater numbers but often had no place to go. O'Connor became part social worker, part attorney. She set up an office at the hospital where patients could see her about getting a place to live or finding out how to recover property that had been lost while they were institutionalized. She drew up rules where either there weren't any or they were "frighteningly disjointed and uncoordinated." O'Connor's regulations established, among other things, fairer procedures for getting inmates released. She also helped draw up legislation that was more protective of the mentally ill. All the while, O'Connor prided herself on maintaining "a very good relationship" with the state hospital directors.

While O'Connor was doing well in her new job, she also was overwhelmed by her responsibilities. Although she had found a new full-time housekeeper, her children were still young. Moreover, contrary to her original intentions, O'Connor had not been able to tear herself away from her philanthropic responsibilities. In 1967, for example, two years into her job as assistant attorney general, O'Connor was nominated as president of the Phoenix chapter of the Junior League. Having proved herself at work, she asked for a three-quarter-day schedule that would allow her to leave the office between three and four in the afternoon, in exchange for two-thirds pay. The attorney general accepted her terms.

Despite her reduced hours, O'Connor took on more responsibilities at the office. She came to represent a number of new state clients, including the welfare, health, and treasury departments. Working for a time with the state auditor, who happened to be a woman, O'Connor found herself in the thick of government, reviewing all the outstanding bills of each agency. She relished the immense responsibility and enjoyed getting "to know the players" and doing every phase of the state's legal work, which sometimes went all the way up to the State Supreme Court. O'Connor had never had so much "fun."

When Richard Nixon appointed Isabel Burgess, who was the state senator from O'Connor's district, to the National Transportation Safety Board, O'Connor was ready. O'Connor made it known to the county board of supervisors that she was interested in the position. And in 1969 she was asked to fill Burgess's seat.

It was never blind ambition that drove O'Connor inexorably up the ladder of Arizona government. "I'm not quite sure why I did that, but I'd been involved in local politics at the grassroots level, so I was interested in the legislature," says O'Connor in the gee-gosh-how'd-that-happen manner that today's formidable Supreme Court justice still cultivates. Bruce Babbitt probably sized up his erstwhile rival best of all: "I . . . think the intense part of her ambition is focused against an internal standard rather than an outside goal or standard."

Indeed, over the years, in decisions ranging from whether to live permanently in Germany with her new husband to whether to run for the governorship of Arizona, O'Connor approached each of life's crossroads with judicious self-restraint and careful consideration. Her overriding goal was to follow Rathbun's admonition to "make a difference" and never stop learning. It helped that O'Connor developed an interest in almost every situation or place in which she found herself.

From her first days in the state legislature, O'Connor's political career was marked by her methodical nature and deep-seated integrity. During her freshman year, for example, she was approached by Bill Jacquin, who was about to become president of the senate, to take his place as majority leader. But O'Connor demurred. It would be presumptuous, she told him, for a rookie senator to take on a such a post. Thus, it wasn't until nearly three years later, in 1973, that O'Connor became the first woman to serve as the majority leader of a state senate. Indeed, the only purely political act any of her colleagues remember her making was the decision to pull her kids out of the private high school down the street and put them in a public school that required a commute by bus or car.

After what seemed like a hectic work schedule at the attorney general's office, O'Connor suddenly found herself thrust into a job that would place round-the-clock demands on her time. It was as a state senator that O'Connor's legendary organizational powers were truly tested. She distinguished herself early as a leader of the senate, while preserving the Rockwellian ideal of family life that she so fervently cherished. Performing both jobs with a quiet, cheerful competence, she miraculously almost never showed signs of stress.

O'Connor's phone never stopped ringing. The calls started at 6:00 A.M. and didn't stop until 11:30 P.M. O'Connor traveled the state, giving several speeches each week, and found her schedule so demanding that she resumed the old habit of getting up before dawn for the only hours of quiet, concentrated work that her routine allowed. To squeeze as much out of her workday as possible, O'Connor almost never went out for lunch, preferring to work at her desk with Bill Jacquin, eating carry-out fried chicken.

Yet O'Connor made sure that her office hours never interfered with her family's schedule. Come 4:30 or 4:45, she would collect her handbag and say in that matter-of-fact way of hers: "I have to go home now and get dinner ready." There were exceptions: During particularly busy periods, at the end of a term, it wasn't unusual for O'Connor to work late into the night, either in the senate chamber or on the phone. But when one legislative session happened to coincide with the day before Jay's departure for summer camp, O'Connor stood up on the house floor and announced that the debate would have to end by 8:00 P.M. because she would have to go home to pack her son's suitcase. The debate ended on time, and another piece of the Sandra Day O'Connor legend fell into place.

After her appointment to the senate, O'Connor rarely got home before dinnertime. Yet her children don't recall her not being there when, as young boys, they arrived home. In the hours between the time school let out and 6:00 P.M., she filled up the boys' schedules with a variety of after-school activities—mostly sports. She hired high school students to take them out to play or to swimming classes at the country club. "When we got home, typically she would be getting there at about the same time we were," says Brian, who would have been entering the third grade when O'Connor first became a senator.

It helped that the O'Connors now had a full-time housekeeper. Although O'Connor had always liked to cook, and continued preparing meals even after she joined the senate, she planned her menus a week ahead of time so that she could do all the grocery shopping on a single day, either after work or on a weekend, usually with her youngest son, Jay, in tow. On her way out in the mornings, she would leave the housekeeper detailed instructions as to which ingredients to prepare for each night's meal. By the time she got home from the office, the prep work would be done. While the kids watched *The Brady Bunch*, O'Connor would produce dinner for five, choosing from any one of thirty or so family favorites, such as leg of lamb or crabmeat enchiladas. Just about the only culinary concession she made to her busy schedule was that she rarely baked or made desserts, and her kids remember weekly outings to a family-style restaurant, usually an inexpensive Mexican eatery called Gene's Buffet. Even when she was nominated to the Supreme Court, O'Connor still didn't hang up her apron: Today the justice, who keeps a coffee-table book entitled *The Washington Hostess* in her chambers, often relaxes after her Saturday-morning meetings at the Supreme Court by preparing meals at home for friends.

Between the end of one workday and the beginning of another, O'Connor kept a schedule that even her sons found exhausting. She helped the kids with their homework, proofreading it for spelling mistakes, and typed all their papers until they took typing class in high school. Every paper would elicit at least one or two well-reasoned questions. The O'Connors regularly attended PTA meetings. And when Scott took up competitive swimming (he would go on to become the state swimming champion), Sandra and John would alternate chauffeuring him to early-morning swim meets, even though frequently they had had only three or four hours' of sleep the night before. Nor did O'Connor forgo her regular Friday-evening tennis games with friends at the Paradise Valley Country Club. "If anything, as kids, we'd joke: 'Hey, Mom, stop being so hyper, settle down, let's just do nothing for a while,' " remembers Brian O'Connor.

But there was a method behind the hyperactive schedule of the O'Connor clan. As much as possible, Sandra O'Connor had tried to create an atmosphere of carefree independence, adventure, and trust such as she had enjoyed on the Lazy B. Although both Sandra and John kept close tabs on their sons' progress—both in school and in sports—they also gave the boys "a ton of independence . . . as long as we didn't blow it," recalls Brian. The O'Connors had moved back to Phoenix, in part, because it was a safe place to raise children. The boys did well in school. By cultivating in them their own avid interest in sports, the O'Connors knew they were providing an extra bit of insurance against the more delinquent exploits of adolescence. Although the house-keeper was usually at home in the afternoons, the boys, when older, had their own keys. If they wanted to visit a friend after school, all they had to do was leave a note or phone their parents to let them know where they could be reached. More than most of their friends, the O'Connor boys were allowed to make their own decisions. They "never micromanaged us," recalls Brian.

At times the O'Connors must have worried that the boys had ab-sorbed a taste for independence all too well. For Sandra, Brian was a particular source of anxiety. He began skydiving in high school. When he came home one day and told his parents that he wanted to go hang gliding, the O'Connors suggested that the new sport was too danger-ous. Not wanting to come down too hard on the boy, Sandra said offhandedly: "I'd rather you jumped out of a plane." The next week, Brian signed up for parachuting lessons, and the O'Connors had no choice but to sign the parental consent forms.

When Brian developed an interest in mountain climbing, his par-ents, at first reluctantly, gave him their backing. "They did it because they knew I was serious and organized," says Brian, who also knew the unasked question that always hung in the air: "God, what's he going to do next?" But Brian also could count on his mother not to stand in his way. Before long, Sandra's son had developed a plan to climb the high-est peak on each continent. His mother watched with a mixture of pride and foreboding as Brian tackled summit after summit. When he set his heart on climbing a forbidding peak in New Guinea that no one had scaled in decades—on an island populated by cannibals—O'Connor actually gave him a leg up: She asked Secretary of State James Baker to intercede with the Indonesian government to help Brian get the required permits.

An Irresistible Candidate

If politics had started out as something "fun," an interest Sandra and John could share and that would help them make a place for themselves in Phoenix, it soon became much more. Within months of O'Connor's joining the state legislature, the Senate leadership identified her as a comer. Jacquin, who died in 1992, tapped her as chairman of the powerful State County and Municipal Affairs Committee.

Before long, it became clear to Republicans and Democrats alike that O'Connor had developed a deep sense of mission. "She worked interminable hours and read everything there was," said Alfredo Gutierrez, a Democratic state senator. "It was impossible to win a debate with her. We [the Democrats] would go on the floor with a few facts and let rhetoric do the rest. Not Sandy. She would overwhelm you with her knowledge."

While most legislators delegated much of their background reading to staff, O'Connor insisted on poring over every piece of legislation herself. Not one for back-room dealmaking, she won her battles the long and arduous way: After doing her homework, O'Connor would sit down with legislators on either side of the aisle and quietly, cogently, argue the good sense of her side. Nor did she shy away from controversy, often embracing legislation that led her to cross party lines. Once she took up a cause, O'Connor rarely lost. By the end of her tenure in the legislature, O'Connor's influence had become so far-reaching that one Arizona columnist noted that no other legislator had ever had as great an impact on state government as Sandra Day O'Connor.

Of course, O'Connor was no radical. During her first few years in the senate, which coincided with the first stirrings of radical feminism and free love, O'Connor opened one speech at a high school by announcing: "I come to you tonight wearing my wedding band and my brassiere." Yet many of the bills with which she came to be identified were socially progressive and grew out of her experience as a woman who had faced prejudice within her profession. They also reflected her exposure to an array of social problems both in the attorney general's office and in private practice. Her work with the state mental hospital had triggered an interest in health care and prompted O'Connor, despite enormous opposition from the Republican party, to join Burton Barr, the house majority leader, in devising a Medicaid enabling act for Arizona—the only state that didn't have one. Although the bill, which was introduced by Scott Alexander, finally passed, it was never funded; in the early 1980s, Arizona adopted an alternative program based on a managed-care model.

O'Connor also became an advocate of women's rights, affirming her conviction that "in family law, property law, and elsewhere, women, particularly black women, [are] relegated to a position that could best be described as second class." She pushed for ratification of the Equal Rights Amendment to the Constitution after it passed Congress in 1972, supported legislation to make community property laws fairer to women, and backed a plan for making "all medically acceptable family-planning methods and information" available to all women—a stance that angered opponents of abortion. She also succeeded in overturning an Arizona statute that limited a woman's workweek to forty hours. After being turned down for a credit card—because she hadn't applied jointly with John—O'Connor also got a bill passed that made it easier for Arizona women to get credit on their own.

Nor was she apt to back away from a tough fight, especially when it came to issues that had strong support among her constituents. When she took on a long-shot battle to pass a constitutional amendment to limit state spending, for example, it didn't bother O'Connor that a similar bill had previously been defeated. In fact, her colleagues were often stunned by the passionate conviction that this normally reserved woman could bring to a legislative battle. "She put her whole heart into it," recalls Barr, referring to the amendment. "I had people in the house in both [parties] who thought that was the dumbest idea. But [we] finally fought that mother through. I'll never forget it. I [was] holding a caucus in the house, going on and on about this subject. [Sandra] was standing outside the door. She had worked herself up to the point where [when] I came out of the room and said you've got it, she put her arms around me"—Barr pauses for emphasis—"and I [had to explain to] her that majority leaders don't kiss."

Indeed, O'Connor developed a reputation for uncompromising integrity and evenhandedness—traits that would be an asset to a judge but could be a liability in the legislature. As chairman of the State County and Municipal Affairs Committee, which handled the lion's share of new legislation, for example, O'Connor eschewed the common practice of pocketing legislation—holding it up so the legislature couldn't vote on it—as a way of leveraging votes. Says Scott Alexander: "[For Sandra] it wasn't a matter of being a lady. It had to do with her perception of what was the right thing to do."

O'Connor's lawyerly penchant for precision and detail, however, sometimes ran up against the catch-as-catch-can nature of the legislature. Known for believing in the importance of "workable" laws, she would take a red pencil to her colleagues' bills if she found them wanting in logic or clarity. Once, she even introduced an amendment to a bill calling for nothing more than the insertion of a comma in the legislative language to make the intent of the law unmistakable. "She was the most particular person when it came to a bill," recalls Barr. "To her a law was sacred. It was more than that—it had to be perfect. The English, the punctuation. She'd call up and say: 'Now, Burton, on line 48, "is" should be "was." ' Or, 'There's no comma here.' No kidding, Sandra. My goal in life was let's just get it passed."

In the hurly-burly of the legislature, such perfectionism often rankled members of her own party, as well as the Democrats. "The bottom line is you can have a Ph.D. in political science, [but this is] a people business, and Psychology 101 may do better than all political science," says Barr. "It's [a question of being able] to make things happen, knowing how to facilitate things, how to handle colleagues. If you didn't really know [Sandra], she might appear a little too professional, a little cold. Too officious. A little [too] all business."

Dignity. Precision. Care. "All the things that make her a great justice, they aren't all the things that make you a [great] majority leader," says Barr. "Not that she wasn't a good majority leader. God, let it never be said that I ever cast an aspersion. But let it also be said that I think she found herself to be [in a] difficult [position]. I think there was a lot of stress for her. I think she saw that it presented a problem for her, that it didn't quite fit her."

Then came 1974, the year of Watergate. The scandal marked a low point for the Republican party. In Arizona, the GOP lost control of the state senate. And several senators decided not to run again—including Jacquin, Alexander, and O'Connor.

O'Connor left the state legislature in 1974, to run for trial judge in the Maricopa County Superior Court, having tired of the incessant demands of her office, the constant legislative battles, and the larger scandal involving her party. Publicly she would only say that she had accomplished much of what she had set out to do as a state senator. "Perhaps more than my share," she would say. "There was another aspect of it too," admits the justice. "As a majority leader, nothing could get through the legislature without some help and cooperation from me. That leads to a lot of flattery, [and] I don't think that's good for a person."

But her record as a legislator was sterling. She had impeccable connections and credentials. She was a woman. And for the struggling Republican party, she was an irresistible candidate. Consequently, for the next few years, in the prelude to virtually every hotly contested political race, whether it was for the U.S. Senate or for the governorship, the Republican party always turned to O'Connor.

O'Connor came close to seeking higher office only once. In the wake of Watergate, as the Arizona Republicans tried to resuscitate the state's party, they asked her to run for governor. Not only had the GOP lost control of the Arizona senate, but during the next four years, a bizarre game of musical chairs in the governor's mansion seemed to keep alive the chaos of the Watergate years; during one ten-month period in 1977 and 1978, one governor quit and another dropped dead, unexpectedly sweeping Bruce Babbitt, who was then attorney general, and who would prove to be a hugely popular politician, into power.

O'Connor had probably been approached as early as 1976 about running for governor on the Republican ticket. But as the elections grew nearer, the GOP became increasingly desperate. Most of all, the party was "scared to death" that a popular Democrat like Babbitt would carry a passel of Democrats into the house and senate on his coattails, stripping the Republicans of their control of the house. In March, a handful of Arizona's leading Republican power brokers got together for lunch at a local club to decide what to do. Barry Goldwater, Governor Paul Fannin, and John Pritzloff, the father-in-law of Governor Syming- ton, were all there. At one time, Jacquin and Barr, two popular young Republicans, would have made the most logical candidates; but Jacquin already had suffered a costly defeat, in 1974, and Barr wasn't interested. To the men in the room there was only one logical alternative, only one Republican who had the special appeal that might yet snatch vic- tory from the jaws of almost certain defeat.

Sandra Day O'Connor was sitting on the bench one day that spring, when a bailiff handed her a scrap of paper. "You'll never guess what happened," she told her friend and then-brother-in-law Scott Alexander later that afternoon. "I got subpoenaed to the Arizona Club." During the lunchtime recess, O'Connor made her way from the court- house to the club, where several local politicians, including Jacquin, pressed her to consider a run for the governorship.

It was then that O'Connor began to realize the full extent of the political opportunities open to her. Later that day, in a conversation with Alexander, O'Connor couldn't hide her excitement at the lobby- ing effort under way to make her a challenger in the race for governor. But if she was looking for encouragement from Alexander, she was dis- appointed. "I'm sure that's all very flattering," he told the young judge, "but I think you have to take a [close] look at the situation. How seri- ous are they about wanting you to be governor? If they're serious, how much money are they willing to put behind the candidate? I wouldn't accept anything but cash on the table."

"You're not being very nice," O'Connor replied, the disappoint- ment audible in her voice.

There was no doubt that O'Connor was tempted. But as Alexander well knew, there was the all-important question of what such a move would mean for her family life. "We also discussed the question and character of the life of a governor. Of having everything on the clothesline all the time. The family would have absolutely no privacy." The boys were now teenagers and no longer needed constant atten- tion. But how would public office change her relationship with Scott and Brian and Jay? What kind of family vacations would they have? How would they celebrate Christmas and Thanksgiving?

The Arizona Club luncheon took place on a Thursday. John was on a business trip and not expected back in town until the following week. Sandra wouldn't make any decision until he got home. In the meantime, that Saturday morning, some half a dozen Republicans gathered in the O'Connors' den to press their case. "We had honed our sales pitch," recalled Jacquin. "John was [still] out of town. He wasn't due back till Monday. We broke up around twelve or twelve-thirty. I went back to Tucson. On Sunday morning, I got a call from Sandra. Her question was: 'If you think so strongly that I should run, why aren't you running?' "

Jacquin ticked off the reasons—excluding the financial concerns that lingered since his last defeat. One, O'Connor had impeccable credentials, both as a legislator and through years of voluntarism. Two, the Republicans were certain that, as a woman, she could win more votes than she would lose from the state's Democratic constituency. Third, through her years of work as a volunteer, she had links to the workforce and to civic groups that none of the other candidates could match. By the time Jacquin hung up the phone, he was certain she was going to say yes.

On Monday, John returned to Phoenix. And on Tuesday, O'Connor called Jacquin to tell him that she had decided not to run for the governorship after all. "My impression was she'd talked to the kids, to John. They had had a family council meeting," said Jacquin.

O'Connor and those who know her well insist that John would never have stood in her way. "I don't know what he thought in his heart of hearts; [but] we weren't at odds," says O'Connor. "He talked about the pluses and minuses, [about] what it would entail. I think he would have supported a decision to go for it." Says Scott Alexander: "John would have supported her all the way. I don't think he discouraged or encouraged her."

It is much more likely that O'Connor had taken a cool, dispassionate measure of her existence, of her "destiny," and the sort of life to which she was best suited, and concluded that there was no compelling reason to disrupt her life in Paradise Valley. The possibility of holding the highest public office in the state, the glamour and flattery of it all, might have overcome a candidate with a weaker ego. O'Connor's life was exceptionally rich precisely because she had a singular ability to find joy and meaning in what she already possessed. For O'Connor knew herself, and knew that she had found fulfillment in her family, in her zest for the law, and in her new position on the bench. Says O'Connor: "My sons were teenagers, [which] didn't mean they didn't need a little attention; [the judiciary] was much more compatible with my family commitments than holding a statewide office."

It was Burton Barr who said it best: "I think she understood who she was; I just don't think Sandra O'Connor wanted the hurly-burly, public attention, day after day," of political office.

In fact, O'Connor's growing celebrity hadn't detracted one iota from her feelings about her personal life. Just as family had remained the central focus of her life, O'Connor also had maintained a wide network of friendships completely unrelated to her professional life. She kept up with her old classmate Beatrice Laws, who had settled in California and become a confirmed Democrat. Since her days at the Junior League, O'Connor also had maintained close ties with a group of Phoenix matrons, most of whom led traditional lives as homemakers. The group called itself the Red Creek Riders, and they would go horseback riding together and occasionally, on weekends, camping. Later, after her appointment to the Supreme Court, O'Connor turned the weekend get-togethers into an annual reunion that would meet during summer recess in places like Switzerland, Maine, or Iron Springs. Even after O'Connor became a justice, and arguably the most powerful woman in the country, during her summer retreats with the Mobile Party Unit—as the women now called themselves—all her energy was focused on her friends. Just about the only difference the women noticed, says Betsy Taylor, a member of the group, was that when "we'd go to bed at around 10:00 P.M., you could see a light under her door." Late at night, O'Connor would take a few hours to read the correspondence that came regularly from the Supreme Court.

One bonus in keeping her job as a judge was that O'Connor could continue to perform marriage rites. Among her friends and family she had become known as an unabashed apostle of marriage. As a judge, she enjoyed officiating at weddings and composed a ceremony that echoed Rathbun's vision of marriage as the principal unit of civilization: "Marriage is far more than an exchange of vows. It is the foundation of the family, mankind's basic unit of society, the hope of the world and the strength of our country. It is the relationship between ourselves and the generations which follow."

To her friends, O'Connor became known as the Yenta of Paradise Valley. "I was single when I was elected to the state senate," recalls Scott Alexander. "And she kept pulling me aside, saying, 'You have to meet my sister.' And I kept saying I don't need to meet anyone; save your sister for someone else." Then, one balmy April day in 1971, O'Connor and Alexander were walking to a budget meeting for the State Highway Department, when Alexander suggested on a whim that they ditch the meeting and go play tennis instead. Since the highway department was federally funded and the meeting just advisory, O'Connor agreed to play hooky and told Alexander to pick her up at home in thirty minutes. O'Connor phoned her sister Ann and told her to get to her house right away. When Alexander arrived to pick up Sandra, "There was Ann." They were married three months later.

As a Supreme Court justice, O'Connor would continue to indulge her yen for matchmaking. One spring in the early 1980s, O'Connor, who schedules monthly social events, such as museum outings and birthday parties, for her Supreme Court staff, noticed that there was nothing scheduled for April. Not too subtly, she suggested to one of her clerks, who was living with his girlfriend at the time: "It would be a good time for an engagement party." The couple were engaged a few months later.

Not even her sons could escape their mother's obsession with conjugal bliss. When Brian was still in high school, O'Connor caused a minor uproar at home when she told one of her friends that he would be delighted to take her daughter to the prom. Nor would she be able to resist, years later, poking around Brian's apartment in search of telltale signs of female companionship. But if finding a dress in Brian's closet gave her hope that her middle son, who would remain a bachelor until he was in his thirties, might soon marry, she thoroughly disapproved of modern courtship. "I was never allowed to go to the cabin on my own until I got married," says Brian, referring to the family's summer house in Iron Springs. "When I was thirty, she still would not allow it; she felt I was going to bring some gals up there, [and] that was just not right in a family environment. Things like that she just had her mind [made up about]. To us it was halfway funny, halfway frustrating. . . . Sometimes we'd make fun of her: 'Earth to Mom, you're supposed to know what's going on out there, it's the 1990s.' "

Though for both Sandra and John O'Connor the family would always come first, by the 1970s Sandra knew that her professional home was in the judiciary. By her first term on the Maricopa County Superior Court, O'Connor recognized that the work was ideally suited to her temperament and interests. It was intellectually challenging and made "quieter demands" on her than had the legislature. It was also work tailor made for a woman who was known for marshaling her facts, weighing the evidence, and making unequivocal decisions. Unlike many lawyers, O'Connor claims she never dreamed of winning a place on the Supreme Court. She knew the appeals court and even a federal district court appointment were good "possibilities." "I assumed I would stay on the bench there in Arizona; I was not focusing ten years ahead," says O'Connor. "Life had gone on happily. There was no reason to worry about my career."

When O'Connor ran for a seat on the Maricopa County Superior Court in 1974, Phoenix had become known as the most crime-ridden city in the country. O'Connor campaigned on a law-and-order platform as "a citizen, a wife, and a mother."

She soon developed a reputation as a tough, fair judge with a penchant for Solomonic efficiency. Presiding over a divorce case in which a couple couldn't agree on the division of their community property, a pack of forty thoroughbred greyhounds, O'Connor cut short what promised to be a long and agonizing hearing; she told the lawyer for one spouse to draw up two comparable lists of twenty greyhounds each, then gave the two lists to the other spouse's lawyer and let him choose between them.

The case that may have posed the greatest test of her legal convictions involved a woman with two small children who had been abandoned by her husband and had pleaded guilty to kiting $3,500 in bad checks. The woman asked for a lenient sentence, begging O'Connor not to separate her from her children by sending her to jail. The judge's response was vintage O'Connor: "You have intelligence, beauty and two small children. . . . You come from a fine and respected family. . . . Someone with all your advantages should have known better." When O'Connor handed down a five-to-ten-year sentence, of which the woman would serve 1.5 years in prison before being paroled, the defendant burst into tears, crying: "What about my babies?" The judge, who quickly left the bench after delivering her sentence, was later found weeping in her chambers.

After Bruce Babbitt was elected governor, he appointed O'Connor to the Arizona Court of Appeals. Arizonans surmise that the savvy Democrat had simply seized the first opportunity to get rid of his most serious opponent in the Republican party. A few years later, when President Jimmy Carter was looking for candidates to fill seats on the federal bench, one of John O'Connor's friends threw Sandra O'Connor's name into the ring. She never did win a federal appellate court appointment. But her reputation as a jurist and the social connections John had cultivated over the years already were paying off in other ways.

Sometime in the late 1970s, Chief Justice Warren Burger was scheduled to come to Flagstaff and give a speech at a national judicial conference. Burger's chief administrative assistant, Mark Cannon, was an Arizonan and a distant relation of John and Gail Driggs, who were close friends of the O'Connors. When Driggs heard that the chief justice was coming to the state, he offered to organize a weekend excursion on a houseboat on Lake Powell. Burger accepted the invitation, and the Driggses suddenly worried about how they would manage to entertain the chief justice for three whole days. Whom could they invite to help show Burger a good time? At first the couple thought of inviting Judge Bloomfield, the chief judge of Maricopa County Superior Court. But they finally decided to invite the O'Connors. So, shortly after hearing from Burger's office, Driggs called John O'Connor at his office to ask whether he and his wife might be interested in joining them for the weekend.

"Boy, would we ever," O'Connor replied.

What ensued was six weeks of intensive advance work worthy of a state visit. The two couples got together several times for "planning meetings," to work out the menus for all three days and to arrange for the park service to meet the boat and take the justice, who was an avid fisherman, on fishing expeditions. They borrowed a houseboat from a friend and brought along the Driggses' motorboat for waterskiing. They arranged for the chief justice's flight from Flagstaff to a small airstrip near Lake Powell.

The Driggses and the O'Connors met together in Flagstaff the night before the trip and flew together to the lake. A friend had offered to pilot the boat. Gail Driggs and Sandra O'Connor did all the cooking. "The chemistry couldn't have been better," says John Driggs, who remembers wide-ranging conversations about everything from family and the law to an hour-long recitation by Burger on how he came to be appointed to the Supreme Court.

Sandra O'Connor and the chief justice got along particularly well. One night after dinner, the Driggses discovered O'Connor and Burger sitting on deck, alone in the moonlight, enmeshed in a conversation about the law. They seemed to be getting along so well, in fact, that Gail Driggs remarked to her husband: "Wouldn't it be something if someday Sandra became a member of the Supreme Court?"

As unlikely as that seemed, Burger was clearly impressed with the young Arizona judge. The next summer, Burger invited O'Connor to attend a month-long international judicial conference in England, asking her to serve as a representative of the state appellate courts. The summer after that, in 1981, O'Connor would be nominated to the Supreme Court. And when the Driggses visited the O'Connors in Washington during her first term on the bench, Chief Justice Burger invited the couple to his chambers and boasted: "I just want you to know that it was on the Lake Powell trip that I sized Sandra up and decided that she should have the next appointment to the court."

Although Ronald Reagan might have been surprised to hear the Chief Justice take sole credit for O'Connor's nomination, the Lake Powell boat trip was clearly the first stop on O'Connor's unlikely journey to the Supreme Court.

·   ·   ·

O'Connor was lying in bed, recovering from a hysterectomy, when she got a call from William French Smith, the U.S. attorney general. Reagan's top law-enforcement official wanted to know if O'Connor could come to Washington to discuss the opening on the Supreme Court. O'Connor already had been scheduled to go to Washington to attend a meeting, but hadn't been sure she would be up for the trip. After consulting her doctor, who told her she could go as long as she promised not to lift anything, she agreed to fly to Washington.

O'Connor's nomination owed much to the political climate in Washington at the time. Since 1971 when Justices Hugo L. Black and John Marshall Harlan left the Court, women's groups had pleaded for a woman justice—but to no avail. Black and Harlan were replaced by Powell and Rehnquist. Similarly, when William O. Douglas retired in 1975, Gerald Ford ignored public pressure and the pleas of his own wife to appoint a woman, and chose John Paul Stevens, instead.

Then, during the 1980 presidential campaign, Ronald Reagan found himself in woman trouble. Public opinion polls showed him badly trailing President Carter among women voters, prompting candidate Reagan to open a speech in Los Angeles, on October 14, with a fervent defense of his views on equal opportunity for women. He went on to say: "It is time for a woman to sit among our highest jurists. . . . I am announcing today that one of the first Supreme Court vacancies in my administration will be filled by the most qualified woman I can find."

In retrospect, the get-acquainted session in July 1981 between the President and O'Connor might just as well have been a formality. Less than a week passed between O'Connor's two days at the White House— an intensive morning of meetings with the attorney general and a long list of Reagan associates, including Bill Clark, Jim Baker, Ed Meese, and Mike Deaver, followed by a forty-five-minute meeting with the President the following day—and her nomination. O'Connor was back at work on the Arizona Court of Appeals a few days after her return from Washington, when she got a call from President Reagan, telling her that she was his choice for the Supreme Court nomination.

"I was flabbergasted," says O'Connor. It had been "a fascinating experience to meet [those] people and see the Oval Office, to talk to the

President. When I left, I still didn't think . . . I did not see how it was likely that I would be asked to do it. I did not have a traditional background, they already had someone from Arizona on the Court. I just assumed that I was one of several people being considered."

O'Connor encountered little resistance to her nomination. Although her tenure on the appeals court had not been marked by any legal landmarks, she had developed a reputation as a tough but scrupulously fair judge. She had sentenced a twenty-three-year-old convicted hit man to death, but she also was known for giving a minimum sentence to a battered wife who had been convicted of murdering her abusive husband and then petitioning the governor to grant clemency for the defendant. In a 1980 Arizona bar judicial poll, she scored well in all areas except judicial temperament and courtesy to litigants and lawyers—O'Connor was known for being impatient with poorly prepared lawyers and, on at least one occasion, advised a litigant to get another counselor. Her nomination would be debated by advocates on both sides of the abortion issue—right-to-lifers worried that she would uphold *Roe* v. *Wade*, while pro-choice advocates were concerned that she would cast her votes with the conservative wing of the Court. But in the end, her nomination won the approval of such legal luminaries as Harvard's Laurence Tribe, who called her a "nominee of potentially great distinction."

John, of course, never doubted that his wife would get the nomination.

To old friends and colleagues, it seemed as though every decision O'Connor had made since leaving the state senate, including her decision not to run for the U.S. Senate or for governor of Arizona, had led inexorably to the Supreme Court. It was as though she had somehow divined that one day she would be "going on the Supreme Court," says Barr. It was as though "she had had a vision."

Of course, John was the first person she phoned after receiving the President's call. If she had any doubts about accepting the appointment, John would almost certainly have dispelled them. For one thing, the children were no longer at home. Although she would have to go through the scrutiny of the confirmation hearings, Supreme Court ap-

pointments had not yet been as politicized as they were to become under George Bush, especially after the nomination of Robert Bork. Once
she got through the confirmation process, she would be far more sheltered from public scrutiny than are politicians.

It probably helped that John O'Connor, who was in his fifties, had
already achieved his ambitions—he was a senior partner at Fennemore
Craig and a leading citizen of Phoenix. Although a move to Washington would mean that he would have to leave his law firm, O'Connor of
all people would have looked on the move not as losing his position in
Phoenix but as gaining one in Washington. Indeed, in the coming
years in Washington, the O'Connors surprised Washingtonians by becoming active members of the capital social circuit, a role that John relished even more than his wife did.

While John O'Connor was almost certainly thrilled with the social
stature his wife's position would now afford them, no one who spent
time with the O'Connors in Phoenix during the days after Sandra Day
O'Connor's appointment could doubt the genuine pleasure he took in
his wife's victory. Within hours of receiving the news of Sandra's nomination, the O'Connors were barraged by phone calls, telegrams, and
visitors. The national press corps descended on the Arizona legislature
to learn what they could about the new justice from Phoenix, whose
name was virtually unknown outside the Grand Canyon State. The
O'Connors retreated up to Iron Springs together with Ann and Scott
Alexander, hauling with them a bag full of congratulatory letters and
telegrams. Their first night at the cabin, after Sandra and Ann had gone
to bed, John and Scott read the letters, drank, and marveled over "what
a wondrous thing it was."

As so often happened, John seemed more excited by his wife's appointment than Sandra herself. For John O'Connor, the occasion unleashed a flood of good humor. He went around town telling anyone
who would listen that he was going to market the John O'Connor
School for How to Succeed as a Woman.

John O'Connor certainly wasn't going to squander the opportunities that had suddenly presented themselves. In the years ahead, he
would become a regular fixture in the formidable judicial chamber,

with its marble columns and its aura of hushed solemnity. There, after watching his wife and eight fellow justices emerge almost mystically from the crimson draperies that hang behind the broad, raised bench of the courtroom, he would listen to oral arguments.

At Sandra Day O'Connor's confirmation hearings, family took center stage once again. More than half of her opening remarks were to be devoted to a lengthy introduction of her husband and her sons. By way of preamble, the future justice began with an excerpt from the marriage ceremony in which she refers to marriage as "the hope of the world and the strength of our country," and she concluded, fittingly, with a tribute to her husband: "John has been totally and unreservedly and enthusiastically supportive of this whole nomination and this endeavor, and for that I am very grateful. Without it, it would not have been possible."

Ronald Reagan had promised he would nominate a woman. To those who had followed the "family values" rhetoric of a Republican administration that would slash the number of new female judicial appointees by nearly half and the number of women on the White House staff by more than fifty percent, the nomination of a woman who looked and sounded like Donna Reed in a black robe might have seemed like an empty gesture. In fact, O'Connor would eventually play a crucial leadership role in creating a moderately conservative center in an ideologically riven court.

In the first year after taking her place on the Supreme Court, in 1981, it took all of O'Connor's legendary powers of concentration and dedication to master the awesome responsibilities of her new job. Having had no training as a federal judge and little experience analyzing the legal ramifications of the federal Constitution, she was initially overwhelmed by the work at hand. "Everything was new," she later recalled. She was painfully aware that there was now "no appeal to a higher court," that her decisions represented "the end of the line" in the legal process. While on the appellate court she had had to work on panels of three; here she would have to "satisfy eight highly intellectually qualified colleagues in the production of an opinion that could speak for" the entire Court. During her first year on the Court, some observers thought that she seemed uncomfortable in her new job, noticing that, on the bench, she read her questions from a prepared list rather than speaking extemporaneously. Her sons noticed that their mother was more tired than they had ever seen her before.

But O'Connor put in place a system for educating herself as quickly as possible and soon regained her characteristic self-confidence. She began reading briefs for pending cases even before her confirmation hearings had been concluded. To review the draft opinions composed by her law clerks, she would have them stack a library cart full of the cases and law review articles they used to bolster their reasoning and would personally check every citation.

O'Connor also brought with her a friend from home—a representative of the old-girl network in Phoenix—to serve as a clerk and a much-needed source of support for her first year on the bench. Ruth MacGregor had worked with John for nearly a decade at Fennemore Craig when Sandra was appointed to the Supreme Court. Although MacGregor and O'Connor had never worked together, the two women met frequently at parties and on the tennis court, and they liked and respected each other enormously. When MacGregor, who had graduated first in her class from the University of Arizona law school in the early 1970s, applied for a position as O'Connor's clerk, the new justice jumped at the chance to hire her. She had inherited three clerks from Potter Stewart, but she seized on a chance to hire someone she "already knew and whose judgment she trusted."

Her clerks soon got to know O'Connor as a quick—but thorough—study who would seek out an array of opinions before she made up her mind about a case. (To select the four clerks who help her draft opinions each term, O'Connor personally pores over the hundreds of applications that flow into her chambers—a task most justices delegate to a screening committee—and takes great pains to select a politically eclectic group, ranging from Libertarians to liberal Democrats. Rehnquist also is known for favoring an eclectic mix of clerks.) Then, on Saturday mornings before oral arguments, she gets together with her clerks, apprising them of her preliminary decision and challenging them to find fault with her reasoning. For O'Connor is a linear thinker, and it is to her clerks that she often turns for creative solutions to problems. Former clerks recall the excitement they felt during those Saturday-morning debates, especially on the days when, in the course of hours-long arguments over bags of popcorn, O'Connor's young advisers could watch as, sometimes, the justice changed her mind.

Just as O'Connor was hitting her stride, a personal crisis threatened to cut short her career on the bench. In 1988, O'Connor was diagnosed with breast cancer. The two weeks between her learning the diagnosis and her deciding on surgery, O'Connor later told her friends, were the worst weeks of her life. Scared and confused, O'Connor uncharacteristically turned to outsiders for help. The day after her surgery, for example, she left a message on the answering machine of Nancy Ignatius, one of several friends who had also suffered breast cancer. "Come," she said. "I need you."

Of course, it was John O'Connor who bore the burden of caring for his wife as she visited doctors, underwent a mastectomy, and then endured chemotherapy. It helped that John was "more optimistic about the outlook" than was Sandra. Making the rounds of doctors' offices, recalls O'Connor, was an experience "so emotionally jarring that I was afraid I wouldn't hear what the doctors were recommending, that it just wouldn't register." So she asked John to attend all the appointments and insisted that both take detailed notes at each consultation, "so he could help me sort out the information."

Thus, O'Connor tackled her disease the way she would a thorny legal issue, convinced that in dissecting the problem, she would find a solution to it. She read every book she could find on the subject and interviewed doctors and friends who were familiar with the disease. Once she had decided on a course of therapy, she did not brood about it. The night before her mastectomy was scheduled, O'Connor made the seven-hour round-trip drive to Lexington, Virginia, to make a speech at Washington and Lee University, a commitment she had made months earlier. At the time, speculation was rife that the combination of her illness and John O'Connor's growing unhappiness with his job in Washington would lead to her resignation. She defied the skeptics by returning to the bench almost immediately after surgery. O'Connor didn't miss a single day of oral arguments at the Court. Less than a month after the mastectomy, she was playing golf and tennis again, even though the pain under her arm caused her to wince every time she hit an overhead. When tests showed that the cancer had spread to her lymph nodes and that she would have to have chemotherapy, O'Connor scheduled the sessions on Fridays so that she would have the weekend to recover and could be back at the Court on Monday morning.

Her friends weren't the least bit surprised by the élan with which O'Connor returned to work. The doctors had given her a clean bill of health after she completed her course of chemotherapy. Just as important, they knew, O'Connor had developed a passionate devotion to her work on the Supreme Court.

At first O'Connor had been viewed as a meek follower of the most conservative wing of the Court, and initially she had voted close to eighty percent of the time with Burger and Rehnquist. But with each passing year, "her self-confidence and mastery have grown exponentially," says a former clerk, and with them her independence from the conservative wing of the court. By the mid 1980s, Justice Blackmun noted: "In the past, I have put Justice O'Connor over there," with Burger and Rehnquist. But, he went on, "there have been a few little intimations that in certain areas she is becoming . . . independent and her own woman."

Increasingly, O'Connor stood apart from both the liberal and the conservative wings of the Court. In a 1984 case involving the display of a nativity scene in Rhode Island, O'Connor joined the conservatives in a five-to-four majority that allowed the display, but refused to sign the majority opinion; instead, she developed separate reasoning, using as her test an assessment of whether the government's actions had amounted to "an endorsement" of religion. Similarly, in 1988, O'Connor joined the liberal wing of the Court, concurring with a five-to-four majority that sought to prevent murderers under sixteen from being executed; but again she refused to join the opinion written by William Brennan, drafting instead a narrower opinion that would not rule out the possibility of such executions in the future.

More than anything else, O'Connor's judicial philosophy would be

informed by an abiding pragmatism and a commitment to the importance of precedent. While she has no more love for the Warren Court
than either her old friend William Rehnquist or Antonin Scalia, she
does not believe it appropriate to roll back unilaterally the decisions
that were made during the great liberal's fifteen-year leadership of the
Court. Indeed, legal experts draw parallels between O'Connor's measured, cautious reasoning and that of Justice Lewis F. Powell, another
conservative who was a firm believer in precedent, and with whom
O'Connor often conferred before his resignation from the Court in
1987.

Unlike several of her male colleagues, O'Connor never presumes to
know all the answers and resists the often aggressive opinions and
"swashbuckling reach" of the far right wing of the Court. She possesses
a fearsome awareness both of the responsibility that has been invested
in her and of the fallibility of even the greatest of justices. Since her
days in the state legislature she has thrived on consensus building.
What could be more sacred than the historic consensus represented by
decades of judicial precedent? Although at heart a conservative, as a
legislator she had been acutely attuned to the social changes of the
times and a stickler for drafting "workable laws." Similarly, as a justice,
one former clerk would note: "She believed the Court was doing its job
best when it was resolving disputes, not creating them."

In her first years on the Court, O'Connor became extremely influential in two areas: in limiting the applicability of affirmative action and
in affirming—and redefining—*Roe* v. *Wade*. O'Connor's decisions on affirmative action were marked by her innate conservatism, for they interpreted the constitutionality of affirmative action programs narrowly.
In *Croson* v. *Richmond*, O'Connor found that affirmative action programs
are valid only when they are intended to remedy current and prior gov-
ernmental misconduct, *not* societal discrimination.

But it was in 1992, in a ruling on *Planned Parenthood* v. *Casey*, that
O'Connor would achieve what will probably be seen as her most important legal milestone. No case would prove a greater test of O'Connor's desire to minimize controversy, her belief in precedent, and how
far she was willing to go in her liberalism on women's issues. The controversial abortion decision would highlight her role in creating a mod-

erately conservative center within what had been a highly polarized Court. Although O'Connor personally abhors abortion and has criticized the legal reasoning behind *Roe*, which centered on an interpretation of the Fourteenth Amendment that sees in it an implicit right to privacy, she repeatedly refused to overturn the law. In its 1992 ruling, the Court upheld *Roe* v. *Wade* in an unusual opinion that was signed by the three centrist justices—O'Connor, Souter, and Kennedy. The opinion was noteworthy in its search for a middle ground: "An entire generation has come of age free to assume Roe's concept of liberty in defining the capacity of women to act in society, and to make reproductive decisions. . . . A decision to overrule Roe's essential holding under the existing circumstances would address error, if error there was, at the cost of both profound and unnecessary damage to the Court's legitimacy, and to the nation's commitment to the rule of law. It is therefore imperative to adhere to the essence of Roe's original decision, and we do so today."

Constitutional scholars believe the two-part decision to have been written jointly by Souter and O'Connor—the former explaining the reason for maintaining *stare decisis*, and O'Connor reinterpreting the reasoning behind *Roe* v. *Wade*. While the Court's decision reaffirmed *Roe* v. *Wade*, it also upheld a Pennsylvania law that placed restrictions on a woman's right to have an abortion—with one key exception: the decision struck down a portion of the law that would have required a woman to inform her husband before having an abortion.

O'Connor's decision in *Planned Parenthood* v. *Casey* was driven by more than just a respect for precedent. Two key factors probably figured into her opinion: First, O'Connor would have been keenly aware of the importance of this decision for women. Had there been a sixth vote in support of *Planned Parenthood* v. *Casey*, some experts believe, O'Connor might have cast her vote with the opposition. But as the swing vote, she could not bring herself to a decision that would put technical legal reasoning ahead of *both* precedent and a milestone for women's rights.

Second, in the federal government's efforts to overturn *Roe* v. *Wade* and to wrest control over this most controversial aspect of reproduction from pregnant women, O'Connor perceived a fundamental attack on personal liberty. "Do you say there is no fundamental right to decide whether to have a child or not?" O'Connor asked Charles Fried, the Justice Department lawyer who represented the Reagan administration in the 1989 case. What if, in a future century, she continued, the country faced a serious overpopulation problem? Would the state then have the right to mandate abortions? If the government could control a woman's right to abort an unwanted pregnancy, might it not, at some later date, use the same power to force women—because of overpopulation, indigency, or a malformed fetus—to abort a *wanted* child?

The attack on *Roe* v. *Wade* saw the convergence of three issues that have been central to O'Connor's philosophy: her fervent belief in individual liberty and self-actualization; a reluctance to concentrate too much power in the hands of the federal government; and, finally, a commitment to protect the rights and freedom of women.

In a 1991 speech at New York University Law School, Justice O'Connor explored the "cult of domesticity" that historically had barred women from the legal profession, citing a Supreme Court ruling in 1872, in which Justice Bradley wrote: "Man is, or should be, woman's protector and defender. The natural and proper timidity and delicacy which belongs to the female sex evidently unfits it for many of the occupations of civil life."

In O'Connor's lifetime, the law would undergo a "revolution" that has seen women come to constitute some thirty percent of the profession, mirroring changes in the workplace overall. That progress, according to O'Connor, has been due in large part to "the explosion of the myth of the 'true woman,'" which cast women as frail, dependent creatures needing male protection.

Yet O'Connor recognizes that societal habits die hard. Women professionals, she noted at NYU, "still have primary responsibility for the children and housekeeping, spending roughly twice as much time in these cares as do their professional husbands . . . [and] time spent at home is time that cannot be billed to clients or spent making contacts at social or professional organizations."

With more women in the profession and the new controversies

over the "mommy track" has come a reinterpretation of feminine in-sight, what O'Connor refers to as a "troubling" and "chilling" tendency of feminists to search for gender-based differences in the way women practice law. Are women attorneys, many of whom are more likely than their husbands to sacrifice career advancement for family obliga-tions, also more likely to mediate disputes than to litigate them? Do women judges favor context over general principles? Are women more compassionate?

Interestingly, O'Connor wouldn't refute the possibility of such gender-based differences. "Asking whether women attorneys speak with a 'different voice' than men do is a question that is both dangerous and unanswerable," she would say. Rather, she prefers to believe, as a female colleague, Justice Jeanne Coyne of the Supreme Court of Okla-homa, once said: "A wise old man and a wise old woman reach the same conclusion."

O'Connor has demonstrated a considerable capacity for wisdom long before reaching anything that could be considered "old age." It is a wisdom that percolated up out of her family's long and valiant strug-gle with the land. It grew out of a girlhood marked by love, loyalty, and the sacrifice of a young girl who was forced to spend long periods of time away from home. But more than anything else, it was shaped by her experience as a conservative Arizona lawyer who also happened to be a woman, a wife, and a mother.

Certainly, the decision to join the Supreme Court altered the well-ordered family life that she had cultivated since moving to Phoenix. However, since her sons were grown and building their own careers and families, her move to the East Coast did not create as wrenching a change in her household as the political offices that she had consid-ered—and rejected—earlier in her career would have done.

What turned out to be far more difficult than either of the O'Connors expected was helping John adjust to the role of "Mr. Justice O'Connor." John missed Phoenix. Although he threw himself into Washington's so-cial life, the professional adjustments he had to make were considerable. O'Connor found it difficult to establish his legal practice in Washington, and after seven years at Miller & Chevalier, the Washington firm he had joined after his wife's appointment, he switched to the Washington office of Bryan, Cave, McPheeters & McRoberts, a Saint Louis–based firm that requires his presence in Phoenix several days a month and allows him to use the vast network of contacts that he cultivated during more than twenty years in Arizona.

So as Sandra Day O'Connor entered her sixties, she found herself in a commuting marriage. Since the O'Connors were as devoted to each other as ever, however, she viewed John's absences as simply an opportunity to get some work done, and a trade-off that was well worth the most rewarding job she had undertaken since motherhood.

Although she would never describe herself as a feminist, over the years Sandra Day discovered the emancipated woman's greatest ally—other women. Despite a happy marriage, a close-knit family life, and a self-reliant nature that rarely found need to ask openly for help, O'Connor surrounded herself with close women friends since childhood. Earlier generations of women had often treated other women as competition—Lee Krasner considered most women artists as inferior rivals, while Maria Mayer scorned all but a handful of her contemporaries. By contrast, O'Connor drew strength from women during key junctures of her life: During her childhood exile in El Paso, she relished the sisterly companionship of Flournoy Manzo. In Cubberly House, she found a welcome feminine refuge from the masculine—and sometimes hostile—environment of law school. During her five-year hiatus from paid employment, the Junior League gave her companionship, a sense of civic purpose, and a place to hone her managerial skills. As a lawyer for the Arizona attorney general, she did some of her most rewarding work alongside a woman executive in the state auditor's office. Countless friendships have carried her through the minor crises of motherhood and the serious trauma of breast cancer. During her first year on the Supreme Court, she found support in a familiar, and trusted, female associate from Phoenix. And even today, her summers would never be the same without the one-week getaways with her friends from Phoenix.

O'Connor's life has never been lived according to the masculine convention of a linear pursuit of fame and fortune. It was a life built on self-knowledge—one in which she allowed herself to follow the ebb and flow of changing passions and interests and her biological destiny. It was filled with the kind of choices that would be thrust upon growing numbers of men and women throughout the 1980s and 1990s. But O'Connor always knew where she was going and what her priorities were. By hewing deliberately to her own unique course, O'Connor defied the odds against women in the law and rose to the pinnacle of her profession.

EPILOGUE

As I followed the progress of the women in this book and looked at my own experiences, as well as those of my unfamous contemporaries, I couldn't help but wonder how far we have actually come since Mileva Maric's day and her trials as Einstein's wife. While many of the cultural and professional barriers that once kept women out of the workplace have fallen, the glass ceiling in most professions remains frustratingly impermeable. Women still are likely to earn less than their husbands. Thus, when children enter the picture, it is the wife's career that often seems most expendable.

There is, however, far more to the picture of modern work and marriage than salary statistics and women's struggle to break into the top echelons of their professions. As women come close to filling half the jobs in the labor force, a sea change is occurring in both the resources that are available to working women and the ways men and women view their priorities and their roles in the family.

In some respects, my own experience seems to represent a common transitional state between the domestic trap that destroyed Maric and the full spectrum of professional opportunities that are available to many women today. I love both my children and my work, and am one of a new breed of hard-charging "mommy trackers." In the four years since I began researching this book, I've left one job, given birth to two daughters, and taken over the reins at home as my husband's international law practice has become increasingly busy. I am, however, definitely not the housewife my mother was. In the final months of my most recent pregnancy, I was putting in ten-to-twelve-hour workdays as I prepared this book for publication and completed various freelance commitments. The baby things for my newborn were gathered together haphazardly between appointments and with considerable help from friends and my mother-in-law. Although my husband is on the road much of the time, he is capable—and willing—to perform an array of domestic tasks, including diaper changing, dishwashing, and preparing a (very occasional) meal.

Within the constraints of a relatively traditional marriage, updated for the 1990s, I've found that a little ingenuity can keep even a busy mom well connected to her profession. Not unlike Sandra Day O'Connor, who discovered help and comfort in a female colleague from Arizona who served as a clerk during her first year on the Supreme Court, many women of my generation have found a critical resource in a wide informal network of women friends and colleagues.

Although most of my career has been spent working in business journalism, a field dominated—certainly at senior levels—by men, my own work life today is increasingly filled with women. My collaborators on this book were all women—one editor is a former college classmate, my agent is the sister of a former (female) colleague from the days when I worked for a national newsmagazine. (I now realize that had I gone overseas or become a newspaper reporter, as I once envisioned, I may never have discovered the satisfaction that I've found immersing myself in the in-depth process of researching and writing books.) Each spring, I spend a semester as an adjunct professor at Columbia University, assisting with a course in international economics; I work there with five women, all of them former colleagues from magazines where we once were employed full time. (I was hired by a woman with whom I've worked on and off for years.) Indeed, it was at Columbia that I became reacquainted with a woman whom I knew only casually a decade ago, when we were both rookie reporters and editors at *Business Week;* she now runs a finance magazine and occasionally asks me to pinch-hit when she is in need of an extra editor. When I first took her up on her offer, I found that the editors of this hard-core financial publication, which caters to a largely male readership, are almost exclusively women, most of whom mold their editing work around the schedules of their small children. Indeed, many of the moms of my generation have achieved an extraordinary balance between pursuing rewarding work—even if it is sometimes different from what they envisioned at the start of their careers—and devoting time to their children.

Women of my generation are even benefiting, in some cases, from the flux and uncertainty of modern life. The very changes that have made the corporate world an unsettling place for anyone seeking stable, long-term employment have placed a premium on professionals who are adaptable and willing to embrace flexible work schedules. Fewer couples can afford the luxury of allowing a wife to abandon her professional credentials. And men who came of age during the last two decades and fell in love during the 1980s are much more likely to have accepted the possibility that their wives' careers might one day take precedence. For my contemporaries, changing aspirations and expectations need not lead to divorce, as they did for my cousin Magda and for many women in their late forties and their fifties.

Yet it is also clear that ambitious wives have far more planning to do than did their forerunners. Even women who today are in their thirties and forties are at a distinct professional disadvantage compared to their male colleagues and husbands, to the extent that so many of them awoke late to the full spectrum of their professional ambitions. In Boston, the first woman to head a major private university hospital in the Northeast recently confessed that she was twenty-two-years old and working in a clinic before she realized a woman could become a doctor. It took her well over another decade to realize that she was capable of—and interested in—running a hospital.

My own experience wasn't any different. Although I had sensed, since my adolescence, that I wanted to be a writer, my thoughts on the subject were for many years dominated as much by relief that I was drawn to a profession that would be compatible with motherhood as by any clear sense of where I wanted my aspirations to lead me. And I am struck again and again by the number of senior-level women I have interviewed over the years who are hard-pressed to identify exactly where they see themselves in the next decade. The same question to a male executive elicits an almost instinctive response: He wants to be the CEO, of course.

Since the realm of work and ambition remains a bit hazy for many young women, they rarely consider their marriage decisions in the context of their professional goals. Although motherhood clearly is not for everyone, I've come across only two women who seriously debated whether to have children and finally concluded that it was *not* for them. Similarly, the smart women I know inevitably look for men who will *at least* match them ounce for ounce when it comes to brainpower and ambition, even though the most ambitious among them might clearly have benefited from marrying men who were willing to put their careers second and their families first.

Still, we unquestionably live in a world very different from that of our parents. Happy families still look very much alike, even if it is Mom bringing home the largest paycheck and Dad getting dinner on the table. By contrast, working moms are bringing inevitable change to the workplace—some because they insist on getting on a mommy track for a few years, others because they trade off career priorities with their husbands, grabbing opportunities for themselves some years and allowing his work to take precedence at other times. In either case, two-career families often defy the linear career trajectories that employers traditionally have been able to take for granted and that long have worked against professional married women. At the same time, they are expanding the opportunities for men and women to enjoy lives that are richer because they are defined by both work and parenthood.

NOTES

INTRODUCTION
Page

xi: poem to George Sand: Bonnie S. Anderson and Judith P. Zinsser, *A History of Their Own: Women in Europe from Prehistory to the Present,* vol. II (New York: Harper & Row, 1989), p. 171.

xii: "a victorious conclusion": *New York Times Book Review,* Nov. 26, 1990. Interview with Robert Schulmann. See also Jurgen Renn and Robert Schulmann, eds., *Albert Einstein/Mileva Maric: The Love Letters* (Princeton, N.J.: Princeton University Press, 1992), pp. 36, 39.

xii: "the rest are details": R.W. Clark, *Einstein: The Life and Times* (New York: Avon Books, 1984), pp. 37, 647.

xiii: lived for another decade: Elizabeth Roboz Einstein, *Hans Albert Einstein: Reminiscences of His Life and Our Life Together* (Iowa City: University of Iowa, 1991), p. 24.

xiii: considerable intellectual promise: Phone conversation with Abraham Pais. Abraham Pais, *"Subtle Is the Lord ..." The Science and the Life of Albert Einstein* (New York: Oxford University Press, 1982), pp. 45, 47, 187, 300–301. Carl Seelig, *Albert Einstein: Leben und Werk Eines Genies Unserer Zeit* (Zurich: Europa Verlag, 1960), pp. 73–74, 95–97. Clark, *Einstein,* pp. 82–83. See also Banesh Hoffmann, *Albert Einstein: Creator and Rebel* (New York: Viking, 1972).

xiv: important biological puzzles: James D. Watson, *The Double Helix,* (London: W.W. Norton & Co, 1980), pp. 14–15, 86, 95–96. Horace Freeland Judson, *The Eighth Day of Creation,* (New York: Simon & Schuster, 1979), pp. 147–148, 159.

xiv: high-priced fertility doctors: Felice Schwartz, "Management Women and the New Facts of Life," *Harvard Business Review,* Jan.–Feb., 1989, pp. 65–76.

xvi: posed for their wives: Anderson and Zinsser, *History of Their Own*, p. 176.

xix: a few generations ago: Interview with Robert Schulmann. See also Renn and Schulmann, *Love Letters*.

xix: a surprise to most wives: Marian Burros, *New York Times*, May 31, 1993, p. A1.

xx: they should marry at all?: Anderson and Zinsser, *History of Their Own*, p. 224.

xx: "Hedgehogs" and "Foxes": Isaiah Berlin, *The Hedgehog and the Fox: An Essay on Tolstoy's View of History* (New York: Simon & Schuster, 1966).

xxii: "light each end [and turn it] about": Francine du Plessix Gray, "Chère Maître," *The New Yorker*, July 26, 1993, pp. 82–88.

xxiii: he was so single-focused: Richard Tarnas, *The Passion of the Western Mind: Understanding the Ideas That Have Shaped Our World View* (New York: Ballantine Books, 1991), p. 364.

Mileva Maric Einstein

Page

3: "one and only beloved man?": Roger Highfield and Paul Carter, *The Private Lives of Albert Einstein* (London: Faber and Faber, 1993), p. 32.

3: a classroom with boys: Einstein, *Reminiscences*, p. 87.

4: her father's favorite: Desanka Trbuhovic-Gjuric, *Im Schatten Albert Einsteins: Das tragische Leben der Mileva Einstein-Maric* (Bern: Verlag Haupt, 1988), p. 18.

4: top student in her class: Einstein, *Reminiscences*, pp. 22–23. See also Trbuhovic-Gjuric, *Im Schatten Albert Einsteins*, pp. 22–26.

4: mastered that language too: Einstein, *Reminiscences*, pp. 22–23. See also Trbuhovic-Gjuric, *Im Schatten Albert Einsteins*, p. 23.

5: both math and physics: Interview with Robert Schulmann. Also Einstein, *Reminiscences*, p. 88.

5: "Wife to her Husband": Anderson and Zinsser, *History of Their Own*, pp. 112–15.

6: graduate from the university: Ibid., pp. 149–50.

6: for a servant and for everyman: Interview with Robert Schulmann.

6: demise of her career: Trbuhovic-Gjuric, *Im Schatten Albert Einsteins*, p. 35.

7: children and exotic cacti: Ibid., p. 175.

7: through the Alps: Renn and Schulmann, *Love Letters*, p. 3.

8: "a sweet voice": Trbuhovic-Gjuric, *Im Schatten Albert Einsteins*, p. 53.

8: her feelings toward Einstein: John Stachel, ed., *The Collected Papers of Albert Einstein*, vol. I: *The Early Years* (Princeton, N.J.: Princeton University Press, 1987), Trbuhovic-Gjuric, *Im Schatten Albert Einsteins*, p. 45.

9: "the Heidelberg professors": Renn and Schulmann, *Love Letters*, p. 3.

9: electron theory of metals: Renn and Schulmann, *Love Letters*, pp. xiv–xv, 4, 82. Interview with Robert Schulmann.

10: Bachtold residence itself: Ibid., pp. 14–15.

10: already had vaulted over: Ibid., pp. 12–13.

10: "such harmless competition": Ibid., p. 14.

10: 6 in electrical engineering: Transcripts from ETH, dated 1896–1900. Stachel, *The Early Years* p. 49.

11: disapproval weighed heavily

on Maric: Renn and Schulmann, *Love Letters*, pp. 19–20, 29.

11: felt his father lacked: High-field and Carter, *Private Lives*, pp. 9–11.

12: letter would not be intercepted: Stachel, *The Early Years*, pp. 248, 257. Trbuhovic-Gjuric, *Im Schatten Albert Einsteins*, p. 65.

12: "poor Dollie [would] cook": Renn and Schulmann, *Love Letters*, p. 32.

13: "[Milana] has come to hate": Stachel, *The Early Years*, p. 303.

13: allowed into a laboratory at all: Renn and Schulmann, *Love Letters*, pp. 51–52. See also Einstein, *Reminiscences*, p. 88.

13: "destiny has determined for us": Stachel, *The Early Years*, pp. 279, 303.

14: dragged down her final grade: Ibid., p. 247. Transcripts from ETH, 1896–1900.

14: "nothing without being punished": Renn and Schulmann, *Love Letters*, p. 48.

14: work on her dissertation: Trbuhovic-Gjuric, *Im Schatten Albert Einsteins*, p. 98.

15: destined to be "punished": Renn and Schulmann, *Love Letters*, p. 63.

15: her death in 1948: Interview with Robert Schulmann.

16: "see what you've written?": Renn and Schulmann, *Love Letters*, pp. 60–61.

16: "a few other ideas on this": Ibid.

16: a few miles outside Schaffhausen: Stachel, *The Early Years*, pp. 316–317. Trbuhovic-Gjuric, *Im Schatten Albert Einsteins*, p. 75.

17: able to cover transportation: Renn and Schulmann, *Love Letters*, p. 99.

17: "I dread the mere thought of it": Ibid., p. 62.

18: "happiest people on earth": Ibid., pp. 66, 68, 73.

18: left with nothing but debts: Highfield and Carter, *Private Lives*, p. 100.

18: "overworked, impractical Johnnie": Renn and Schulmann, *Love Letters*, p. 68.

19: lasting side effects: Einstein, *Reminiscences*, p. 91.

19: "Your poor Dollie": Renn and Schulmann, *Love Letters*, p. 78.

19: "problems don't arise for her later": Renn and Schulmann, *Love Letters*, p. 78.

19: suffering would have been worth it: Clark, *Einstein*, p. 83.

20: a month before Lieserl's birth: Renn and Schulmann, *Love Letters*, pp. 72–73.

20: lived for a time with the Einsteins: Trbuhovic-Gjuric, *Im Schatten Albert Einsteins*, pp. 83, 90. See also Einstein, *Reminiscences*, p. 93.

20: ascribing the 1905 papers to "Einstein-Marity": Trbuhovic-Gjuric, *Im Schatten Albert Einsteins*, p. 97. Highfield and Carter, *Private Lives of Albert Einstein*, p. 111.

20: watched the children: Trbuhovic-Gjuric, *Im Schatten Albert Einsteins*, pp. 104–6.

21: work she was doing with Einstein: Ibid., pp. 93–94.

21: "work that will make my husband world famous": Einstein, *Reminiscences*, p. 93.

21: from financial worries: Trbuhovic-Gjuric, *Im Schatten Albert Einsteins*, pp. 104–6.

21: complaining of the "inappropriate" correspondence: Highfield and Carter, *Private Lives*, pp. 124–25.

22: anti-Semitism everywhere: Clark, *Einstein*, p. 178. Highfield and Carter, *Private Lives*, p. 134.

22: convocation of the world's leading physicists: Highfield and Carter, *Private Lives*, pp. 139–41.

22: a man and his "employee": Ibid., p. 164.

23: failed dreams and strained marriage: Trbuhovic-Gjuric, *Im Schatten Albert Einsteins*, pp. 120–21. See also Einstein, *Reminiscences*, p. 97.

23: to marry Friedrich: Interview with Robert Schulmann. See also Highfield and Carter, *Private Lives*, pp. 142, 185–186. Trbuhovic-Gjuric, *Im Schatten Albert Einsteins*, pp. 111–112.

24: return to Zurich with her sons: Highfield and Carter, *Private Lives*, pp. 165–67. See also Einstein, *Reminiscences*, p. 128.

24: one of his letters: Highfield and Carter, *Private Lives*, pp. 170–71.

25: "human beings included in it": Clark, *Einstein*, p. 37.

25: "as good at mathematics as Marcel [Grossman].": Trbuhovic-Gjuric, *Im Schatten Albert Einsteins*, pp. 113–14, 120–21. Einstein, *Reminiscences*, p. 98.

26: borrowing money from friends: Ibid., pp. 132, 156–60.

26: battle for the custody of their children: Highfield and Carter, *Private Lives*, pp. 172, 175–77, 181.

26: relented when she was hospitalized: Trbuhovic-Gjuric, *Im Schatten Albert Einsteins*, pp. 138–39. Albert Einstein and Michelangelo Besso, *Correspondence 1903–1955* (Paris: Hermann, 1972), p. 80.

26: hospitalized repeatedly during subsequent years: Trbuhovic-Gjuric, *Im Schatten Albert Einsteins*, pp. 138–39.

Einstein and Besso, *Correspondence*, p. 80.

27: treated with consideration and respect: Highfield and Carter, *Private Lives*, p. 158.

27: proud of their father: Einstein and Besso, *Correspondence*, pp. 90, 144–45.

28: until the time of her death: Clark, *Einstein*, pp. 82–83. See also Einstein, *Reminiscences*, pp. 36–37.

28: showed any affection were cats: Trbuhovic-Gjuric, *Im Schatten Albert Einsteins*, p. 148.

28: deluge of hate mail: Ibid.

29: never see either of them again: Interview with Robert Schulmann. See also Highfield and Carter, *Private Lives*, p. 182.

29: became ill and died: Trbuhovic-Gjuric, *Im Schatten Albert Einsteins*, pp. 191–92. Highfield and Carter, *Private Lives*, pp. 252–53. Einstein, *Reminiscences*, pp. 33–34.

29: rushed to the hospital: Trbuhovic-Gjuric, *Im Schatten Albert Einsteins*, p. 199.

30: accepted his marital detours: Highfield and Carter, *Private Lives*, p. 204.

31: "more attached to human beings than I": Clark, *Einstein*, pp. 632–35, 644–47.

31: speak of his mother again: Trbuhovic-Gjuric, *Im Schatten Albert Einsteins*, pp. 203–5.

31: no mention at all: Ibid.

31: active in her profession: Einstein, *Reminiscences*, p. 59.

Lee Krasner

Page

36: the face that she deserved:

Interviews with Jeffrey Potter, Patsy Southgate, and Clement Greenberg.

37: "the visual equivalent of perfect pitch": Eleanor Green, *John Graham: Artist and Avatar* (Washington, D.C.: The Phillips Collection, 1987), p. 19.

37: their counterparts in Europe: Ibid. John Graham, *Systems and Dialectics of Art* (Baltimore: Johns Hopkins Univ. Press, 1971), p. 154.

38: "your last large painting": Postcard from John Graham to Lee Krasner. Interview with Eleanor Green.

39: "snag her genius": Interview with Clement Greenberg.

39: her parents' reunion in New York: B. H. Friedman, *Jackson Pollock: Energy Made Visible* (New York: McGraw-Hill,1972), pp. 66–67. Handwritten notes by Lee Krasner, Archives of American Art. Interview with Ruth K. Stein.

40: nurtured in Russia: Interviews with Ruth K. Stein and Ronnie Stein. See also Naifeh and White Smith, *Jackson Pollock*, p. 367.

40: long hours away from home: Interview with Ruth K. Stein. See also Friedman, *Jackson Pollock*, pp. 66–67.

40: contest for Irving's affections: Interview with Ruth K. Stein. See also Naifeh and White Smith, *Jackson Pollock*, pp. 367, 369.

41: none resorted to divorce either: Interviews with Rena Kanokogi, Ruth Stein, and Ronnie Stein.

41: moved to Manhattan: Friedman, *Jackson Pollock*, pp. 67–69.

41: "too sure of herself": Ellen Landau, *Lee Krasner's Early Career, Part Two: The 1940s.*

42: one of his textbooks: Charles Moritz, *Current Biography Yearbook*

(New York: H. W. Wilson, 1974), pp. 215–18. See also Freidman, *Jackson Pollock,* p. 68 and Naifeh and White Smith, *Jackson Pollock*, pp. 375, 376.

42: their most truculent student: Naifeh and White Smith, *Jackson Pollock*, p. 376.

43: "attracted to her per se": Ibid., pp. 378, 393. Also interview with B. H. Friedman.

43: "that face?" he once exclaimed: Naifeh and White Smith, *Jackson Pollock*, p. 381. Off-the-record interview.

44: summers after Pollock's death: Ibid., pp. 378–79. Also interviews with Sanford Friedman and Ronnie Stein. Note from Igor Pantuhoff to Lee Krasner.

44: equivalent of the Prix de Rome: Naifeh and White Smith, *Jackson Pollock*, pp. 377, 855.

44: a dress he had just bought for her: Interview with Jeanne Bultman.

45: not to be charmed by him: Interviews with Ruth K. Stein and Rena Kanokogi.

45: on the lower West Side: Naifeh and White Smith, *Jackson Pollock*, pp. 380–81.

45: feathers for her hair: Ibid., p. 379.

45: its toll on their relationship: Ibid., pp. 387–388.

46: New Deal public assistance programs: Barbara Rose, *Lee Krasner: A Retrospective* (New York: Museum of Modern Art, 1983), p. 17.

46: "as Matisse himself": Ibid., p. 23.

46: "done by a woman": Friedman, *Jackson Pollock*, p. 70. Rose, *Lee Krasner*, p. 13.

47: "further than anyone else":

Interview with Josephine Little. Hermine Benheim Freed, *Lee Krasner: East Hampton Studio*, video interview, Lee Krasner, circa 1973. Also interview with Fritz Bultman by Irving Sandler, for Archives of American Art.

47: the photographer Herbert Matter: Rose, *Lee Krasner*, pp. 35–38. Friedman, *Jackson Pollock*, p. 70.

47: to stay with his family: Naifeh and White Smith, *Jackson Pollock*, p. 388.

47: Lee had remained unchanged: Interview with Jeanne Bultman.

48: "shift to New York": Interview with Ronnie Stein. Also transcript of interview with Lee Krasner, for Archives of American Art, August 7, 1977.

48: love of boogie-woogie, had danced together: Rose, *Lee Krasner*, pp. 40–43.

48: the subconscious, and spontaneous gesture: Barbara Rose, "Lee Krasner and the Origins of Abstract Expressionism," *Arts Magazine*, Feb. 1977, pp. 96–100.

49: already working as a serious painter: April Kingsley, *The Turning Point: The Abstract Expressionists and the Transformation of American Art* (New York: Simon & Schuster, 1992), pp. 179–89. Interview with Ted Dragon. See also *Art International*, Sept. 1967, and Robert Hughes "Bursting out of the shadows," *Time*, Nov. 14, 1983.

49: "Do you like to fuck?" Naifeh and White Smith, *Jackson Pollock*, p. 298. Kay Larson, "The Odd Couple," *New York*, Nov. 23, 1981, p. 73. Dan Rattiner, "Lee Krasner, Jackson Pollock, The Legend," *East Hampton Summer Sun*, Sept. 4, 1981, pp. 1–11.

50: Krasner had concluded that he was: Naifeh and White Smith, *Jackson Pollock*, pp. 392–93.

50: and, finally, Lee: Jeffrey Potter, *To a Violent Grave: An Oral Biography of Jackson Pollock* (Wainscott, N.Y.: Pushcart Press, 1987), p. 57.

51: moved in almost immediately thereafter: Naifeh and White Smith, *Jackson Pollock*, pp. 400–401.

51: Stuart Davis and one by John Graham: Sidney Janis, *Abstract & Surrealist Art in America* (New York: Arno Press, 1944), p. 50. Rose, *Lee Krasner*, p. 49.

52: connoisseurs who came into his orbit: Peggy Guggenheim, *Confessions of an Art Addict* (New York: Macmillan, 1960), p. 69. See also Hermine Benham Freed, *Archives of American Art*.

52: artists, including Pollock: Hermine Benheim Freed, paper on Howard Putzel, *Archives of American Art*.

52: "ones of the highest quality": Guggenheim, *Confessions*, p. 69.

53: lobbied Guggenheim for months: Freed, paper on Howard Putzel. Also Guggenheim, *Confessions*, pp. 104–5.

53: declined the offer: Guggenheim, *Out of This Century* (New York: Dial Press, 1946). Naifeh and White Smith, *Jackson Pollock*, p. 449.

53: get Pollock into bed: Whitney Chadwick and Isabelle de Cortivron, *Significant Others: Creativity and Intimate Partnership* (New York: Charles Scribners and Sons, 1968), pp. 98–99. Naifeh and White Smith, *Jackson Pollock*, p. 461.

53: whom he asked to join: Freed, paper on Howard Putzel. Edward Alden Jewell, "Toward Abstraction or Away?" *New York Times*, July 1, 1945.

54: later revised his opinion: Freed, paper on Howard Putzel.

54: leading exponent of the new "ism": Guggenheim, *Confessions of an Art Addict*, pp. 104–106. Robert Coates, "The Art Galleries; From Moscow to Harlem," *The New Yorker*, May 29, 1943.

55: further her lover's career: Naifeh and White Smith, *Jackson Pollock*, pp. 460–61.

55: banish Krasner from the apartment: Interview with Jeanne Bultman. Naifeh and White Smith, *Jackson Pollock*, pp. 367–68.

56: view of the universe: Michael Cannell, "An Interview with Lee Krasner," *Arts Magazine*, Sept. 1984, pp. 87–89. Rose, *Lee Krasner*, pp. 50, 66.

56: "my mother and my brother," recalls Ruth: Interview with Ruth Stein.

56: called his death a suicide: Freed, paper on Howard Putzel.

56: artists during the go-go sixties: Freed, paper on Howard Putzel.

57: without a strong artistic ally: Barbara Rose, *The Long View*, documentary, 1978. Also interview with William Lieberman.

57: "married enough": Marriage certificate, Archives of American Art. Potter, *To a Violent Grave*, pp. 86–87. Friedman, *Jackson Pollock*, p. 82.

57: "essentially nerve endings": Interviews with Ronnie Stein and Jeffrey Potter.

58: "What beast must one adore?": Ray Mathew, "A Record on Canvas," *Art World*, Jan. 15–Feb. 15, 1985, pp. 1–2.

58: "I wanted to get away": Barbara Rose, "The Long View," documentary.

59: area after World War II: Interview with Ted Dragon. Potter, *To a Violent Grave*, p. 88. Naifeh and White Smith, *Jackson Pollock*, pp. 506–8.

59: Indians, particularly welcoming: Potter, *To a Violent Grave*, p. 85. Naifeh and White Smith, *Jackson Pollock*, p. 509.

59: Pollock's five-by-seven-foot canvases: Freed, *Lee Krasner: East Hampton Studio*. Naifeh and White Smith, *Jackson Pollock*, p. 509.

60: games of penny-ante poker: Naifeh and White Smith, *Jackson Pollock*, p. 516. Rattiner, "Lee Krasner, Jackson Pollock."

60: turn Pollock into a popular legend: Naifeh and White Smith, *Jackson Pollock*, p. 552. Potter, *To a Violent Grave*, p. 90.

60: special refuge for Krasner: Francis Valentine O'Connor and Eugene Victor Thaw, *Pollock: A Catalogue Raisonné of Paintings, Drawings, and Other Works* (New Haven: Yale University Press, 1978), pp. 44–45.

61: "made life possible for me": Interview with Josephine Little. Rose, *The Long View*.

61: "I don't think many people knew Lee's work": Interviews with Jeffrey Potter and B. H. Friedman.

61: directly influenced by it: Ellen Landau, "Lee Krasner's Early Career, Part Two: The 1940s," *Arts Magazine*, Nov. 1981, pp. 80–89. Cindy Nemser, "Lee Krasner's Paintings 1946–49," *Artforum*, Dec. 1973, pp. 61–65.

62: "No. 2 on the scene": Interview with Clement Greenberg.

62: "terrified it might fall through": Interview with Jeffrey Potter.

62: letting him drive to a bar: Naifeh and White Smith, *Jackson Pollock*, p. 693.

62: first all-over paintings: Rose, *Lee Krasner*, pp. 53–54.

63: tightly woven patterns: Ibid.

63: images on her small canvases: Rose, *The Long View*.

64: "affected by these works": Friedman, *Jackson Pollock*, p. 80. Ellen Landau, "Lee Krasner's Past Continuous." *Art News*, Feb. 1984. Landau, "Lee Krasner's Early Career, Part Two," pp. 80–89. Interviews with William Rubin and Bryan Robertson. Letter from William Lieberman to Professor Franco Russoli, dated Oct. 15, 1970. Kay Larson, "Lee Krasner's Enduring Gestures," *New York*, Jan. 14, 1985, pp. 48–51.

64: "not the same kind of encouragement": Freed, *Lee Krasner: East Hampton Studio*.

65: "the student of my student": Cynthia Goodman, *Hans Hofmann* (New York: Abbeville Press, 1986), p. 52. Rose, *Lee Krasner*, pp. 20–26.

65: "bigness that she didn't achieve before": Letter by Jackson Pollock, June 7, 1951.

66: found objects in his paintings: Rose, *Lee Krasner*, p. 61. Ellen Landau, *Jackson Pollock* (New York: Harry N. Abrams, 1989), pp. 174–75.

66: "wife of the painter J. Pollack [*sic*]": Rose, *Lee Krasner*, p. 61. Naifeh and White Smith, *Jackson Pollock*, p. 571. Potter, *To a Violent Grave*, p. 96.

66: function in the art world: Naifeh and White Smith, *Jackson Pollock*, p. 571.

67: keep paying the stipend until February: Ibid., pp. 544–47.

67: same last name and the same address: Ibid., p. 274.

67: paintings he actually sold: Ibid., p. 545–47.

68: Montauk, didn't pan out: Ibid., pp. 548, 557, 570.

68: Pollock's biographers Naifeh and White Smith: Naifeh and White Smith, *Jackson Pollock*, p. 560. O'Connor and Thaw, *Catalogue Raisonné*, p. 48.

69: only she knew how to do it properly: Interviews with Ronnie Stein, Jason McCoy, and Darby Cardansky. Simone de Beauvoir, *The Second Sex* (New York: Vintage Books, 1989), pp. 450–53.

69: "maternal bone in her body," recalled one friend: Naifeh and White Smith, *Jackson Pollock*, p. 388, off-the-record interview.

69: looked at Stein's work: Interviews with Ronnie Stein and Jason McCoy.

70: "their failed marriages": Musa Mayer, *Night Studio: A Memoir of Philip Guston*.

70: very nearly impossible: Interview with Arloie McCoy.

70: Ford sometime in 1948: Interview with Patsy Southgate.

70: "a bleeding wreck": Ibid.

70: running after other women: Naifeh and White Smith, *Jackson Pollock*, p. 568.

71: "How old are you, Lee?" Interview with Jeffrey Potter.

71: lied about for years was her age: Amei Wallach, "Krasner's Triumph," *Vogue*, Nov. 1983, pp. 444–502.

71: front page of the *New York Times*: Kingsley, *The Turning Point*, pp. 160–61. Interview with B. H. Friedman.

72: include her in the group either: Naifeh and White Smith, *Jackson Pollock*, pp. 602–603. Kingsley, *The Turning Point*, pp. 160–61.

73: seen him in a drunken rage:

Friedman, *Jackson Pollock*, p. 165. Interview with Ted Dragon. Naifeh and White Smith, *Jackson Pollock*, p. 651–653.

73: behavior alienated many friends: Naifeh and White Smith, *Jackson Pollock*, pp. 656, 672, 710–15. Interview with Jeffrey Potter.

74: turned his rage on Krasner: Irving Sandler, *The New York School* (New York: Harper & Row, 1978), pp. 27–28, 67, 69. Interview with Ted Dragon.

74: Krasner had stopped giving parties: Naifeh and White Smith, *Jackson Pollock*, p. 695.

74: if he hadn't died first: Potter, *To a Violent Grave*, pp. 225, 228, 233. Interview with Clement Greenberg. Naifeh and White Smith, *Jackson Pollock*, pp. 531, 672, 773–777.

75: searching for a new dealer: Naifeh and White Smith, *Jackson Pollock*, pp. 677–79.

75: help "control" Pollock: Ibid., pp. 677–79, 683–85.

75: modicum of freedom and mobility: Interview with Patsy Southgate.

75: "long-necked, long-legged personages": Rose, *Lee Krasner*, pp. 68–70. Friedman, *Jackson Pollock*, p. 185.

76: not a single piece sold: Rose, *Lee Krasner*, pp. 68–70. Friedman, *Jackson Pollock*, p. 185.

76: more than six feet in height: Rose, *Lee Krasner*, pp. 76, 79, 83, 86.

76: "remarkably advanced works": Ibid., pp. 76, 79, 83, 86. Fairfield Porter, "Reviews and Previews," *Art News*, Nov. 1955, vol. 54, pp. 66–67. Interviews with William Rubin and Clement Greenberg.

76: more than she could bear: Rose, *Lee Krasner*, pp. 93–95.

77: conceal his affair from Lee: Potter, *To a Violent Grave*, pp. 228–29. Interviews with B. H. Friedman and Jeanne Bultman.

77: think about the future: Interview with Ted Dragon.

77: "(How are you Jackson?)": Letter from Lee Krasner to Jackson Pollock, Archives of American Art.

78: she and her husband could get out: Interviews with Abby and B. H. Friedman.

78: convulsed with uncontrollable weeping: Interview with Clement Greenberg. Rose, *Lee Krasner*, p. 95.

78: charge of the funeral arrangements: Interviews with Patsy Southgate, B. H. Friedman, and Ronnie Stein.

79: alone during the service: Interviews with Ronnie Stein, Clement Greenberg, and Jeffrey Potter.

80: Krasner's early widowhood: Interviews with Ted Dragon, Sanford Friedman, and Richard Howard.

80: Jackson's attraction to Ruth Kligman: Interview with B. H. Friedman.

80: destroyed his copy of the note: Interview with B. H. Friedman.

80: soar to $50 million: Interviews with B. H. Friedman and David Gibbs.

81: wielding undue influence: Harold Rosenberg, "The Art Establishment," *Esquire*, Jan. 1965, p. 43. Friedman, *Jackson Pollock*, p. 246.

81: one of her own canvases: Interview with Helen Harrison.

81: "nothing but her art to live for": Wallach, "Krasner's Triumph," pp. 442. Rose, *Lee Krasner*, pp. 97–98.

82: banished color from her paintings: Interview with Sanford Friedman.

82: "he was terrific at it": Tom Wolfe, *The Painted Word* (New York: Bantam Books, 1975), p. 63. Interview with Clement Greenberg. Lee Krasner Chronology, Archives of American Art.

82: change his mind at the last minute: Interview with Clement Greenberg.

83: his lover Helen Frankenthaler: Michael Cannell, "An Interview with Lee Krasner," *Arts Magazine*, Sept. 1984. Interview with Clement Greenberg. Barbara Rose, *Frankenthaler*, pp. 23–24, 29–30.

83: "French isn't going to show 'em' ": Interview with Clement Greenberg.

83: "favor" to a dear old friend: Ibid.

83: "promised show never came off": Eleanor Munro, *Art World*, Feb. 16–Mar. 16, 1979.

83: "[my criticism] would have given pause": Interview with Clement Greenberg.

83: wouldn't see him again for several years: Ibid.

84: "when I saw them again": Ibid.

84: "that's how I felt": Ibid.

84: "[one picture] hit it": Ibid.

84: bookcases and the ceiling: Ibid.

84: "first bad show [was] in 1953": Ibid.

85: damaged his reputation: Edith Evans Asbury, "Rothko Oil Prices Stir Arguments," *New York Times* Mar. 6, 1974. Edith Evans Asbury, "Stamos Defends Shift to Gallery," *New York Times*, Mar. 13, 1974. John Russell, "Principles, Art and Money Form a Background to 'Rothko Trial,' " *New York Times*, June 21, 1974.

85: "secret cartel at work": Interviews with Bryan Robertson, Eugene V. Thaw, and David Gibbs. Also off-the-record interview.

86: weighed down on Lee after Jackson's death: Interview with Ruth K. Stein.

86: taxes associated with the estate: Interview with David Gibbs.

86: first large picture she had ever sold: Ibid.

86: close enough to break her heart: Ibid.

87: show in New York, in 1964: Ibid.

87: "love, not power politics": Friedman, *Jackson Pollock*, p. 246.

88: Heller backed out of the arrangement: Interview with William Rubin.

88: *Autumn Rhythm*, for $350,88: Friedman, *Jackson Pollock*, pp. 242–43.

88: between London and New York: Interviews with Bryan Robertson, B. H. Friedman, Ted Dragon, and Eugene Thaw.

89: "My God—is this Lee?": Interviews with Abby and B. H. Friedman and Ted Dragon.

89: "nice to the woman he was with": Interviews with Ted Dragon and Bryan Robertson.

89: "want to see you": Letters from David Gibbs to Lee Krasner.

89: lush, fertile plant life: Marcia E. Vetrocq, "An Independent Tack: Lee Krasner," *Art in America*, May 1984, pp. 137–39. Wallach, "Krasner's Triumph."

90: a brain aneurysm: Letter from Sanford Friedman to David Gibbs, Jan. 4, 1963.

90: "quite a marvelous spectacle": Ibid., Jan. 22, 1963.

90: her doctor for years: Letter from Lee Krasner to David Gibbs, Feb. 1964.

91: "artificial and dissatisfying": Letter from Lee Krasner (via Sanford Friedman) to David Gibbs, Feb. 20, 1963.

91: "never bother us again": Letter from Fritz Bultman to Lee Krasner.

91: getting away with it: Interviews with Ted Dragon and Sanford Friedman.

91: paintings like *August Petals*: Wallach, "Krasner's Triumph."

92: Krasner retrospective: Interview with Bryan Robertson.

92: rose-and-green *Earth Green*: Interview with Bryan Robertson.

93: "get down to the painting— *NOW*": Letter from Bryan Robertson to Lee Krasner, June 15.

93: *Right Bird Left* and *Combat*: Interviews with Bryan Robertson and Ellen Landau.

93: ready to set sail: Interviews with Jeanne Bultman, B. H. Friedman, Sanford Friedman, and Ted Dragon.

94: "like no one else": Richard Howard, "Grand Street," p. 184.

94: Virginia Woolf's lighthouse: Rose, *Lee Krasner*, p. 132. Interview with Bryan Robertson. Letter from Bertrand Russell to Mrs. Jackson Pollock, Oct. 7, 1965.

94: "I go into a rage": Amei Wallach, "The Fierce Legacy of Lee Krasner," *Newsday*, June 24, 1984.

95: in the Olympic Games: Interviews with Ronnie Stein and Rena Kanokogi.

95: supplied with lox and bagels: Interview with Rena Kanokogi.

95: "surrendering to their power": Howard, "Grand Street," p. 185.

96: listening to Netter's sermons: Interview with Terrance Netter.

96: how the work will come out: Sandler, *The New York School*, p. 53. Interview with Terrance Netter.

97: "pay homage to Pollock, did you?": Interview with Terrance Netter.

97: during dinner with his old aunt: Interviews with Diana and Jason McCoy.

98: support of other women: Interviews with Ronnie Stein and Nancy Graves.

98: not a single Jackson Pollock: Interviews with Darby Cardonsky and Ted Dragon.

98: Pollock/Krasner House: Interviews with Eugene V. Thaw and Terrance Netter.

99: with her when death came: Interviews with Eugene V. Thaw and Diana and Jason McCoy.

Maria Goeppert Mayer

Page

103: "I had just gotten engaged": Interview with Faye Ajzenberg-Selove.

104: salaried position at a university: Spencer R. Weart and Melba Phillips, *History of Physics* (New York: American Institute of Physics, 1985), pp. 115–21.

104: collaborate with her husband: Interviews with Maria M. Wentzel and Jim Arnold.

105: colleagues at the University of Göttingen: Victor Weisskopf, *The Joy of Insight* (New York: Basic Books, 1991), pp. 64–68.

106: "men you are now going to school with": Vivian Gornick, *Women in Science* (New York: Simon & Schuster, 1983), p. 78.

106: family life and physics: Weart and Phillips, *History of Physics*, pp. 149–57. Daniel J. Kevles, *The Physicists* (New York: Alfred A. Knopf, 1978), p. 205.

107: "the admission of ambition": Carolyn Heilbrun, *Writing a Woman's Life* (New York: Norton, 1988), p. 24. Weart and Phillips, *History of Physics*, p. 191.

107: before her marriage: Joan Dash, *A Life of One's Own: Three Gifted Women and the Men They Married* (New York: Paragon House, 1988), p. 236.

108: bike rides into the countryside: Ibid., pp. 236–40, 243.

108: virtually worthless currency: Ibid., pp. 238, 242.

109: chances with an early *Abitur*: Ibid., p. 242.

109: Mayer was the youngest of them: Ibid., pp. 243–44.

109: she never received a salary: Max Born, *My Life: Recollections of a Nobel Laureate* (New York: Charles Scribner's Sons, 1978), p. 205, 208. Dash, *Life of One's Own*, p. 250.

110: cradle of quantum mechanics: Dash, *Life of One's Own*, p. 275.

110: "succeed even without mathematics": Interviews with Victor Weisskopf and Edward Teller.

110: "niece of the scientific community": Interview with Gustav Born. Audiotape of Eugene Wigner, American Physical Society Annual Meeting, Maria Mayer Memorial Session, Jan. 31, 1973. Dash, *Life of One's Own*, pp. 245, 248.

111: rustic dinner at one of the local inns: Born, *My Life*, p. 227. Dash, *Life of One's Own*, p. 252.

111: "have to be learned, almost every day": Born, *My Life*, p. 227. Kevles, *The Physicists*, p. 201.

111: Göttingen between 1926 and 1927: Weart and Phillips, *History of Physics*, p. 22. Kevles, *The Physicists*, p. 217.

112: "embarrassed her a little": Weisskopf, *Joy of Insight*, p. 30. Kevles, *The Physicists*, p. 163. Audiotape of Eugene Wigner, American Physical Society Annual Meeting.

112: "God does not play dice": Kevles, *The Physicists*, p. 162. Max Born, *My Life and My Views* (New York: Charles Scribner's Sons, 1968), p. 105. Weisskopf, *Joy of Insight*, p. 35. Stephen W. Hawking, *A Brief History of Time* (New York and Toronto: Bantam Books, 1988), pp. 54–56.

113: the interruptions ceased: Born, *My Life*, p. 229.

113: a common one on campus: Interviews with Maria M. Wentzel and Gustav Born.

114: first mentor—in America: Born, *My Life*, p. 241. Interviews with Maria M. Wentzel, Robert Sachs, and Gustav Born. Dash, *Life of One's Own*, p. 269.

114: "faultless Cambridge English": Born, *My Life*, p. 240. Notes of Joseph E. Mayer; interview with Robert Sachs.

115: "Heads I win, tails you lose": Dash, *Life of One's Own*, pp. 259–60.

115: Maria accepted his proposal: Ibid. Interview with Victor Weisskopf.

115: complete her dissertation: Interviews with Peter Mayer and Maria M. Wentzel.

116: absorbing two photons simultaneously: Dash, *Life of One's Own*, p. 262. Interviews with Robert Sachs and Marianne Wentzel. Karen E. Johnson, "Maria Goeppert Mayer:

Atoms, Molecules and Nuclear Shells," *Physics Today*, Sept. 1986, pp. 2–7.

116: her mathematical prowess: Audiotape of Eugene Wigner, American Physical Society Annual Meeting. Interview with Robert Sachs. Johnson, "Maria Goeppert Mayer." Born, *My Life*, p. 235.

116: eventually become Nobelists: Interview with Robert Sachs. Born, *My Life*, p. 235 Dash, *Life of One's Own*, pp. 264–65.

117: lively conversation about physics: Weart and Phillips, *History of Physics*, pp. 115–21. Kevles, *The Physicists*, p. 216.

117: to a new country: Dash, *Life of One's Own*, pp. 266, 267.

118: forced to leave her homeland: Interview with Edward Teller. Letters from Maria Mayer to Frau Goeppert, Jan. 30 and Mar. 4, 1933.

119: possessed a Ph.D.: Letters from Maria Mayer to Frau Goeppert, Oct. 14 and Oct. 19, 1931. Dash, *Life of One's Own*, p. 269.

119: "even be able to save a little": Letters from Maria Mayer to Frau Goeppert, Oct. 14, Oct. 19, and Nov. 5, 1931.

120: "greatest favor you could do for me": Ibid., Jan. 30 and Mar. 4, 1933.

120: "could never abide hen parties": Ibid., Oct. 31 and Nov. 9, 1931, Feb. 17, 1932.

120: take Mayer under his wing: Dash, *Life of One's Own*, pp. 269–70.

121: agonized for weeks before telling him: Letters from Maria Mayer to Frau Goeppert, Nov. 22, and Dec. 1, 1932.

121: "unbelievably kind and civil": Dash, *Life of One's Own*, p. 271.

121: Hopkins some twenty years later: Ibid., p. 271.

121: albeit without a salary: Letter from Maria Mayer to Frau Goeppert, Jan. 15, 1932.

122: Bloody Marys on Christmas morning: Interviews with Jacob Bigeleisen, Maria M. Wentzel, and Robert Sachs. Dash, *Life of One's Own*, p. 282.

122: feast for Thanksgiving Day: Letter from Maria Mayer to Frau Goeppert, Nov. 2, 1931.

123: let them into the house: Ibid., Feb. 27, 1932.

123: long after her child was born: Ibid., Nov. 1932. Gornick, *Women in Science*, pp. 101–2.

124: "remuneration would be $1,000": Letter from Karl Herzfeld to Joseph Ames, July 13, 1935.

124: "wind up going bankrupt": Letter from Maria Mayer to Frau Goeppert, Jan. 15, 1932.

124: "much less tiring": Ibid., Dec. 11, 1934.

125: course in quantum mechanics: Ibid., Apr. 9, 1935.

125: once again virtually broke: John C. French, *The History of the University Founded by Johns Hopkins* (Baltimore: Johns Hopkins Press, 1946), pp. 95–101, 375. Interview with Robert Sachs.

125: émigrés, Jews, Catholics, women, and Communists: Interviews with Robert Sachs and Brian Harrington. Lloyd William Stephenson, "Dean Edward Wilber Berry," *Johns Hopkins Alumni Magazine*, June 1946, pp. 109–13.

126: decided to leave Germany: Born, *My Life*, p. 251. Interviews with Robert Sachs and Jacob Bigeleisen. *Baltimore Sun*, Feb. 18, 1935.

126: the accommodating Polly-anna: Letter from Joseph Mayer to Frau Goeppert, Oct. 6, 1935 (1936?).

126: "Everything is really very strange": Letter from Maria Mayer to Frau Goeppert, Dec. 6, 1936?

127: highest levels of the administration: Interview with Robert Sachs.

128: name on the title page: Interviews with Maria M. Wentzel and Jacob Bigeleisen. Dash, *Life of One's Own*, pp. 288–289.

128: "never do great science": Gornick, *Women in Science*, p. 36.

128: supermarket in a neighboring town: Interview with Jacob Bigeleisen. Dash, *Life of One's Own*, pp. 288–89.

129: "overlooked the Japanese," wrote Laura Fermi: Laura Fermi, *Atoms in the Family* (Chicago: University of Chicago Press, 1954), pp. 170–71.

129: cause the Mayers special conflicts: Dash, *Life of One's Own*, pp. 284, 290.

130: uranium for use in atomic weapons: Letter from C. Warren to Maria Mayer, Apr. 18, 1942. Dash, *Life of One's Own*, p. 292.

130: during a nuclear explosion: Interviews with Jacob Bigeleisen and Robert Sachs. Dash, *Life of One's Own*, p. 292.

130: after five every night: Interview with Jacob Bigeleisen.

130: rest of the scientific community: Interviews with Edward Teller and Robert Sachs.

131: a hair from her head: Interview with Jacob Bigeleisen.

132: "made her very unhappy": Ibid. Dash, *Life of One's Own*, p. 300.

132: dinners or the department seminars: Dash, *Life of One's Own*, p. 301.

132: "She was a perfectionist": Interview with Jacob Bigeleisen.

132: mother's full attention: Interviews with Jacob Bigeleisen, Maria M. Wentzel, and Robert Sachs.

133: pressure on his mother: Interviews with Maria M. Wentzel and Peter Mayer.

133: "leave her the way my mother left me": Interviews with Maria M. Wentzel, Peter Mayer, and Jacob Bigeleisen.

133: in German, others in English: Letter from Maria Mayer to Frau Goeppert, circa Dec. 1934.

134: "shame over me—I cannot remember": Max Born to Maria Mayer, Jan. 20, 1943. Dash, *Life of One's Own*, pp. 279–280.

134: "speaking German all along": Dash, *Life of One's Own*, pp. 279–80.

135: "befriending her parents again": Letter from Maria Mayer to Frau Goeppert, Oct. 19, 1934.

136: someone to care for his children: Interviews with Maria M. Wentzel, Peter Mayer, and Jacob Bigeleisen.

136: "then it would fade": Interview with Maria M. Wentzel.

136: their children could understand: Ibid.

137: during the course of the war: Ibid.

137: working on during the entire war: Ibid. Dash, *Life of One's Own*, pp. 299–300.

138: without even a nominal salary: Ibid., p. 303.

139: "one of the boys": Interview with Jacob Bigeleisen. Dash, *Life of One's Own*, p. 309.

139: "disappearing in odd couples": Interviews with Jim Arnold, Jacob and Grace Bigeleisen.

139: "no support at all": Interview with Robert Sachs.

140: son's attachment to Libby: Interviews with Peter Mayer and Maria M. Wentzel.

140: talking about divorce: Interviews with Peter Mayer and Gustav Born.

141: "get started [in nuclear physics]": Interview with Robert Sachs.

141: didn't wholly understand: Interview with Jacob Bigeleisen.

141: problems tossed out by Teller and Fermi: Interview with Robert Sachs.

142: "didn't have that kind of drive": Interview with Robert Sachs.

142: "everything came to me": Interview with Peter Mayer.

142: like manna from heaven: Interview with Robert Sachs.

143: new ones to the known list: Dash, *Life of One's Own*, pp. 311–12. Interview with Robert Sachs.

143: interested in her work: Dash, *Life of One's Own*, p. 312.

143: more abundant in nature than others: Ibid., p. 315. Interview with Karen Johnson.

144: account for the magic numbers: Interview with Jacob Bigeleisen.

144: body of his work in physics: Interview with Edward Teller. Dash, *Life of One's Own*, pp. 311–12.

144: " 'you can explain it to me' ": Robert Sachs, *Maria Goeppert Mayer, 1906–1972: A Biographical Memoir* (Washington D.C.: The National Academy of Sciences of the United States, 1979) p. 322.

144: orbital angular momentum: Interviews with Jacob Bigeleisen and Karen Johnson.

145: "write it down," he de-

manded: Interview with Peter Mayer.

145: "riding on his coattails": Interview with Maria M. Wentzel. Dash, *Life of One's Own*, p. 324.

146: obscure her own contribution: Dash, *Life of One's Own*, pp. 319, 321. Rosalynd Pflaum, *Grand Obsession: Madame Curie and Her World* (New York: Doubleday, 1989), pp. 67–68.

146: Bohr and Heisenberg: Letter from Hans Jensen to Maria Mayer, Nov. 2, 1949.

147: in the Mayers' house: Letter from Maria Mayer to Hans Jensen, June 28, 1950. Letters from Hans Jensen to Maria Mayer, May 17, 1951, July 30, 1951, and Feb. 6, 1952.

147: were having an affair: Interview with Victor Weisskopf.

147: " 'quicker if you don't have your way' ": Letter from Hans Jensen to Maria Mayer, Nov. 7, 1951.

147: "the scamp, the spoiled boy. . .": Ibid., Nov. 27, 1951.

148: "your twin brother": Interview with Maria M. Wentzel and Peter Mayer. Letters from Hans Jensen to Maria Mayer, Nov. 27, 1951 and Jan. 11, 1952.

148: says the outspoken physicist: Interviews with Robert Sachs and Maria M. Wentzel. Interview with Edward Teller.

148: "consequences of the shell model": Interview with Robert Sachs.

149: willing to overlook his politics: Interview with Edward Teller.

149: would change their minds: Dash: *A Life of One's Own*, p. 304.

149: "been completely isolated": Interview with Edward Teller.

149: "dreamt the whole thing": Interview with Maria M. Wentzel.

Dash, *Life of One's Own*, pp. 337, 339.

150: Joe had burst into tears: Dash, *Life of One's Own*, pp. 231–33, 338.

150: "seeing it work out!": Ibid., p. 139.

150: obvious affection and approval: Ibid., p. 137.

150: around Stockholm like a dandy: Ibid., p. 339.

151: within six months of his wife's death: Interview with Peggy Griffin.

151: had family responsibilities: Interviews with Peter Mayer and Maria M. Wentzel.

151: never been anything but a lady: Interview with Faye Ajzenberg-Selove. Audiotape of the American Physical Society Annual Meeting.

152: "before winning the Nobel Prize": Ibid.

152: university to grant her tenure: Ibid.

Denise Scott Brown

Page

160: a pretty good brain: Interview with Steven Izenour.

160: most illustrious and influential level: Interview with Rosemarie Haag Bletter and Martin Filler.

161: "collaboration with my husband": Ellen Perry Berkeley and Matilda McQuaid, eds., *Architecture: A Place for Women* (Washington, D.C.: Smithsonian Institution Press, 1989), p. 243. Interview with Philip Finkelpearl.

163: agreed to finance her studies: Interview with Denise Scott Brown. David Bertugli, "Designing Woman," *Inside*, Winter 1990, pp. 80–126.

163: their daughter Denise on October 3, 1931: Interview with Denise Scott Brown.

163: second-class nonwhites: Ibid.

164: cousins also lived nearby: Ibid.

164: "subordinated to his moods": Interviews with Robin Middleton and Denise Scott Brown.

165: three feet would do just as well: Ibid.

165: world of Johannesburg's bourgeoisie: Interview with Denise Scott Brown.

165: hills around Johannesburg: Interviews with Diana Goldstein and Denise Scott Brown.

166: her absolute opposite: Ibid.

166: Ruth followed her there: Interview with Robin Middleton.

167: and an anti-Semite: Interviews with Denise Scott Brown and Diana Goldstein.

167: his half-Jewish mother: Interview with Diana Goldstein.

167: "evenings and on vacations": Interview with Denise Scott Brown.

168: "all the conversation he's got?": Ibid.

168: preparations for "Manmade Johannesburg": Ibid.

168: for over a week: Ibid.

168: still quite proud of her daring: Ibid.

169: "we talked about it," endlessly: Ibid.

169: architect's office in Natal: Ibid.

170: become part of the campaign: Ibid. Denise Scott Brown, *Urban Concepts* (New York: St. Martin's Press, 1990), p. 9.

170: declaration of love and loyalty: Interview with Denise Scott Brown.

170: "Brick Wall Brown": Ibid.

170: would, of course, be taking her: Ibid.

171: her relationship with Robert: Ibid.

171: miasma of lovesick despair: Ibid.

171: exclaimed the very next day: Ibid.

171: she acknowledges, "scared" and embarrassed her: Ibid.

172: principle for design and planning: Scott Brown, *Urban Concepts*, p. 9.

172: expenses at the AA: Interview with Denise Scott Brown.

172: he wouldn't even touch her!: Ibid.

173: "finished on time," she recalls: Ibid.

173: the man for her: Ibid.

173: collaborate on a thesis project: Ibid.

174: "cavity fillers, by the faculty": Ibid. Scott Brown, *Urban Concepts*, p. 9.

174: honors from her diploma: Interview with Denise Scott Brown.

175: "studying with Robert": Ibid.

175: worked together on school projects: Ibid.

175: "I knew he'd be interested": Ibid.

175: thought he was too young: Interviews with Denise Scott Brown and Diana Goldstein.

176: keep up with her: Interview with Denise Scott Brown.

176: firm up his resolve: Ibid.

177: Zulu war dance: Ibid.

177: together as husband and wife: Ibid.

177: Kahn was teaching at the time: Ibid.

177: jobs in an architect's office: Ibid.

178: and the special intimacy of the piazzas: Ibid. Robert Venturi, Denise Scott Brown, and Steven Izenour, *Learning from Las Vegas: The Forgotten Symbolism of Architectural Form* (Cambridge, Mass.: The MIT Press, 1977), p. 6.

178: made a great deal of sense: Interview with Denise Scott Brown. Scott Brown, *Urban Concepts*, p. 10.

178: monotony of look-alike houses: Interviews with Denise Scott Brown. Scott Brown, *Urban Concepts*, p. 10.

179: the famous Lou Kahn: Scott Brown, *Urban Concepts*, pp. 10, 11. Interview with Denise Scott Brown.

180: "no place for him to exist": Interviews with Denise Scott Brown, Chester Rapkin, Robin Middleton, and Robert Venturi.

180: "place would be behind her husband": Interview with Denise Scott Brown.

181: died on the way to the hospital: Ibid.

181: to his demise: Interviews with Denise Scott Brown and Diane Goldstein.

182: ready to do anything for her: Interviews with Denise Scott Brown and Steven Izenour.

183: "beginning city planners": Interviews with Denise Scott Brown and G. Holmes Perkins.

183: urban fabric of their subject: Interview with Fred Schwartz.

184: showers for the homeless: Interviews with Denise Scott Brown and Fred Schwartz.

184: "quite wonderful," according to Denise: Interview with Denise Scott Brown.

185: "I have saved one street":

Scott Brown, *Urban Concepts*, pp. 9, 34. Interview with Denise Scott Brown.

185: plea to save the structure: Interview with Denise Scott Brown and G. Holmes Perkins. Donald L. Miller, *The Lewis Mumford Reader* (New York: Pantheon Books, 1986), p. 60.

186: "why didn't you speak up?" she demanded: Interviews with Denise Scott Brown, Robert Venturi, and Steven Izenour.

187: young woman named Vanna Luisi: Frederic Schwartz, ed., *Mother's House: The Evolution of Vanna Venturi's House in Chestnut Hill* (New York: Rizzoli International Publications, 1992), p. 17.

187: picked up from his mother: Interview with Denise Scott Brown. Schwartz, *Mother's House*, p. 17.

188: "She is stronger than he": Schwartz, *Mother's House*, p. 41.

188: "Now I'll show you how to do it": Interview with Philip Finkelpearl. Schwartz, *Mother's House*, p. 17.

188: Palladio's Villa Rotondo: Interview with Philip Finkelpearl.

188: margins of his schoolbooks: Schwartz, *Mother's House*, p. 59.

189: she and Bob would eventually marry: Interview with Denise Scott Brown.

189: weren't going to tell them the score: Ibid.

189: considered marriage again: Ibid.

190: drawings for his mother's house: Interviews with Denise Scott Brown, Robert Venturi, and Robert A. M. Stern.

190: Vanna Venturi House: Interviews with Denise Scott Brown and Steven Izenour. Schwartz, *Mother's House*, pp. 22–23.

190: "most important building of the late 20th century": Schwartz, *Mother's House*, p. 16. Interview with Steven Izenour.

191: *"Vers une Architecture*, of 1923": Robert Venturi, *Complexity and Contradiction in Architecture* (New York: Museum of Modern Art, 1977), p. 12.

191: sophistication, ambiguity, and distortion: Ibid., p. 16.

191: "grew together [only] after she left" Penn: Interview with Robert Venturi.

191: "he was giving to this little girl": Interview with Denise Scott Brown.

192: "he was a very simpatico person": Ibid.

192: friends of his in Los Angeles: Ibid.

192: Bob didn't say a word: Ibid.

192: "I can't remember what it is": Ibid.

192: kiss landed, instead, on her ear: Ibid.

192: "no intention of marrying Bob": Interviews with Denise Scott Brown and Steven Izenour.

193: Las Vegas for the first time: Interview with Denise Scott Brown.

193: "it became a real relationship": Ibid.

194: piazzas attracted pedestrians in Florence: Venturi, Scott Brown, and Izenour, *Learning from Las Vegas*, pp. 6, 18–35. Interview with Daniel Scully.

194: "ornament is applied independently": Venturi, Scott Brown, and Izenour, *Learning from Las Vegas*, p. 87. Interview with Denise Scott Brown.

194: Robert A.M. Stern, a prominent New York architect: Venturi, *Complexity and Contradiction*, p. 17. Interview with Robert A. M. Stern.

194: "challenged and read," Gary Wolf, review of *Learning from Las Vegas*, *Journal of the Society of Architectural Historians*, Oct. 1973, pp. 258–60. Laurence B. Holland, "Rear-guard Rebellion," *Yale Review*, Spring 1973, pp. 456–61.

195: responsible for the firm's "excesses": Robert Venturi and Denise Scott Brown, *A View from the Campidoglio: Selected Essays, 1953–1984* (New York: Harper & Row, 1984), pp. 34–37. Interviews with Rosemarie Haag Bletter and Martin Filler.

195: referring to the Las Vegas study: Interview with Steven Izenour. Rosemarie Haag Bletter, "Transformation of the American Vernacular: The Work of Venturi, Rauch, & Scott Brown," *Venturi, Rauch & Scott Brown: A Generation of Architecture* (Krannert Art Museum, Urbana Champaign: Univ. of Illinois, 1984), pp. 2–19. Schwartz, *Mother's House*, p. 21.

196: continued to give her his backing: Interview with Denise Scott Brown.

196: same institutions as their husbands: Ibid.

197: pavement of a wide Manhattan avenue: Ibid.

197: "yes," replied the perennial bachelor: Ibid.

197: formal functions they must attend: Ibid.

197: battle she had had to fight to win tenure: Ibid.

198: a civil marriage ceremony: Ibid.

198: wide lapels and a wide zooty tie: Ibid.

199: "was going to have a baby": Ibid.

199: ensconced full time at the firm: Ibid.

200: could do to a marriage: Ibid. Berkeley and McQuaid, *Architecture*, p. 239.

200: as his mother would say: Interviews with Denise Scott Brown and Jimmie Venturi.

202: partnership in the firm and a salary: Scott Brown, *Urban Concepts*, pp. 34–35.

202: her contributions to the firm: Interview with Denise Scott Brown.

203: " 'why must you bring up trivia?' ": Interviews with Denise Scott Brown and Robert Venturi.

203: it wasn't nearly that long: Interview with Robert Venturi.

203: a place on the letterhead: Interview with Denise Scott Brown.

204: awards for both designs: *Progressive Architecture* Annual Awards, 1980, 1982.

204: "man-made nature": Rosemarie Haag Bletter, p. 16. Interview with Denise Scott Brown.

205: district in Toulouse, France: Bertugli, "Designing Woman." Interviews with Denise Scott Brown and Steven Izenour.

205: not recognize her as his mother: Interview with Denise Scott Brown.

206: that lasted for years: Interviews with Denise Scott Brown and Robin Middleton.

206: Jimmie's first week in kindergarten: Interview with Denise Scott Brown.

207: "I dropped out of school": Interviews with Jimmie Venturi and Denise Scott Brown.

207: original Penn Station in New York: Interview with Robert Venturi.

207: as far away as Ann Arbor, Michigan: Interviews with Denise Scott Brown and Jimmie Venturi.

208: whirring around their heads: Ibid.

208: The two remain close friends: Interviews with Jimmie Venturi and Fred Schwartz.

209: Denise was his real mother: Interviews with Denise Scott Brown and Jimmie Venturi.

209: a love of electronics: Interview with Jimmie Venturi.

209: "at least not while she is living": Ibid.

210: "meshes most with what I'm interested in": Ibid.

210: accepted the need for a change: Interview with Philip Finkelpearl.

210: collaborator and principal critic: Interviews with Denise Scott Brown, Robert Venturi, and Steven Izenour.

211: bills off a money roll to pay for them: Interview with Denise Scott Brown. Denise Scott Brown, "My Miami Beach," Interview, Sept. 1986, pp. 156–58.

211: "rare in world architecture": Scott Brown, "My Miami Beach."

211: "elderly and poor residents": Ibid.

212: finally won the competition: Ibid.

212: planting a median strip: Interview with Denise Scott Brown. Scott Brown, "My Miami Beach."

212: "elsewhere in the Deco District": Interview with Denise Scott Brown. Scott Brown, "My Miami Beach."

213: synonymous with Miami: Interview with Denise Scott Brown. Scott Brown, "My Miami Beach."

213: in which they lived and shopped: Scott Brown, "My Miami Beach."

213: highway construction plans:

Interviews with Denise Scott Brown and Gabrielle London.

214: vilified rather than praised: Colin Amery, A Celebration of Art and Architecture: The National Gallery Sainsbury Wing (London: National Gallery Publications, 1991), pp. 46–49.

215: draw a single line: Interviews with Denise Scott Brown and Robert Venturi.

215: one of London's great squares: Interview with Robert Venturi.

215: a British public school: Lecture by Carol Duncan in Amery, Celebration of Art and Architecture, pp. 19, 24–28.

216: emerging merchant class: Ibid., pp. 19, 24.

216: wing's ever being built: Interviews with Denise Scott Brown, Robert Venturi, Colin Amery, and Simon Sainsbury.

217: architectural adviser to the project: Interviews with Colin Amery and Simon Sainsbury.

217: the client hated the idea: Interview with Colin Amery.

217: if it hadn't been for Denise: Interviews with Colin Amery and Simon Sainsbury.

217: curved, fluted pilaster: Interviews with Robert Venturi, Colin Amery, and Denise Scott Brown.

217: most delicious controversy in recent architectural history: Amery, A Celebration of Art and Architecture, p. 132.

218: Denise had plenty of company: Interview with Steven Izenour.

218: "It didn't go down very well": Interview with Colin Amery.

219: "I suppose she's never been domesticated": Ibid.

219: "flying around the buildings": Ibid.

219: "Why does he send this surrogate?": Berkeley and McQuaid, p. 239. Interview with Rosemarie Haag Bletter and Martin Filler.

219: "More than I would care to know": Interviews with Rosemarie Haag Bletter, Martin Filler, and off-the-record source.

219: "Less is a bore": Venturi, *Complexity and Contradiction*, pp. 17–19.

220: Venturi declined to join the group: Interviews with Denise Scott Brown, Robert Venturi, Rosemarie Haag Bletter, and Martin Filler.

220: "it was Denise's work": Interview with Fred Schwartz.

221: praises her work: Interviews with Elizabeth Plater-Zyberk and phone conversation with Vincent Scully.

221: "I prefer the darning and the mending": Interview with Denise Scott Brown. Bertugli, "Designing Woman."

222: never shown in a unified exhibition: Interview with Jim Hartmann.

222: toward the end of the planning process: Interview with Lewis I. Sharp.

223: representatives of city government and community groups: Interviews with Lou Sharp, Jim Hartmann, and Denise Scott Brown.

223: "She didn't kill ideas, she encouraged them": Interview with Jim Hartmann.

224: amenity for Denverites: Interview with Denise Scott Brown.

224: residents closer to downtown: Ibid.

225: the boa had to go: Author's notes and transcript of a meeting of the Commission of Fine Arts, Feb. 1992.

225: "stepped on his toe or something": Ibid.

225: " 'but fear itself' ": Interview with Denise Scott Brown.

226: constituents who couldn't travel to the center: Interviews with Ann Trowbridge and Denise Scott Brown.

227: "safe use of fire and smoke": Venturi Scott Brown & Assoc's, *The Way of the People: Master Facilities Programming Phase I, National Museum of the American Indian, Smithsonian Institution*, Revised Draft Report, Nov. 22, 1991, pp. 7, 9.

227: "directives to the design architects": Transcript of a meeting of the Commission of Fine Arts, Feb. 1992.

227: "Commission would be dead against": Ibid.

227: "I think would be too bad": Ibid.

227: upcoming events at the civic center: Interviews with Denise Scott Brown and Steven Izenour.

230: that defines urban relationships: Interview with William Morrish. Herbert Muschamp, "Two for the Roads: A Vision of Urban Design," *New York Times*, Feb. 13, 1994, Section C, p. 1.

Sandra Day O'Connor

Page

235: I doubt you can ever make a living: Cited in a speech by Sandra Day O'Connor, "Portia's Progress," James Madison Lecture, 1991, New York University Law School, Oct. 29, 1991.

235: traditional role limitations: Sandra Day O'Connor, "Portia's

Progress," James Madison Lecture, 1991, New York University Law School, Oct. 29, 1991.

235: burned down several years ago: Interview with Alan Day.

236: in search of scarce water and grass: Ibid.

236: homesteaders and Indians: Ibid.

236: nothing more than the federal government: Ibid.

237: trek from the Mexican border: Ibid.

237: almost in slow motion: Ibid.

237: child of a Lazy B neighbor: Ibid.

237: from the government—was trouble: Ibid.

238: throughout most of her schooling: Ibid.

239: respite from the dry desert temperatures: Interview with Sandra Day O'Connor.

240: too arduous to make twice a day: Interviews with Alan Day and Ann Hernandez.

240: wouldn't have sent him to jail: Interviews with Alan Day and Sandra Day O'Connor.

241: regain full control of the ranch: Interview with Alan Day.

241: "survived that period": Interview with Sandra Day O'Connor.

241: *Saturday Evening Post*: Interviews with Alan Day and Sandra Day O'Connor. Al Kamen and Marjorie Williams, "Woman of the Hour," *Washington Post Magazine*, June 11, 1989.

242: "that's just the way it was": Interviews with Alan and Sue Day.

242: "given that money to my dad": Interview with Alan Day.

242: harassed late payers: Interview with Sandra Day O'Connor.

243: never saw a penny of that deposit again: Interview with Alan Day.

243: leaving her without any assets: Interview with Sandra Day O'Connor.

244: O'Connor would say years later: Ibid.

244: she agreed to return to El Paso: Interviews with Alan Day and Sandra Day O'Connor.

245: "blue-ribbon preparation": Interview with Alan Day.

245: after Henry Clay's death: Peter Huber, *Sandra Day O'Connor* (New York: Chelsea House, 1990), p. 27. Interview with Sandra Day O'Connor.

245: Republicans in the state: Interviews with Alan Day and Scott Alexander.

246: "impact on the court and the nation": Interview with Alan Day.

246: "not the way of the world": Ibid.

246: key to the survival of mankind: Harry J. Rathbun, *Creative Initiative: Guide to Fulfillment* (Palo Alto: Creative Initiative Foundation, 1976), p. 121.

247: a "fabulous" insight: Interview with Sandra Day O'Connor.

247: "values upon which meaningful survival depends": Rathbun, *Creative Initiative*, pp. 100–1.

247: "make a new world": Ibid., pp. 102–3.

248: live life to its fullest: Interview with Sandra Day O'Connor.

248: put their law degrees to use: Interview with Beatrice Challiss Laws.

248: "without skipping a beat": Ibid.

249: "not unusual for a cowgirl": Interviews with Beatrice Challiss Laws and Sandra Day O'Connor.

249: highest ten percent of each class: Ibid. Huber, *Sandra Day O'Conner*, p. 31.

249: "easy to get to know": Interview with Professor Samuel D. Thurman.

249: up-and-coming Republican elite: Off-the-record interview.

250: schoolwork was beginning to suffer: Interview with Sandra Day O'Connor.

250: "always comes up with funny things": Ibid.

250: "interested in hiring a woman": Ibid.

250: "get busy looking elsewhere": Ibid.

251: brief interruptions for child-bearing: Interview with Beatrice Challiss Laws.

251: "But he accepted that": Interview with Sandra Day O'Connor.

251: country and western band: Harry Day, "A Country Wedding," *Arizona Cattlelog*, Jan. 1953, pp. 24–27. Interview with Beatrice Challiss Laws.

251: "we just worked it all out": Interview with Sandra Day O'Connor.

252: vision of the ideal family: Off-the-record interview.

252: New Mexico border and the Lazy B: Interview with Sandra Day O'Connor.

252: become a lawyer instead: Interview with Sandra Day O'Connor.

253: "lost their links with the U.S.": Ibid.

253: training ground for national office: Ibid.

253: "wasn't too big" either: Interview with Beatrice Challiss Laws.

253: "have been swallowed up," says Laws: Ibid.

253: mayor of San Francisco: Interviews with Sandra Day O'Connor and Scott Alexander.

254: "most important things in his life": Interviews with Scott Alexander.

254: her sister Ann's ex-husband: Interviews with Scott Alexander and Alan Day.

254: "He's just self-satisfied": Interview with Jerome Lewkowitz.

254: "negative about her goals": Interview with Alan Day.

255: what John thrives on: Interviews with Sandra Day O'Connor and Alan Day.

255: its way through the legislature: Interview with Scott Alexander.

255: jobs simply weren't there for women: Interview with Sandra Day O'Connor.

256: apt to sing Sandra's praises: Interviews with Jay O'Connor, Alan Day, and Scott Alexander.

256: "she's always building him up": Interviews with Alan Day and Jerome Lewkowitz.

256: "impact of her career on their marriage": Interview with Ruth McGregor.

256: "if left to his own devices": Interview with Jay O'Connor.

256: after just a few weeks: Interview with Sandra Day O'Connor. Huber, *Sandra Day O'Connor*, p. 37.

257: "darling with the children": Interview with Sandra Day O'Connor.

257: "life of a suburban housewife": Ibid.

257: "for women to be hired in law firms": Ibid.

257: less egregious cases: Ibid.

258: all the more "fascinating to do": Ibid.

258: mentors, during this period: Interviews with Scott Alexander and Sandra Day O'Connor.

258: "I had to get baby-sitters constantly": Ibid. Huber, *Sandra Day O'-Connor*, p. 37.

259: hospital for the mentally ill: Interview with Sandra Day O'Connor.

259: "good relationship" with the state hospital directors: Interviews with Sandra Day O'Connor and Jerome Lewkowitz.

259: attorney general accepted her terms: Ibid.

260: never had so much "fun": Interview with Sandra Day O'Connor.

260: appointed to Burgess's seat: Gene Witzeman, "Job Assessment: Quality not Sex," *Phoenix Gazette*, Jan. 9, 1973. Interview with Sandra Day O'Connor.

260: "outside goal or standard": Kamen and Williams, "Woman of the Hour." Interview with Sandra Day O'Connor.

260: commute by bus or car: Interview with Bill Jacquin.

261: eating carry-out fried chicken: Interviews with Sandra Day O'Connor and Bill Jacquin.

261: O'Connor legend fell into place: Interview with Bill Jacquin.

261: when O'Connor first became a senator: Interviews with Sandra Day O'Connor and Brian O'Connor.

262: meals at home for friends: Interviews with Jay O'Connor and Sandra Day O'Connor. Evan Thomas, "Here Comes La Judge, Heading Toward the Supreme Court with Tea and Sympathy," *Time*, Sept. 21, 1981, p. 12.

262: " 'let's just do nothing for a while' ": Interviews with Sandra Day O'Connor and Brian O'Connor.

263: They "never micromanaged us": Interview with Brian O'Connor.

263: sign the parental consent forms: Ibid.

263: help Brian get the required permits: Ibid.

264: State County and Municipal Affairs Committee: Interview with Scott Alexander.

264: "overwhelm you with her knowledge": Huber, *Sandra Day O'Connor*, pp. 40–41.

264: impact on state government as Sandra Day O'Connor: Interview with Burton Barr.

265: program based on a managed-care model: Interviews with Burton Barr and Scott Alexander. Huber, *Sandra Day O'Connor*, p. 42.

265: woman's workweek to forty hours: O'Connor, "Portia's Progress." Jana Bommersbach, "A Republican Darling Becomes a Political Hot Potato," *New Times*, July 15–21, 1981, p. 7. Huber, *Sandra Day O'Connor*, p. 43.

265: "majority leaders don't kiss": Interview with Burton Barr.

266: "the right thing to do": Interview with Scott Alexander.

266: "let's just get it passed": Interview with Burton Barr. Kamen and Williams, "Woman of the Hour." Huber, *Sandra Day O'Connor*, p. 39.

266: "a little [too] all business": Interview with Burton Barr.

266: "it didn't quite fit her": Ibid.

267: "I don't think that's good for a person": Interview with Sandra Day O'Connor.

267: popular politician, into power: Interview with Scott Alexander.

268: from the jaws of almost certain defeat: Interviews with Scott Alexander and Burton Barr.

268: a run for the governorship: Interview with Scott Alexander.

268: "cash on the table": Ibid.

268: disappointment audible in her voice: Ibid.

268: celebrate Christmas and Thanksgiving?: Ibid.

269: " 'why aren't you running?' ": Interview with Bill Jacquin.

269: he was certain she was going to say yes: Ibid.

269: "family council meeting": Ibid.

269: "discouraged or encouraged her": Interviews with Sandra Day O'Connor and Scott Alexander.

270: "holding a statewide office": Interview with Sandra Day O'Connor.

270: "public attention, day after day": Interview with Burton Barr.

270: came regularly from the Supreme Court: Interviews with Sandra Day O'Connor and Betsy Taylor.

271: "the generations which follow": Mersky and Jacobstein, *Supplement on Sandra Day O'Connor*, p. 58.

271: married three months later: Interview with Scott Alexander.

271: engaged a few months later: Off-the-record interview.

272: " 'it's the 1990s' ": Interview with Brian O'Connor.

272: "no reason to worry about my career": Interview with Sandra Day O'Connor.

272: "a citizen, a wife, and a mother": Huber, *Sandra Day O'Connor*, p. 45.

272: choose between them: Ibid., pp. 48–49.

273: weeping in her chambers: Ibid., p. 46.

273: paying off in other ways: Interview with Sandra Day O'Connor.

273: joining them for the weekend: Interview with John Driggs.

273: "Boy, would we ever": Interview with John Driggs.

274: airstrip near Lake Powell: Ibid.

274: appointed to the Supreme Court: Interviews with John Driggs and Sandra Day O'Connor.

274: "Sandra became a member of the Supreme Court?": Interview with John Driggs.

275: "most qualified woman I can find": Elder Witt, *A Different Justice: Reagan and the Supreme Court*, Washington, D.C.: *Congressional Quarterly*, 1986, pp. 30–32.

275: choice for the Supreme Court nomination: Interview with Sandra Day O'Connor.

276: "one of several people being considered": Ibid.

276: "nominee of potentially great distinction":

276: "she had had a vision": Interview with Burton Barr.

277: "what a wondrous thing it was": Interview with Scott Alexander.

277: School for How to Succeed as a Woman: Ibid.

278: "it would not have been possible": Roy M. Mersky and J. Myron Jacobstein, compilers, *The Supreme Court of the United States: Hearings and Reports on Successful and Unsuccessful Nominations of Supreme Court Justices by the Senate Judiciary Committee, 1916–1981. 1983 Supplement on Sandra Day O'Connor* (Washington, D.C.: William S. Hein, 1983), p. 58–59.

278: center in an ideologically riven court: Susan Faludi, *Backlash: The Undeclared War Against American Women* (New York: Crown Publishers, 1991), pp. 257.

279: more tired than they had ever seen her before: Interviews with Sandra Day O'Connor and Brian O'Connor. Kamen and Williams, "Woman of the Hour."

279: personally check every citation: Kamen and Williams, "Woman of the Hour."

279: "whose judgment she trusted": Interviews with Ruth MacGregor and off-the-record source.

280: the justice changed her mind: Off-the-record interview with Sandra Day O'Connor. Kamen and Williams, "Woman of the Hour."

280: "Come," she said. "I need you": Ibid.

280: "help me sort out the information": Interview with Sandra Day O'Connor.

281: back at the Court on Monday morning: Interview with Betsy Taylor.

281: "independent and her own woman": Off-the-record interview. Al Kamen, "Justice Sees O'Connor Becoming Independent," *Washington Post*, Nov. 4, 1985.

281: rule out such executions in the future: Kamen and Williams, "Woman of the Hour."

282: before his resignation from the Court in 1987: Off-the-record interview.

282: "resolving disputes, not creating them": Off-the-record interview. Linda Greenhouse, "Changed Path for Court?" *New York Times*, June 26, 1992, p. A1.

282: *not* societal discrimination: Interview with Henry Monaghan.

283: "and we do so today": Linda Greenhouse, "High Court, 5–4, Affirms Right to Abortion but Allows Most of Pennsylvania's Limits," *New York Times*, June 30, 1992, p. A1.

284: to abort a *wanted* child?: Ellen Goodman, "Justice O'Connor's Question," *Washington Post*, Apr. 29, 1989, p. A25.

284: "occupations of civil life": Sandra Day O'Connor, "Portia's Progress."

284: dependent creatures needing male protection: Ibid.

285: Are women more compassionate?: Ibid.

285: "reach the same conclusion": Ibid.

SELECTED BIBLIOGRAPHY

Books

Ajzenberg-Selove, Fay. *A Matter of Choices.* New Brunswick: Rutgers University Press, 1994.

Amery, Colin. *A Celebration of Art and Architecture: The National Gallery Sainsbury Wing.* London: National Gallery Publications Ltd., 1991.

Anderson, Bonnie S., and Judith P. Zinsser. *A History of Their Own: Women in Europe from Prehistory to the Present,* vol. II. New York: Harper & Row, 1989.

Bateson, Mary Catherine. *Composing a Life.* New York: Penguin Books, 1989.

————. *With A Daughter's Eye.* New York: Washington Square Press, 1984.

Beauvoir, Simone de. *The Second Sex.* New York: Vintage Books, 1989.

Berkeley, Ellen Perry, and Matilda McQuaid, eds. *Architecture: A Place for Women.* Washington: Smithsonian Institution Press, 1989.

Berlin, Isaiah. *The Hedgehog and the Fox: An Essay on Tolstoy's View of History.* New York: Simon & Schuster, 1966.

Born, Max. *My Life: Recollections of a Nobel Laureate.* New York: Charles Scribner's Sons, 1978.

————. *My Life and My Views.* New York: Charles Scribner's Sons, 1968.

Brandon, Ruth. *The New Women and the Old Men: Love, Sex and the Woman Question.* New York: W.W. Norton & Co., 1990.

Chadwick, Whitney, and Isabelle De Courtivron. *Significant Others: Creativity and Intimate Partnership*. London: Thames and Hudson, 1993.

Clark, R. W. *Einstein: The Life and Times*. New York: Avon Books, 1984.

Conway, Jill Kerr, ed. *Written by Herself: Autobiographies of American Women, An Anthology*. New York: Vintage Books, 1992.

Dash, Joan. *A Life of One's Own: Three Gifted Women and the Men They Married*. New York: Paragon House Publishers, 1988.

Einstein, Albert, and Michele Besso. *Correspondence 1903–1955*. Paris: Hermann, 1972.

Einstein, Elizabeth Roboz. *Hans Albert Einstein: Reminiscences of His Life and Our Life Together*. Iowa City: University of Iowa, 1991.

Faludi, Susan. *Backlash: The Undeclared War Against American Women*. New York: Crown Publishers, 1991.

Fermi, Laura. *Atoms in the Family*. Chicago: University of Chicago Press, 1954.

———. *Illustrious Immigrants*. Chicago: University of Chicago Press, 1971.

French, John C. *The History of the University Founded by Johns Hopkins*. Baltimore: Johns Hopkins Press, 1946.

Friedman, B. H. *Jackson Pollock: Energy Made Visible*. New York: McGraw-Hill, 1972.

Friedman, Sanford. *A Haunted Woman*. New York: E. P. Dutton, 1968.

Geldzahler, Henry. *New York Painting and Sculpture: 1940–1970*. New York: E. P. Dutton, 1969.

Goodman, Cynthia. *Hans Hofmann*. New York: Abbeville Press, 1986.

Gornick, Vivian. *Women in Science*. New York: Simon & Schuster, 1983.

Green, Eleanor. *John Graham: Artist and Avatar*. Washington, D.C.: The Phillips Collection, 1987.

Greenberg, Clement. *Art and Culture: Critical Essays*. Boston: Beacon Press, 1961.

Guggenheim, Peggy. *Confessions of an Art Addict*. New York: Macmillan, 1960.

———. *Out of This Century: The Informal Memoirs of Peggy Guggenheim*. New York: The Dial Press, 1946.

Haag Bletter, Rosemarie. "Transformation of the American Vernacular: The Work of Venturi, Rauch & Scott Brown," *Venturi, Rauch & Scott Brown: A Generation of Architecture*, Krannert Art Museum, Urbana Champaign: University of Illinois, 1984.

Hawking, Stephen W. *A Brief History of Time*. New York and Toronto: Bantam Books, 1988.

Heilbrun, Carolyn. *Writing a Woman's Life*. New York: W.W. Norton, 1988.

Hepworth, Barbara. *A Pictorial Autobiography*. New York: Frederick A. Praeger, 1970.

Highfield, Roger, and Paul Carter. *The Private Lives of Albert Einstein*. London: Faber and Faber, 1993.

Hobbs, Robert. *Lee Krasner*. New York: Abbeville Press, 1993.

Huber, Peter. *Sandra Day O'Connor*. New York: Chelsea House Publishers, 1990.

Janis, Sidney. *Abstract & Surrealist Art in America*. New York: Arno Press, 1944.

Judson, Horace Freeland. *The Eighth Day of Creation*. New York: Simon & Schuster, 1979.

Kevles, Daniel J. *The Physicists*. New York: Alfred A. Knopf, 1978.

Kingsley, April. *The Turning Point: The Abstract Expressionists and the Transformation of American Art*. New York: Simon & Schuster, 1992.

Landau, Ellen. *Jackson Pollock*. New York: Harry N. Abrams, 1989.

Mayer, Musa Guston. *Night Studio: A Memoir of Philip Guston*. London: Thames & Hudson, 1991.

Mersky, Roy M., and J. Myron Jacobstein, compilers. *The Supreme Court of the United States: Hearings and Reports on Successful and Unsuccessful Nominations of Supreme Court Justices by the Senate Judiciary Committee, 1916–1981. 1983 Supplement on Sandra Day O'Connor*. Washington, D.C.: William S. Hein, 1983.

Miller, Donald L. *The Lewis Mumford Reader*. New York: Pantheon Books, 1986.

Naifeh, Steven, and Gregory White Smith. *Jackson Pollock: An American Saga*. New York: Clarkson N. Potter, 1989.

O'Brian, John, ed. *Clement Greenberg: The Collected Essays and Criticism*. Vol. I, *Perceptions and Judgments, 1939–1944*. Chicago: University of Chicago Press, 1986.

O'Connor, Francis Valentine, and Eugene Victor Thaw. *Pollock: A Catalogue Raisonné of Paintings, Drawings and Other Works*. New Haven: Yale University Press, 1978.

Pais, Abraham. *"Subtle Is the Lord . . ." The Science and the Life of Albert Einstein*. New York: Oxford University Press, 1982.

Pflaum, Rosalynd. *Grand Obsession: Madame Curie and Her World*. New York: Doubleday, 1989.

Potter, Jeffrey. *To a Violent Grave: An Oral Biography of Jackson Pollock*. Wainscott, N.Y.: Pushcart Press, 1987.

Rathbun, Harry J. *Creative Initiative: Guide to Fulfillment*. Palo Alto: Creative Initiative Foundation, 1976.

Renn, Jurgen, and Robert Schulmann, eds. *Albert Einstein / Mileva Maric: The Love Letters*. Princeton, N.J.: Princeton University Press, 1992.

Rose, Barbara. *American Art Since 1900: A Critical History.* New York: Frederick A. Praeger, 1967.

———. *Frankenthaller.* New York: Harry N. Abrams, 1971.

———. *Lee Krasner: A Retrospective.* New York: Museum of Modern Art, 1983.

Rose, Phyllis. *Parallel Lives: Five Victorian Marriages.* New York: Vintage Books, 1984.

Rosenberg, Harold. *The De-definition of Art: Action Art to Pop to Earthworks.* Chicago: University of Chicago Press, 1972.

Sachs, Robert. *Maria Goeppert Mayer, 1906–1972: A Biographical Memoir.* Washington, D.C.: The National Academy of Sciences of the United States, 1979.

Sandler, Irving. *The New York School.* New York: Harper & Row, 1978.

Satchel, John, ed. *The Collected Papers of Albert Einstein.* Vol. I, *The Early Years.* Princeton, N.J.: Princeton University Press, 1987.

Schwartz, Frederic, ed. *Mother's House: The Evolution of Vanna Venturi's House in Chestnut Hill.* New York: Rizzoli International Publications, 1992.

Scott Brown, Denise. *Urban Concepts.* New York: St. Martin's Press, 1990.

Scully, Vincent. *American Architecture and Urbanism.* New York: Henry Holt, 1988.

Smithson, Alison, ed. *The Emergence of Team 10 out of C.I.A.M.* London: Architectural Association, 1982.

Tarnas, Richard. *The Passion of the Western Mind: Understanding the Ideas That Have Shaped Our World View.* New York: Ballantine Books, 1991.

Trbuhovic-Gjuric, Desanka. *Im Schatten Albert Einsteins: Das tragische Leben der Mileva Einstein-Maric.* Bern: Verlag Haupt, 1988.

Venturi, Robert. *Complexity and Contradiction in Architecture.* New York: Museum of Modern Art, 1977.

———, and Denise Scott Brown. *A View from the Campidoglio: Selected Essays, 1953–1984.* New York: Harper & Row, 1984.

Venturi, Robert, Denise Scott Brown, and Steven Izenour. *Learning from Las Vegas: The Forgotten Symbolism of Architectural Form.* Cambridge, Mass.: The MIT Press, 1977.

Watson, James D. *The Double Helix.* London: W.W. Norton & Co., 1980.

Weart, Spencer R., and Melba Phillips. *History of Physics.* New York: American Institute of Physics, 1985.

Weisskopf, Victor. *The Joy of Insight.* New York: Basic Books, 1991.

Weld, Jaqueline B. *Peggy: The Wayward Guggenheim.* New York: E.P. Dutton, 1986.

Witt, Elder. *A Different Justice: Reagan and the Supreme Court.* Washington, D.C.: Congressional Quarterly, 1986.

Wolfe, Tom. *The Painted Word*. New York: Bantam Books, 1975.

Woolfe, Virginia. *A Room of One's Own*. New York: Harcourt Brace Javanovichs, 1929.

Articles

Asbury, Edith Evans. "Rothko Oil Prices Stir Arguments." *New York Times*, Mar. 6, 1974.

————. "Stamos Defends Shift to Gallery." *New York Times*, Mar. 13, 1974.

Bertugli, David. "Designing Woman." *Inside*, Winter 1990.

Cannell, Michael. "An Interview with Lee Krasner." *Arts Magazine*, Sept. 1984.

Coates, Robert. "The Art Galleries: From Moscow to Harlem." *The New Yorker*, May 29, 1943.

Day, Harry. "A Country Wedding." *Arizona Cattlelog*, Jan., 1953.

Glazer, Vera. "Justice O'Connor: The Supreme Court's First Woman is Tough, Smart—and a Lady." *The Boston Globe*, Mar 13, 1984.

Goldberger, Paul. "Less Is More—Mies van der Rohe; Less Is a Bore—Robert Venturi." *New York Times*, October 17, 1979, p. 34.

Goodman, Ellen. "Justice O'Connor's Question." *The Boston Globe*, Apr. 29, 1989.

Greenhouse, Linda. "Changed Path for Court?" *New York Times*, June 26, 1992.

————. "High Court, 5–4, Affirms Right to Abortion but Allows Most of Pennsylvania's Limits." *New York Times*, June 30, 1992.

Holland, Laurence B. "Rear-guard Rebellion." *Yale Review*, Spring 1973.

Hughes, Robert. "Bursting Out of the Shadows." *Time*, Nov. 14, 1983.

Johnson, Karen E. "Maria Goeppert Mayer: Atoms, Molecules and Nuclear Shells." *Physics Today*, Sept. 1986.

Kamen, Al, and Williams, Marjorie. "Woman of the Hour." *Washington Post Magazine*, June 11, 1989.

Landau, Ellen. "Lee Krasner's Early Career, Part Two: The 1940s." *Arts Magazine*, Nov. 1981.

Larson, Kay. "Lee Krasner's Enduring Gestures." *New York*, January 14, 1985.

Magnuson, Ed. "The Brethren's First Sister; A Supreme Court nominee—and a triumph for common sense." *Time*, July 20, 1981.

Mathew, Ray. "A Record on Canvas." *Art World*, Jan. 15–Feb. 15, 1985.

Muschamp, Herbert. "Two for the Roads: A Vision of Urban Design." *New York Times*, February 13, 1994, Section C, p. 1.

Nemser, Cindy. "Lee Krasner's Paintings, 1946–49." *Artforum*, Dec. 1973.

————. "A Conversation with Lee Krasner." *Arts,* April 30, 1973.

Rose, Barbara. "Lee Krasner and the Origins of Abstract Expressionism." *Arts Magazine,* Feb. 1977.

Rosenberg, Harold. "The Art Establishment." *Esquire.* Jan. 1965.

Russell, John. "Principles, Art and Money Form a Background to 'Rothko Trial.' " *New York Times,* June 21, 1974.

Schwartz, Felice. "Management Women and the New Facts of Life." *Harvard Business Review,* Jan.–Feb. 1989.

Vetrocq, Marcia E. "An Independent Tack: Lee Krasner." *Art in America,* May 1984.

Wallach, Amei. "Krasner's Triumph." *Vogue,* Nov., 1983.

————. "The Fierce Legacy of Lee Krasner." *Newsday,* June 24, 1984.

Witzeman, Gene. "Job Assessment: Quality not Sex." *Phoenix Gazette,* Jan. 9, 1973.

Wolf, Gary. Review of *Learning from Las Vegas. Journal of the Society of Architectural Historians,* Oct. 1973.

Unpublished Articles and Letters.

Freed, Hermine Benheim. Paper on Howard Putzel. Archives of American Art/Smithsonian Institution, 1972.

Letter from Karl Herzfeld to Joseph Ames, July 13, 1935.

Ferdinand Hamburger, Jr. Archives of The Johns Hopkins University, Record Group 02.001, Office of the President, Series 1, File #47, Box 25.

Lee Krasner Papers. Archives of American Art/Smithsonian Institute.

Maria Mayer Papers. MSS 20. Mandeville Department of Special Collections, University of California at San Diego.

Venturi Scott Brown & Associates. *The Way of the People:* Master Facilities Programming Phase I, National Museum of the American Indian, Smithsonian Institution, Revised Draft Report, Philadelphia: Nov. 22, 1991.

Venturi Scott Brown & Associates. *Civic Center Cultural Complex,* Denver, Colorado. Emerging Policies and Options: Data Gathering, Analysis, and Synthesis II, Philadelphia, Nov. 16, 1991.

Audio and Videotapes

Freed, Hermine Benheim. Lee Krasner: East Hampton Studio. Video interview with Lee Krasner, circa 1973. Oral History Collection, Pollock-

Krasner House and Study Center, East Hampton, NY/Gift of Hermine Freed.

Rose, Barbara. *Lee Krasner: The Long View*, 1978.

American Federation of Arts Film Program, 1978.

Wigner, Eugene. Audiotape, American Physical Society Annual Meeting, Maria Mayer Memorial Session, Jan. 31, 1973.

Collection of miscellaneous audio recordings, Niels Bohr Library, American Institute of Physics.

INDEX

FOR THE BEST IN PAPERBACKS, LOOK FOR THE

In every corner of the world, on every subject under the sun, Penguin represents quality and variety—the very best in publishing today.

For complete information about books available from Penguin—including Puffins, Penguin Classics, and Arkana—and how to order them, write to us at the appropriate address below. Please note that for copyright reasons the selection of books varies from country to country.

In the United Kingdom: Please write to *Dept. JC, Penguin Books Ltd, FREEPOST, West Drayton, Middlesex UB7 0BR.*

If you have any difficulty in obtaining a title, please send your order with the correct money, plus ten percent for postage and packaging, to *P.O. Box No. 11, West Drayton, Middlesex UB7 0BR*

In the United States: Please write to *Consumer Sales, Penguin USA, P.O. Box 999, Dept. 17109, Bergenfield, New Jersey 07621-0120.* VISA and MasterCard holders call 1-800-253-6476 to order all Penguin titles

In Canada: Please write to *Penguin Books Canada Ltd, 10 Alcorn Avenue, Suite 300, Toronto, Ontario M4V 3B2*

In Australia: Please write to *Penguin Books Australia Ltd, P.O. Box 257, Ringwood, Victoria 3134*

In New Zealand: Please write to *Penguin Books (NZ) Ltd, Private Bag 102902, North Shore Mail Centre, Auckland 10*

In India: Please write to *Penguin Books India Pvt Ltd, 706 Eros Apartments, 56 Nehru Place, New Delhi 110 019*

In the Netherlands: Please write to *Penguin Books Netherlands bv, Postbus 3507, NL-1001 AH Amsterdam*

In Germany: Please write to *Penguin Books Deutschland GmbH, Metzlerstrasse 26, 60594 Frankfurt am Main*

In Spain: Please write to *Penguin Books S. A., Bravo Murillo 19, 1° B, 28015 Madrid*

In Italy: Please write to *Penguin Italia s.r.l., Via Felice Casati 20, I-20124 Milano*

In France: Please write to *Penguin France S. A., 17 rue Lejeune, F–31000 Toulouse*

In Japan: Please write to *Penguin Books Japan, Ishikiribashi Building, 2–5–4, Suido, Bunkyo-ku, Tokyo 112*

In Greece: Please write to *Penguin Hellas Ltd, Dimocritou 3, GR–106 71 Athens*

In South Africa: Please write to *Longman Penguin Southern Africa (Pty) Ltd, Private Bag X08, Bertsham 2013*